D1672429

Knowing and Seeing

(Fourth Revised Edition)

Talks and Questions&Answers
at a Meditation Retreat in Taiwan

by
the Pa-Auk Tawya Sayadaw

A GIFT – NOT FOR SALE

©(First Edition) W.K.Ng (Private), Kuala Lumpur, Malaysia:
1999: Free Distribution
(First Reprint) *WAVE Publications*, Kuala Lumpur, Malaysia:
1999: Free Distribution
(Second Reprint) Penang Buddhist Association, Penang, Malaysia:
2000: Free Distribution
© (Revised Edition: Second Edition)
WAVE Publications, Kuala Lumpur, Malaysia:
2003: a gift in the public domain, the material cannot be copyrighted.
© (Revised Edition II: Third Edition)
Pa-Auk Meditation Centre, Singapore
2008: a gift in the public domain, the material cannot be copyrighted.
© (Fourth Revised Edition)
Pa-Auk Meditation Centre, Singapore
2010: a gift in the public domain, the material cannot be copyrighted.

The material in this book may be reproduced without the author's permission. It is recommended, however, that unauthorized changes and other misrepresentation of the Most Venerable Pa-Auk Tawya Sayadaw's teachings be avoided.

It is further recommended that before publishing a new edition, one contact Pa-Auk Tawya Meditation Centre in Myanmar and inquire whether there is a later text to the book: typing or other errors may have been corrected, additional information may have been added, etc.

It is also the Most Venerable Sayadaw's express wish that there not be his photograph or biography. He says: 'There is only the Dhamma.' Please respect the Sayadaw's wish.

Any inquiries regarding this book may please be addressed to the author.

A GIFT – NOT FOR SALE

CONTENTS

TABLES

CONTENTS
(in Detail)

---

[1] See index of questions from yogis, p.291.

[2] See index of questions from yogis, p.291.

[3] See index of questions from yogis, p.291.

[4] See index of questions from yogis, p.291.

[5] For untranslated Pali, see Appendix 1, p.283

FOREWORD
(First Edition)

As most of us know, the three trainings of morality, concentration, and wisdom, are the three stages of Buddhist practice. Through the practice of the three trainings, an ordinary person can attain supreme Nibbāna,[6] and become a Noble One.

The *Visuddhi·Magga* compiled by the Venerable Buddhaghosa is an exposition of the three trainings. It is based on the Pali texts and commentaries, and explains the seven stages of purification, and sixteen vipassanā knowledges. But how to attain them has been a difficult question for all Buddhists over many generations. For this, we are fortunate to have the Venerable Pa-Auk Tawya Sayadaw of Pa-Auk Forest Monastery. His teaching is the same as, indeed it is in much more detail than, what is described in the *Visuddhi·Magga*. Based on the very same sources, the Pali texts, commentaries and the *Visuddhi·Magga* itself, the Sayadaw teaches yogis, step by step, how to attain those stages of purification, and vipassanā knowledges.

The goal of the teaching at Pa-Auk Forest Monastery is, in accordance with the ancient texts, to realize Nibbāna in this very life. To achieve that end, yogis must comprehend all mentality-materiality, also known as the five aggregates, as impermanence, suffering, and non-self. As for the objects of vipassanā meditation, they are not only the internal and external five aggregates, but also the five aggregates of past, future and present, gross and subtle, superior and inferior, far and near. Only after comprehending all of them penetratively as impermanence, suffering, and non--self, can yogis attain the Noble Paths and Fruitions, and thereby gradually eradicate or reduce various defilements. After having seen Nibbana for the first time, yogis can see clearly that they have attained the First Path and Fruition; what defilements they have abandoned; and what defilements they still need to abandon.[7] Then they continue to practise vipassanā to attain the higher Paths and Fruitions up to Arahantship, whereby they are no longer subject to rebirth, and will attain final Nibbāna after death.

It is very fortunate that I still have the opportunity, in this age wherein Buddhism is degenerating, to practise the original system of Buddhist meditation. It makes me feel as if I were back in the Buddha's time. For this I am very grateful to the Sayadaw, who spent many years practising

---

[6] For untranslated Pali, see Appendix 1, p.283.

[7] For details on how the yogi sees this, see further p.226.

in the forest, and studying the Pali texts and commentaries to rediscover this teaching. It is out of compassion that he sacrifices much of his time to teach meditation for the benefit of humankind. His teaching is markedly clear and detailed throughout the seven stages of purification. This is a rare teaching and hard to come by, not only in Taiwan, but in the whole world.

From April to June, the Sayadaw conducted a two-month meditation retreat for the first time in Taiwan, at Yi-Tung Temple. Among many Taiwanese, his teaching will definitely arouse interest in the original meditation. It is also a great help to fill in some gaps in Mahāyāna meditation. Hopefully the reader will, after reading the profound talks, and answers to questions, given in Taiwan by the Sayadaw, be able to have a deeper understanding of the Buddha's teachings.

May the true Dhamma endure long. May the publication of this book help provide a refuge for those who wish to know what the rounds of birth&death are, and who wish to attain liberation. May this book guide more people onto the right path to liberation, so that they can realize for themselves: 'All formations are impermanent, all dhammas are non-self, and Nibbāna is utterly peaceful.' To see that is certainly not something impracticable, but something absolutely practical. Only one who sees it knows it, and only one who experiences it can enjoy the bliss of the Dhamma.

A Taiwanese Bhikshuni [8]

---

[8] Yogi at said retreat, who then went to Pa-Auk Tawya Monastery to continue.

Namo Tassa,	**Homage to Him,**
Bhagavato,	**the Blessed One,**
Arahato,	**the Worthy One,**
Sammā-	**the Perfectly**
Sambuddhassa.	**Self-Enlightened One.**

INTRODUCTION[9]

THE BUDDHA'S DISPENSATION

On one occasion, the Blessed One was dwelling among Vajjians at Koṭigāma. There the Blessed One addressed the bhikkhus[10] thus:[11]

It is, bhikkhus, because of not understanding *(an·anubodhā)* **and not penetrating** *(a·ppaṭivedhā)* **the Four Noble Truths** *(Catunnaṁ Ariya·Saccānaṁ)* **that you and I have for a long time wandered the round of rebirth. What four?**

[1] **It is, bhikkhus, because of not understanding and not penetrating the Noble Truth of Suffering** *(Dukkhassa Ariya·Saccassa)* **that you and I have for a long time wandered the round of rebirth.**

[2] **It is, bhikkhus, because of not understanding and not penetrating the Noble Truth of the Origin of Suffering** *(Dukkha·Samudayassa Ariya·Saccassa)* **that you and I have for a long time wandered the round of rebirth.**

[3] **It is, bhikkhus, because of not understanding and not penetrating the Noble Truth of the Cessation of Suffering** *(Dukkha·Nirodhassa Ariya·Saccassa)* **that you and I have for a long time wandered the round of rebirth.**

[4] **It is, bhikkhus, because of not understanding and not penetrating the Noble Truth of the Path Leading to the Cessation of Suffering** *(Dukkha·Nirodha·Gāminiya Paṭipadāya Ariya·Saccassa)* **that you and I have for a long time wandered the round of rebirth.**

The Four Noble Truths are thus the foundations of The Buddha's Teaching, His Dispensation. He then explains:

[1] **The Noble Truth of Suffering, bhikkhus, has been understood and penetrated.**

[2] **The Noble Truth of the Origin of Suffering has been understood and pentrated.**

[3] **The Noble Truth of the Cessation of Suffering has been understood and penetrated.**

[4] **The Noble Truth of the Path Leading to the Cessation of Suffering has been understood and penetrated.**

Craving for existence has been cut off; the tendency to existence has been destroyed; now there is no more renewed existence.

Let us then see how the Four Noble Truths are related to each other.

---

[9] This introduction is an addition to *Knowing and Seeing Revised Edition.*

[10] For untranslated Pali, see Appendix 1 'Glossary of Untranslated Pali Terms', p.283*ff.*

[11] S.V.XII.iii.1 *'Paṭhama·Koṭigāma·Suttaṁ'* ('The First Koṭigāma Sutta') For bibliographical abbreviations and source references, see 'Bibliographical Abbreviations etc.' p.281.

WHAT NEEDS TO BE FULLY REALIZED

The Buddha taught the Four Noble Truths for us to realize the Third Noble Truth, Nibbāna, which is to put a complete end to rebirth and therefore suffering. But that is not possible without the right conditions. In the *'Kūṭāgāra'* sutta ('The Peaked-House Sutta'), The Buddha explains first the conditions that make it impossible to put a complete end to suffering:[12]

Indeed, bhikkhus, if anyone said: 'Without having built the lower structure of a peaked house, I shall erect the upper structure', such a thing is impossible. So too, if anyone said:

[1] **'Without penetrating the Noble Truth of Suffering as it really is;**

[2] **'without penetrating the Noble Truth of the Origin of Suffering as it really is;**

[3] **'without penetrating the Noble Truth of the Cessation of Suffering as it really is;**

[4] **'without penetrating the Noble Truth of the Path Leading to the Cessation of Suffering as it really is,**

'I shall put a complete end to suffering', such a thing is impossible.

This means that we cannot put a complete end to suffering (we cannot attain the Third Noble Truth, Nibbāna) unless we have first fully realized the First Noble Truth (suffering *(dukkha)*), and fully realized the Second Noble Truth (the origin of suffering *(samudaya)*). Only then are we able to realize also the supramundane Fourth Noble Truth, the Supramundane Noble Eightfold Path..

The only way to attain these realizations is to first practise the mundane Fourth Noble Truth, the mundane path truth *(lokiya magga·sacca)*, which is the mundane Noble Eightfold Path, the threefold training:

1) Morality *(sīla)*
2) Concentration *(samādhi)*
3) Wisdom *(paññā)*[13]

For bhikkhus, morality is *Pāṭimokkha* restraint, and for laypeople, it is the eight or five precepts. When we are established in morality, we can develop access-concentration and absorption concentration *(appanā·samādhi)*, which is jhāna *(jhāna)*, and can then proceed to develop wisdom, which is vipassanā meditation. Vipassanā meditation is nothing other than to real-

---

[12] S.V.XII.v.4: a peaked house is here a single-storied house with four outside pillars that are surmounted with beams that support a high roof that peaks.

[13] This is explained in the commentary to M.I.iv.3 *'Mahā·Gopālaka·Suttaṁ'* ('The Great Cowherd Sutta'), where The Buddha explains the eleven qualities in a bhikkhu that make it impossible for him to progress in the Dhamma-Vinaya.

ize the impermanent, suffering, and non-self nature of the Noble Truth of Suffering and Noble Truth of the Origin of Suffering. Only when we practise vipassanā well and thoroughly, and fully realize these two Noble Truths, are we able to realize the supramundane Fourth Noble Truth, the Noble Eightfold Path associated with supramundane Path Truth *(Lokuttarā Magga·Sacca)*: the Path *(Magga)* of Stream-Entry *(Sot·Āpatti)*, Once-Return *(Sakad·Āgāmi)*, Non-Return *(An·Āgāmi)*, and Arahantship.

In summary: the aim of the Fourth Noble Truth (the Eightfold Noble Path) is to realize the Third Noble Truth (Nibbāna), which is achieved only by fully realizing the First and Second Noble Truths (Suffering and the Origin of Suffering).

THE FIRST AND SECOND NOBLE TRUTH

But what is the First Noble Truth, the Noble Truth of Suffering? In the *'Dhamma·Cakka·Ppavattana'* sutta ('The Dhamma-Wheel Setting-in-Motion Sutta'), the Buddha explains:[14]

Now this, bhikkhus, is the Noble Truth of Suffering: birth is suffering; ageing is suffering; illness is suffering; death is suffering; being united with the unloved is suffering; being separated from the loved is suffering; not to get what one wants is suffering: in brief, the five clinging-aggregates *(pañc·upādāna·kkhandhā)* **are suffering.**

When The Buddha teaches the Noble Truth of Suffering, He teaches the five aggregates; He teaches us to know and see the five aggregates. Our human world is the five-constituent existence *(pañca·vokāra·bhava)* (the world of five aggregates), and unless we know and see the five aggregates, we cannot realize The Buddha's Teaching. This He explains in the *'Puppha'* sutta ('The Flower Sutta'):[15]

And what is the ultimate reality of the world *(loke loka·dhammo)* **that the Tathāgata has realized with perfect and complete knowledge?**

[1] **Materiality** *(rūpa)*... [2] **Feeling** *(vedanā)*.... [3] **Perception** *(saññā)*.... [4] **Mental formations** *(saṅkhārā)*[16].... [5] **Consciousness** *(viññāṇa)*, **bhikkhus, is the ultimate reality of the world that the Tathāgata has realized with perfect and complete knowledge.**

---

[14] S.V.XII.ii.1 'The Dhamma-Wheel Setting-in-Motion Sutta'

[15] S.III.II.v.2 'The Flower Sutta'

[16] formations: *(saṅkhāra)* The meaning of this term depends on the context. 1) As the cause of consciousness (here), it refers to the formation of kamma: volitional formation by body, speech or mind. 2) As the fourth clinging-aggregate, it refers to all the mental factors (except the two mental factors feeling and perception) associated with any kind of consciousness (resultant-, functional- or kamma consciousness): mental formations. In yet other contexts, the term has yet other meanings.

Having done so, He explains it, teaches it, proclaims it, establishes it, discloses it and elucidates it. When it is thus explained, taught, disclosed, analysed and elucidated by the Tathāgata, if there is someone who does not know and see, how can I do anything with that foolish common person, blind and sightless, who does not know and does not see?

The realities of the world that The Buddha is here explaining are the five aggregates, which are the Noble Truth of Suffering and the Noble Truth of the Origin of Suffering. And in the *Mahā·Sati·Paṭṭhāna'* sutta ('The Great Mindfulness-Foundation Sutta') He explains:[17]

And how, bhikkhus, in short, are the five clinging-aggregates *(pañc·upādāna·kkhandhā)* **suffering? They are as follows:**

[1] **the materiality clinging-aggregate** *(rūp·upādāna·kkhandho)***;**
[2] **the feeling clinging-aggregate** *(vedan·upādāna·kkhandho)***;**
[3] **the perception clinging-aggregate** *(saññ·upādāna·kkhandho)***;**
[4] **the mental formations clinging-aggregate** *(saṅkhār·upādāna·kkhandho)***;**
[5] **the consciousness clinging-aggregate** *(viññāṇ·upādāna·kkhandho)***.**

And in, for example, the *'Khandha'* sutta ('The Aggregates Sutta'), He explains that the aggregates are aggregates of eleven categories:[18]

And what, bhikkhus, are the five clinging-aggregates? Whatever kind of materiality *(rūpa)* **there is, whether**

[1-3] **past, future, or present** *(atīt·ānāgata·paccuppannaṁ)***;**
[4-5] **internal or external** *(ajjhattaṁ vā bahiddhā vā)***;**
[6-7] **gross or subtle** *(oḷārikaṁ vā sukhumaṁ vā)***;**
[8-9] **inferior or superior** *(hīnaṁ vā paṇītaṁ vā)***;**
[10-11] **far or near** *(yaṁ dūre santike vā)*

that is tainted *(sāsava)***, that can be clung to** *(upādāniya)***, it is called the materiality clinging-aggregate. Whatever kind of feeling.... perception.... mental formations....**

Whatever kind of consciousness there is, whether past, future, or present; internal or external; gross or subtle; inferior or superior; far or near that is tainted, that can be clung to, it is called the consciousness clinging-aggregate.

These, bhikkhus, are called the five clinging-aggregates.

These five clinging-aggregates are the First Noble Truth, the Noble Truth of Suffering, and, as The Buddha explains, they comprise each an aggregate of eleven categories. This means that to know and see the five aggregates is to know and see these eleven categories of materiality, feelings, perceptions, formations, and consciousness.

---

[17] D.ii.9 'The Great Mindfulness-Foundation Sutta' (Also M.I.i.10)

[18] S.III.I.v.6. In M.III.i.9 *'Mahā·Puṇṇama·Suttaṁ'* ('The Great Fullmoon-Night Sutta'), a bhikkhu asks The Buddha why the aggregates are called aggregates, and He explains that the eleven categories constitute the aggregation of each aggregate.

The first of the five clinging-aggregates (materiality) is also called just materiality *(rūpa)*, and the remaining four clinging-aggregates (feeling, perception, mental formations, and consciousness are together also called just mentality *(nāma)*. Thus, the five clinging-aggregates are also called just mentality-materiality *(nāma·rūpa)*.[19]

To know and see mentality-materiality as they really are, we need also to know and see how they are connected, that is, we need to know and see that in the five-constituent existence *(pañca·vokāra·bhava)*, mentality depends on materiality. The five-constituent existence is the world of five aggregates, and it is explained by The Buddha in the *'Loka'* sutta ('The World Sutta'). Here, He explains mentality-materiality as eighteen elements *(dhātu)*: the six sense doors, six sense objects and six types of consciousness *(viññāṇa)*. He says:[20]

And what, bhikkhus, is the origin of the world?

[1] **Dependent on the eye and colour** *(cakkhuñ·ca paṭicca rūpe*[21] *ca)*, **there arises eye consciousness** *(cakkhu·viññāṇaṁ)*.
With the meeting of the three there is contact *(phasso)*.

- **Because of contact, feeling** *(vedanā)* [comes to be];
- **because of feeling, craving** *(taṇhā)*;
- **because of craving, clinging** *(upādāna)*;
- **because of clinging, existence** *(bhava)*;
- **because of existence, birth** *(jāti)*;
- **because of birth, ageing&death** *(jarā·maraṇa)*, **sorrow** *(soka)*, **lamentation** *(parideva)*, **suffering** *(dukkha)*, **grief** *(domanassa)* **and despair** *(upāyāsa)* **come to be.**

[2] **Dependent on the ear and sounds, ear consciousness arises....**
[3] **Dependent on the nose and odours, nose consciousness arises....**
[4] **Dependent on the tongue and flavours, tongue consciousness arises....**
[5] **Dependent on the body and tangibles, body consciousness arises.**
[6] **Dependent on the mind and dhammas,**[22] **mind consciousness arises....**

---

[19] From another point-of-view, mentality-materiality are by The Buddha referred to as the six bases (*sāl·āyatana*: six internal and six external), which is a term He also uses when explaining dependent origination. Throughout His Teaching, The Buddha explains phenomena according to the inclination and understanding of his listeners. Hence, He explains mentality-materiality in many different ways, although they refer ultimately to the same things. See also Q&A 2.2, p.72, and footnote 474, p.248.

[20] S.II.I.v.4

[21] Here, *rūpa* refers to colour, without which the object cannot be seen.

[22] Here, as He is speaking of the eighteen elements of the world, *dhammas* refers to the sixteen kinds of subtle materiality, and all associated mental factors. When speaking of *dhammas* in other contexts, The Buddha means all objects, which include Nibbāna and concepts *(paññatti)*. But as the latter are not the world (are neither mentality nor materiality, and are therefore not the First and Second Noble Truths) they are not included in the

(Please see further next page.)

To know and see mentality-materiality we need thus to know and see:

1) The sense doors
2) The objects that strike upon the sense doors
3) The thereby arisen consciousnesses and associated mental factors.

As explained by The Buddha, there are six sense doors:

1) Eye door .... *(cakkhu·dvāra)*	4) Tongue door .... *(jivhā·dvāra)*
2) Ear door .... *(sota·dvāra)*	5) Body door .... *(kāya·dvāra)*
3) Nose door .... *(ghāna·dvāra)*	6) Mind door (bhavaṅga) .. *(mano·dvāra)*

The first five sense doors are materiality *(rūpa)*, and are therefore the same as the five sense bases *(vatthu)*,[23] but the sixth sense door, the mind door (bhavaṅga), is mentality *(nāma)*. It depends on the sixth material base, the heart base *(hadaya·vatthu)*.

The five material doors take only their respective material object, whereas the mental mind door takes those five objects and its own objects. This is explained by The Buddha in the *'Uṇṇābha·Brāhmaṇa'* sutta, although the term He uses is faculty *(indriya)*:[24]

These five faculties *(indriya)*, **Brahmin, have each a different sphere** *(visaya)*, **a different field** *(gocara)*, **and do not experience** *(paccanubhontānaṁ)* **each others field. What five?**

[1] **The eye faculty** .... *(cakkh·undriyaṁ)*,	[4] **The tongue faculty** ...... *(jivh·indriyaṁ)*,
[2] **The ear faculty** .... *(sot·indriyaṁ)*,	[5] **The body faculty** .... *(kāy·indriyaṁ)*.
[3] **The nose faculty** .... *(ghān·indriyaṁ)*,	

Now, Brahmin, these five faculties, having separate spheres and separate fields, not experiencing each other's sphere and field, have the mind *(mano)* **as their refuge** *(paṭisaraṇaṁ)*, **and the mind experiences** *(paccanubhoti)* **their spheres and fields.**

When the material objects strike upon their material sense door, they strike at the same time upon the mind door (bhavaṅga):[25] All other objects strike upon the mind door alone. The objects that strike upon the mind

'World Sutta'. See further footnote 474, p.248.

[23] sense base: the five physical sense bases are called either *vatthu* or *āyatana*. The sixth sense base (the immaterial mind base *(man·āyatana)*) is called only *āyatana*. But the physical base of the sixth base is called *vatthu*, as in *hadaya·vatthu* (heart base). All six sense bases may also be called the six elements *(dhātu)*.

[24] Faculty *(indriya)* is here the same as 'base', 'door', 'element' etc. elsewhere. The Brahmin to whom The Buddha is here speaking, used 'five faculties' in his introductory question. (S.V.IV.v.2 'Uṇṇābha Brahmin Sutta')

[25] The Most Venerable Pa-Auk Tawya Sayadaw refers to the simile in the *Aṭṭhasālinī* §114 (*The Expositor* p.96): when a bird lands on the branch of a tree, its shadow strikes the ground at the same time. In the same way, when the object strikes the material door, it strikes the mind door at the same time.

door alone include also those that are not mentality-materiality, that are not the world. We have thus six types of object.

1) Colour objects ...... *(rūp·ārammaṇa)*
2) Sound objects .... *(sadd·ārammaṇa)*
3) Odour objects .. *(gandh·ārammaṇa)*
4) Flavour objects .... *(ras·ārammaṇa)*
5) Touch objects[26] *(phoṭṭhabb·ārammaṇa)*
6) Dhamma objects .. *(dhamm·ārammaṇa)*

Dhamma objects are all objects apart from the previous five material types of object: all other objects in the world, which can be cognized only by the mind. They comprise six types:

1) Five kinds of translucent materiality *(pasāda·rūpa)*: the eye-, ear-, nose-, tongue-, and body translucency.[27] They are gross materiality *(oḷārika-·rūpa)*.[28]
2) Sixteen kinds of subtle materiality *(sukhuma·rūpa)*[28]
3) Six kinds of consciousness element *(viññāṇa·dhātu)*[29]
4) Fifty-two kinds of mental factor *(cetasika)*[30]
5) The Nibbāna element, the Unformed Element *(Asaṅkhata·Dhātu)*
6) The infinite number of concepts *(paññatti)*: e.g. the concept of the breath, the kasiṇa object, and names for the ultimate realities, without which we cannot communicate.

---

[26] More precisely: 1) visible-/chromatic-, 2) auditory-, 3) olfactory-, 4) gustatory-, and 5) tangible/tactile objects.

[27] translucent/translucency: see dictionary definition, footnote 504, p.276.

[28] gross/subtle materiality: two divisions of the twenty-eight types of materiality. Gross materiality *(oḷārika·rūpa)* is considered so because it is impingeing materiality *(sappaṭigha-·rūpa)* <materiality that impinges upon other materiality>. It is of twelve types: 1-5) the five translucencies (just mentioned); 6-9) colour, sound, odour, and flavour; 10-12) the earth-, fire-, and wind element. The translucencies are cognized by mind-door consciousness; the remainder by both mind-door- and five-door consciousness: they are easily discerned by insight. Subtle materiality *(sukhuma·rūpa)* is considered so because it is non-impingeing materiality *(a·ppaṭigha·rūpa)*. It is of sixteen types: 1) the water element; 2-6) nutritive-essence, life faculty, heart base-, and female/male sex-materiality; 7-16) the ten types of unconcrete materiality (See Table 2a ' The Twenty-Eight Types of Materiality', p.137). Subtle materiality is cognized only by mind consciousness, and is not easily discerned by insight.

[29] consciousness element: eye-, ear-, nose-, tongue-, body-, and mind-consciousness element.

[30] fifty-two kinds of mental factors: VARIABLES: seven universals and six occasionals; UNWHOLESOME: fourteen universals, ten occasionals; WHOLESOME: nineteen beautiful universals, three abstinences, two illimitables and non-delusion. For the wholesome, see, for example, the thirty-three mental factors of the first jhāna, table p.162.

As The Buddha explained, when one of the six sense doors comes together with its appropriate object, consciousness arises. We have thus six types of consciousness:

1) Eye consciousness... *(cakkhu·viññāṇa)*	4) Tongue consciousness. *(jivhā·viññāṇa)*
2) Ear consciousness......... *(sota·viññāṇa)*	5) Body consciousness....... *(kāya·viññāṇa)*
3) Nose consciousness.. *(ghāna·viññāṇa)*	6) Mind consciousness..... *(mano·viññāṇa)*

As The Buddha also explained to the Brahmin, when an object strikes upon one of the five material sense doors, it strikes also upon the mental sense door. When you have developed strong and powerful concentration, you will be able to see that the object is reflected in the mind door (bhavaṅga) as in a mirror.

Then will you also be able to see that the consciousnesses that arise in one of the material sense doors are very weak. They 'just pick up' the object *(abhinipātamattā)*. The actual knowing of the object is done by a series of mind consciousnesses *(mano·viññāṇa)* that arise later.[31]

For example, when a material object such as colour strikes the materiality of the eye door, and strikes at the same time the mind door (the bhavaṅga), a mind consciousness arises followed by an eye consciousness: they do not 'know' the object; they do not know that it is colour. The object is known by mind consciousnesses that arise afterwards.

We may thus understand that to know mentality-materiality we need to know each type of mentality, each type of materiality, and how they work together. We need to know:

1) The materiality of the door.
2) The materiality of the object.
3) The mentality that arises in the material door and mind door.

We need to know and see the eye door, its object (colour), and the mind consciousnesses and eye consciousness that arise when colour strikes the eye door. And we need to know and see that without the materiality of the eye door, no eye consciousness arises, without the materiality of the heart base no mind consciousness arises either, and without the materiality of the object (colour), no eye- or mind consciousness arises either. We need to know and see this for the ear, the nose, the tongue, and body too, and need to know and see that there are objects known by mind consciousnesses alone, which also arise dependent on heart-base materiality.

But these realities are not to be known only as concepts, because that is only to know and see things as they appear, which means we remain what

---

[31] See table '1b: The Mind-Door Process', p.164, and quotation p.125, from *Dispeller of Delusion.*

The Buddha called a **foolish common person, blind and sightless, who does not know and does not see.**

To know and see these things as they really are we need to penetrate to ultimate reality *(paramattha·sacca)*; we need to know and see ultimate mentality-materiality *(paramattha·nāma·rūpa)*.

KNOWING AND SEEING THE FIRST NOBLE TRUTH

We need to know and see each and every type of mentality. We need to see that in the five sense bases arises one of two types of consciousness, 'two times five consciousness' *(dve·pañca·viññāṇa)*:

1) Wholesome resultant consciousnesses *(kusala ·vipāka·viññāṇa)*: that is, eye-, ear-, nose-, tongue-, and body consciousness: five types of consciousness.
2) Unwholesome resultant consciousnesses *(akusala·vipāka·viññāṇa)*: that is also, eye-, ear-, nose-, tongue-, and body consciousness: again five types of consciousness.

That is in total ten types of consciousness. And in the heart base arise all other types of consciousness:

- Twelve types of unwholesome consciousness *(akusala·citta)*: eight greed-rooted, two hatred-rooted, and two delusion-rooted.
- Eighteen types of rootless consciousness *(a·hetuka·citta)*: ten are the same as the ten types of 'two times five consciousness' that we just mentioned. There are also the two types of receiving consciousness, the three types of investigating consciousness, the five-door adverting consciousness, the mind-door adverting consciousness, and the Arahant's smile-producing consciousness.
- Twenty-four types of sensual-sphere beautiful consciousness *(kāma·sobhaṇa·citta)*: that is eight types of sensual-sphere wholesome consciousness, eight types of sensual-sphere resultant consciousness, and the Arahant's eight types of sensual-sphere functional consciousness.
- Fifteen types of fine-material sphere consciousness *(rūp·āvacara·citta)*: that is, the five types of jhāna wholesome consciousness, the five types of jhāna resultant consciousness, and the Arahant's five types of jhāna functional consciousness.
- Twelve types of immaterial-sphere consciousness *(arūp·āvacara·citta)*: that is, the four types of immaterial-jhāna wholesome consciousness, the four types of immaterial-jhāna resultant consciousness, and the Arahant's four types of immaterial-jhāna functional consciousness.

- Eight types of supramundane consciousness *(lokuttarā·citta)*: that is, the four types of Path Consciousness and four types of Fruition Consciousness.

This gives eighty-nine types of consciousness. And whenever one of these types of consciousness arises, there arise also a number of associated mental factors, of which there are fifty-two in total. Mentality comprises thus eighty-nine types of consciousness and fifty-two types of associated mental factors.[32] They are included in the Noble Truth of Suffering.

So long as we are yet unenlightened, however, we are able to discern only fifty-four of the eighty-nine types of consciousness and their mental factors. That is:

- Twelve types of unwholesome consciousness *(akusala·citta)*
- Only seventeen types of rootless consciousness *(a·hetuka·citta)* (we cannot yet discern the rootless Arahant smiling-consciousness)
- Only sixteen types of sensual-sphere wholesome consciousness (we cannot yet discern the eight types of sensual-sphere functional consciousness, because they are found only in an Arahant)
- Only the five types of fine-material sphere wholesome consciousness (we cannot yet discern the five types of fine-material resultant and five types of fine-material functional consciousness)
- Only the four types of immaterial-sphere wholesome consciousness (we cannot yet discern the four types of immaterial-sphere resultant and four types of immaterial-sphere functional consciousness).

To know and see the Noble Truth of Suffering as it really is, we need thus to directly know and directly see these fifty-four types of consciousness and associated mental factors. But as The Buddha explained, in this our five aggregates world, mentality arises dependent on materiality; the individual consciousness arises dependent on its respective base. That means we need to directly know and directly see also the materiality.

To know and see materiality as it really is we need to know and see how materiality consists of sub-atomic particles that are in Pali called *rūpa-kalāpas*.[33] They arise and perish very quickly, but that is only conceptual reality *(vijjamāna·paññatti)*, not ultimate materiality *(paramattha·rūpa)*. To know

---

[32] When doing *nāma·kammaṭṭhāna* (mentality meditation) one knows and sees these things directly (see also p.159*ff*). Until then, one is referred to the Abs.

[33] sub-atomic: The Most Venerable Pa-Auk Tawya Sayadaw is here using the term 'sub-atomic' to indicate what kind of reality one is looking at: he is not making any kind of equation between the hypotheses of modern science and the realities that one sees in the Buddha's ancient science.

and see materiality as it really is, we need to penetrate the concept of rūpa-kalāpas (penetrate the delusion of compactness[34]) and see the ultimate realities *(paramattha·saccā)*, the different types of ultimate materiality *(paramattha·rūpa)*, that comprise the individual types of rūpa-kalāpa.

In the *'Mahā·Gopālaka'* sutta,[35] The Buddha explains the knowledge of materiality that is necessary for a bhikkhu to progress in the Dhamma and Vinaya:

How does a bhikkhu have knowledge of materiality *(rūp·aññū)***? Here a bhikkhu understands as it really is: 'All materiality of whatever kind consists of the four great essentials** *(cattāri mahā·bhūtāni)***, and materiality derived from the four great essentials** *(catunna·ñca mahā·bhūtānaṁ upādāya·rūpaṁ)***.'**

That is how a bhikkhu has knowledge of materiality.

And He says that without this knowledge the bhikkhu is

incapable of growth, increase, and fulfilment in this Dhamma-Vinaya.

This means we need to know and see all twenty-eight types of materiality. That is, the four great essentials *(mahā·bhūta)*:

1) earth element *(pathavī·dhātu)*	3) fire element *(tejo·dhātu)*
2) water element *(āpo·dhātu)*	4) wind element *(vāyo·dhātu)*

And the twenty-four types of derived materiality *(upādāya·rūpa)*, such as:[36]

- The five types of translucent materiality *(pasāda·rūpa)*: the eye-, ear-, nose-, tongue-, and body translucency, which comprise the five physical sense doors.
- The four types of sense-field materiality *(gocara·rūpa)*: colour, sound, odour, flavour.
- Nutritive essence *(ojā)*
- Life faculty *(jīvit·indriya)*
- Heart materiality *(hadaya·rūpa)*: the material base for mind consciousnesses *(mano·viññāṇa)* and their associated mental factors.

[34] For details about penetrating the delusion of compactness, see Q&A 1.3, p.49, and 'How You Analyse the Rūpa-Kalāpas', p.124.

[35] M.I.iv.3 *'Mahā·Gopālaka·Suttaṁ'* ('The Great Cowherd Sutta')

[36] For a complete list of the twenty-eight types of materiality, see Table 2a 'The Twenty-Eight Types of Materiality', p.137.

HOW YOU KNOW AND SEE THE FIRST AND SECOND NOBLE TRUTH

YOU DEVELOP CONCENTRATION

To be able to see the individual types of materiality of individual rūpa-kalāpas is to be able to see ultimate materiality, and that requires strong and powerful concentration. Only strong and powerful concentration is able to know and see things as they really are.[37] It is explained by The Buddha in, for example, the *'Samādhi'* sutta ('The Concentration Sutta') of the *'Sacca·Saṁyutta'* ('Section on the Truths'):[38]

Develop concentration *(samādhi)*, **bhikkhus. Concentrated** *(samāhito)*, **bhikkhus, a bhikkhu understands according to reality. And what does he understand according to reality ?**

[1] **He understands 'This is suffering' according to reality;**

[2] **He understands 'This is the origin of suffering' according to reality.**

[3] **He understands 'This is the cessation of suffering,' according to reality.**

[4] **He understands 'This is the path leading to the cessation of suffering' according to reality.**

Develop concentration *(samādhi)*, **bhikkhus. Concentrated** *(samāhito)*, **bhikkhus, a bhikkhu according to reality understands.**

That is why, at Pa-Auk, we teach first to develop the strong and powerful concentration of the jhānas (absorption concentration *(appanā·samādhi)*) using, for example, mindfulness-of-breathing *(ān·āpāna·sati)* and the ten kasiṇas, or access concentration *(upacāra·samādhi)*[39] using four-elements meditation *(catu-dhātu vavatthāna)*.[40]

[37] This is what is called vipassanā-basis jhāna *(vipassanā·pādaka·jjhāna)*: see footnote 330, p. 173. It is mentioned in many suttas, for example, D.i.2 *'Sāmañña·Phala·Suttaṃ'* ('The Asceticism-Fruit Sutta'). There, The Buddha explains how the bhikkhu develops the four jhānas, and then: 'With consciousness thus concentrated *(samāhite citte)*, purified *(parisuddhe)*, cleansed *(pariyodāte)*, unblemished *(anaṅgaṇe)*, with contaminations gone *(vigat·ūpakkilese)*, become flexible *(mudu·bhūte)*, wieldy *(kammaniye)*, fixed *(ṭhite)*, attained to imperturbability *(āneñja·ppatte)*, he directs and turns his consciousness towards knowledge and vision *(ñāṇa·dassananāya cittaṃ abhinīharati abhininnāmeti)*.'

[38] S.V.XII.i.1 'The Concentration Sutta'

[39] For a discussion about the different types of concentration, see Q&A 3.1, p.95.

[40] For mindfulness-of-breathing, see 'How You Develop Mindfulness-of-Breathing' p.33*ff*, for the ten kasiṇas, see 'How You Develop the Ten Kasiṇas', p.61*ff*; for four-elements meditation, see 'How You Develop Four Elements Meditation', p.116*ff*.

YOU DEVELOP THE LIGHT OF WISDOM

Strong and powerful concentration produces strong and powerful light, and it is by that strong and powerful light that you are able to penetrate to ultimate truth *(paramattha·sacca)*. It is explained by The Buddha in the *'Ābhā·Vagga'* ('Splendour Chapter') of the *Aṅguttara·Nikāya*:[41]

- **There are, bhikkhus, four splendours. What four? The splendour of the moon, of the sun, of fire, and of wisdom** *(paññ·ābhā)*.
- **There are, bhikkhus, four radiances. What four? The radiance of the moon, of the sun, of fire, and of wisdom** *(paññā·pabhā)*.
- **There are, bhikkhus, four lights. What four? The light of the moon, of the sun, of fire, and of wisdom** *(paññ·āloko)*.
- **There are, bhikkhus, four brilliances. What four? The brilliance of the moon, of the sun, of fire, and of wisdom** *(paññ·obhāso)*.
- **There are, bhikkhus, four brightnesses. What four? The brightness of the moon, of the sun, of fire, and of wisdom** *(paññā·pajjoto)*.

And He refers to the light also in His very first teaching, the *'Dhamma·Cakka·Ppavattana'* sutta, when He explains His enlightenment:[42]

...thus, bhikkhus, in regard to things *(dhammā)* **unheard before, there arose in me vision** *(cakkhu)*, **knowledge** *(ñāṇa)*, **wisdom** *(paññā)*, **true knowledge** *(vijjā)* **and light** *(āloko)*.

Consciousnesses of mundane vipassanā produce strong and powerful 'light of enlightenment' *(vipassan·obhāso)*, but consciousnesses of supramundane vipassanā produce light that is even more strong and powerful: for example, the light of the Enlightened One's enlightenment spread throughout the ten-thousand-fold world system.[43]

How does this light arise? The deeply concentrated consciousness is associated with wisdom *(paññā)*. Such consciousness produces many generations of consciousness-born materiality *(cittaja·rūpa)* of great brightness.[44] Using that light, we are able to penetrate to ultimate truth *(paramattha·sacca)*;

---

[41] A.IV.III.v.1-5 *'Ābhā-', 'Pabhā-', 'Āloka-', 'Obhā-',* and *'Pajjota·Suttaṁ'*

[42] S.V.XII.ii.1 'The Dhamma-Wheel Setting-in-Motion Sutta'

[43] VsM.xx.634 *'Vipassan·Upakkilesa·Kathā'* ('Vipassanā Imperfection Discussion') PP.-xx.107. The light is the result of wholesome dhammas and is in itself not an imperfection. But it can be the basis for imperfection *(uppakilesa·vatthu)* if the yogi who experiences it becomes very attached to it, and develops the wrong view that he has thereby attained Path and Fruition. See also SA.V.XII.ii.1 *'Dhamma·Cakka·Ppavattana·Suttaṁ'* ('The Dhamma-Wheel Setting-in-Motion Sutta'), and 'How You Overcome the Ten Imperfections', p.222.

[44] For details about the light that arises with very deep concentration and vipassanā meditation, see 'Consciousness-born Materiality', p.112, and Q&A 4.10, p.156.

to see things as they really are. It is like going into a dark room: we need light to see the objects there.[45]

YOU PROTECT YOUR CONCENTRATION

But it is not enough just to develop deep concentration, because to be able to penetrate to ultimate reality is deep and profound, and is an opportunity we must not lose. We teach therefore also how you protect yourself and your meditation by developing the four sublime abidings *(brahma·vihāra)* up to jhāna or access concentration:[46]

1) Loving-kindness *(mettā)* to overcome anger and hatred.[47]
2) Compassion *(karuṇā)* to overcome ill-will and cruelty.
3) Sympathetic joy *(muditā)* to overcome envy.
4) Equanimity *(upekkhā)* to overcome indifference towards beings.

For the same reason, we teach also the four Protective Meditations *(catur·ārakkha·bhāvanā)* up to jhāna or access concentration:[48]

1) Lovingkindness *(mettā)* to protect you against dangers from other beings.[49]

---

[45] In S.IV.I.xvi.5 *'Jīvak·Amba·Vana·Samādhi·Suttaṁ'* ('The Jīvaka's-Mango-Grove Concentration Sutta'), The Buddha explains this in accordance with the six bases: 'Develop concentration, bhikkhus. When concentrated *(samāhitassa)*, bhikkhus, things become manifest to the bhikkhu, according to reality. And what becomes manifest according to reality? The eye becomes manifest according to reality as impermanent. Sights… Eye consciousness… Eye contact… And any feeling that arises because of eye contact, be it pleasant, unpleasant, or neither unpleasant nor pleasant… [the ear, nose, tongue, body, mind, their objects, respective consciousnesses, contact, and feelings: the same as "the all" referred to in quotation, p.152].' SA explains that 'become manifest' *(okkhāyati)* means they become manifest *(paccakkhāyati)*, knowable *(paññāyati)*, and evident *(pākataṁ)*: *paccakkha* (discernible, perceivable, known to the senses, manifest) is the opposite of *anumāna* (inference). And in S.V.III.i.4 *'Sāla·Suttaṃ'* ('The Sāla Sutta'), The Buddha explains that newly ordained bhikkhus should be trained to abide contemplating the four foundations of mindfulness 'of unified *(ekodibhūtā)* clear consciousness *(vippasanna·cittā)*, concentrated *(samāhitā)*, of one-pointed consciousness *(ek·agga·cittā)*, in order to know… [the four foundations of mindfulness] according to reality *(kāyassa yathā·bhūtaṃ ñāṇāya)*.'

[46] See The Buddha's analysis of the four divine abidings, A.VI.I.ii.3 *'Nissāraṇīya·Suttaṁ'* ('The Escape Sutta'), and M.II.ii.2 *'Mahā·Rāhul·Ovāda·Suttaṁ'* ('The Great Advice-to-Rāhula Sutta'), and Q&A 2.2, p.72.

[47] See The Buddha's advice, U.iv.1 *'Meghiya·Suttaṁ'* ('The Meghiya Sutta'), discussed also 'Summary', p.93, and Q&A 7.13, p.235.

[48] These are also called the four protective meditation subjects *(ārakkha·kammaṭṭhāna)*.

[49] See The Buddha's explanation of the benefits of loving-kindness practice, A.XI.ii.5 *'Metta·Suttaṁ'* ('The Loving-Kindness Sutta'): quoted p.87. For an example of this meditation's efficacy, see also Q&A 2.2, p.72.

2) Buddha Recollection *(Buddh·Ānussati)* to protect you against fear,[50] and dangers from other beings.
3) Foulness meditation *(asubha·bhāvanā)* to protect you against lust and desire.[51]
4) Death Recollection *(maraṇ·ānussati)* to protect you against laziness in meditation: to fire you with a sense of urgency *(saṁvega)*.[52]

With the jhāna concentration or access concentration that you have already developed, these subjects do not take long to develop.[53]

YOU PENETRATE TO ULTIMATE REALITY

PENETRATING TO ULTIMATE MATERIALITY

If you are a samatha yogi, with strong and powerful concentration that is well protected, we then teach you how to know and see materiality as it really is, using four-elements meditation *(catu-dhātu vavatthāna)*.[54] But if you prefer not to develop samatha, and prefer to develop only access concentration, you go straight to four-elements meditation.

We teach the discernment of materiality first for several reasons. One reason is that to discern materiality is very subtle and profound. But although materiality changes billions of times per second, it does not change as quickly as mentality does. This means that once you have completed the profound discernment of materiality, the more profound discernment of mentality becomes easier for you to do. Another reason is that mentality depends on materiality, and unless one can see the specific materiality that a consciousness depends upon, one cannot see the mentality at all. To be able to see it, one needs to see its arising.[55]

[50] See The Buddha's advice, S.I.XI.i.3 *'Dhajagga·Suttaṁ'* ('The Standard Sutta').

[51] For details on this meditation, see p.92*f.*

[52] See The Buddha's advice, A.VI.ii.10&11 *'Paṭhama-'* & *'Dutiya·Maraṇassati·Suttaṁ'* ('The First-' & 'Second Death-Recollection Sutta').

[53] For the sublime abidings and protective meditations see Talk 3 'How You Develop the Sublime Abidings and Protective Meditations', p.81*ff.*

[54] For four-elements meditation, see 'How You Develop Four Elements Meditation', p.116*ff.*

[55] This is explained VsM.xviii.669-671 *'Nāma·Rūpa·Pariggaha·Kathā'* ('Mentality-Materiality Definition Discussion') PP.xviii.16-23, where is added that if one does not complete the discernment of materiality before proceeding to discern mentality, one 'falls from one's meditation subject like the [foolish] mountain cow…'. (A.IX.I.iv.4 *'Gāvī-Upamā·Suttaṁ'* ('The Cow Simile Sutta') mentioned p.46.). But this refers only to sensual sphere mentality, not fine-material sphere mentality (jhāna). See also p.160.

Four-elements meditation means you discern the four elements in materiality, and you start with the materiality that is your own body, that is, you start with materiality that The Buddha called internal *(ajjhatta)*. The Buddha explains four-elements meditation in the *'Mahā·Sati·Paṭṭhāna'* sutta:[56]

Again, bhikkhus, a bhikkhu reviews this body, however it may be placed or disposed, in terms of the elements *(dhātu)*: **'There are in this body**

[1] **earth element**... *(pathavī·dhātu)*, | [3] **fire element**............ *(tejo·dhātu)*,
[2] **water element**......... *(āpo·dhātu)*, | [4] **wind element**........ *(vāyo·dhātu)*.

It is easier to start with one's own materiality because it is easier to know that one's own materiality is hot or cold or hard or soft than it is to know it in external materiality such as the materiality of another being. But once you have become skilled in discerning internal materiality, you will need to discern also the remaining ten categories of materiality enumerated by The Buddha: past, future, present, external, gross, subtle, inferior, superior, far and near.[57]

The Buddha taught four-elements meditation in order that we may be able to know and see ultimate materiality. First, you develop the ability to know and see the different characteristics of the four elements in your body as one compact mass of materiality, as one lump. As your skill and concentration develops you will eventually be able to see the rūpa-kalāpas, and then, using the light of concentration that you have developed, you will then be able to penetrate the delusion of compactness,[58] penetrate to ultimate materiality, to know and see, to identify and analyse the individual types of materiality in the different types of rūpa-kalāpa.

PENETRATING TO ULTIMATE MENTALITY

Having now truly known and seen the different types of ultimate materiality, you can proceed to knowing and seeing ultimate mentality, which is meditation on mentality *(nāma·kammaṭṭhāna)*.

We can discern mentality either by way of the six sense bases or by way of the six sense doors.[59] But, since you discerned materiality by way of the

---

[56] D.ii.9 'The Great Mindfulness-Foundation Sutta' (Also M.I.i.10). See also M.II.ii.2 *'Mahā·Rāhul·Ovāda·Suttaṁ'* ('The Great Advice-to-Rāhula Sutta').

[57] See *'Khandha·Suttaṁ'* ('The Aggregates Sutta') quoted, p.4.

[58] For details regarding the delusion of compactness, see Q&A 1.3, p.49, and 'How You Analyse the Rūpa-Kalāpas', p.124.

[59] When you discern by way of the sense bases, you discern the consciousnesses and associated mental factors that arise dependent on each of the sense bases. (E.g. you discern the

(Please see further next page.)

sense doors, the *Visuddhi·Magga* says you should do the same for mentality:[60] **When he has discerned materiality thus, the immaterial states become plain to him in accordance with the sense doors.** And the sub-commentary says further that to discern mentality by way of the doors is to be **free from confusion.**[61]

The six sense doors and their objects were mentioned earlier, and are:

1) The eye door, which takes colour objects.
2) The ear door, which takes sound objects.
3) The nose door, which takes odour objects.
4) The tongue door, which takes flavour objects.
5) The body door, which takes touch objects.
6) The mind door (bhavaṅga), which takes the previous five objects of the five material sense doors, and dhamma objects.[62]

When one of the six types of object strikes its respective door, a series of consciousnesses *(citta)* arise, and with each consciousness arise also a number of associated mental factors *(cetasika)*: this is according to the natural law of consciousness *(citta·niyāma)*. Such a series of consciousnesses and associated mental factors is called a mental process *(citta·vīthi)*, and there are accordingly six types:

1) Eye-door process *(cakkhu·dvāra·vīthi)*
2) Ear-door process *(sota·dvāra·vīthi)*
3) Nose-door process *(ghāna·dvāra·vīthi)*
4) Tongue-door process *(jivhā·dvāra·vīthi)*
5) Body-door process *(kāya·dvāra·vīthi)*
6) Mind-door process *(mano·dvāra·vīthi)*

When a material object strikes upon its material door, a mental process of the first five doors arises: this is called a five-door process *(pañca·dvāra·vīthi)*. But a mental process of the sixth door, the mind door (the bhavaṅga), is called a mind-door process *(mano·dvāra·vīthi)*.

---

eye base (the eye-translucent element), and then the eye consciousness (1) and associated mental factors (7) that arise dependent on the eye base.) When you discern by way of the six sense doors, you discern the different types of consciousness in the mental processes of each door. For example, the different consciousness and associated mental factors of the eye-door process. See also p.9 and following.

[60] VsM.xviii.664 *'Nāma·Rūpa·Pariggaha·Kathā'* ('Mentality-Materiality Definition Discussion') PP.xviii.8

[61] VsMṬ.ibid. For each of the five sense bases only one such type of consciousness arises, but for the heart base, there arise all other types of consciousness. Unless one is well familiar with the Abhidhamma's explanation of the different types of consciousnesses in the different types of mental process, this may be very confusing to the beginning yogi.

[62] See p.7 for explanation of 'dhamma objects'.

As also mentioned before, when one of the five types of material object strikes upon its material door, it strikes at the same time upon the mind door (bhavaṅga):[63] both a five-door- and a mind-door process arise. When, for example, a colour object strikes upon the eye door, it strikes at the same time upon the mind door (bhavaṅga), which gives rise first to an eye-door process, and then to many mind-door process.[64] This too takes place according to the natural law of consciousness *(citta·niyāma)*.

It is thus clear that to know and see mentality, we need first to know and see materiality, because to know and see these mental processes, we need first to know and see the sense doors and their objects. This you did when you discerned materiality.[65]

When discerning mentality, you first discern the different types of mental process, which means you discern how many consciousness moments *(citta·kkhaṇa)* there are in each mental process, and discern the different types of consciousness moment. But that is not ultimate mentality *(paramattha·nāma)*. Just as you with materiality had to break down the delusion of compactness that is the rūpa-kalāpa, so do you here need to break down the delusion of compactness that is the mental process.[66]

Each mental process comprises what we call consciousness moments *(citta·kkhaṇa)*, and each consciousness moment is the time it takes for one consciousness *(citta)* and its associated mental factors *(cetasika)* to arise, stand and perish. A consciousness does not arise alone: it arises always together with associated mental factors. Likewise, associated mental factors do not arise alone: they arise always together with a consciousness. Hence, a consciousness and its associated mental factors arise as a compact group. To break down this compactness, you need to analyse each type of consciousness moment and know and see the individual consciousness and its associated mental factors. That is knowing and seeing the different types of ultimate mentality *(paramattha·nāma)*. It is far subtler than knowing and seeing the different types of ultimate materiality. But you can do it because of the strong and powerful light of concentration that you have developed, and because of the power of discernment that you developed when discerning materiality.

---

63 See 'Uṇṇābha Brahmin Sutta' (quoted) etc., p.6*ff.*

64 For details, see tables 1b and 1c, p.164*ff.*

65 See 'How You Analyse the Translucencies', p.129*ff.*

66 For details regarding the delusion of compactness, see also Q&A 1.3, p.49.

Mentality comprises, as mentioned,[67] eighty-nine types of conscious and fifty-two types of associated mental factors. But eight of those consciousnesses are supramundane *(lokuttarā)*: four Paths and four Fruitions), and arise only when you do vipassanā practice on one of the remaining eighty-one types of consciousness (all mundane), and its associated mental factors. In other words, the objects of vipassanā are only the mundane eighty-one types of consciousness, and their associated mental factors, whereas the results of that vipassanā are the eight supramundane consciousnesses.

Furthermore, included in those eighty-one types of mundane consciousnesses are the jhānas. But you cannot discern unless you have attained them. Should you therefore be a pure-vipassanā yogi, you leave out the discernment of jhāna consciousnesses.

What you will now be able to discern is explained by the Buddha in the *'Mahā·Sati·Paṭṭhāna'* sutta:[68]

Again and further, bhikkhus, how does a bhikkhu abide contemplating consciousness as consciousness? Here, bhikkhus, a bhikkhu understands:

[1] **lustful consciousness** *(sa·raga·citta)* **as lustful consciousness,**
[2] **unlustful consciousness** *(vita·raga·citta)* **as unlustful consciousness,**
[3] **hateful consciousness** *(sa·dosa·citta)* **as hateful consciousness,**
[4] **unhateful consciousness** *(vita·dosa·citta)* **as unhateful consciousness,**
[5] **deluded consciousness** *(sa·moha·citta)* **as deluded consciousness,**
[6] **undeluded consciousness** *(vita·moha·citta)* **as undeluded consciousness,**
[7] **contracted consciousness** *(samkhitta·citta)* **as contracted consciousness,**
[8] **distracted consciousness**[69] *(vikkhitta·citta)* **as distracted consciousness,**
[9] **exalted consciousness**[69] *(mahaggata·citta)* **as exalted consciousness,**
[10] **unexalted consciousness** *(a·mahaggata·citta)* **as unexalted consciousness,**
[11] **surpassed consciousness**[69] *(sa·uttara·citta)* **as surpassed consciousness,**
[12] **unsurpassed consciousness** *(an·uttara·citta)* **as unsurpassed consciousness,**
[13] **concentrated consciousness**[69] *(samahita·citta)* **as concentrated consciousness,**
[14] **unconcentrated consciousness** *(a·samahita·citta)* **as unconcentrated consciouness,**
[15] **liberated consciousness**[69] *(vimutta·citta)* **as liberated consciousness,**

---

[67] See p.10*f.*

[68] 'The Great Mindfulness-Foundation Sutta' (Also M.I.i.10)

[69] D.ii.9: CONTRACTED shrunken, slothful and torpid, without interest in the object; DISTRACTED agitated, restless, worried; EXALTED of a fine-material/immaterial sphere (jhāna); UNEXALTED of the sensual sphere; SURPASSED of the sensual sphere; UNSURPASSED of a fine-material/immaterial sphere (jhāna); CONCENTRATED of access-concentration or jhāna; UNCONCENTRATED otherwise; LIBERATED at this stage, this refers to a consciousness that is temporarily liberated owing to wise attention or because the hindrances have been suppressed by concentration; UNLIBERATED not so. The pairs 9-10, 11-12, 13-14, 15-16, each cover all types of mundane consciousness.

[16] **unliberated consciousness** *(a·vimutta·citta)* **as unliberated consciousness.**

- **Thus he abides contemplating mind as mind internally** *(ajjhattaṁ)*,
- **or he abides contemplating mind as mind externally** *(bahiddhā)*,
- **or he abides contemplating mind as mind** [both] **internally and externally** *(ajjhatta·bahiddhā)*.

Here, The Buddha explains mentality as comprising sixteen types of consciousness. That means you should know and see each pair, such as a consciousness associated with lust,and one dissociated from lust, as they really are, by way of each of the six sense doors, and do it internally, externally and both internally and externally. Then will you have penetrated to ultimate mentality, and know and see it as it really is.

THE THREE PURIFICATIONS

Having now known and seen mentality-materiality as they really are, you have realized what is called the three purifications.[70] The *Visuddhi·Magga*,[71] explains:[72]

[1] **...morality purification** *(sīla·visuddhi)* **is the quite purified fourfold morality beginning with *Pāṭimokkha* restraint**

[2] **...consciousness purification** *(citta·visuddhi)*, **namely, the eight attainments** [the jhānas] **together with access concentration**[73]

[3] **...view purification** *(diṭṭhi·visuddhi)* **is the correct seeing of mentality-materiality.**

KNOWING AND SEEING THE SECOND AND THIRD NOBLE TRUTH

To attain Nibbāna, however, we need to know and see also the Noble Truth of the Origin of Suffering. The Noble Truth of the Origin of Suffering is explained by The Buddha in the *'Dhamma·Cakka·Ppavattana'* sutta:[74]

---

[70] See further Q&A 2.3, p.77.

[71] *Visuddhi·Magga (Purification Path)*: authoritative and extensive instruction manual on meditation, compiled from ancient, orthodox Sinhalese translations of the even earlier Pali Commentaries (predominantly 'The Ancients' *(Porāṇā)*, dating back to the time of The Buddha and the First Council) as well as later Sinhalese Commentaries, and translated back into Pali by Indian scholar monk Venerable Buddhaghosa (approx. 500 A.C.).

[72] VsM.xviii.587 *'Diṭṭhi·Visuddhi·Niddesa'* ('View-Purification Description') PP.xviii.1-2

[73] For how concentration purifies the mind, see also Q&A 7.8, p.232.

[74] S.V.XII.ii.1 'The Dhamma-Wheel Setting-in-Motion Sutta'

Now this, bhikkhus, is the Noble Truth of the Origin of Suffering: it is this craving *(taṇhā)* **that leads to renewed existence, accompanied by delight and lust, seeking delight here and there; that is,**

[1] **craving for sensual pleasures** *(kāma·taṇhā)*,

[2] **craving for existence** *(bhava·taṇhā)*,

[3] **craving for non-existence** *(vibhava·taṇhā)*.

In more detail, The Buddha explains the Noble Truth of the Origin of Suffering as dependent origination *(paṭicca·samuppāda)*:[75]

And what, bhikkhus, is the Noble Truth of the Origin of Suffering *(Dukkha·Samudayaṁ Ariya·Saccaṁ)***?**

[1] **Because of ignorance** *(avijjā)*, **formations** [arise] *(saṅkhārā)*;

[2] **because of formations, consciousness** *(viññāṇa)*;

[3] **because of consciousness, mentality-materiality** *(nāma·rūpa)*;

[4] **because of mentality-materiality, the six bases** *(saḷ·āyatana)*;

[5] **because of the six bases, contact** *(phassa)*;

[6] **because of contact, feeling** *(vedanā)*;

[7] **because of feeling, craving** *(taṇhā)*;

[8] **because of craving, clinging** *(upādāna)*;

[9] **because of clinging, existence** *(bhava)*;

[10] **because of existence, birth** *(jāti)*;

[11] **because of birth,**

[12] **ageing&death** *(jarā·maraṇa)*, **sorrow** *(soka)*, **lamentation** *(parideva)*, **pain** *(dukkha)*, **grief** *(domanassa)* **and despair** *(upāyāsā)* **arise.**

Such is the origin of this whole mass of suffering.

This is called, bhikkhus, the Noble Truth of the Origin of Suffering *(Idaṁ vuccati, bhikkhave, Dukkha·Samudayaṁ Ariya·Saccaṁ)*.

Also this needs to be known and seen as it really is, which is to know and see how five causes in one life (ignorance, volitional formations, craving, clinging and existence[76]) give rise to rebirth, which is five results (consciousness, mentality-materiality, the six sense bases, contact and feeling). You need to see how this ongoing process continues from life to life.

---

[75] A.III.II.ii.1 *'Titth·Āyatana·Suttaṁ'* ('The Sectarian Doctrines Sutta')

[76] There are two types of existence *(bhava)*: 1) kamma-process existence *(kamma·bhava)*, which is the production of kamma; 2) rebirth-process existence *(upapatti·bhava)*, which is the result of kamma (rebirth in any sphere of existence). See quotation, footnote 364, p.192.

But it is not enough to see dependent origination only as the arising of formations; you need also to see it as the perishing and cessation of formations:[77]

And what, bhikkhus, is the Noble Truth of the Cessation of Suffering *(Dukkha·Nirodhaṁ Ariya·Saccaṁ)* **?**

[1] **With ignorance's remainderless fading away and cessation** *(avijjāya tveva asesa·virāga·nirodhā)*,
[2] **volitional formations cease** *(saṅkhāra·nirodho)*;
[3] **with volitional formations' cessation, consciousness ceases** *(viññāṇa·nirodho)*;
[4] **with consciousness's cessation, mentality-materiality ceases** *(nāma·rūpa·nirodho)*;
[5] **with mentality-materiality's cessation, the six sense bases cease** *(saḷ·āyatana-·nirodho)*;
[6] **with the six sense bases' cessation, contact ceases** *(phassa·nirodho)*;
[7] **with contact's cessation, feeling ceases** *(vedanā·nirodho)*;
[8] **with feeling's cessation, craving ceases** *(taṇhā·nirodho)*;
[9] **with craving's cessation, clinging ceases** *(upādāna·nirodho)*;
[10] **with clinging's cessation, existence ceases** *(bhava·nirodho)*;
[11] **with existence's cessation, birth ceases** *(jāti·nirodho)*;
[12] **with birth's cessation, ageing&death, sorrow, lamentation, pain, grief and despair cease** *(jarā·maraṇaṁ, soka·parideva·dukkha·domanass·upāyāsā nirujjhanti)*.

Such is the cessation of this whole mass of suffering.

This is called, bhikkhus, the Noble Truth of the Cessation of Suffering *(Idaṁ vuccati, bhikkhave, Dukkha·Nirodhaṁ Ariya·Saccaṁ)*.

You need to see the momentary cessation of formations that takes place from consciousness moment to consciousness moment, which is knowing and seeing the (mundane) Truth of Suffering. And you need to continue until you see that you in the future attain Arahantship and later attain Parinibbāna.

When you in the future attain Arahantship, ignorance (1) will have been destroyed, and there will have been the remainderless cessation *(an·avasesa·nirodhā)* of volitional formations (2), craving (8), and clinging (9): the causes for suffering will have ceased. But suffering itself will not have ceased, because the results of past kamma still operate: you will still be possessed of the five aggregates.[78] (Even The Buddha was possessed of the five aggregates, and suffered pleasant and unpleasant feelings.[79]) It is only at

[77] A.III.II.ii.1 *'Titth·Āyatana·Suttaṁ'* ('The Sectarian Doctrines Sutta')

[78] The five aggregates = consciousness (3), mentality-materiality (4), the six sense bases (5), contact (6), and feeling (7).

[79] The Buddha suffered, for example, because of a back pain (see p.241), and at old age

(Please see further next page.)

your Parinibbāna that the five aggregates cease without remainder: it is only at your Parinibbāna that suffering ceases. This means there are two types of cessation:

1) the cessation at your attainment of Arahantship
2) the cessation at your Parinibbāna

The cause for these two cessations is the Arahant Path Knowledge, which knows and sees (the Unformed *(A·Saṅkhata)*) Nibbāna, the Noble Truth of the Cessation of Suffering *(Nirodha Ariya·Sacca)*. But this does not mean that when you now look into the future and know and see your attainment of Arahantship and Parinibbāna, you know and see Nibbāna: you do not at this stage know and see Nibbāna. At this stage you know and see only when the five causes that give rise to formations cease, there are no more formations. With that knowledge, you understand that your Parinibbāna will have been realized.

Without seeing this, says The Buddha, you cannot realize Nibbāna, the goal of asceticism and Brahminhood:[80]

Those, bhikkhus, ascetics or Brahmins *(samaṇā vā brāhmanā vā)*

[1] **who do not understand ageing&death,**
[2] **who do not understand ageing&death's origin** *(samudaya)*,
[3] **who do not understand ageing&death's cessation** *(nirodha)*,
[4] **and who do not understand the way leading to ageing&death's cessation** *(nirodha·gāmini·paṭipadaṁ)*;

who do not understand birth... existence...clinging... craving... feeling... contact... the six sense bases... mentality-materiality... consciousness... volitional formations, their origin, their cessation, and the way leading to their cessation: these I do not consider to be ascetics among ascetics or Brahmins among Brahmins, and such venerable ones do not, by realizing it for themselves with direct knowledge, in this very life enter and dwell in the goal of asceticism or the goal of Brahminhood.

But you can enter and dwell in the goal of asceticism, you can see these things, because you have developed strong and powerful concentration. The Buddha explains in the *'Samādhi'* sutta ('The Concentration Sutta') of the *'Khandha·Saṁyutta'* ('The Aggregate-Section'):[81]

because of ageing (see quotation p.252).

[80] S.II.I.ii.3 *'Samaṇa·Brāhmaṇa·Suttaṁ'* ('The Ascetics and Brahmins Sutta'). In M.II.iii.10 *'Vekhanassa·Suttaṁ'* (Vekhanassa is a wanderer's name), The Buddha also explains: 'If any, Kaccāna, ascetics and brahmins, without knowing the past, without seeing the future, claim "Birth is destroyed, the holy life has been lived, what had to be done has been done, there is no more coming into any state of being," such with this, in accordance with the Dhamma, are confuted.'

[81] S.III.I.i.5

Develop concentration, bhikkhus *(Samādhiṁ, bhikkhave, bhāvetha)*. **Concentrated, bhikkhus, a bhikkhu according to reality understands** *(yathā·bhūtaṁ pajānāti)*. **And what according to reality does he understand?**

[1] **Materiality's appearance and disappearance;**
[2] **feeling's appearance and disappearance;**
[3] **perception's appearance and disappearance;**
[4] **formations' appearance and disappearance;**
[5] **consciousness's appearance and disappearance.**

YOU KNOW AND SEE DEPENDENT ORIGINATION

The splendour, radiance, light, brilliance and brightness of wisdom that you have developed enables you to go back along the line of successive mentality-materiality from the present to the moment of your rebirth in this life, to the moment of your death in your past life, and further back in the same way to as many lives as you can discern, and then also look into the future, to the time of your own Parinibbāna.[82] By looking at the individual constituents of mentality-materiality, you will be able to identify the causes and effects.

At the time of practising diligently and with a mind that is purified by strong and powerful concentration, engaged in the deep and profound practice of discerning ultimate mentality-materiality, you will see that in the future there is the attainment of final cessation: Nibbāna. But if you stop meditating etc., the conditions will have changed, in which case the future results will also have changed.

An example of this is Mahādhana the Treasurer's Son and his wife.[83] They both inherited very much wealth, but Mahādhana squandered it on drink and entertainment. Finally, he and his wife had nothing at all, and were begging in the streets. The Buddha explained to Ānanda that if Mahādhāna had become a bhikkhu when young, he would have become an Arahant; if he had become a bhikkhu when middle-aged, he would have become a Non-Returner; and if he had become a bhikkhu when elderly, he would have become a Once-Returner: such were his *pāramī*. But because of drink, he attained nothing at all, and was now a beggar. This shows that our future is determined all the time by our present. That is why, at the time of practising deep and profound meditation continuously over a period, you will see your own Parinibbāna either in this life or in the future.

---

[82] For details see 'How You Discern Your Future', p.191, and Table 1d 'Death and Rebirth', p.188.

[83] DhP.A.xi.9 *'Mahādhana·Seṭṭhi·Putta·Vatthu'* ('The Case of Mahādhana the Lord-Son')

Without seeing past lives and future lives it is impossible for you to understand dependent origination as it really is: to know and see how past causes have given results in the present, and present causes will give results in the future, and how the cessation of the causes gives the cessation of the results. And without knowing and seeing dependent origination, it is impossible to know and see the Noble Truth of the Origin of Suffering as it really is. It is explained in the *Visuddhi·Magga*:[84]

There is no one, even in a dream, who has got out of the fearful round of rebirths, which is ever destroying like a thunderbolt, unless he has severed with the knife of knowledge well whetted on the stone of sublime concentration, this Wheel of Existence, which offers no footing owing to its great profundity, and is hard to get by owing to the maze of many methods. And this has been said by the Blessed One:

This dependent origination is profound, Ānanda, and profound it appears. And, Ānanda, it is through not understanding, through not penetrating it, that this generation has become a tangled skein, a knotted ball of thread, matted as the roots in a bed of reeds, and finds no way out of the round of rebirths, with its states of loss, unhappy destinations... perdition.[85]

Once you have known and seen the Second Noble Truth (the Noble Truth of the Origin of Suffering) as it really is, you will have overcome doubt about the three divisions of time: present, past, and future. It is explained in the *Visuddhi·Magga*:[86]

When he has thus seen that the occurrence of mentality-materiality is due to conditions *(paccayato)*, **then he sees** *(samanupassati)* **that, as now, so in the past too its occurrence was due to conditions, and in the future too its occurrence will be due to conditions.**

Having reached this stage, you have realized the Doubt-Overcoming Purification *(Kaṅkhā·Vitaraṇa Visuddhi)*.[87] It is only at this stage that you can begin to practice Vipassāna, because it is only at this stage that you know and see ultimate reality: you cannot practise vipassanā until you have seen dhammas[88] as they really are.

---

[84] VsM.xvii.659 *'Bhava·Cakka·Kathā'* ('The Wheel of Existence Discussion') PP.xvii.314: the quotation is from D.ii.2 *'Mahā·Nidāna·Suttaṁ'* ('The Great Causation Sutta').

[85] This passage is quoted and analysed p.79.

[86] VsM.xix.679 *'Paccaya·Pariggaha·Kathā'* ('Cause-Apprehending Discussion') PP.xix.5

[87] For the discernment of dependent origination/cessation, and past and future mentality/materiality, see Talk 6 'How You See the Links of Dependent Origination', p.183*ff.*

[88] For *dhammas*, see footnote 22, p.5.

YOU PRACTISE VIPASSANĀ

When practising vipassanā, you go back and again know and see the Noble Truth of Suffering as it really is, and the Noble Truth of the Origin of Suffering as it really is: you know and see the arising and perishing of all eleven categories of mentality-materiality. But this time you know and see them as impermanence *(anicca)*, suffering *(dukkha)* and without a self, non-self *(an·atta)*. You know and see formations as they really are, and reflect on them according to the instructions given by The Buddha in His second teaching, the *'An·Atta·Lakkhaṇa'* sutta ('The Non-Self Characteristic Sutta'), which He taught to the group of five bhikkhus *(pañca·vaggiyā bhikkhū)*:[89]

[1] **What do you think, bhikkhus, is materiality permanent or impermanent** *(niccaṁ vā aniccaṁ vā)*? **(Impermanent, Venerable Sir.)**

[2] **That which is impermanent, is it suffering or happiness** *(dukkhaṁ vā taṁ sukhaṁ vā)*? **(Suffering, Venerable Sir.)**

[3] **Is that which is impermanent, suffering and subject to change, fit to be regarded thus: 'This is mine** *(etaṁ mama)*; **this I am** *(esohamasmi)*; **this is my self** *(eso me attā)*'? **(No, Venerable Sir.)**

Therefore, bhikkhus,

[1] **whatever kind of materiality there is, whether past, future, or present; internal or external; gross or subtle; inferior or superior; far or near, all materiality should be seen as it really is with right wisdom thus: 'This is not mine** *(netaṁ mama;)*; **this I am not** *(nesohamasmi;)*; **this is not my self** *(na meso attā)*'.

[2] **Whatever kind of feeling there is whether past, future, or present; internal or external; gross or subtle; inferior or superior; far or near, all feeling....**

[3] **Whatever kind of perception there is whether past, future, or present; internal or external; gross or subtle; inferior or superior; far or near, all perception....**

[4] **Whatever kind of mental formations there are whether past, future, or present; internal or external; gross or subtle; inferior or superior; far or near all mental formations....**

[5] **Whatever kind of consciousness there is whether past, future, or present; internal or external; gross or subtle; inferior or superior; far or near, all consciousness should be seen as it really is with right wisdom thus: 'This is not mine; this I am not; this is not my self'.**[90]

In other words, formations *(saṅkhārā)*, which is mentality-materiality and their causes, perish as soon as they arise, which is why they are

---

[89] S.III.I.II.i.7

[90] The commentary to the *'Chann·Ovāda·Suttaṁ'* ('The Advice-to-Channa Sutta'); M.III.v.2) explains that 'This is not mine' is a reflection on impermanence; 'This I am not' is a reflection on suffering; 'This is not my self' is a reflection on non-self.

impermanent *(anicca)*; they are subject to constant arising and perishing, which is why they are suffering *(dukkha)*; they have no self *(atta)*, or stable and indestructible essence, which is why they are non-self *(anatta)*.

YOU KNOW AND SEE THE UNFORMED

Through a series of exercises in which you contemplate the rising and perishing of formations, and then only the perishing of formations, you progress through the remaining Knowledges *(Ñāṇa)*, after which you will eventually know and see the Unformed *(A·saṅkhata)*, which is Nibbāna. When you know and see the unformed, you know and see the Deathless *(A·mata)*. This is explained by The Buddha:[91]

Let him look on the world as void:
Thus, Mogharāja, always mindful,
He may escape the clutch of death
By giving up belief in self.
For King Death cannot see the man
Who looks in this way on the world.

When The Buddha says we must know and see the world as void, He means that we must know and see it as void of permanence *(nicca)*, void of happiness *(sukha)* and void of self *(atta)*.[92] In ordinary language, we may say that you must see absolute zero.

But this does not mean that your consciousness is absolute zero: your consciousness is fully aware: it is the object that your consciousness knows and sees which is absolute zero. The object that your consciousness is fully aware of and knows and sees is the Nibbāna element: the Unformed Element *(A·saṅkhata·Dhātu)*.[93] This is realization of the Supramundane Eightfold Noble Path, when all eight factors take Nibbāna as object.[94]

---

[91] SuN.v.15 *'Mogharāja·Māṇava·Pucchā'* ('The Student Mogharāja's Questions'), quoted VsM.xxi.765 *'Saṅkhār·Upekkhā·Ñāṇa·Kathā'* ('Equanimity-Towards-Formations-Knowledge Discussion') PP.xxi.60.

[92] Further to the perception of voidness, see also Q&A 5.9, p.181.

[93] For a discussion of the inevitable full awareness at the realization of Nibbāna, see Q&A 3.2, p.97.

[94] For the realization of Nibbāna, see 'You Know and See Nibbāna', p.224.

YOU FULLY REALIZE THE FOUR NOBLE TRUTHS

It is at this stage that you will have realized the Four Noble Truths as they really are, and that has been possible only because the necessary conditions for doing so have been present. In the *'Kūṭāgāra'* sutta ('The Peaked-House Sutta') mentioned previously, the Buddha explains also how those conditions make it possible to put a complete end to suffering:[95]

Indeed, bhikkhus, if anyone said: 'Having built the lower structure of a peaked house, I shall erect the upper structure', such a thing is possible. So too, if anyone said:

[1] **'Having realized the Noble Truth of Suffering as it really is;**
[2] **'having realized the Noble Truth of the Origin of Suffering as it really is;**
[3] **'having realized the Noble Truth of the Cessation of Suffering as it really is;**
[4] **'having realized the Noble Truth of the Path Leading to the Cessation of Suffering as it really is, 'I shall put a complete end to suffering'; such a thing is possible.**

And He adds:

[1] **Therefore, bhikkhus, an exertion should be made** *(yogo karaṇīyo)* **to understand: 'This is suffering** *(idaṁ dukkhan'ti)*.**'**
[2] **Therefore, bhikkhus, an exertion should be made to understand: 'This is the origin of suffering** *(idaṁ dukkha·samudayan'ti)*.**'**
[3] **Therefore, bhikkhus, an exertion should be made to understand: 'This is the cessation of suffering** *(idaṁ dukkha·nirodhan'ti)*.**'**
[4] **Therefore, bhikkhus, an exertion should be made to understand: 'This is the path leading to the cessation of suffering** *(idaṁ dukkha·nirodha·gāminī·paṭipadā'ti)*.**'**

May all beings find the opportunity to make the necessary exertion to fully realize the Four Noble Truths, and put a complete end to suffering.

Pa-Auk Tawya Sayadaw
Pa-Auk Tawya Monastery

---

95 S.V.XII.v.4 'The Peaked-House Sutta'.

Talk 1

How You Develop Mindfulness-of-Breathing to Absorption

INTRODUCTION

We are very happy to have come to Taiwan, at the invitation of some Taiwanese monks and nuns who stayed at Pa-Auk Forest Monastery, near Mawlamyine in Myanmar.[96] While in Taiwan we should like to teach you something about the system of meditation taught at Pa-Auk Forest Monastery. It is based upon instructions found in the Pali[97] Buddhist texts and the *Visuddhi·Magga*.[98] We believe that the meditation taught in the Pali Buddhist texts is the same as the meditation practised by The Buddha Himself, and taught by Him to His disciples during His lifetime.

WHY MEDITATE?

First we should ask ourselves, 'Why did The Buddha teach meditation?' or, 'What is the purpose of meditation?'

The purpose of Buddhist meditation is to attain Nibbāna. Nibbāna is the cessation of mentality *(nāma)* and materiality *(rūpa)*. To reach Nibbāna, therefore, we must completely destroy both wholesome volitional formations, rooted in non-greed, non-hatred, and non-delusion, and unwholesome mental formations, rooted in greed, hatred, and delusion, all of which produce new birth, ageing, sickness and death. If we destroy them totally with the Path Knowledge *(Ariya·magga)*, then we will have realized Nibbāna. In other words, Nibbāna is release and freedom from the suffering of the round of rebirths *(saṁsāra)*, and is the cessation of rebirth, ageing, sickness, and death. We are all subject to the suffering of rebirth, ageing, sickness, and death, and so to free ourselves from the many forms of suffering we need to meditate. Since we wish to be free from all suffering, we must learn how to meditate in order to attain Nibbāna.

WHAT IS MEDITATION?

So what is meditation? Meditation consists of samatha and vipassanā meditation, which must both be based upon moral conduct of body and

---

[96] *Pa-Auk Tawya* = Pa-Auk Forest

[97] For untranslated Pali terms, see Appendix 1, p.283.

[98] *Visuddhi·Magga*: see footnote 71, p.20.

speech. In other words, meditation is the development and perfection of the Noble Eightfold Path *(Ariya Aṭṭhaṅgika Magga)*. The Noble Eightfold Path is:

1) Right View .... *(Sammā·Diṭṭhi)*	5) Right Livelihood .... *(Sammā·Ājīva)*
2) Right Thought ... *(Sammā·Saṅkappa)*	6) Right Effort .... *(Sammā·Vāyāma)*
3) Right Speech .... *(Sammā·Vācā)*	7) Right Mindfulness .... *(Sammā·Sati)*
4) Right Action ..... *(Sammā·Kammanta)*	8) Right Concentration .. *(Sammā·Samādhi)*

Right View is two types of view: Vipassanā Right-View *(Vipassanā·Sammā·Diṭṭhi)* and Path Right-View *(Magga·Sammā·Diṭṭhi)*. Right View and Right Thought are together called the training of wisdom *(paññā)*.

Right Speech, Right Action, and Right Livelihood are together called the training of morality *(sīla)*.

Right Effort, Right Mindfulness, and Right Concentration are together called the training of concentration *(samādhi)*, which is samatha meditation *(samatha·bhāvanā)*.

THE NOBLE EIGHTFOLD PATH

Now, let us look a little bit more at each of the eight factors of the Noble Eightfold Path.

The first factor is Right View *(Sammā·Diṭṭhi)*. What is Right View? Right View consists of four kinds of knowledge:

1) Vipassanā knowledge of the Noble Truth of Suffering, which is the five clinging-aggregates.
2) Vipassanā knowledge of the Noble Truth of the Origin of Suffering, which discerns the causes for the five clinging-aggregates, in other words, it is the vipassanā knowledge of dependent origination.
3) Realization and knowledge of the Cessation of Suffering, which is the cessation of the five clinging-aggregates, Nibbāna.
4) Knowledge of the Noble Truth of the Path Leading to the Cessation of Suffering, which is the way of practice leading to realization of Nibbāna, the Noble Eightfold Path.

The second factor of the Noble Eightfold Path is Right Thought *(Sammā·Saṅkappa)*. Right Thought too is four-fold:

1) Application to the object of the Noble Truth of Suffering, which is the five clinging-aggregates.
2) Application to the object of the Noble Truth of the Origin of Suffering, which is the causes for the five clinging-aggregates.
3) Application to the object of the Noble Truth of the Cessation of Suffering, which is Nibbāna.

4) Application to the object of the Noble Truth of the Path Leading to the Cessation of Suffering, which is the Noble Eightfold Path.

Thus, Right Thought applies the mind to the object of the Truth of Suffering, the five clinging-aggregates, and Right View understands it as it really is. These two factors work together to apply the mind to each of the Four Noble Truths, and to understand them. Since they work together in this way, they are called the training of wisdom *(paññā sikkhā)*.

The third factor of the Noble Eightfold Path is Right Speech *(Sammā·Vācā)*. Right Speech is to abstain from lying, slander, harsh speech, and useless talk.

The fourth factor of the Noble Eightfold Path is Right Action *(Sammā·Kammanta)*. Right Action is to abstain from killing, from theft, from sexual misconduct, and from taking beer&wine liquor and other intoxicants.[99]

The fifth factor of the Noble Eightfold Path is Right Livelihood *(Sammā·Ājīva)*. Right Livelihood is to abstain from obtaining a living by wrong speech or wrong actions, such as killing, stealing, or lying. For laypeople it includes to abstain from the five types of wrong trade: trade in weapons, humans, animals for slaughter, liquor and other intoxicants, and poisons.

The three factors of Right Speech, Right Action, and Right Livelihood are called the training of morality *(sīla sikkhā)*.

The sixth factor of the Noble Eightfold Path is Right Effort *(Sammā·Vāyāma)*. Right Effort is also of four kinds:

1) The effort to prevent the arising of unwholesome states that have not yet arisen;
2) The effort to remove unwholesome states that have already arisen;
3) The effort to arouse the arising of wholesome states that have not yet arisen;
4) The effort to increase wholesome states that have already arisen.

In order to develop these four types of Right Effort, we must practise and develop the three trainings of morality, concentration, and wisdom.

The seventh factor of the Noble Eightfold Path is Right Mindfulness *(Sammā·Sati)*. Right Mindfulness is also of four kinds, the four foundations of mindfulness *(sati·paṭṭhāna)*:

1) Body-contemplation *(kāy·ānupassanā sati·paṭṭhāna)*
2) Feelings-contemplation *(vedan·ānupassanā sati·paṭṭhāna)*
3) Consciousness-contemplation *(citt·ānupassanā sati·paṭṭhāna)*
4) Dhammas-contemplation *(dhamm·ānupassanā sati·paṭṭhāna)*

---

[99] beer&wine liquor: see footnote 471, p.246.

Here, dhammas are the fifty-one associated mental factors excluding feeling, or the five clinging-aggregates, or the twelve internal and external sense bases, or the eighteen elements, or the seven enlightenment-factors, or the Four Noble Truths, etc. But the four types of mindfulness can in fact be reduced to just two, mindfulness of materiality and mindfulness of mentality.

The eighth factor of the Noble Eightfold Path is Right Concentration *(Sammā·Samādhi)*. Right Concentration is the first jhāna (absorption), second jhāna, third jhāna, and fourth jhāna. These are called Right Concentration according to the *'Mahā·Sati·Paṭṭhāna'* sutta, 'The Great Mindfulness-Foundation Sutta'.[100] In the *Visuddhi·Magga*,[101] Right Concentration is explained further as the four jhānas *(rūpa·jhāna)*, the four immaterial jhānas *(a·rūpa·jhāna)* and access concentration *(upacāra·samādhi)*.

Some people have a great accumulation of *pāramī*, and can attain Nibbāna by simply listening to a brief or detailed talk on the Dhamma. Most people, however, do not have such *pāramī*, and must practise the Noble Eightfold Path in its gradual order. They are called person-to-be-led *(neyya·puggala)*, and must develop the Noble Eightfold Path step by step, in the order of morality, concentration, and wisdom. After purifying their morality they must train in concentration, and after purifying their mind by way of concentration practice, they must train in wisdom.

HOW YOU DEVELOP CONCENTRATION

How should you develop concentration? There are forty subjects of samatha meditation, and a person can develop any of these to attain concentration.

Those who cannot decide which meditation subject to develop should start with *ān·āpāna·sati* (mindfulness-of-breathing). Most people succeed in meditation by using either *ān·āpāna·sati* or four-elements meditation. Therefore, let us now look briefly at how to practise *ān·āpāna·sati*.

---

[100] D.ii.9 (Also M.I.i.10) For bibliographical abbreviations and source references, see p.281.

[101] Vis.xviii.662 *'Diṭṭhi-Visuddhi Niddesa'* ('Description of View Purification') PP.xviii.1. Here, the *Visuddhi·Magga* explains that 'Purification of Consciousness' is 'the eight attainments together with access concentration': this is the same as Right Concentration.

HOW YOU DEVELOP MINDFULNESS-OF-BREATHING

The development of *ān·āpāna·sati* (mindfulness-of-breathing) is taught by The Buddha in the *'Mahā·Sati·Paṭṭhāna'* sutta[102] He begins:

And how then, bhikkhus, does a bhikkhu abide contemplating the body as a body?

Here, bhikkhus, a bhikkhu (gone to the forest, or gone to the foot of a tree, or gone to a secluded place) sits down, having crossed his legs, set his body straight, having mindfulness established before him [established upon his meditation subject]**.**

Then The Buddha explains mindfulness-of-breathing *(ān·āpāna·sati)*:

- **He mindfully breathes in; mindfully breathes out.**
- **Breathing in long, he understands: 'I breathe in long;'**
- **breathing out long, he understands: 'I breathe out long.'**
- **Breathing in short, he understands: 'I breathe in short;'**
- **breathing out short, he understands: 'I breathe out short.'**
- **'Experiencing the whole** [breath] **body, I shall breathe in': thus he trains;**
- **'experiencing the whole** [breath] **body, I shall breathe out': thus he trains.**
- **'Tranquillizing the body-formation, I shall breathe in': thus he trains;**
- **'tranquillizing the body-formation, I shall breathe out': thus he trains.**

To begin meditating, sit in a comfortable position and try to be aware of the breath as it enters and leaves the body through the nostrils. You should be able to feel it either just below the nose or somewhere around the nostrils: that is called the touching-point. Do not follow the breath into the body or out of the body, because then you will not be able to perfect your concentration. Just be aware of the breath at the most obvious place it brushes against or touches, either the top of the upper lip or around the nostrils. Then you will be able to develop and perfect your concentration.

Do not pay attention to the natural characteristics *(sabhāva·lakkhaṇa)*, general characteristics *(sammañña·lakkhaṇa)*,[103] or colour of the nimitta (sign of concentration). The natural characteristics are the characteristics of the four elements in the breath: hardness, roughness, flowing, heat, supporting, pushing, etc. The general characteristics are the impermanent *(anicca)*, suffering *(dukkha)*, and non-self *(an·atta)* characteristics of the breath. This means, do not note 'in-out-impermanent', or 'in-out-suffering', or 'in-out-non-self'. Simply be aware of the in&out breath as a concept.

---

[102] D.ii.9 'The Great Mindfulness-Foundation Sutta' (Also M.I.i.10)

[103] natural characteristic *(sabhāva·lakkhaṇa)*: the characteristic peculiar to one type of ultimate reality, be it materiality or mentality: also called individual characteristic *(paccatta·lakkhaṇa)*; general characteristic *(samañña·lakkhaṇa)*: the three characteristics general to all formations, be they material or mental: impermanence, suffering, non-self.

The concept of the breath is the object of *ān·āpāna·sati*. It is this object you must concentrate on to develop concentration. As you concentrate on the concept of the breath in this way, and if you practised this meditation in a previous life, and developed some *pāramī*, you will easily be able to concentrate on the in&out breath.

If not, the *Visuddhi·Magga* suggests counting the breaths. You should count after the end of each breath: 'In-out-one, in-out-two,' etc.[104]

Count up to at least five, but to no more than ten. We suggest you count to eight, because that reminds you of the Noble Eightfold Path, which you are trying to develop. So you should count, as you like, up to any number between five and ten, and determine that during that time you will not let your mind drift, or go elsewhere, but be only calmly aware of the breath. When you count like this, you find that you are able to concentrate your mind, and make it calmly aware of only the breath.

After concentrating your mind like this for at least half an hour, you should proceed to the first and second stage of the meditation:

[1] **Breathing in long, he understands: 'I breathe in long** *(dīghaṁ assasāmi)***;' breathing out long, he understands: 'I breathe out long** *(dīghaṁ passasāmi)***.'**

[2] **Breathing in short, he understands: 'I breathe in short** *(rassaṁ assasāmi)***;' breathing out short, he understands: 'I breathe out short** *(rassaṁ passasāmi)***.'**

At this stage, you have to develop awareness of whether the in&out breaths are long or short. 'Long' or 'short' here do not refer to length in feet and inches, but length in time, the duration. You should decide for yourself what length of time you will call 'long', and what length of time you will call 'short'. Be aware of the duration of each in&out breath. You will notice that the breath is sometimes long in time, and sometimes short. Just knowing this is all you have to do at this stage. Do not note, 'In-out-long, In-out-short', just 'In-out', and be aware of whether the breaths are long or short. You should know this by being just aware of the length of time that the breath brushes against and touches the upper lip, or around the nostrils, as it enters and leaves the body. Sometimes the breath may be long throughout the sitting, and sometimes short, but do not purposely try to make it long or short.

At this stage the nimitta may appear, but if you are able to do this calmly for about one hour, and no nimitta appears, you should move on to the third stage;

---

104 VsM.viii.223*ff* *'Ān·Āpāna·Sati·Kathā'* ('Mindfulness-of-Breathing Discussion') PP.viii.90*ff*

[3] **'Experiencing the whole** [breath] **body** *(sabba·kāya·paṭisaṁvedī)*, **I shall breathe in** *(assasissāmi)*:**' thus he trains.**
'Experiencing the whole [breath] **body** *(sabba·kāya·paṭisaṁvedī)*, **I shall breathe out** *(passasissāmī)*:**' thus he trains.**

Here The Buddha is instructing you to be aware of the whole breath from beginning to end. As you do this the nimitta may now appear. If it does, do not immediately shift your mind to it, but stay with the breath.

If you are calmly aware of the breath from beginning to end for about an hour, and no nimitta appears, you should move on to the fourth stage:

[4] **'Tranquillizing the body-formation** *(passambhayaṁ kāya·saṅkhāraṁ)*, **I shall breathe in** *(assasissāmi)*'**: thus he trains.**
'Tranquillizing the body-formation *(passambhayaṁ kāya·saṅkhāraṁ)*, **I shall breathe out** *(passasissāmi)*'**: thus he trains.**

To do this, you should decide to make the breath tranquil, and go on being continuously aware of the breath from beginning to end. You should do nothing else, otherwise your concentration will break and fall away.

The *Visuddhi·Magga* gives four factors for making the breath tranquil:[105]

1) Concern .... *(ābhoga)*	3) Attention .... *(manasikāra)*
2) Reaction .... *(samannāhāra)*	4) Reviewing .... *(paccavekkhaṇa)*

And they are explained first with a simile:

Suppose a man stands still after running or after descending from a hill, or putting down a load from his head; then his in-breaths and out-breaths are gross, his nostrils become inadequate, and he keeps on breathing in and out through his mouth. But when he has rid himself of his fatigue and has bathed and drunk and put a wet cloth on his chest, and is lying in the cool shade, then his in-breaths and out-breaths eventually occur so subtly that he has to investigate whether they exist or not.

Likewise, says the *Visuddhi·Magga*, the bhikkhu's in&out-breaths are gross to begin with, become increasingly subtle, after which **he has to investigate whether they exist or not.**

To further explain why the bhikkhu needs to investigate the in&out-breaths, the *Visuddhi·Magga* says:

Because previously, at the time when the yogi had not yet discerned the [in&out breath] **there was no concern in him, no reaction, no attention, no reviewing, to the effect that** [he knew]: **'I am progressively tranquillizing each grosser bodily formation** [the in&out breath].**' But once he has discerned** [the in&out breath], **there is. So his bodily formation** [the in&out breath] **at the time when he has discerned** [it] **is subtle in comparison with what it was at the time when he had not** [discerned it].

[105] VsM.viii.220 *'Ān·Āpāna·Sati·Kathā'* ('Mindfulness-of-Breathing Discussion') PP.viii.178

1) Concern *(ābhoga)*: you pay initial attention to the breath, you apprehend the breath, you advert the mind towards the breath, to the effect: 'I will try to make the breath tranquil.'
2) Reaction *(samannāhāra)*: you continue to do so, i.e. you pay sustained attention to the breath that way, do it again and again, keep the breath in the mind, to the effect: 'I will try to make the breath tranquil.'
3) Attention *(manasikāra)*: literally 'deciding to make the breath tranquil'. Attention is the mental factor that makes the mind advert towards the object. Attention makes the mind conscious of the breath and know the breath.
4) Reviewing *(paccavekkhaṇa)*:[106] you review *(vīmaṁsa)* the breath, make it clear to the mind, to the effect: 'I will try to make the breath tranquil.'

So all you need to do at this stage is to decide to tranquil the breath, and to be continuously aware of it. That way, you will find the breath becomes more tranquil, and the nimitta may appear.

Just before the nimitta appears, a lot of yogis encounter difficulties. Mostly they find that the breath becomes very subtle and unclear; they may think the breath has stopped. If this happens, you should keep your awareness where you last noticed the breath, and wait for it there.

A dead person, a foetus in the womb, a drowned person, an unconscious person, a person in the fourth jhāna, a person in the attainment of cessation *(nirodha·samāpatti)*[107], and a brahmā: only these seven types of person do not breathe. Reflect on the fact that you are not one of them, that you are in reality breathing, and that it is just your mindfulness which is not strong enough for you to be aware of the breath.

When it is subtle, you should not make the breath more obvious, as the effort will cause agitation, and your concentration will not develop. Just be aware of the breath as it is, and if it is not clear, simply wait for it where you last noticed it. You will find that, as you apply your mindfulness and wisdom in this way, the breath will reappear.

---

[106] Here, *vimaṁsa* is synonymous with *paccavekkhaṇa*, and is the term employed in the sub-commentary's discussion.

[107] When consciousness, associated mental factors, and materiality produced by consciousness are suspended. For details regarding this attainment, see Q&A 5.1, p.173.

THE NIMITTA

For some yogis, there is first light before the nimitta appears, for others, the nimitta appears directly. They are not the same thing. They are different just as the sun is different from sunlight.

The nimitta of *ān·āpāna·sati* varies according to the individual yogi. To some the nimitta is pure and fine like cotton wool, or drawn out cotton, moving air or a draught, a bright light like the morning star Venus, a bright ruby or gem, or a bright pearl. To others it is like the stem of a cotton plant, or a sharpened piece of wood. To yet others it is like a long rope or string, a wreath of flowers, a puff of smoke, a stretched out cobweb, a film of mist, a lotus, a chariot wheel, a moon, or a sun.

In most cases, a pure white nimitta like cotton wool is the *uggaha-nimitta* (taken-up sign or learning sign), and is usually dull and opaque. When the nimitta becomes bright like the morning star, brilliant and clear, it is the *paṭibhāga-nimitta* (counterpart sign). When like a dull ruby or gem, it is the *uggaha-nimitta*, but when bright and sparkling, it is the *paṭibhāga-nimitta*. The other images should be understood in this way too.

So, even though *ān·āpāna·sati* is a single meditation subject, it produces various types of nimitta: the nimitta appears differently to different people.

The *Visuddhi·Magga* explains that this is because the nimitta is produced by perception.[108] And the sub-commentary of the *Visuddhi·Magga* explains that it is the different perceptions which the different yogis had before the nimitta arose.[109]

Thus, the nimittas are different because of perception. But perception does not arise alone. It is a mental formation that arises always together with the individual consciousness and other mental formations: these mental formations associated with the individual consciousness are called associated mental factors *(cetasika)*.[110] So, for example, if a yogi concentrates on the *ān·āpāna* nimitta with a happy mind, the mental factors are not only the one perception, but are altogether thirty-three, such as, contact, volition, one-pointedness, attention, application, sustainment, decision, effort, and desire: not only perception differs, but also all the other mental factors differ.

---

[108] VsM.viii.231 *'Ān·Āpāna·Sati·Kathā'* ('Mindfulness-of-Breathing Discussion') PP.viii.216

[109] VsMṬ.ibid.

[110] For the mental formations of jhāna, see table, p.162.

This is in fact explained elsewhere in the *Visuddhi·Magga*, in its explanation of the attainment of the base of neither perception nor non-perception *(neva·saññā·n·āsaññ·āyatana)*, the fourth immaterial jhāna.[111]

There, the *Visuddhi·Magga* explains that the perception in that jhāna is very subtle, which is why we call it the attainment of neither perception nor non-perception. But it is not only the perception that is very subtle. The feelings, the consciousness, the contact and all the other mental formations are also very subtle. Thus, says the *Visuddhi·Magga*, in the attainment of neither perception nor non-perception there is also neither feeling nor non-feeling, neither consciousness nor non-consciousness, neither contact nor non-contact, etc.[112]

So, when the commentaries say the nimittas are different because of perception, they are merely explaining the *ān·āpāna-nimitta* from the single point-of-view of perception, in terms of perception *(saññāsīsa)*, using perception as their example.

But, whatever the shape or colour of your nimitta, whatever your perception of the in&out breath, it is important not to play with your nimitta. Do not let it go away, and do not intentionally change its shape or appearance. If you do, your concentration will not develop any further and your progress will stop. Your nimitta will probably disappear. So when your nimitta first appears, do not move your mind from the breath to the nimitta. If you do, you will find it disappears.

If you find that the nimitta is stable, and your mind by itself has become fixed on it, then just leave your mind there. If you force your mind to come away from it, you will probably lose your concentration.

If your nimitta appears far away in front of you, ignore it, as it will probably disappear. If you ignore it, and simply concentrate on the breath at the place where the breath touches, the nimitta will come and stay there.

If your nimitta appears at the place where the breath touches, is stable, and appears as the breath itself, and the breath as the nimitta, then forget about the breath, and be aware of just the nimitta. By moving your mind from the breath to the nimitta, you will be able to make further progress. As you keep your mind on the nimitta, the nimitta becomes whiter and whiter, and when it is white like cotton wool, it is the *uggaha-nimitta*.

You should determine to keep your mind calmly concentrated on the white *uggaha-nimitta* for one, two, three hours, or more. If you can keep your mind fixed on the *uggaha-nimitta* for one or two hours, it should

---

[111] For details regarding this jhāna, see p.68.

[112] VsM.x.287 *'Neva-Saññā-N-Āsaññ-Āyatana·Kathā'* ('Neither-Perception-Nor-Non-Perception Base Discussion') PP.x.50

become clear, bright, and brilliant. This is then the *paṭibhāga-nimitta* (counterpart sign). Determine and practise to keep your mind on the *paṭibhāga-nimitta* for one, two, or three hours. Practise until you succeed.

At this stage you will reach either access *(upacāra)* or absorption *(appanā)* concentration. It is called access concentration because it is close to and precedes jhāna. Absorption concentration is jhāna.

Both types of concentration have the *paṭibhāga-nimitta* as their object. The only difference between them is that in access concentration the jhāna factors are not fully developed. For this reason bhavaṅgas still occur, and one can fall into bhavaṅga (life-continuum consciousness). The yogi will say that everything stopped, and may even think it is Nibbāna. In reality the consciousness has not stopped, but the yogi is just not sufficiently skilled to discern this, because the bhavaṅgas are very subtle.

HOW YOU BALANCE THE FIVE CONTROLLING FACULTIES

To avoid dropping into bhavaṅga and to develop further, you need the help of the five controlling faculties *(pañc·indriyā)* to push the mind and fix it on the *paṭibhāga-nimitta*. The five controlling faculties are:

1) Faith .... *(saddhā)*
2) Effort .... *(vīriya)*
3) Mindfulness .... *(sati)*
4) Concentration .... *(samādhi)*
5) Understanding .... *(paññā)*

The five controlling faculties are the five powers that control the mind, and keep it from straying off the path of samatha (tranquillity) and vipassanā (insight) that leads to Nibbāna. If one or more of the controlling faculties are in excess, there will be an imbalance.

The first controlling faculty is faith in what one should have faith in, such as the Triple Gem, or faith in kamma and its results. It is important to have faith in the enlightenment of The Buddha, because without it, a person will regress from his work in meditation. It is also important to have faith in the teaching of The Buddha, namely the Four Paths, the Four Fruitions, Nibbāna, etc. The teaching of The Buddha shows us the way of meditation, so at this stage it is important to have complete faith in it.

Let us say the yogi thinks, 'Can jhāna really be attained by just watching the in-breath and out-breath? Is it really true that the *uggaha-nimitta* is like white cotton wool, and the *paṭibhāga-nimitta* like clear ice or glass?' If these kinds of thought persist, they result in views such as, 'Jhāna cannot be attained in the present age,' and the yogi's faith in the teaching will decline, and he will be unable to stop himself from giving up the development of samatha.

So a person who is developing concentration with a meditation subject like *ān·āpāna·sati* needs to have strong faith. He should develop *ān·āpāna·sati* without any doubts. He should think, 'Jhāna can be achieved if I follow the instructions of The Fully Enlightened Buddha systematically.'

If, however, a person lets his faith become excessive, and here it is faith in the meditation *paṭibhāga-nimitta*, his concentration will decrease. Excessive faith contains excessive joy *(pīti)*, which leads to emotions. This means the yogi's mind is disturbed by joyful excitement, and wisdom is unable to understand the *paṭibhāga-nimitta*. Then, because excessive faith has decided on the object, wisdom is not clear and firm, and also the remaining faculties, effort, mindfulness and concentration are weakened: effort is unable to raise associated mental formations to the *paṭibhāga-nimitta*, and keep them there; mindfulness is unable to establish knowledge of the *paṭibhāga-nimitta*; concentration is unable to prevent the mind from going to another object; and wisdom is unable to see the *paṭibhāga-nimitta* penetratively. Thus excessive faith leads actually to a decrease in faith.

If effort is too strong, the remaining faculties, faith, mindfulness, concentration, and wisdom, will be unable to respectively decide, establish, prevent distraction, and develop penetrative discernment. Thus excessive effort causes the mind not to stay calmly concentrated on the *paṭibhāga-nimitta*.

This can be illustrated by the case of the Venerable Soṇa. In the city of Rājagaha, he heard the Buddha teach, and winning faith, he got his parents' consent and ordained. The Buddha taught him a subject for meditation, and he went to the monastery Sītavana. He worked very hard, but pacing up and down in meditation with great energy, he developed painful sores on his feet. He did not lie down and sleep, and when he could no longer walk, he crawled on his hands and knees. He worked so hard that his meditation path was stained with blood. Even so, he won no attainment and was filled with despair.

The Buddha, on *Gijjha·Kūta* (*Vulture Peak* mountain), became aware of his despair and visited him. And The Buddha reminded him that when he as a layman had played the *vīṇā* (a type of Indian lute), the lute was not tuneful or playable if the strings were strung either too tight or too loose: they had to be strung evenly. The Buddha explained that in the same way, too much energy or effort ends in flurry, and too little energy or effort ends in idleness. The Venerable Soṇa profited from the lesson, because not long afterwards, having reflected on the lesson, he became an Arahant.

To balance faith with wisdom, and concentration with effort, is praised by the wise. If, for instance, faith is strong and wisdom is weak, a person will develop faith in, and respect for objects without use and essence. For instance, he will develop faith in, and reverence for objects revered and respected by religions outside orthodox Buddhism, such as guardian spirits or protective deities.

If, on the other hand, wisdom is strong and faith is weak, a person can become quite crafty. Without meditating, he will spend his time simply passing judgements. This is as difficult to cure as to cure a disease caused by an overdose of medicine.

If faith and wisdom are balanced, however, a person will have faith in objects he should have faith in: the Triple Gem, kamma, and its effects. He will believe that if he meditates in accordance with The Buddha's instructions, he will be able to attain the *paṭibhāga-nimitta*, and jhāna.

Again, if concentration is strong and effort is weak, a person can become lazy. For example, if, when the yogi's concentration improves, he pays attention to the *ān·āpāna paṭibhāga-nimitta* with a relaxed mind, without knowing it penetratively, he may become lazy. The five jhāna-factors will in that case not be strong enough to maintain the high level of concentration, which means his mind will very often fall into bhavaṅga.

But if effort is strong, and concentration weak, however, he can become agitated. When concentration and effort are balanced, he will become neither lazy, nor agitated, and will be able to attain jhāna.

When a person wishes to cultivate a samatha subject, it is in any case good to have very strong faith. If he thinks, 'I will certainly reach jhāna, if I develop concentration on the *paṭibhāga-nimitta*', then by the power of that faith, and by concentrating on the *paṭibhāga-nimitta*, he will definitely achieve jhāna. This is because jhāna is based primarily on concentration.

For a person developing vipassanā it is good that wisdom be strong, because when wisdom is strong he will be able to know and see the three characteristics of impermanence, suffering, and non-self penetratively.

Only when concentration and wisdom are balanced can mundane jhānas *(lokiya·jjhāna)* arise. The Buddha taught that this applies equally to supramundane jhānas *(lokuttara·jjhāna)*, which further require that concentration and wisdom be balanced with effort and faith.

Mindfulness is necessary under all circumstances, because it protects the mind from agitation due to excess faith, effort, or wisdom, and from laziness due to excess concentration. It balances faith with wisdom, concentration with effort, and concentration with wisdom.

So mindfulness is always necessary, as is the seasoning of salt in all sauces, and a prime minister for all the king's affairs. Hence the ancient commentaries say The Blessed One said, 'Mindfulness is always necessary in any meditation subject.' Why? Because it is a refuge and protection for the meditating mind. Mindfulness is a refuge, because it helps the mind arrive at special and high states it has never reached or known before. Without mindfulness the mind is incapable of attaining any special and extraordinary states. Mindfulness protects the mind, and keeps the object of meditation from becoming lost. That is why to one discerning it with vipassanā knowledge, mindfulness appears as that which protects the object of meditation, as well as the mind of the yogi. Without mindfulness, a person is unable to lift the mind up or restrain the mind, which is why The Buddha said it is necessary in all instances.[113]

HOW YOU BALANCE THE SEVEN ENLIGHTENMENT-FACTORS

If one is to achieve jhāna using *ān·āpāna·sati*, it is also important to balance the seven enlightenment-factors *(bojjh·aṅga)*. They are:

1) Mindfulness *(sati)*: remembers the *paṭibhāga-nimitta* and discerns it again and again.
2) Investigation of Phenomena *(dhamma·vicaya)*: understands the *paṭibhāga-nimitta* penetratively.
3) Effort *(vīriya)*: brings the enlightenment factors together, and balances them on the *paṭibhāga-nimitta*; and especially reinforces itself, and the Factor of Investigation of Phenomena.
4) Joy *(pīti)*: gladness of the mind when experiencing the *paṭibhāga-nimitta*.
5) Tranquillity *(passaddhi)*: tranquillity of the mind and associated mental factors, that have the *paṭibhāga-nimitta* as their object.
6) Concentration *(samādhi)*: one-pointedness of the mind on the *paṭibhāga-nimitta*.
7) Equanimity *(upekkhā)*: evenness of mind that neither becomes excited, nor withdraws from the *paṭibhāga-nimitta*.

A yogi must develop and balance all seven enlightenment factors. With insufficient effort the mind will fall away from the object of meditation, in this case the *paṭibhāga-nimitta*. Then one should not develop tranquillity, concentration, and equanimity, but instead develop investigation of phenomena, effort, and joy. That way the mind is raised up again.

---

[113] See also VsM.iv.62 *'Dasa·Vidha·Appanā Kosallaṁ'* ('The Ten Kinds of Skill in Absorption') PP.iv.45-49, and VsMṬ.ibid.

When there is too much effort, however, the mind will become agitated and distracted. Then one should do the opposite, and not develop investigation of phenomena, effort, and joy, but instead develop tranquillity, concentration, and equanimity. This way the agitated and distracted mind becomes restrained and tranquillized.

This is how the five controlling faculties, and seven enlightenment-factors are balanced.

HOW YOU ATTAIN JHĀNA

When the five controlling faculties, faith, effort, mindfulness, concentration, and understanding are sufficiently developed, concentration will go beyond access, up to jhāna, absorption concentration. When you reach jhāna, your mind will know the *paṭibhāga-nimitta* without interruption. This can continue for several hours, even all night, or for a whole day.

When your mind stays continuously concentrated on the *paṭibhāga-nimitta* for one or two hours, you should try to discern the area in the heart where the bhavaṅga consciousness rests, that is the heart materiality. The bhavaṅga consciousness is bright and luminous, and the commentaries explain that it is the mind door *(mano·dvāra)*. If you try many times, again and again, you will eventually discern both the mind door (bhavaṅga), and *paṭibhāga-nimitta* as it appears there. You should then discern the five jhāna factors one at a time. With continued practice, you will be able to discern them all at once. In the case of *ān·āpāna·sati*, the five jhāna factors are:

1) Application *(vitakka)*: directing and placing the mind on the *ān·āpāna paṭibhāga-nimitta.*
2) Sustainment *(vicāra)*: maintaining the mind on the *ān·āpāna paṭibhāga-nimitta.*
3) Joy *(pīti)*: liking for the *ān·āpāna paṭibhāga-nimitta.*
4) Bliss *(sukha)*: happiness about the *ān·āpāna paṭibhāga-nimitta.*
5) One-pointedness *(ek·aggatā)*: one-pointedness of mind on the *ān·āpāna paṭibhāga-nimitta.*

1a: **The Jhāna-Attainment Process** *(jhāna·samāpatti·vīthi)*[1]

- One consciousness lasts one consciousness-moment *(citta·kkhaṇa)*, with three stages: arising *(uppāda)* ↑, standing *(ṭhiti)* |, dissolution *(bhaṅga)* ↓.
- In between each mental process arises a number of life-continuum consciousnesses (see table 1d: 'Death and Rebirth').
- Cognition follows a fixed procedure, according to the natural law of the mind *(citta·niyāmā)*.

CONSCIOUSNESS MOMENT *Citta·Kkhaṇa*	(Before the mental process) ⇒⇒⇒⇒⇒⇒	⇒	⇒
OBJECT *Ārammaṇa*	Previous life's near-death object		
CONSCIOUSNESS *Citta*	Life-Continuum *Bhavaṅga* ↑|↓	Trembling Life-Continuum *Bhavaṅga·Calana* ↑|↓	Arrest Life-Continuum *Bhavaṅg·Upaccheda* ↑|↓
Sphere *Āvacara*	Sensual/Fine-/Immaterial *Kāma·/Rūpa·/Arūpa·*		

CONSCIOUSNESS MOMENT *Citta·kkhaṇa*	3⇒	4⇒	5⇒	6⇒	7⇒	⇒⇒⇒⇒⇒⇒⇒...⇒⇒⇒⇒⇒⇒⇒	(After the mental process) ⇒⇒⇒⇒⇒⇒⇒⇒⇒
OBJECT *Ārammaṇa*	Jhāna Object *Jhān·Ārammaṇa*						Previous life's near-death object.
CONSCIOUSNESS *Citta*	Mind-Door Adverting *Mano·Dvār·Āvajjana* ↑|↓	1st Impulsion *Javana* ↑|↓	2nd Impulsion *Javana* ↑|↓	3rd Impulsion *Javana* ↑|↓	4th Impulsion *Javana* ↑|↓	Very Many Thousand Million Impulsions *Javana* ↑|↓↑|↓↑|↓↑|↓...↑|↓↑|↓↑|↓↑|↓	Life-Continuum *Bhavaṅga* ↑|↓
		Preparation *Parikamma*	Access *Upacāra*	Conformity *Anuloma*	Change-of-Lineage *Gotrabhu*	Absorption *Appanā*	
Sphere *Āvacara*	Sensual *Kāma·*					Fine-Material/Immaterial *Rūpa·/Arūpa·*	Sensual/Fine-/Immaterial *Kāma·/Rūpa·/Arūpa·*

[1] The jhāna-attainment process is a mind-door process that can take place on any of the three planes: sensual-, fine-material-, or immaterial plane. All details given here are based on VsM.iv.69 *'Paṭhama·Jjhāna·Kathā'* ('Explanation of the First Jhāna') PP.iv.74-78

Further Notes for Table 1a 'The Jhāna-Attainment Process'

- The procedure of the jhāna-attainment process is:

1) A mind-door adverting consciousness: it takes as object the counterpart sign *(paṭibhāga·nimitta)* of the meditation subject.

2-4) Three preparatory impulsions with that same object:
(i) Preparation- (ii) Access- (iii) Conformity Knowledge
Their application, sustainment, happiness, joy and one-pointedness are stronger than normal sensual-sphere consciousnesses. Thus they prepare the way for absorption, are in the access of jhāna, and conform to the consciousness preceding them, and the succeeding Change of Lineage. (In one of keen faculties, the preparation consciousness does not arise: there are only three preparatory impulsions.)

5) Change of Lineage Knowledge: it marks the transition from consciousness of the limited lineage *(paritta·gotta)* of sensual-sphere consciousness to the exalted lineage *(mah·aggata·gotta)*, of fine-material- or immaterial-sphere jhāna consciousness.

6) Countless absorption impulsion consciousnesses (mental formations *(saṅkh-ārā)*), with the same object; each cognition reinforcing the next.[114] The number of absorption impulsions depends on how long the jhāna attainment lasts, which depends on the yogi's practice and skill: it may last only some fractions of a second, it may last an hour, it may last several days. The yogi who has developed the five masteries of jhāna determines beforehand how long the jhāna attainment will last. But when the beginner first attains jhāna, there arises only one jhāna.

This same procedure is followed when one enters into the supramundane Fruition Attainment.[115]

- In a five-door-, and mind-door process of the sensual sphere, the impulsions are all the same, but in a jhāna-attainment process (which is of the fine-material- or immaterial sphere) the impulsions are different. The fifth impulsion, which is the actual jhāna consciousness, is not only one, but many thousand million, and they are all the same. If one is in the same jhāna for a longer period, the number of fifth impulsions is uncountable.
- The yogi enters the jhāna attainment in accordance with the way the mind is conveyed *(yath·ābhinīhāra·vasena)*: the yogi decides which jhāna to attain.
- The wholesome kamma of a jhāna attainment becomes a wholesome weighty kamma when it is maintained up to the near-death mental process.

The jhāna factors are together called jhāna. When you are just beginning to practise jhāna, you should practise entering jhāna for a long

[114] For the mental-formations of each absorption consciousness, see 'How You Discern Jhāna Mental-Processes', p.161.

[115] See 'You Know and See Nibbāna', p.224.

time, and not spend too much time discerning the jhāna factors. You should develop mastery *(vasī-bhāva)* of the jhānas.

There are five masteries:

1) To enter jhāna whenever desired.
2) To resolve *(adhiṭṭhāna)* to stay in jhāna for a determined duration, and-carry out the resolve.
3) To emerge from jhāna at the determined time.
4) To advert to the jhāna factors.
5) To review the jhāna factors.[116]

In the *'Pabbateyya·Gāvī'* sutta of the *Aṅguttara·Nikāya,*[117] The Buddha says one should not try going to the second jhāna before mastering the first jhāna. He explains that if one does not master the first jhāna completely, and tries to go to higher jhānas, one will lose the first jhāna, as well as be unable to attain the other jhānas. One will lose all the jhānas.

When you have mastered the first jhāna, you can try to progress to the second jhāna. You need to enter the now familiar first jhāna, emerge from it, reflect on its faults, and reflect on the advantages of the second jhāna. That is: the first jhāna is close to the five hindrances, and has the gross jhāna factors of applied and sustainment, making it less tranquil than the second jhāna, which is without them. So, with no desire now for those two jhāna factors, a desire for only joy, happiness, and one-pointedness, you should again concentrate on the *paṭibhāga-nimitta,* and attain the first jhāna. When you now emerge from the first jhāna, and again review the jhāna factors with mindfulness and full awareness, the two jhāna factors of application and sustainment will appear gross to you, while joy, happiness or bliss and one-pointedness appear peaceful. So, in order to abandon the gross factors and obtain the peaceful factors, you should again concentrate on the *paṭibhāga-nimitta.*

This way you will be able to attain the second jhāna, possessed of only those three factors, joy, bliss, and one-pointedness. You should then develop the five masteries of the second jhāna.

When you have succeeded, and want to develop the third jhāna, you should emerge from the now familiar second jhāna, reflect on its faults,

---

[116] Adverting and reviewing occur in the same mind-door process *(mano·dvāra·vīthi).* Adverting is performed by the mind-door adverting consciousness *(mano·dvār·āvajjana),* which in this case takes as object one of the five jhāna factors. It is followed by the four, five, six, or seven reviewing impulsion consciousnesses, which have the same object. For details, see table '1b: The Mind-Door Process', p.164.

[117] A.IX.I.iv.4 'The Mountain Cow Sutta', also called *'Gāvī-Upamā·Suttaṁ'* ('The Cow Simile Sutta').

and reflect on the advantages of the third jhāna. That is: the second jhāna is close to the first jhāna, which has the gross jhāna factor of applied- and sustainment. And the second jhāna itself has the gross jhāna factor of joy,[118] making it less tranquil than the third jhāna, which is without it. So, with no desire now for that gross factor, a desire for only the peaceful factors, you should again concentrate on the *paṭibhāga-nimitta*, and attain the second jhāna. When you now emerge from the second jhāna, and again review the jhana factors, the jhāna factor of joy will appear gross to you, while bliss and one-pointedness appear peaceful. So, in order to abandon the gross factor and obtain the peaceful factors, you should again concentrate on the *paṭibhāga-nimitta*. This way you will be able to attain the third jhāna, possessed of only happiness and one-pointedness. You should then develop the five masteries of the third jhāna.

When you have succeeded, and want to develop the fourth jhāna, you should emerge from the now familiar third jhāna, reflect on its faults, and reflect on the advantages of the fourth jhāna. That is, the third jhāna is close to the second jhāna, which has the gross jhāna factor of joy. And the third jhāna itself has the gross jhāna factor of happiness, making it less tranquil than the fourth jhāna, which is without it. With the desire now to attain the fourth jhāna, you should again concentrate on the *paṭibhāga-nimitta* and attain the third jhāna. When you now emerge from the third jhana, and again review the jhāna factors, the jhāna factor of bliss will appear gross to you, while equanimityand one-pointedness appear peaceful. So, in order to abandon the gross factor and obtain the peaceful factors, you should again concentrate on the *paṭibhāga-nimitta*.This way you will be able to attain the fourth jhāna, possessed of only equanimity and one-pointedness. You should then develop the five masteries of the fourth jhāna.

With the attainment of the fourth jhāna, the breath stops completely. This completes the fourth stage in the development of *ān·āpānā·sati*:

[4] **'Tranquillizing the body-formation, I shall breathe in': thus he trains.**
'Tranquillizing the body-formation, I shall breathe out': thus he trains.

This stage began just before the nimitta appeared, and as concentration developed through the four jhānas, the breath became progressively more and more tranquil, until it stopped in the fourth jhāna. The four jhānas are also called fine-material-sphere jhānas *(rūp·āvacara·jhāna)*, because they

[118] The Most Venerable Pa-Auk Tawya Sayadaw explains that the jhāna factor of joy *(pīti)* is a contributory factor towards developing attachment for jhāna happiness *(jhāna·sukha)*, which, because the object is very subtle, cannot develop into sensual happiness *(rāga)*; it is only subtle *(pīha)*.

may cause rebirth in the fine-material realm. But here we do not encourage you to develop jhānas for the sake of attaining rebirth in the fine-material realm, but for the sake of using them to develop vipassanā meditation.

When a yogi has reached the fourth jhāna by using *ān·āpāna·sati*, and has developed the five masteries, the light of concentration is bright, brilliant and radiant, and he can, if he wishes, move on to develop vipassanā meditation. The yogi can, on the other hand, continue to develop samatha meditation. That will be the subject of our next talk, namely, how you develop samatha meditation on the thirty-two parts of the body, the skeleton, ten kasiṇas, etc.

Questions and Answers 1

Question 1.1 How do we, in the four stages of *ān·āpāna·sati* (mindfulness-of-breathing), decide when to go from one stage to another?

Answer 1.1 The Buddha taught *ān·āpāna·sati* step by step: long breath, short breath, whole breath and subtle breath, only for easy understanding. At the time of actual practice, all four stages may occur at the same time.

Then, if you can concentrate on the whole long breath, and the whole short breath for about one hour, then (as your concentration improves) the breath will automatically become subtle, and you can change to concentrate on the subtle breath. When the subtle breath is long, you should try to know the whole, long, subtle breath; when the subtle breath is short, you should try to know the whole, short, subtle breath.

If the breath does not become subtle by itself, you should concentrate on it (attention *(manāsikāra)*) with the decision that it should be subtle.[119] That way it will become subtle, but you must not make the breath subtle on purpose, nor make it long or short on purpose; just decide that it should be tranquil. In this way, long breath, short breath, whole breath and subtle breath, all the four stages, are included in a single stage.

At the early part of the fourth stage, the breath becomes only very subtle. It does not cease entirely. The breath ceases entirely only at the fourth jhāna. This is the subtlest stage.

Question 1.2 Is it necessary, in meditation, to have a nimitta?

Answer 1.2 In some meditation subjects *(kammaṭṭhāna)* like *ān·āpāna·sati* (mindfulness-of-breathing), kasiṇa meditation and repulsiveness meditation *(asubha)*, a nimitta is necessary. If one wants to attain jhāna in other meditation subjects, like Buddha Recollection *(Buddh·Ānussati)*, a nimitta is not possible. In loving-kindness meditation *(mettā·bhāvanā)*, breaking down the barriers is called the nimitta.[120]

Question 1.3 Some say that while practising *ān·āpāna·sati* (mindfulness-of-breathing) their soul goes out of the body. Is that true, or are they on the wrong path?

Answer 1.3 A concentrated mind can usually create a nimitta. When concentration is deep, strong, and powerful, then because of different perceptions, different nimittas appear. For example, if you want the nimitta to be long, it will be long; if you want it to be short, it will be short; if you want it to be round, it will be round; if you want it to be red, it will be red. So, various perceptions may arise while practising *ān·āpāna·sati*. You may

---

[119] For more details about tranquillizing the breath, see p.35.

[120] Only a name, for it is in fact not a nimitta.

perceive yourself as outside the body. It is simply a mental creation, not because of a soul. It is not a problem. Just ignore it, and return to being mindful of your breath.

Only when you discern ultimate mentality-materiality *(paramattha·nāma·rūpa)* internally and externally, can you solve the problem of a soul: you will not find a soul anywhere. So, you need to break down the compactness *(ghana)* of mentality and materiality, and realize ultimate mentality and materiality.

Nānādhātuyo vinibbhujitvā ghanavinibbhoge kate anattalakkhaṇaṁ yāthāvasarasato upaṭṭhāti.

When compactness is broken down with the breaking down into different elements, the non-self characteristic *(an·atta·lakkhaṇa)* **in its true nature will arise.**[121]

It is because of the perception of compactness, that the perception of a soul arises.

In the case of materiality, there are three types of compactness *(ghana)*:[122]

1) Continuity compactness *(santati·ghana)*: because materiality seems to be one compact continuity, a continuous whole, one may think one's body and limbs have actual existence. And one may think the same self 'migrates' from life to life, taking different forms. To overcome this delusion, we need to resolve the seeming compactness of the body. We need to see that the body comprises rūpa kalāpas that arise and perish. That way, we see that a kalāpa has no continuity; as soon as it arises, it perishes. There is no time for a kalāpa to go anywhere, not from life to life, not even from second to second.
2) Synthesis compactness *(samūha·ghana)*: because materiality seems to be a synthetic whole, one may think the kalāpas are ultimate materiality. And one may think they are one's self. To overcome this delusion, we need to resolve the seeming compactness of the individual type of kalāpa: we need to analyse the individual type of kalāpa. That way, we see that a kalāpa comprises elements: earth element, water element, fire element, wind element, colour, odour, flavour,

[121] VsM.xxi.739 *'Upakkilesa·Vimutta-Udaya·Bbaya·Ñāṇa·Kathā'* ('Imperfections-Free Arise&Peris Knowledge Discussion') PP.xxi.4

[122] In VsM.xi.306 *'Catu·Dhātu·Vavatthāna·Bhāvanā·Vaṇṇanā'* ('Description of the Four-Elements Definition Meditation') PP.xi.30, reference is made to the Buddha's simile of the butcher who has killed a cow and cut it into pieces: in D.ii.9 *'Mahā·Sati·Paṭṭhāna·Suttaṁ'* ('The Great Mindfulness-Foundation Sutta'), and M.I.i.10 *'Sati·Paṭṭhāna·Suttaṁ'* ('The Mindfulness-Foundation Sutta'). The Subcommentaries to these texts explain how this involves resolving the three kinds of compactness.

nutritive-essence, life faculty, etc. There is no synthetic whole anywhere.

3) Function compactness *(kicca·ghana)*: because of insufficient understanding about ultimate materiality, one may think the elements rest upon a self, like seeds and plants rest upon earth. To overcome this delusion, we need to see that each element has its own characteristic *(lakkhaṇa)*, function *(rasa)*, manifestation *(paccupaṭṭhāna)*, and proximate cause *(padaṭṭhāna)*: it does not depend on any external thing such as a self.

How do you break down the compactness of materiality? You must first discern the rūpa-kalāpas (small particles). Then you must analyse the different rūpa-kalāpas, and see that they comprise different types of materiality, which are at least eight in each rūpa-kalāpa. And then you need to analyse each type of materiality. Without doing this the perception of a soul will not disappear.

Similarly, without breaking down the compactness of mentality, the perception of a soul will not disappear. For example, when your mind wanders, you may think that the wandering mind is your soul.

There are four types of compactness in such a mental process that need to be broken down by vipassanā knowledge:[123]

1) Continuity compactness *(santati·ghana)*: because mentality seems to be one compact continuity, a continuous whole, one may think it is the same 'mind' that cognizes objects through the eye, ear, nose, tongue, body, and mind. And one may think it is the same self, the same 'mind', the same 'pure consciousness', etc., that 'migrates' from life to life, entering different bodies. And in this life, one may think one's mind wanders outside the body. To overcome this delusion, we need to resolve the seeming compactness of the mind. We need to see that cognition takes place by way of mental processes that arise and perish. That way, we see that the mind has no continuity; as soon as it arises, it perishes. There is no time for consciousness to go anywhere, not from life to life, not even from second to second.
2) Synthesis compactness *(samūha·ghana)*: because mentality seems to be a synthetic whole, one may think it is pure consciousness that cognizes the object. And one may think it is one's self. To overcome this delusion, we need to resolve the seeming compactness of the individual type of consciousness: we need to analyse the individual type of consciousness in each type of mental process. That way, we

[123] VsMṬ.xxi.739 *'Upakkilesa·Vimutta-Udaya·Bbaya·Ñāṇa·Kathā·Vaṇṇanā'* ('Description of Explanation of the Corruption-Freed Arise&Perish Knowledge')

see that a consciousness comprises consciousness and a given number mental factors, such as feeling, perception, and volition, and application, and sustainment, or hatred, delusion, wrong view, conceit, and scepticism, or non-greed, non-hatred, non-delusion, happiness, mindfulness, faith and Right View. There is no synthetic whole anywhere.

3) Function compactness *(kicca·ghana)*: because of insufficient understanding about ultimate mentality, one may think the elements rest upon a self, like seeds and plants rest upon earth. To overcome this delusion, we need to see that each consciousness and mental factor has its own characteristic, function, manifestation, and proximate cause: it does not depend on any external thing such as a self.
4) Subject compactness *(ārammaṇa·ghana)*: having penetrated the previous three compactnesses, one may think, for example, 'I saw ultimate materiality and mentality', or, '"the knowing self" saw ultimate materiality and mentality.'[124] To overcome this delusion, we need to resolve the three types of compactness in the vipassanā mental-processes that penetrated the three types of compactness, with subsequent vipassanā knowledge. We need to see that the mentality that is the object of our vipassanā knowledge was also the subject of vipassanā knowledge: it penetrated the three types of compactness of mentality that also was a subject with an object.

And how do you break down the compactness of mentality? Take, for example a mind-door process of access concentration that has the *ān·āpāna paṭibhāga-nimitta* as object.

Such a mental process has one mind-door adverting consciousness and seven impulsion consciousnesses *(javana)*. In the mind-door adverting consciousness moment there are twelve mental formations, and in each impulsion moment there are thirty-four mental formations.

If you break down the four types of compactness of mentality this way, you will see only the rapid arising and perishing of consciousnesses and their associated mental factors.

With that perception of impermanence, one can no longer think one's consciousness is one's soul, because with the perception of impermanence comes the perception of non-self. As said by The Buddha, in the *'Meghiya'* sutta:[125]

---

[124] Other variations of this delusion would be, for example, 'the knower knows', 'the doer knows', 'that which knows knows', etc. One may also think 'ultimate materiality and mentality change, but "the knowing mind" does not change'.

[125] U.iv.1 (also A.IX.I.i.3)

Anicca·saññino meghiya an·atta·saññā saṇṭhāti.

For those who have powerful vipassanā knowledge of impermanence, vipassanā knowledge of non-self will also appear clearly.

Question 1.4 Where does the [*ān·āpāna*] nimitta come from? What makes it appear?

Answer 1.4 Most mind states that arise dependent upon the heart base produce breathing. A real *ān·āpāna-nimitta* comes from the breath. But not every mind state produces a nimitta. Only a deeply concentrated mind produces a nimitta. Therefore, the breath produced by a deep and concentrated mind makes an *ān·āpāna-nimitta* appear. If the nimitta is far from the nostrils, it is not a real nimitta. A nimitta may appear because of concentration, but not necessarily the real *ān·āpāna-nimitta*. If the nimitta produces jhāna, we call it an *ān·āpāna-nimitta*. But if it does not produce jhāna, it is not the real *ān·āpāna-nimitta*. If you concentrate on that nimitta, jhāna will not arise. Usually the concentration cannot become strong and powerful. If you meditate on that nimitta, it will very soon disappear.

Question 1.5 What are the seven stages of purification and sixteen vipassanā knowledges?

Answer 1.5 The seven stages of purification are:

1) Morality Purification *(Sīla·Visuddhi)*
2) Consciousness Purification *(Citta·Visuddhi)*
3) View Purification *(Diṭṭhi·Visuddhi)*
4) Doubt-Overcoming Purification *(Kaṅkhā·Vitaraṇa·Visuddhi)*
5) Path&Non-Path Knowledge&Vision Purification *(Magg·Āmagga·Ñāṇa·-Dassana·Visuddhi)*
6) Practice Knowledge&Vision Purification *(Paṭipadā·Ñāṇa·Dassana·Visuddhi)*
7) Knowledge&Vision Purification *(Ñāṇa·Dassana·Visuddhi)*

And the sixteen vipassanā knowledges are:

1) Mentality-Materiality Definition Knowledge *(Nāma·Rūpa·Pariccheda·Ñāṇa)*
2) Cause-Apprehending Knowledge *(Paccaya·Pariggaha·Ñāṇa)*
3) Comprehension Knowledge *(Sammasana·Ñāṇa)*
4) Arise&Perish Knowledge *(Udaya·bbaya·Ñāṇa)*
5) Dissolution Knowledge *(Bhaṅga·Ñāṇa)*
6) Fearsomeness Knowledge *(Bhaya·Ñāṇa)*
7) Danger Knowledge *(Ādīnava·Ñāṇa)*
8) Disenchantment Knowledge *(Nibbidā·Ñāṇa)*
9) Liberation-Longing Knowledge *(Muñcitu·kamyatā·Ñāṇa)*
10) Reflection Knowledge *(Paṭisaṅkhā·Ñāṇa)*
11) Formations-Equanimity Knowledge *(Saṅkhār·upekkhā·Ñāṇa)*

12) Conformity Knowledge *(Anuloma·Ñāṇa)*
13) Change-of-Lineage Knowledge *(Gotrabhu·Ñāṇa)*
14) Path Knowledge *(Magga·Ñāṇa)*
15) Fruition Knowledge *(Phala·Ñāṇa)*
16) Reviewing Knowledge *(Paccavekkhaṇa·Ñāṇa)*

Now you know the names of the vipassanā knowledges: have you experienced them? No. That is why to have only theoretical knowledge is not enough; you must practise with great effort to also realize them.

[At the end of this talk the Most Venerable Pa-Auk Tawya Sayadaw added the following comment on the five hindrances.]

Now let us discuss briefly the five hindrances *(nīvaraṇa)*:

1) sensual desire *(kāma·cchanda)*	4) restlessness&remorse *(uddhacca·kukkucca)*
2) ill-will *(byāpāda)*	5) doubt *(vicikicchā)*
3) sloth&torpor *(thina·middha)*	

The first hindrance, sensual desire *(kāma·cchanda)*, is attachment to property or people. It is the desire for sense objects. For example, you may get attached to your *kuṭi*[126] or room. While meditating you may think, 'Oh, it would be good if my *kuṭi* were beautiful.' Or you may think, 'Oh, it would be good if the whole room belonged to me!' If you are overwhelmed by sensual desire, you will not be able to concentrate well on your meditation object. You must exert strong mindfulness and make effort to stop the arising of sensual desire.

The second hindrance is ill-will *(byāpāda)*. It is hatred for or dissatisfaction with people or things. For example, if the yogi sitting next to you, while sitting down, makes a noise with his robes, you may become angry and think, 'Oh, why is he making so much noise!!' If your mind is overwhelmed by hatred or dissatisfaction, you will not be able to concentrate well on your meditation object either.

The third hindrance is sloth and torpor *(thina·middha)*. If the mind is weak, or not interested in the meditation object, sloth and torpor can occur. Sometimes, however, sleepiness may be due to tiredness, illness, or lack of rest.

The fourth hindrance is restlessness and remorse *(uddhacca·kukkucca)*. If your mind is restless, it will be like a heap of ashes hit by a stone, flying about and scattering. The mind is scattered. While meditating, you must not relax the mind, and let it leave your meditation object. If you do, restlessness will occur. Remorse is to regret bad deeds done, and good deeds

[126] A *kuṭi* is a monastic dwelling for one, a cell or lodge.

not done in the past. Here too, you must exert strong mindfulness, and make great effort to stop the arising of restlessness and remorse.

The fifth hindrance is doubt *(vicikicchā)*. It is having doubts about eight things:

1) The Buddha
2) The Dhamma
3) The Saṅgha
4) The three trainings: morality, concentration, and wisdom.
5) The past five aggregates *(khandhā)*, which is past lives.
6) The future five aggregates, which is future lives.
7) Both the past and future five aggregates, which is past and future lives.
8) Dependent Origination *(paṭicca·samuppāda)*, which includes the present five aggregates.

If you have doubts about the training in concentration, you cannot meditate well. For example, you may think: 'Is it possible to attain jhāna through *ān·āpāna·sati* (mindfulness-of-breathing)? Can jhāna be attained by concentrating on the *ān·āpāna-nimitta*?'

The five hindrances are opposite jhāna concentration.

How You Develop Absorption on Other Subjects

In the previous talk we discussed how to develop the meditation subject of *ān·āpāna·sati* (mindfulness-of-breathing) up to the fourth jhāna, and how to develop the five masteries. As discussed, the light of concentration is then bright, brilliant and radiant, which means the yogi can, if he wishes, move on to develop vipassanā meditation.

But at this point the yogi can also go on to develop his samatha meditation further. Today, we shall discuss how to develop other samatha subjects: meditation on the thirty-two parts of the body, the skeleton, ten kasiṇas, etc.

HOW YOU DEVELOP THE THIRTY-TWO PARTS OF THE BODY

If you want to develop meditation on the thirty-two parts of the body, you should first re-establish the fourth *ān·āpāna* jhāna so the light of concentration is bright, brilliant, and radiant. You should then use the light to try to discern the thirty-two parts of the body, one at a time. The thirty-two parts of the body are twenty parts with predominantly the earth element, and twelve parts with predominantly the water element. The twenty earth-element parts should be discerned in four sets of five:

I	II	III	IV
1. head hairs	6. flesh	11. heart	16. intestines
2. body hairs	7. sinews	12. liver	17. mesentery[127]
3. nails	8. bones	13. membrane	18. gorge[127]
4. teeth	9. bone marrow	14. spleen	19. faeces
5. skin	10. kidneys	15. lungs	20. brain

The twelve water-element parts should be discerned in two sets of six:

I		II	
1. bile	4. blood	7. tears	10. snot
2. phlegm	5. sweat	8. grease	11. synovia[127]
3. pus	6. fat	9. saliva	12. urine

[127] MEMBRANE: the white, net-like membrane that separates the different sections of flesh throughout the body; MESENTERY: the fastenings of the bowels; GORGE: undigested food, contents of the stomach; SYNOVIA: unctuous fluid, oil in the joints.

Discern the parts in the given order, but one at a time. Try to see each part as distinctly as you would see your face in a clean mirror.

If, while doing this, the light of concentration should fade, and the part of the body being discerned become unclear, you should re-establish the fourth *ān·āpāna* jhāna, so the light is again bright and strong. Then return to discerning the parts of the body. Do this whenever the light of concentration fades.

Practise so that you are, from head hairs down to urine, or from urine back to head hairs, able to see each one clearly and with penetrating knowledge; keep practising until you become skilful.

Then, again using the light of concentration and with your eyes still closed, you should try to discern another being close by. It is especially good to discern someone in front of you. Discern the thirty-two parts of the body in that person or being, from head hairs down to urine, and from urine back to head hairs. Discern the thirty-two parts forwards and backwards many times. When you have succeeded, discern the thirty-two parts once internally, that is in your own body, and once externally, that is in the other person's body; do this many times, again and again.

When you are able to discern internally and externally like this, the power of meditation will increase. You should thus gradually extend your field of discernment bit by bit, from near to far. Do not think that you cannot discern beings far away. Using the brilliant light of the fourth jhāna, you can easily see beings far away, not with the naked eye, but with the eye of wisdom *(ñāṇa·cakkhu)*. You should be able to extend your field of discernment in all ten directions: above, below, east, west, north, south, north east, south east, north west, south west. Take whomever you discern, be they human, animal or other beings, in those ten directions, and discern the thirty-two parts, once internally and once externally, one person or other being at a time.

When you no longer see men, women, devas, or buffaloes, cows, and other animals as such, but see only groups of thirty-two parts, whenever and wherever you look, internally or externally, then can you be said to be successful, skilful, and expert in discerning the thirty-two parts of the body.

THE THREE ENTRANCES TO NIBBĀNA

Here, let us look at what is called the three entrances to Nibbāna. In the *'Mahā·Sati·Paṭṭhāna'* sutta,[128] The Buddha teaches that the four founda-

[128] D.ii.9 'The Great Mindfulness-Foundation Sutta' (Also M.I.i.10)

tions of mindfulness is the only way to Nibbāna. The commentary explains further that there are three entrances to the way to Nibbāna. They are the samatha subjects of the colour kasiṇas *(vaṇṇa·kasiṇa)*, repulsiveness *(paṭikkūla·manasikāra)*, and voidness of self *(suññatā)*, which is four-elements meditation.[129]

Therefore, when a person has become proficient in discerning the thirty-two parts of the body, internally and externally, he can choose to develop any of those three entrances. The first entrance we shall discuss is repulsiveness meditation.

HOW YOU DEVELOP SKELETON MEDITATION

To develop meditation on repulsiveness *(paṭikkūla·manasikāra)* you take as object either all thirty-two parts of the body or only one part. Let us look at how to meditate on, for example, the skeleton, the bones, which is one of the thirty-two parts of the body.

You should first re-establish the fourth *ān·āpāna* jhāna, so the light is bright, brilliant and radiant. Then use the light to discern the thirty-two parts in your own body, and then in a being nearby. Discern thus internally and externally once or twice. Then take the internal skeleton as a whole, and discern it with wisdom. When the whole skeleton is clear, take the repulsiveness of the skeleton as object, that is the concept, and note it again and again as either: 'repulsive - repulsive'; or 'repulsive skeleton - repulsive skeleton'; or 'skeleton - skeleton.

Note it in any language you like. You should try to keep your mind calmly concentrated on the object of repulsiveness of the skeleton for one or two hours. Be careful to see the colour, shape, position and delimitation of the skeleton, so that its repulsive nature can arise.

Because of the strength and momentum of the fourth-jhāna concentration based on *ān·āpāna·sati* (mindfulness-of-breathing), you will find that this meditation will also become deep and fully established: you will be able to produce, sustain and develop the perception and knowledge of repulsiveness.

---

129 The entrance of colour kasiṇas is mentioned in the *'Mahā Parinibbāna·Suttaṁ'* ('The Great Parinibbāna Sutta' D.ii.3), the *'Abhibh·Āyatana·Suttaṁ'* ('The Mastery-Base Sutta' A.VIII.V.ii.5), and the *'Abhibh·Āyatana·Kathā'*('Discussion of the Mastery Base' DhSA.1). The entrance of repulsiveness and voidness (of self) are mentioned in the *'Mahā Satipaṭṭhāna·Suttaṁ'* ('The Great Mindfulness-Foundation Sutta' D.ii.9) in the section *'Kāy·Ānupassanā'* ('Body-Contemplation'). Further to the perception of voidness, see p.27, and Q&A 5.9, p.181.

Once your concentration on the repulsiveness of the skeleton is established, you should drop the perception of 'skeleton', and just be mindful of the repulsiveness. According to the *Visuddhi·Magga*, seeing the colour, shape, position, and delimitation of a part is seeing the *uggaha-nimitta*. Seeing and discerning the repulsiveness of that part is seeing the *paṭibhāga-nimitta*.[130]

By concentrating on the *paṭibhāga-nimitta* of the repulsiveness of the skeleton, you can attain the first jhāna, at which time the five jhāna factors will be present. They are:

1) Application *(vitakka)*: directing and placing the mind on the *paṭibhāga-nimitta* of the repulsiveness of the skeleton.
2) Sustainment *(vicāra)*: maintaining the mind on the *paṭibhāga-nimitta* of the repulsiveness of the skeleton.
3) Joy *(pīti)*: liking for the *paṭibhāga-nimitta* of the repulsiveness of the skeleton.
4) Bliss *(sukha)*: happiness associated about the *paṭibhāga-nimitta* of the repulsiveness of the skeleton.
5) One-pointedness *(ek·aggatā)*: one-pointedness of mind on the *paṭibhāga-nimitta* of the repulsiveness of the skeleton.

You can, in a similar way, attain the first jhāna on the repulsiveness of one of the other parts of the body.

A question arises: 'How can joy and happiness arise with the repulsiveness of the skeleton as object?' The answer is that, although you are concentrating on the repulsiveness of the skeleton, and experience it as really repulsive, there is joy because you have undertaken this meditation, because you have understood the benefits of it, and because you have understood that it will help you to eventually attain freedom from ageing, sickness, and death. Joy and happiness can arise also because you have removed the defilements of the five hindrances, which make the mind hot and tired.

It is just like a scavenger would be delighted to see a big heap of garbage, thinking, 'I will earn a lot of money from this.' Or like a person who is severely ill would be happy and joyful when relieved by vomiting or having diarrhoea.

The *Abhidhamma Commentary* explains that whoever has attained the first jhāna on the repulsiveness of the skeleton should go on to develop the five masteries of the first jhāna. After that, the yogi should here too

---

[130] VsM.viii.214 *'Kāya·Gatā·Sati·Kathā'* ('Body-Related Mindfulness Discussion') PP.viii.141

take the nearest being, best of all a person sitting in front of him, and with his light of concentration take that person's skeleton as object. He should concentrate on it as repulsive, and develop this until the jhāna factors become prominent. Even though they are prominent, it is, according to the commentary, neither access concentration *(upacāra·samādhi)* nor absorption concentration *(appanā·samādhi)*, because the object is living.[131] If, however, you concentrate on the external skeleton as if it were dead, you can, according to the sub-commentary to the *Abhidhamma*, the *Mūla·Ṭīkā*, attain access concentration.[132]

When the jhāna factors are clear, you should again concentrate on the internal skeleton as repulsive. Do this alternately, once internally then once externally, again and again. When you have meditated like this on the repulsiveness of the skeleton, and it has become deep and fully developed, you should extend your field of discernment in all ten directions. Taking one direction at a time, wherever your light of concentration reaches, develop each direction in the same way. You should apply your penetrating knowledge both near and far, in all directions, once internally and once externally. Practise until wherever you look in the ten directions, you see only skeletons. Once you have succeeded, you are ready to develop the white kasiṇa meditation.

HOW YOU DEVELOP THE TEN KASIṆAS

THE COLOUR KASIṆAS

There are four colours used for kasiṇa meditation: blue, yellow, red, and white. 'Blue' *(nīla)* can also be translated as 'black', or 'brown'. All four kasiṇas can be developed up to the fourth jhāna by using as object the colours of different parts of the body.

According to the *Abhidhamma Commentary*, the head hairs, body hairs, and irises of the eyes can be used for the blue, brown, or black kasiṇa up to the fourth jhāna; fat and urine can be used for the yellow kasiṇa; blood and flesh can be used for the red kasiṇa; and the white parts, the bones, teeth, and nails can be used for the white kasiṇa.[133]

---

[131] VbhA.vii.1 *'Suttanta·Bhājanīya Kāy·Ānupassanā·Niddesa'* ('Sutta-Classification Body-Contemplation Description')

[132] VbhṬ.ibid.

[133] VbhA.ibid.

HOW YOU DEVELOP THE WHITE KASIṆA

It says in the suttas, that the white kasiṇa is the best of the four colour kasiṇas, because it makes the mind clear and bright.[134] For that reason, let us first discuss how to develop the white kasiṇa.

You should first re-establish the fourth *ān·āpāna* jhāna, so the light of concentration is bright, brilliant, and radiant. You should then use the light to discern the thirty-two parts of the body internally and then externally in a being nearby. Then discern just the skeleton. If you want to discern it as repulsive you can, if not, simply discern the external skeleton.

Then take either the whitest place in that skeleton, or, if the whole skeleton is white, the whole skeleton, or the back of the skull, and concentrate on it as 'white - white'.

Alternatively, if you want to, and your concentration is really sharp, you can, if you have seen the internal skeleton as repulsive and reached the first jhāna, take the skeleton as white, and use that as your preliminary object.

You can also discern first the repulsiveness in an external skeleton, and make that perception stable and firm, thus making the white of the skeleton more evident. Then, you can change to the perception of it to 'white - white', and instead develop the white kasiṇa.

With one of the objects of white in the external skeleton as object, you should practise to keep the mind calmly concentrated for one or two hours.

Because of the strength and momentum of the fourth-jhāna concentration based on *ān·āpāna·sati* (mindfulness-of-breathing), you will find that your mind will stay calmly concentrated on the object of white. When you are able to concentrate on the white for one or two hours, you will find that the skeleton disappears and only a white circle remains.

When the white circle is white as cotton wool, it is the *uggaha-nimitta* (taken-up sign). When it is bright and clear like the morning star, it is the *paṭibhāga-nimitta* (counterpart sign). Before the *uggaha-nimitta* arises, the skeleton nimitta from which it arises is the *parikamma-nimitta* (preparatory sign).

Continue to note the kasiṇa as 'white - white' until it becomes the *paṭibhāga-nimitta*. Continue concentrating on the *paṭibhāga-nimitta* until you enter the first jhāna. You will find, however, that this concentration is not very stable and does not last long. In order to make it stable and last a long time, you need to expand the nimitta.

---

134 A.X.I.iii.9 *'Paṭhama·Kosala·Suttaṁ'* ('The First Kosala Sutta')

To do this, you should concentrate on the white *paṭibhāga-nimitta* for one or two hours. Then determine to expand the white circle by one, two, three, or four inches, depending on how much you think you are able to expand it. See if you succeed, but do not try to expand the nimitta without first determining a limit: make sure to determine a limit of one, two, three, or four inches.

While expanding the white circle, you may find that it becomes unstable. Then go back to noting it as 'white - white' to make it stable. But as your concentration increases the nimitta will become stable and tranquil.

When the first expanded nimitta has become stable, you should repeat the process, that is, again determine to expand it by a few inches. This way you can expand the nimitta in stages, until it is one yard in size, then two yards, and so on. Do this until it extends in all ten directions around you, without limit, and so that wherever you look, you see only white. Do it till you see not even a trace of materiality, whether internal or external.

If you developed the white kasiṇa in a past life, during this or a previous Buddha's dispensation, that is, if you have white kasiṇa pāramī, then you will not need to expand the *paṭibhāga-nimitta*, because as you concentrate on it, it will automatically expand in all ten directions.

You should in either case now keep your mind calmly concentrated on the expanded white kasiṇa. And when it is stable, then just as if you were to hang a hat on a hook in a wall, put your mind on one place in that white kasiṇa. Keep your mind there, and continue to note 'white - white'.

When your mind is tranquil and stable, the white kasiṇa will also be tranquil and stable, and will be exceedingly white, bright, and clear. This too is a *paṭibhāga-nimitta*, produced by expanding the original white kasiṇa *paṭibhāga-nimitta*.

You must continue to meditate, until you can concentrate on that white kasiṇa *paṭibhāga-nimitta* continuously for one or two hours. Then the jhāna factors will become very prominent, clear, and strong in your mind, and you will have reached the first jhāna. The five jhāna factors are:

1) Application *(vitakka)*: directing and placing the mind on the *paṭibhāga-nimitta* of the white kasiṇa.
2) Sustainment *(vicāra)*: maintaining the mind on the *paṭibhāga-nimitta* of the white kasiṇa.
3) Joy *(pīti)*: joy at the *paṭibhāga-nimitta* of the white kasiṇa.
4) Bliss *(sukha)*: blissful about the *paṭibhāga-nimitta* of the white kasiṇa.
5) One-pointedness *(ek·aggatā)*: one-pointedness of mind on the *paṭibhāga-nimitta* of the white kasiṇa.

The jhāna factors are together called jhāna. In the way described in the talk on *ān·āpāna·sati* (mindfulness-of-breathing), develop the five masteries[135] of the first white kasiṇa jhāna, and then develop the second, third, and fourth jhānas, and the masteries of them too.

HOW YOU DEVELOP THE REMAINING COLOUR KASIṆAS

If you have developed the white kasiṇa meditation up to the fourth jhāna using the white of an external skeleton, then you will also be able to develop the brown, blue, or black kasiṇa using external head hairs, the yellow kasiṇa using external fat or urine, and the red kasiṇa using external blood, etc. You can also use those parts in your own body.

When you have succeeded, you can develop the colour kasiṇas using the colour of also flowers, or other external objects. All blue and brown flowers are calling out, inviting you to develop the blue kasiṇa. All yellow flowers are calling out, inviting you to develop the yellow kasiṇa. All red flowers are calling out, inviting you to develop the red kasiṇa. All white flowers are calling out, inviting you to develop the white kasiṇa. Thus, a skilled yogi can use whatever he sees to develop kasiṇa concentration and vipassanā, be it animate or inanimate, internal or external.

According to the Pali texts, The Buddha taught ten kasiṇas. They are the mentioned four colour kasiṇas, plus a further six: the earth, water, fire, wind, space, and light kasiṇas.[136]

Now, let us discuss how to develop the remaining six types of kasiṇa.

HOW YOU DEVELOP THE EARTH KASIṆA

To develop the earth kasiṇa, you should find a piece of plain earth, which is reddish brown like the sky at dawn, and with no sticks, stones, or leaves. Then with a stick or some other instrument, draw a circle about one foot across. That is your meditation object: an earth kasiṇa. You should concentrate on it, and note it as 'earth - earth'. Concentrate on it for a while with your eyes open, and then close them, and visualize the earth kasiṇa. If unable to visualize the nimitta in this way, you should re-establish the fourth *ān·āpāna-*, or white kasiṇa-jhāna. Then use the light of concentration to look at the earth kasiṇa. When you see the nimitta of

---

[135] See p.46.

[136] M.II.iii.7 *'Mahā·Sakuludāyī·Suttaṁ'* ('The Great Sakuludāyī Sutta') & Dhs.I *'Aṭṭha-·Kasiṇaṁ Soḷasa·Kkhattukaṁ'* ('Eight Kasiṇas & Sixteen Times')

earth as clearly as if you were looking at it with your eyes open, and it is thus an *uggaha-nimitta*, you can go and develop it somewhere else.

You should not concentrate on the colour of the earth nimitta, or the characteristics of hardness, roughness, etc. of the. earth element, but concentrate on only the concept of earth. Continue to develop this *uggaha-nimitta* until it becomes pure and clear, and is the *paṭibhāga-nimitta.*

You should then expand the *paṭibhāga-nimitta* a little at a time, in all ten directions, and develop this meditation up to the fourth jhāna.

HOW YOU DEVELOP THE WATER KASIṆA

To develop the water kasiṇa, you should use a bowl, bucket or well of pure, clear water. Concentrate on the concept of water as 'water - water' till you get the *uggaha-nimitta*, and then develop it as you did the earth kasiṇa.

HOW YOU DEVELOP THE FIRE KASIṆA

To develop the fire kasiṇa, you should use a candle, a fire, or any other flames you remember seeing. If unable to visualize it, you can make a screen with a circular hole in it about one foot across. Put the screen in front of a wood- or grass-fire, so you see only the flames through the hole.

Ignoring the smoke, and burning wood or grass, concentrate on the concept of fire as 'fire - fire' till you get the *uggaha-nimitta*, and then develop it in the usual way.

HOW YOU DEVELOP THE WIND KASIṆA

The wind kasiṇa is developed through the sense of touch, or sight. You should concentrate on the wind coming in through a window or door, touching the body; or the sight of leaves or branches moving in the wind. Concentrate on the concept as 'wind - wind' till you get the *uggaha-nimitta.* You can discern the nimitta of the wind by re-establishing the fourth jhāna with another kasiṇa object, and using the light of concentration see this movement externally. The *uggaha-nimitta* looks like steam coming off hot milk rice, but the *paṭibhāga-nimitta* is motionless. Develop the nimitta in the usual way.

HOW YOU DEVELOP THE LIGHT KASIṆA

To develop the light kasiṇa, you should look at rays of light, as they stream into a room through, for example, a crack in the wall, and fall on the floor or as they stream through the leaves of a tree and fall on the ground. You can also look up through the branches of a tree, at the light in the sky above. If unable to visualize it, you can put a candle or lamp inside an earthen pot, and place the pot in such a way that rays of light come out of the opening of the pot, and fall upon the wall. Concentrate on the circle of light on the wall as a concept, as 'light - light' till you get the *uggaha-nimitta*, and then develop it in the usual way.

HOW YOU DEVELOP THE SPACE KASIṆA

To develop the space kasiṇa, you should look at the space in a doorway, window, or keyhole. If unable to visualize it, you can make a circular hole in a piece of board, about eight inches to one foot across. Hold the board up so you see only the sky through the hole, no trees or other objects. Concentrate on the space within that circle as a concept, as 'space - space', and develop the nimitta in the usual way.

THE FOUR IMMATERIAL JHĀNAS

Once you have attained the four jhānas with each of the ten kasiṇas, you can proceed to develop the four immaterial jhānas *(arūpa jhāna)*, also called the four immaterial states. They are:

1) The Base of Boundless Space *(ākāsānañc·āyatana)*
2) The Base of Boundless Consciousness *(viññāṇañc·āyatana)*
3) The Base of Nothingness *(ākiñcaññ·āyatana)*
4) The Base of Neither Perception nor Non-Perception *(neva·saññā·n·āsaññ-·āyatana)*

You can develop them with all the kasiṇas except the space kasiṇa.[137]

HOW YOU DEVELOP THE BASE OF BOUNDLESS SPACE

To develop the four immaterial jhānas, you should first reflect upon the disadvantages of materiality. The human body produced by the sperm and egg of your parents is called the produced body *(karaja·kāya)*. Since you have a produced body, you are open to assault with weapons such as

[137] See footnote 138, p.67.

knives, spears, and bullets, and to being hit, beaten, and tortured. The produced body is also subject to many diseases of, for example, the eyes, ears, and heart. So you should consider with wisdom that because you have a produced body made of materiality, you are subject to various kinds of suffering, and that if you can be free of that materiality, you can also be free of the suffering.

Even though a fourth fine-material jhāna surpasses gross physical materiality, it is still based on it. Thus you need to surmount the kasiṇa materiality. Having considered this, and with no desire now for the kasiṇa materiality, you should re-establish the fourth jhāna with one of the nine kasiṇas,[138] such as the earth kasiṇa, emerge from it, and reflect on its disadvantages: it is based on materiality, which you no longer desire; it has joy of the third jhāna as its near enemy; and it is grosser than the four immaterial jhānas. But you do not need to reflect on the disadvantages of the mental formations (the two jhāna factors) in the fourth jhāna, because they are the same as in the immaterial jhānas. With no desire now for the fourth fine-material jhāna, you should also reflect on the more peaceful nature of the immaterial jhānas.

Then expand your nimitta, say, of the earth kasiṇa, so that it is boundless, or as much as you wish, and replace the kasiṇa materiality with the space it occupies, by concentrating on the space as 'space - space' or 'boundless space - boundless space'. What remains is the boundless space formerly occupied by the kasiṇa.

If unable to do so, you should discern and concentrate on the space of one place in the earth-kasiṇa nimitta, and then expand that up to the infinite universe. As a result, the entire earth-kasiṇa nimitta is replaced by boundless space.

Continue to concentrate on the boundless space nimitta, until you reach jhāna, and then develop the five masteries. This is the first immaterial jhāna, also called the base of boundless space *(ākāsānañc·āyatana)*.

HOW YOU DEVELOP THE BASE OF BOUNDLESS CONSCIOUSNESS

The second immaterial jhāna, also called the base of boundless consciousness *(viññāṇañc·āyatana citta)*, has as its object the base-of-boundless-space consciousness *(ākāsānañc·āyatana citta)*, which had boundless space as its object.

---

[138] Since space is not materiality, the space kasiṇa cannot be used to surmount the kasiṇa materiality to attain an immaterial jhāna.

To develop the base of boundless consciousness, you should reflect on the disadvantages of the base of boundless space: it has the fourth fine-material jhāna as its near enemy, and is not as peaceful as the base of boundless consciousness. With no desire now for the base of boundless space, you should also reflect on the more peaceful nature of the base of boundless consciousness. Then concentrate again and again on the consciousness that had boundless space as its object, and note it as 'boundless consciousness - boundless consciousness' or just 'consciousness - consciousness'.

Continue to concentrate on the boundless-consciousness nimitta, until you reach jhāna, and then develop the five masteries. This is then the second immaterial jhāna, also called the base of boundless consciousness.

HOW YOU DEVELOP THE BASE OF NOTHINGNESS

The third immaterial jhāna, also called the base of nothingness *(ākiñcaññ-·āyatana)*, has as its object the absence of the consciousness that had boundless space as its object, and which was itself the object of the base of boundless consciousness.

To develop the base of nothingness, you should reflect on the disadvantages of the base of boundless consciousness: it has the base of boundless space as its near enemy and is not as peaceful as the base of nothingness. With no desire now for the base of boundless consciousness, you should also reflect on the more peaceful nature of the base of nothingness. Then concentrate on the absence of the consciousness that had boundless space as its object. There were two jhāna consciousnesses: first the consciousness of base of boundless space *(ākāsānañc·āyatana citta)* and then that of the base of boundless consciousness *(viññāṇañc·āyatana citta)*. Two consciousnesses cannot arise in one consciousness moment *(citta·kkhaṇa)*. When the consciousness of the base of boundless space was present, the other consciousness could not be present too, and vice versa. So, you take the absence of the consciousness of the base of boundless-space as object, and note it as 'nothingness - nothingness' or 'absence - absence'.

Continue to concentrate on that nimitta, until you reach jhāna, and develop the five masteries. This is then the third immaterial jhāna, also called the base of nothingness.

HOW YOU DEVELOP
THE BASE OF NEITHER PERCEPTION NOR NON-PERCEPTION

The fourth immaterial jhāna is also called the base of neither perception nor non-perception *(neva·saññā·n·āsaññ·āyatana)*. That is because the perception in this jhāna is extremely subtle. In fact, all the mental formations in this jhāna are extremely subtle; there is also neither feeling nor non-feeling, neither consciousness nor non-consciousness, neither contact nor non-contact etc. But the jhāna is explained in terms of perception, and it has as object the consciousness of the base of nothingness.[139]

To develop the base of neither perception nor non-perception, you should reflect on the disadvantages of the base of nothingness: it has the base of boundless consciousness as its near enemy, and is not as peaceful as the base of neither perception nor non-perception. Furthermore, perception is a disease, a boil and a dart. With no desire now for the base of nothingness, you should also reflect on the more peaceful nature of the base of neither perception nor non-perception. Then concentrate again and again on the consciousness of the base of nothingness as 'peaceful - peaceful'. Continue to concentrate on the 'peaceful - peaceful' nimitta, until you reach jhāna, and develop the five masteries. This is then the fourth immaterial jhāna, also called the base of neither-perception-nor non-perception.

Today we discussed how to develop the ten kasiṇas, and the eight attainments: the four fine-material jhānas and the four immaterial jhānas. In the next talk, we shall discuss how to develop the four sublime abidings *(brahma·vihāra)* of loving-kindness, compassion, sympathetic-joy, and equanimity; and the four protective meditations *(catur·ārakkha·bhāvanā)* of loving-kindness, Buddha Recollection, foulness meditation and death recollection.

[139] This is discussed in connection also with the different nimittas in mindfulness of breathing *(ān·āpāna·sati)*, p.38.

Questions and Answers 2

Question 2.1 How should beginners balance the faculties *(indriya)* of concentration and wisdom? How should they practise wisdom in *ān·āpāna·sati* (mindfulness-of-breathing)?

Answer 2.1 We already talked about balancing the five controlling faculties in the very first talk, but we can summarize what was said. It is not so important for beginners to balance concentration and wisdom. This is because they are only beginners, and their five controlling faculties are not yet developed. In the beginning of meditation, there is usually much restlessness in the mind. So the faculties are not yet strong and powerful. Only when they are strong and powerful is it necessary to balance them. But if beginners are able to balance the faculties already at the beginning stage, that is of course also good.

For example, you are now practising *ān·āpāna·sati*; *ān·āpāna·sati* is mindfulness-of-breathing. Knowing the breath is wisdom *(paññā)*. Being mindful of the breath is mindfulness *(sati)*. One-pointedness of mind on the breath is concentration *(samādhi)*. The effort to know the breath clearly is effort *(vīriya)*. Having faith that *ān·āpāna·sati* can lead to jhāna is faith *(saddhā)*.

Beginners must try to develop strong and powerful controlling faculties. Their faith in *ān·āpāna·sati* must be strong enough. Their effort to know the breath clearly must be strong enough. Their mindfulness of the breath must be strong enough. Their concentration on the breath must be strong enough. They must see the breath clearly. They must try to make their five controlling faculties strong and powerful, as well as try to balance them. If one is excessive, the others cannot function properly.

For example, if faith is too strong and powerful, it produces emotion. This means that the effort faculty cannot maintain associated mental formations on the breath; mindfulness cannot become established on the breath; the concentration faculty too, cannot concentrate deeply on the breath; and wisdom cannot know the breath clearly.

When, for example, effort is excessive, it makes the mind restless, so the other controlling faculties become again weak, and cannot function properly. When mindfulness is weak, you cannot do anything, because you cannot concentrate on the breath, will make little or no effort to discern the breath, and may have no faith.

Now you are practising samatha. In samatha meditation, strong and powerful concentration is good, but excessive concentration produces laziness. With laziness, the other faculties become again very weak, and cannot function properly.

At this stage wisdom is very dull or inferior. It knows only the natural breath. So for the beginner who is practising samatha meditation, it is enough just to know the breath clearly. When the uggaha or *paṭibhāga-nimitta* appears, wisdom knows the uggaha or *paṭibhāga-nimitta*. Too much general knowledge apart from this is not good, as you may always be discussing and criticizing. If a yogi discusses and criticizes *ān·āpāna-·sati* too much, we can say his wisdom is excessive, which also makes the other controlling faculties weak, and unable to function properly.

So, even though it is not yet very important, it is still good for a beginner to balance his five controlling faculties. How to balance them? We must practise with strong and powerful mindfulness and effort to know the breath clearly, and concentrate on the breath with faith.

Question 2.2 Why don't we, after attaining the fourth jhāna, go straight to discern the five aggregates, their nature of impermanence, suffering, and non-self, and attain Nibbāna? Why do we before attaining Nibbāna need to practise meditation on the thirty-two parts of body, skeleton, white kasiṇa, four elements, materiality, mentality, dependent origination, and vipassanā?

Answer 2.2 The Buddha taught the five-aggregates method of practising vipassanā to three types of person: those who have sharp wisdom, those whose vipassanā knowledge of mentality is not clear, and those who prefer to practise vipassanā in the brief way.

What are the fiveaggregates? What is the difference between the five aggregates and mentality-materiality? Do you know the answer?

Before answering your second question, let us discuss mentality-materiality and the five aggregates. There are four ultimate realities *(paramattha sacca)*: consciousnesses *(cittā)*, associated mental factors *(cetasikā)*, materiality *(rūpa)*, and Nibbāna.

To attain Nibbāna, the fourth ultimate reality, we must see the impermanent, suffering and non-self nature of the other three, that is, we must see:[140]

1) Eighty-nine types of consciousness *(viññāṇa)*
2) Fifty-two types of associated mental factors *(cetasika)*
3) Twenty-eight types of materiality *(rūpa)*[141]

The eighty-nine types of consciousness are called the consciousness aggregate *(viññāṇa·kkhandha)*. Of the fifty-two associated mental factors, feeling

[140] The Most Venerable Sayadaw is here making only a general statement: see 'Knowing and Seeing The First Noble Truth', p.9.

[141] For a full list, see table '2a: The Twenty-Eight Types of Materiality', p.137.

is the feeling aggregate *(vedanā·kkhandha)*; perception is the perception aggregate *(saññā·kkhandha)*; and the remaining fifty associated mental factors are the formations-aggregate *(saṅkhāra·kkhandha)*. Sometimes the consciousnesses *(cittā)* and associated mental factors *(cetasikā)* together are called mentality *(nāma)*. Sometimes they are seen as four aggregates, the feeling aggregate, the perception aggregate, the formations aggregate and the consciousness aggregate, which together are the mentality-aggregate *(nāma·kkhandha)*. The materiality aggregate *(rūpa·kkhandha)* is the twenty-eight types of materiality. The consciousnesses, associated mental factors and materiality together are called 'mentality-materiality' *(nāma·rūpa)*. They are sometimes also called the five aggregates: materiality, feeling, perception, formations, and consciousness. Their causes are also only mentality-materiality.

These five clinging-aggregates are *Dukkha·Sacca·dhammā*: dhammas of the Noble Truth of Suffering. They need to be understood as such.

In the *'Mahā·Nidāna'* sutta of the *Dīgha·Nikāya*, The Buddha explains:

This dependent origination is profound, Ānanda, and profound it appears. And, Ānanda, it is through not knowing, through not penetrating this Dhamma, that this generation has become a tangled skein, a knotted ball of thread, matted as the roots in a bed of reeds, and finds no way out of the round of rebirths with its states of loss, unhappy destinations...perdition.[142]

With regard to this statement, the commentaries explain:

There is no one, even in a dream, who has got out of the fearful round of rebirths, which is ever destroying [beings] **like a thunderbolt, unless he has severed with the knife of knowledge, well whetted on the stone of sublime concentration, this Wheel of Existence** [Dependent Origination], **which offers no footing owing to its great profundity and is hard to get by owing to the maze of many methods.**[143]

This means that the yogi who does not know, and has not penetrated Dependent Origination by the different stages of vipassanā knowledge, cannot escape from the round of rebirths.

And in the *'Titth·Āyatana'* sutta of the *Aṅguttara·Nikāya*, this was said by The Buddha:[144]

And what, bhikkhus, is the Noble Truth of the Origin of Suffering *(Dukkha·Samudayaṁ Ariya·Saccaṁ)***?**

[1] **Because of ignorance** *(avijjā)*, **formations** [arise] *(saṅkhārā)*;
[2] **because of formations, consciousness** *(viññāṇa)*;
[3] **because of consciousness, mentality-materiality** *(nāma·rūpa)*;

---

[142] D.ii.2 *'Mahā·Nidāna·Suttaṁ'* ('The Great Causation Sutta')

[143] VbhA.vi.1 *'Suttanta·Bhājanīya·Vaṇṇanā'* ('Sutta-Classification Description'). VsM.xvii.661 *'Bhava·Cakka·Kathā'* ('The Wheel of Existence Discussion') PP.xvii.344

[144] A.III.II.ii.1 *'Titth·Āyatana·Suttaṁ'* ('The Sectarian-Doctrines Sutta')

[4] **because of mentality-materiality, the six bases** *(saḷ·āyatana)*;
[5] **because of the six bases, contact** *(phassa)*;
[6] **because of contact, feeling** *(vedanā)*;
[7] **because of feeling, craving** *(taṇhā)*;
[8] **because of craving, clinging** *(upādāna)*;
[9] **because of clinging, existence** *(bhava)*;
[10] **because of existence, birth** *(jāti)*;
[11] **because of birth,**
[12] **ageing&death** *(jarā·maraṇa)*, **sorrow** *(soka)*, **lamentation** *(parideva)*, **pain** *(dukkha)*, **grief** *(domanassa)* **and despair** *(upāyāsā)* **arise.**

Such is the origin of this whole mass of suffering.

This is called, bhikkhus, the Noble Truth of the Origin of Suffering *(Idaṁ vuccati, bhikkhave, Dukkha·Samudayaṁ Ariya·Saccaṁ)*.

This is also called dependent origination. And The Buddha says dependent origination is the Noble Truth of the Origin of Suffering *(Samudaya Sacca)*.

The Noble Truth of Suffering, which is the five clinging aggregates, and the Noble Truth of the Origin of Suffering, which is dependent origination, are called formations *(saṅkhārā)*. They are the object of vipassanā, vipassanā knowledge. At the different stages of vipassanā knowledge you comprehend these formations as impermanence *(anicca)*, as suffering *(dukkha)*, and as non-self *(an·atta)*. Without knowing and penetrating them, how can you comprehend them that they are impermanent etc.? That is why we teach vipassanā systematically.

To know ultimate materiality, the materiality clinging-aggregate, you must practise four-elements meditation till you see that materiality consists of small particles that we call *rūpa-kalāpas*, and you need to see the four elements in those small particles.[145] And you need to discern both the base and its object together.[146] Without discerning materiality this way, you cannot discern mentality, the four mental clinging-aggregates. That is why we teach vipassanā stage by stage.

Now your second question. According to the Theravāda tradition, there are two types of meditation subject *(kammaṭṭhāna)*: *pārihāriya·kammaṭṭhāna* and *sabbatthaka·kammaṭṭhāna*. *Pārihāriya·kammaṭṭhāna* is the meditation subject by which the individual yogi develops concentration to be used for vipassanā. The yogi must always use that meditation subject as his foundation. *Sabbatthaka·kammaṭṭhāna*, on the other hand, is the medi-

[145] See further 'Introduction', p.107.
[146] See further quotation, p.5.

tation subjects to be developed by all yogis alike.[147] They are the four protective meditations:

1) Loving-kindness meditation *(mettā·bhāvanā)*
2) Buddha Recollection *(Buddh·Ānussati)*
3) Death recollection *(maraṇ·ānussati)*
4) Foulness meditation *(asubha·bhāvanā)*

So although a yogi uses *ān·āpāna·sati* (mindfulness-of-breathing) as his *pārihāriya·kammaṭṭhāna*, he must practise the four protective meditations before going on to vipassanā. This is the orthodox procedure.

To develop loving-kindness meditation up to jhāna, it is better if the yogi has already developed the white-kasiṇa meditation up to the fourth jhāna. An example of this is the five hundred bhikkhus to whom The Buddha taught the *'Karaṇīya·Mettā'* sutta.[148] Those bhikkhus were expert in the ten kasiṇas and eight attainments *(samāpatti)*, had practised vipassanā up to the Arise&Perish Knowledge *(Udaya·Bbaya·Ñāṇa)*, and had gone to the forest to meditate further. But they returned to the Buddha, because the devas resident in the forest had become annoyed and had frightened the bhikkhus. The Buddha taught the bhikkhus the *'Karaṇīya·Mettā'* sutta both as a meditation subject and as a protective chant *(paritta)*. As a meditation subject it is for those who have already attained loving-kindness jhāna *(mettā jhāna)*, and have broken down the barriers between the different types of person.[149] The *'Karaṇīya·Mettā'* sutta is a more specialized practice of loving-kindness, in which one practises up to the third jhāna by extending loving-kindness to eleven categories of beings with the thought: *'Sukhino vā khemino hontu, sabbe sattā bhavantu sukhitattā'* (May all beings be happy and secure etc.). The Texts say The Buddha knew those five hundred bhikkhus would very easily be able to do this, because they were already expert in the ten kasiṇas. And how is loving-kindness jhāna made easier by kasiṇa meditation?

In the *Aṅguttara·Nikāya*, The Buddha taught that of the four colour kasiṇas, the white kasiṇa is best.[150] The white kasiṇa makes the yogi's mind clear and bright. A clear and tranquil mind is superior and powerful. If a yogi practises loving-kindness meditation with a clear mind, free

---

[147] For how and why you must protect your meditation, see p.14; for details, see Talk 3 'How You Develop the Sublime Abidings and Protective Meditations'.

[148] SuN.i.8 *'Karaṇīya·Mettā·Suttaṃ'* ('To-Be-Done Loving-Kindness Sutta'), also called *'Mettā·Suttaṃ'* ('Loving-Kindness Sutta').

[149] For details about loving-kindness jhāna, see 'How You Develop Loving-Kindness', p.81.

[150] A.X.I.iii.9 *'Paṭhama·Kosala·Suttaṁ'* ('The First Kosala Sutta')

from defilements, he usually attains loving-kindness jhāna within one sitting. So if one enters the fourth white-kasiṇa jhāna, and after emerging from it, practises loving-kindness jhāna, it is very easy to succeed.

In order to attain the fourth white-kasiṇa jhāna, a yogi should first practise skeleton meditation internally and externally, because this makes the white-kasiṇa meditation very easy. Therefore, after the fourth *ān·āpāna* jhāna we usually teach yogis to do the thirty-two parts of the body, skeleton meditation and white-kasiṇa meditation. In our experience, most yogis say that the fourth white-kasiṇa jhāna is better than the fourth *ān·āpāna* jhāna, because it produces a clearer, brighter and more tranquil mind, which is also very helpful for practising other meditation subjects. So we usually teach white-kasiṇa meditation before loving-kindness meditation.

There is also a problem common to beginners. You may have practised loving-kindness meditation. Did you attain jhāna? In practice, if a yogi wants to extend loving-kindness to someone of the same sex, he should first take the smiling face of that person as object, and then develop loving-kindness towards him with: 'May this good person be free from mental suffering, etc.' With a beginner that smiling face very soon disappears. He cannot continue his loving-kindness meditation, because there is no object, and so he cannot attain loving-kindness jhāna or anything.

If he uses the fourth white-kasiṇa jhāna, it is different. He emerges from the jhāna, and when he develops loving-kindness, then, because of the preceding concentration, the smiling face will not fade away. He is able to concentrate deeply on that image, and able to attain up to the third loving-kindness jhāna within one sitting. If he practises systematically up to the breaking down of barriers between the different types of person, he can even practise the eleven ways of the *'Karaṇīya·Mettā'* sutta, and five hundred and twenty-eight ways mentioned in the *Paṭisambhidā·Magga* Pali Text.[151] For this reason too, we usually teach the white-kasiṇa meditation before loving-kindness meditation.

You may also have practised Buddha Recollection *(Buddh·Ānussati)*. Did you attain access concentration? When those who have succeeded in loving-kindness jhāna practise Buddha Recollection, they are able to reach access concentration within one sitting, again because of the preceding concentration. Foulness meditation *(asubha)* too becomes easy. If a yogi practises foulness meditation up to the first jhāna, and then death recollection *(maraṇ·ānussati)*, he is able to succeed within one sitting.

---

151 PsM.II.iv *'Mettā·Kathā'* ('Loving-Kindness Discussion')

That is why we teach the white-kasiṇa meditation before the four protective meditations. If, however, a yogi wants to go straight to vipassanā, without practising the four protective meditations, he can do so: no problem.

Question 2.3 Why, after having discerned materiality and mentality, must one practise the first and fifth methods of dependent origination *(paṭicca·samuppāda)*? What are the first and fifth methods?[152]

Answer 2.3 There are, according to the Theravāda tradition, seven stages of purification *(visuddhi)*. The first five are:

1) Morality Purification *(Sīla·Visuddhi)*: that is morality *(sīla)* of four types:[153]
    i) Pātimokkha restraint *(pātimokkhā·saṁvara·sīla)*
    ii) Sense restraint *(indriya·saṁvara·sīla)*
    iii) Livelihood purification *(ājīva·pārisuddhi·sīla)*
    iv) With regard to requisites *(paccaya·sannissita·sīla)*
2) Consciousness Purification *(Citta·Visuddhi)*: that is access concentration *(upacāra·samādhi)* and the eight attainments *(samāpatti)*: absorption concentration *(appanā·samādhi)*.[154]
3) View Purification *(Diṭṭhi·Visuddhi)*: that is Mentality-Materiality Definition Knowledge *(Nāma·Rūpa·Pariccheda·Ñāṇa)*.
4) Doubt-Overcoming Purification *(Kaṅkhā·Vitaraṇa·Visuddhi)*: that is Cause-Apprehending Knowledge *(Paccaya·Pariggaha·Ñāṇa)*, in other words, seeing dependent origination *(paṭicca·samuppāda)*.
5) Path&Non-Path Knowledge&Vision Purification *(Magg·Āmagga·Ñāṇa·Dassana·Visuddhi)*: that is Comprehension Knowledge *(Sammasana·Ñāṇa)* and Arise&Perish Knowledge *(Udaya·Bbaya·Ñāṇa)*, which is the beginning of vipassanā.

So before vipassanā there are four purifications. Why? Vipassanā is to comprehend the impermanence, suffering, and non-self nature of mentality-materiality and their causes. Without knowing mentality-materiality and their causes, how can we comprehend that they are impermanent, suffering, and non-self? How can we practise vipassanā? It is only after we have thoroughly discerned mentality-materiality and their causes, that we can practise vipassanā meditation.

---

[152] For details about how you practise the first and fifth methods of dependent origination, see 'The Fifth Method', p.183*ff.*

[153] VsM.i.13*ff* *'Sīla·Ppabheda·Kathā'* ('Morality-Classification Discussion') PP.i.42 for details.

[154] Vis.xviii.662 *'Diṭṭhi-Visuddhi Niddesa'* ('Description of View-Purification') PP.xviii.1

Mentality-materiality and their causes are called 'formations' *(saṅkhārā)*. They perish as soon as they arise, which is why they are impermanent; they are subject to constant arising and perishing, which is why they are suffering; they have no self *(atta)*, or stable and indestructible essence, which is why they are non-self.

Comprehending impermanence, suffering, and non-self in this way is real vipassanā. So before vipassanā, we teach yogis to discern mentality, materiality and dependent origination. The commentaries explain it as, '*aniccanti pañca·kkhandhā.*',[155] and '*aniccanti khandha pañcakaṁ.*'[156] That means, 'impermanence is the five aggregates.' The five aggregates are, in other words, mentality-materiality and their causes. So, real vipassanā requires that you know the five aggregates, and their causes and effects.

The Buddha taught according to the character of his listeners, and taught four methods for discerning dependent origination. In the *Paṭisambhidā·Magga*, there is yet another method.[157] Altogether there are five methods. The first of the methods taught by The Buddha is to discern dependent origination in forward order:

Avijjā·paccayā saṅkhārā, saṅkhāra·paccayā viññāṇaṁ, viññāṇa·paccayā nāma·rūpaṁ, [etc.]

Because of ignorance *(avijjā)*, **formations** *(saṅkhārā)* [arise]; **because of formations, consciousness** *(viññāṇaṁ)*; **because of consciousness, mentality-materiality** *(nāma·rūpa)*, [etc.]

The first method is popular in Theravāda Buddhism, but may be very difficult for those who have no Abhidhamma knowledge. Even yogis with good Abhidhamma knowledge may have many difficulties.

The fifth method taught by the Venerable Sāriputta, and recorded in the *Paṭisambhidā·Magga* Pali Text, is easy for beginners. It is to discern that five past causes have produced five present effects, and that five present causes will produce five future effects. This is the main principle in the fifth method. If you want to know it with direct experience, you should practise up to this stage.

After practising the fifth method systematically, you will not have much difficulty in practising the first method. For this reason we teach the fifth

---

[155] VsM.viii.236 *'Ān·Āpāna·Sati·Kathā'* (Mindfulness-of-Breathing Discussion) PP.viii.234. VsM.xxi.740 *'Upakkilesa·Vimutta-Udaya·Bbaya·Ñāṇa·Kathā'* ('Imperfections-Free Arise&Perish Knowledge Discussion') PP.xxi.6

[156] VbhA.ii.1 *'Suttanta·Bhājanīya·Vaṇṇanā'* ('Sutta-Classification Description')

[157] PsM.I.i.4 *Dhamma·Ṭṭhiti·Ñāṇa·Niddeso* ('Standing-on-Phenomena Knowledge Description')

method before the first method. We teach all five methods to those who have time, and want to practise further. But although The Buddha taught dependent origination according to the character of his listeners, one method is enough to attain Nibbāna. Even so, because the first method is popular in Theravāda Buddhism, we teach both the fifth and first methods.

One day, the Venerable Ānanda practised dependent origination in all four ways. In the evening, he went to The Buddha and said: **It is wonderful, Venerable Sir, it is marvellous how profound this dependent origination is, and how profound it appears! And yet it appears to me as clear as clear!**

The Buddha replied:[158]

Do not say so, Ānanda! Do not say so, Ānanda!

This dependent origination is profound *(gambhīro)*, **and appears profound** *(gambhīr·āvabhāso)*.

It is through not understanding *(an·anubodhā)*, **not penetrating this truth** *(a·ppaṭi·vedhā)*, **that the world has become like a tangled skein, matted like a bird's nest, tangled like reeds, unable to pass beyond the states of woe, the woeful destination, ruin, and the round of rebirths.**

This means that without knowing dependent origination, with the *Anubodha·Ñāṇa* and the *Paṭivedha·Ñāṇa*, one cannot escape the round of rebirths *(saṁsāra)*, and four woeful realms *(apāya)*. The *Anubodha·Ñāṇa* is the Mentality-Materiality Definition Knowledge *(Nāma·Rūpa·Pariccheda·Ñāṇa)*, and Cause-Apprehending Knowledge *(Paccaya·Pariggaha·Ñāṇa)*. The *Paṭivedha·Ñāṇa* is all the vipassanā knowledges *(Vipassanā·Ñāṇa)*. So without knowing dependent origination with the *Anubodha·Ñāṇa* and *Paṭivedha·Ñāṇa*, one cannot attain Nibbāna. With this quotation, the commentary says that without knowing dependent origination, no one can escape from the round of rebirths, even in a dream.[159]

---

158 D.ii.2 *'Mahā·Nidāna·Suttaṁ'* (Great Causation Sutta')

159 See quotation p.25.

How You Develop
the Sublime Abidings and Protective Meditations

INTRODUCTION

Today let us look at how you develop the four sublime abidings *(cattāro brahmavihārā)*, and four protective meditations *(catur·ārakkha·bhāvanā)*. The four sublime abidings are:

1) Loving-kindness .... *(mettā)*
2) Compassion .... *(karuṇā)*
3) Sympathetic joy .... *(muditā)*
4) Equanimity .... *(upekkhā)*

The four protective meditations *(catur·ārakkha·bhāvanā)* are:

1) Loving-kindness *(mettā)*
2) Buddha Recollection *(Buddh·ānussati)*
3) Foulness meditation *(asubha·bhāvanā)*
4) Death Recollection *(maraṇ·ānussati)*

HOW YOU DEVELOP LOVING-KINDNESS

INTRODUCTION

To develop the sublime abiding of loving-kindness *(mettā)*, you need first of all be aware that it should not be developed towards a person of the opposite sex *(liṅga·visabhāga)*, or a dead person *(kālakata·puggala)*.

A person of the opposite sex should not be used as object, because lust towards him or her will probably arise. After you have attained jhāna, however, it is possible to develop loving-kindness towards the opposite sex as a group with, for example, 'May all women be happy.' A dead person should at no time be used, because you cannot attain loving-kindness jhāna with a dead person as object.

The people you should develop loving-kindness towards are:

1) Yourself *(atta)*
2) A dear person *(piya·puggala)*: someone you like and respect.
3) An indifferent person *(majjhatta·puggala)*: someone your are indifferent towards.
4) A hated person *(verī·puggala)*

In the very beginning, though, you should develop loving-kindness towards only the first two, yourself and the person you like and respect. This means that in the very beginning, you should not develop loving-kindness towards the following types of person: a person you do not like *(appiya·puggala)*, a person very dear to you *(atippiyasahāyaka·puggala)*, a person you are indifferent to *(majjhatta·puggala)*, and a person you hate *(verī·puggala)*.

A person you do not like is one who does not do what is beneficial to you, or to those you care for. A person you hate is one who does what is detrimental to you, or to those you care for. They are in the beginning both difficult to develop loving-kindness towards, because anger may arise. It is in the beginning also difficult to develop loving-kindness towards a person to whom you are indifferent. In the case of a person who is very dear to you, you may be too attached to that person, and be filled with concern and grief, and even cry if you hear something has happened to him or her. So these four should not be used in the very beginning. Later, though, once you have attained loving-kindness jhāna, you will be able to develop loving-kindness towards them.

You cannot attain jhāna using yourself as object even if you were to develop that meditation for a hundred years. So why begin by developing loving-kindness to yourself? It is not to attain even access concentration, but because when you have developed loving-kindness towards yourself, with the thought, 'May I be happy', then are you able to identify yourself with others; to see that just as you want to be happy, do not want to suffer, want to live long, and do not want to die, so too do all other beings want to be happy, not want to suffer, want to live long, and not want to die.

Thus you are able to develop a mind that desires the happiness and prosperity of other beings. In the words of The Buddha:[160]

> *Sabbā disā anuparigamma cetasā,*
> *Nevajjhagā piyatara mattanā kvaci.*
> *Evaṁ piyo puthu attā paresaṁ,*
> *Tasmā na hiṁse paramattakāmo.*

Having searched in all directions with the mind, one cannot find anyone anywhere whom one loves more than oneself. In this same way do all beings in all directions love themselves more than anyone else, therefore, one who desires his own welfare should not harm others.

So in order to identify yourself in this way with others and make your mind soft and kind, you should first develop loving-kindness towards yourself with the following four thoughts:

1) May I be free from danger *(ahaṁ avero homi)*
2) May I be free from mental pain *(abyāpajjo homi)*
3) May I be free from physical pain *(anīgho homi)*

---

[160] S.I.III.i.8 *'Mallikā·Suttaṁ'* ('The Mallikā Sutta')

4) May I be well and happy *(sukhī attānaṁ pariharāmi)*

If one's mind is soft, kind, understanding, and has empathy for others, one should have no difficulty developing loving-kindness towards another. So it is important that the loving-kindness you have developed towards yourself be strong and powerful. Once your mind has become soft, kind, understanding, and has empathy for other beings, then can you begin to develop loving-kindness towards them.

HOW YOU DEVELOP LOVING-KINDNESS PERSON BY PERSON

If you have attained the fourth *ān·āpāna-*, or white kasiṇa-jhāna, you should re-establish it so the light is bright, brilliant, and radiant. With the light of particularly the fourth white-kasiṇa jhāna, it is really very easy to develop loving-kindness meditation *(mettā·bhāvanā)*.[161] The reason is that with the concentration of the fourth jhāna, the mind is purified of greed, hatred, delusion, and other defilements. After having emerged from particularly the fourth white-kasiṇa jhāna, the mind is pliant, workable, pure, bright, brilliant and radiant, and because of this, you will in a very short time be able to develop powerful and perfect loving-kindness *(mettā)*.

So, with the strong and bright light, you should direct your mind towards a dear person of your own sex, whom you like and respect: maybe your teacher or a fellow yogi. You will find that the light spreads out around you in all directions, and that whomever you pick as object becomes visible. You then take an image of that person, sitting or standing, and select the one you like most, and which makes you the happiest. Try to recall the time when he or she was the happiest you ever saw, and choose that image. Make it appear about two yards in front of you: so you can see the whole body. When you can see the image clearly before you, develop loving-kindness towards him or her with the four thoughts:

1) May this good person be free from danger *(ayaṁ sa·ppuriso avero hotu)*
2) May this good person be free from mental pain *(ayaṁ sa·ppuriso abyāpajjo hotu)*
3) May this good person be free from physical pain *(ayaṁ sa·ppuriso anīgho hotu)*
4) May this good person be well and happy *(ayaṁ sa·ppuriso sukhī attānaṁ pariharatu)*

Extend loving-kindness towards that person with these four phrases three or four times, and then select the one you like most, for example, 'May this good person be free from danger'. Then, with a new image of

[161] In this regard, see further Q&A 2.2, p.72*ff.*

that person, in this case free from danger, extend loving-kindness using the corresponding thought, in this case, 'May this good person be free from danger - may this good person be free from danger'. Do it again and again, until the mind is tranquil and steadily fixed on the object, and you can discern the jhāna factors. Then, keep practising until you reach the second and third jhānas. After that take each of the other three phrases and develop loving-kindness up to the third jhāna. You should have an appropriate image for each of the four phrases, that is, when thinking 'May this good person be free from danger', you should have a particular image of that person as free from danger; when thinking 'May this good person be free from mental pain', you should have another image, one of that person as free from mental pain, and so on. In this way you should develop the three jhānas, and remember in each case to practise the five masteries *(vasī-bhāva)*.

When you have succeeded with one person you like and respect, do it again with another person of your own sex whom you like and respect. Try doing this with about ten people of that type, until you can reach the third jhāna using any of them. By this stage you can safely go on to people, still of your own sex, who are very dear to you *(atippiyasahāyaka)*. Take about ten people of that type, and develop loving-kindness towards them one by one, in the same way, until the third jhāna.

Then you can also take about ten people of your own sex whom you are indifferent to, and in the same way develop loving-kindness towards them until the third jhāna.

You will by now have mastered the loving-kindness jhāna to such an extent that you can in the same way develop it towards about ten people of your own sex whom you hate. If you are a type of Great Being like the Bodhisatta when he was Mahākapi, the monkey king, who never hated anyone who harmed him and you really neither hate, nor despise anyone, then do not look for someone to use here. Only those who have people they hate or despise can develop loving-kindness towards that type.

Practising loving-kindness in this way, that is, by developing concentration up to the third jhāna on each type of people, progressively from one to the next, from the easiest to the more difficult, you make your mind increasingly soft, kind and pliant, until you are finally able to attain jhāna on any of the four types: those you respect, those very dear to you, those you are indifferent to, and those you hate.

HOW YOU BREAK DOWN THE BARRIERS

As you continue to thus develop loving-kindness, you will find that your loving-kindness towards those you like and respect, and those very dear to you, becomes even, and you can take them as one, as just people you like. Then you will be left with only these four types of person:

1) Yourself
2) People you like
3) People you are indifferent to
4) People you hate

You will need to continue developing loving-kindness towards these four, until it becomes balanced and without distinctions. Even though you cannot attain loving-kindness jhāna with yourself as object, you still need to include yourself in order to balance the four types.

To do this, you need to re-establish the fourth *ān·āpāna-*, or white kasiṇa-jhāna. With the strong and bright light, extend loving-kindness to yourself for about a minute or even a few seconds; then towards someone you like, then someone you are indifferent to, and then someone you hate, each one up to the third jhāna. Then again yourself briefly, but the other three types must now each be a different person. Remember to develop them with each of the four phrases, 'May this good person be free from danger' etc. each, up to the third jhāna.

Thus you should every time change the person of each of the three types: a person you like, one you are indifferent to, and one you hate. Do this again and again, with different groups of four, many times, so that your mind is continuously developing loving-kindness without interruption, and without distinctions. When you are able to develop loving-kindness jhāna towards any of the three persons without distinction, you will have achieved what is called 'breaking down the barriers' *(sīmā·sambheda)*. With the barriers between types and individuals broken down, you will be able to further develop your loving-kindness meditation, by taking up the method taught by the Venerable Sāriputta; recorded in the *Paṭisambhidā·Magga.*[162]

THE TWENTY-TWO CATEGORIES

The method in the *Paṭisambhidā·Magga* involves twenty-two categories by which to extend one's loving-kindness: five unspecified categories

[162] PsM.II.iv *'Mettā·Kathā'* ('Loving-Kindness Discussion')

(anodhiso pharaṇā), seven specified categories *(odhiso pharaṇā)*, and ten directional categories *(disā pharaṇā)*. The five unspecified categories are:

1) All beings .... *(sabbe sattā)*
2) All breathers .... *(sabbe pāṇā)*
3) All creatures .... *(sabbe bhūtā)*
4) All people .... *(sabbe puggalā)*
5) All possessing individuality *(sabbe attabhāva·pariyāpannā)*

The seven specified categories are:

1) All women .... *(sabbā itthiyo)*
2) All men .... *(sabbe purisā)*
3) All Noble Ones .... *(sabbe ariyā)*
4) All who are not Noble Ones ... *(sabbe an·ariyā)*
5) All devas .... *(sabbe devā)*
6) All human beings ...... *(sabbe manussā)*
7) All in the lower realms .... *(sabbe vinipātikā)*

The ten directional categories are:

1) In the eastward direction *(puratthimāya·disāya)*
2) In the westward direction *(pacchimāya·disāya)*
3) In the northward direction *(uttarāya·disāya)*
4) In the southward direction *(dakkhiṇāya·disāya)*
5) In the eastward intermediate direction *(puratthimāya·anu·disāya)*
6) In the westward intermediate direction *(pacchimāya anu·disāya)*
7) In the northward intermediate direction *(uttarāya anu·disāya)*
8) In the southward intermediate direction *(dakkhiṇāya anu·disāya)*
9) In the downward direction *(heṭṭhimāya·disāya)*
10) In the upward direction *(uparimāya·disāya)*

HOW YOU DEVELOP THE UNSPECIFIED/SPECIFIED CATEGORIES

To develop this method of loving-kindness meditation, you should as before re-establish the fourth jhāna with the white kasiṇa, and develop loving-kindness towards yourself, a person you respect or who is dear to you, one you are indifferent to, and one you hate, until there are no barriers between them and you.

Then use the bright and brilliant light to see all the beings in as big an area as possible around you, around the building or monastery. Once they are clear, you can develop loving-kindness towards them according to the five unspecified categories, and seven specified categories: twelve in total. You should at each category pervade loving-kindness in four ways:

1) May they be free from danger,
2) May they be free from mental pain,
3) May they be free from physical pain,
4) May they be well and happy.

'They' is in each case one of your twelve categories, all beings, all devas, etc. Thus you will be pervading loving-kindness in a total of forty-eight ways ((5+7) x 4 = 48).

The beings in each category should be clearly visible in the light of concentration and understanding. For example, when you extend loving-kindness to all women, you should actually see, in the light, the women within the determined area. You should actually see the men, devas, beings in lower realms etc., in the determined area.[163] You must develop each category up to the third jhāna before moving on to the next. You should practise in this way until you become proficient in pervading loving-kindness in all forty-eight ways.

Once proficient, you should expand the determined area to include the whole monastery, the whole village, the whole township, the whole state, the whole country, the whole world, the whole solar system, the whole galaxy, and the whole of the infinite universe. Develop each of the expanded areas in the forty-eight ways up to the third jhāna.

Once proficient you may proceed to the ten directional categories.

HOW YOU DEVELOP THE TEN DIRECTIONAL CATEGORIES

The ten directional categories of loving-kindness involve the previously discussed forty-eight categories in each of the ten directions.

You should see all beings in the whole of the infinite universe to the east of you, and extend loving-kindness to them in the forty-eight ways. Then do the same thing to the west of you, and so on in the other directions.

This gives a total of four hundred and eighty ways to extend loving-kindness (10 x 48 = 480). When we add the original forty-eight categories of pervasion, we get five hundred and twenty-eight ways to extend loving-kindness (480 + 48 = 528).

Once you master these five hundred and twenty-eight ways of pervading loving-kindness, you will experience the eleven benefits of practising loving-kindness, which The Buddha taught in the *Aṅguttara·Nikāya*:[164]

When the mind-deliverance of loving-kindness, bhikkhus, is cultivated, developed, much practised, made the vehicle, made the foundation, established, consolidated, and properly undertaken, eleven benefits can be expected. What are the eleven?

---

[163] This does not mean that the yogi can actually see every single woman, man, deva etc. within the determined area: it means that the yogi should extend loving-kindness with the intention that it is for every single woman, man, deva etc., and that insofar as he can, he should see them all.

[164] A.XI.ii.5 *'Mettā·Suttaṁ'* ('The Loving-Kindness Sutta')

[1] **One sleeps in comfort;**
[2] **one wakes in comfort; and**
[3] **one dreams no evil dreams;**
[4] **one is dear to human beings;**
[5] **one is dear to non-human beings;**
[6] **devas guard one;**
[7] **fire, poison and weapons do not affect one;**
[8] **one's mind is easily concentrated;**
[9] **one's complexion becomes bright;**
[10] **one dies unconfused; and**
[11] **if one penetrates no higher, one will be reborn in the Brahma World.**

HOW YOU DEVELOP COMPASSION

Once you have developed loving-kindness as just described, it should not be difficult to develop the sublime abiding of compassion *(karuṇā)*. To develop compassion, you should first select a living person of your own sex who is suffering. You should arouse compassion for him or her by reflecting on his or her suffering.

Then re-establish the fourth jhāna with the white kasiṇa, so the light is bright and clear, and use the light to see that person, and then develop loving-kindness up to the third jhāna. Emerge from it, and develop compassion towards that suffering person with the thought, 'May this good person be released from suffering' *(ayaṁ sa·ppuriso dukkhā muccatu)*. Do this many times, again and again, until you attain the first, second, and third jhānas, and the five masteries of each. After that, you should develop compassion as you did loving-kindness, that is, towards yourself, towards a person you like, one you are indifferent to, and one you hate: and with those three persons, you develop loving-kindness up to the third jhāna, until the barriers have been broken down.

To develop compassion towards beings who are not suffering in any apparent way, you should reflect on the fact that all unenlightened beings are liable to experience the results of the evil they have done while wandering through the round of rebirths: all unenlightened beings are liable therefore to be reborn in the lower realms. Furthermore, every being is worthy of compassion, because they are not free from the suffering of ageing, sickness, and death.

After reflecting thus, you should also here develop compassion as you did loving-kindness: towards yourself and the usual three types of person: and with those three persons, you develop loving-kindness up to the third jhāna, until the barriers have been broken down.

After that you should develop compassion in the same hundred and thirty-two ways you developed loving-kindness, namely: five unspecified categories, seven specified categories, and one hundred and twenty directional categories (5 + 7 + (10 x 12) = 132).

HOW YOU DEVELOP SYMPATHETIC JOY

To develop the sublime abiding of sympathetic joy *(muditā)*, you should select a living person of your own sex who is happy, the sight of whom makes you happy, and whom you are very fond of and friendly with.

Then re-establish the fourth jhāna with the white kasiṇa, so the light is bright and clear, and use the light to see that person, and then develop the third loving-kindness jhāna. Emerge from it and develop compassion jhāna. Emerge from that, and develop sympathetic joy towards the happy person with the thought: 'May this good person not be separated from the prosperity he has attained,' *(ayaṁ sa·ppuriso yathā·laddha·sampattito mā·vigacchatu)*. Do this many times, again and again, until you attain the first, second and third jhānas, and the five masteries of each.

Then develop sympathetic-joy jhāna towards yourself and the usual three types of person: and with those three persons, you develop loving-kindness up to the third jhāna, until the barriers have been broken down. Finally develop sympathetic-joy towards all beings in the infinite universe in the hundred and thirty-two ways.

HOW YOU DEVELOP EQUANIMITY

To develop the sublime abiding of equanimity *(upekkhā)*, you should first re-establish the fourth jhāna with the white kasiṇa. Then choose a living person of your own sex, towards whom you are indifferent, and develop loving-kindness, compassion, and sympathetic joy, each up to the third jhāna. Then emerge from the third jhāna and reflect on the disadvantages of those three sublime abidings, namely their closeness to affection, to like and dislike, and to elation and joy. Afterwards reflect on the fourth jhāna based on equanimity as peaceful. Then develop equanimity towards a person you are indifferent to with the thought: 'This good person is heir to his own kamma *(ayaṁ sa·ppuriso kamma·ssako)*'. Do this many times, again and again, until you attain the fourth jhāna and the five masteries of it. With the support of the third jhānas of loving-kindness, compassion, and sympathetic-joy, it should not take you long to develop the fourth jhāna of equanimity. Afterwards develop it towards a person you respect or who is dear to you, one who is very dear to you, and one you hate. Then again towards yourself, a person you respect or who is dear to you, one you are indifferent to, and one you hate, until you have broken down the barriers between you. Finally develop equanimity towards all beings in the infinite universe in the previously mentioned hundred and thirty-two ways.

This completes the development of the four sublime abidings.

HOW YOU DEVELOP THE FOUR PROTECTIVE MEDITATIONS

The four meditation subjects of loving-kindness, Buddha Recollection, foulness meditation and death recollection are called the 'Four Protections', or the 'Four Protective Meditations'. This is because they protect the yogi from various dangers. It is for this reason worthwhile to learn and develop them before proceeding to vipassanā meditation. We have already discussed how to develop loving-kindness, so we need now only discuss how to develop the other three protective meditations. Let us begin with Buddha Recollection.

HOW YOU DEVELOP BUDDHA RECOLLECTION

Buddha Recollection *(Buddh·Ānussati)* can be developed by looking at the nine qualities of The Buddha, using a formula He gives frequently in the suttas:[165]

Itipi So Bhagavā (**The Blessed One is such**):

[1] *Arahaṁ*	[6] *Anuttaro Purisadamma·Sārathi*
[2] *Sammā·Sambuddho*	[7] *Satthā Deva·Manussānaṁ*
[3] *Vijjā-Caraṇa·Sampanno*	[8] *Buddho*
[4] *Sugato*	[9] *Bhagavā'ti.*
[5] *Loka·vidū*	

This can be explained as:

1) This Blessed One, having destroyed all defilements, is a worthy one: *Arahaṁ.*
2) He has attained perfect enlightenment by Himself: *Sammā·Sambuddho.*
3) He is perfect in knowledge and morality: *Vijjā-Caraṇa·Sampanno.*

---

[165] D.iii.1 *'Pathika·Suttaṁ'* ('The Traveller Sutta'); *Vinaya*.I.1 *'Verañja·Kaṇḍa'* ('Verañja Section'); VsM.vii.125-130 *'Buddh·Ānussati·Kathā'* ('Recollection of The Buddha Discussion') PP.vii.4-25

4) He speaks only what is beneficial and true: *Sugato.*
5) He knows the worlds: *Loka·vidū.*
6) He is the unsurpassed tamer of men fit to be tamed: *Anuttaro Purisdamma·Sārathi.*
7) He is the teacher of devas and human beings: *Satthā Deva·Manussānaṁ.*
8) He is an Enlightened One: *Buddho.*
9) He is the most fortunate possessor of the results of previous meritorious actions: *Bhagavā.*

Let us discuss how to develop concentration with, for example, the first quality, *Arahaṁ*. According to the *Visuddhi·Magga*, the Pali word *Arahaṁ* has five definitions:

1) Since He has removed totally, without remainder, all defilements and habitual tendencies, and has thereby distanced Himself from them, The Buddha is a worthy one: *Arahaṁ.*
2) Since He has cut off all defilements with the sword of the Arahant Path, The Buddha is a worthy one: *Arahaṁ.*
3) Since He has broken and destroyed the spokes of the wheel of dependent origination, led by ignorance and craving, The Buddha is a worthy one: *Arahaṁ.*
4) Since His virtue, concentration, and wisdom are unsurpassed, The Buddha is paid the highest reverence by brahmās, devas, and men, and is a worthy one: *Arahaṁ.*
5) Since He does not, even when in seclusion and unseen, do any evil by body, speech, or mind, The Buddha is a worthy one: *Arahaṁ.*

To develop this meditation, you should memorize these five definitions well enough to recite them. Then re-establish the fourth *ān·āpāna-*, or white kasiṇa-jhāna, so the light is bright and clear. Then use the light to visualize a Buddha image you remember, like, and respect. When it is clear, see it as the real Buddha and concentrate on it as such.

If you were in a past life fortunate enough to meet The Buddha, His image may re-appear. If so, you should concentrate on also the qualities of The Buddha; not just His image. If the image of The real Buddha does not appear, then first see the visualized image as The real Buddha, and then recollect His qualities. You can choose the definition of *Arahaṁ* you like most, take the meaning as object, and recollect it again and again as '*Arahaṁ-Arahaṁ*'.

As your concentration develops and becomes stronger, the image of The Buddha will disappear, and you should simply remain concentrated on the chosen quality. Continue to concentrate on that quality until the jhāna factors arise, although you can with this meditation subject attain only access-concentration *(upacāra·samādhi)*. You can concentrate on the remaining qualities of The Buddha too.

HOW YOU DEVELOP FOULNESS MEDITATION

The second protective meditation is foulness meditation *(asubha·bhāvanā)* on a corpse. To develop it you should re-establish the fourth *ān·āpāna-*, or white kasiṇa-jhāna, so the light is bright and clear. Then use the light to visualize the foulest corpse of your own sex that you remember seeing. Use the light to see the corpse exactly as it was when you really saw it in the past. When it is clear, make it appear as repulsive as possible. Concentrate on it, and note it as, 'repulsive - repulsive' *(paṭikkūla, paṭikkūla)*.[166] Concentrate on the object of the repulsiveness of the corpse until the *uggaha-nimitta* (taken-up sign) becomes the *paṭibhāga-nimitta* (counterpart sign). The *uggaha-nimitta* is the image of the corpse as you really saw it in the past, and is a hideous, dreadful, and frightening sight, but the *paṭibhāga-nimitta* is like a man with big limbs, lying down after having eaten his fill. Continue to concentrate on that nimitta, until you reach the first jhāna, and then develop the five masteries.

HOW YOU DEVELOP DEATH RECOLLECTION

The third protective meditation is death recollection *(maraṇ·ānussati)*. According to the *'Mahā·Sati·Paṭṭhāna'* sutta[167] and the *Visuddhi·Magga*,[168] death recollection too can be developed using a corpse you remember seeing. Therefore, you should re-establish the first jhāna with the repulsiveness of a corpse, and with that external corpse as object, reflect: 'This body of mine is also of a nature to die. Indeed, it will die just like this one. It cannot avoid becoming like this.' By keeping the mind concentrated on and mindful of your own mortality, you will also find that the sense of urgency *(saṁvega)* develops. With that knowledge, you will probably see your own body as a repulsive corpse. Perceiving that the life faculty has in that image been cut off, you should concentrate on the absence of the life faculty with one of the following thoughts:

---

[166] Here, *asubha* (foulness) and *paṭikkūla* (repulsiveness) are synonyms.
[167] D.ii.9 'The Great Mindfulness-Foundation Sutta' (also M.I.i.10)
[168] VsM.viii.168 *'Maraṇ·Ānussati·Kathā'* ('Death-Mindfulness Discussion') PP.viii.6-7

1) My death is certain *(maraṇaṁ me dhuvaṁ)*; my life is uncertain *(jīvitaṁ me a·dhuvaṁ)*.
2) I shall certainly die *(maraṇaṁ me bhavissati)*.
3) My life will end in death *(maraṇa·pariyosānaṁ me jīvitaṁ)*.
4) Death - death *(maraṇaṁ - maraṇaṁ)*.

Choose one and note it in any language. Continue to concentrate on the image of the absence of the life faculty in your own corpse, until the jhāna factors arise, although you can with this meditation subject attain only access concentration.

SUMMARY

As mentioned earlier, the four meditation subjects of loving-kindness, Buddha Recollection, foulness, and death recollection are called the Four Protections, or the Four Protective meditations, because they protect the yogi from various dangers.

In the *'Meghiya'* sutta of the *Khuddaka·Nikāya* it says:[169]

- *A·subhā bhāvetabbā rāgassa pahānāya;*
- *mettā bhāvetabbā byāpādassa pahānāya;*
- *ān·āpānassati bhāvetabbā vitakk·upacchedāya.*

- **For the removal of lust, meditation on foulness should be developed;**
- **for the removal of ill-will, loving-kindness should be developed;**
- **mindfulness-of-breathing should be developed for the cutting off of discursive thought.**

According to this sutta, foulness meditation is the best weapon for removing lust. If you take a corpse as object, and see it as repulsive, it is called 'foulness of a lifeless body' *(a·viññāṇaka asubha)*. To take the thirty-two parts of the body of a being, and see them as repulsive (as taught in the *'Girimānanda'* sutta of the *Aṅguttara·Nikāya*[170]) is called 'foulness of a living body' *(sa·viññāṇaka asubha)*. Both these forms of foulness meditation are weapons for removing lust.

The best weapon for removing ill-will is to develop loving-kindness, and for removing discursive thought *ān·āpāna·sati* is the best weapon.

Furthermore, when faith in meditation slackens, and the mind is dull, the best weapon is to develop Buddha Recollection. When the sense of urgency is lacking, and you are bored with striving in meditation, the best weapon is death recollection.

---

[169] U.iv.1 *'Meghiya·Suttaṁ'* ('The Meghiya Sutta') (also A.IX.I.i.3)

[170] A.X.II.i.10

Today we discussed how to develop the four sublime abidings and Four Protective meditations. In the next talk, we shall discuss how to develop vipassanā meditation, beginning with the four-elements meditation, and analysis of the various kinds of materiality.

BENEFITS OF SAMATHA

Before ending, we should like to discuss briefly the relation between samatha and vipassanā.

In the *'Samādhi'* sutta of the *'Khandha·Vagga'* in the *Saṁyutta·Nikāya*, The Buddha said:[171]

Develop concentration, bhikkhus *(Samādhiṁ, bhikkhave, bhāvetha)*. **Concentrated, bhikkhus, a bhikkhu according to reality understands** *(yathā·bhūtaṁ pajānāti)*. **And what according to reality does he understand?**

[1] **Materiality's appearance and disappearance;**
[2] **feeling's appearance and disappearance;**
[3] **perception's appearance and disappearance;**
[4] **formations' appearance and disappearance;**
[5] **consciousness's appearance and disappearance.**

Therefore, a bhikkhu who is concentrated knows the five aggregates and their causes, and their arising and perishing. He sees clearly that because of the arising of their causes the five aggregates arise, and because of the complete cessation of their causes, the five aggregates also completely cease.

The samatha we discussed in the first two talks and today produces strong concentration. It is the light of this concentration (the light of wisdom) that lets you see ultimate mentality-materiality for vipassanā. With that deep, strong and powerful concentration, you can see clearly the impermanent, suffering, and non-self nature of mentality-materiality and their causes. This clarity is a great benefit coming from samatha.

Samatha also gives you a resting-place. There is much to discern in vipassanā and tiredness may occur. In that case, you can stay in one of the jhānas for a long time. That rests and refreshes your mind, and then you can go back to vipassanā. Whenever tiredness occurs, you can again enter jhāna to rest.

It is good to remember these benefits of samatha, when in the following talks we discuss vipassanā.

---

171 S.III.I.i.5, quoted also p.23, and mentioned Q&A 4.6, p.149.

QUESTIONS AND ANSWERS 3

Question 3.1 In *ān·āpāna·sati* (mindfulness-of-breathing), there are the *parikamma-nimitta*, the *uggaha-nimitta*, and the *paṭibhāga-nimitta*. What is the *parikamma-nimitta*? Is the *parikamma-nimitta* always grey? What is the difference between the *parikamma-nimitta* and the *uggaha-nimitta*?

Answer 3.1 In *ān·āpāna·sati*, there are three types of nimitta, three types of concentration *(samādhi)* and three types of meditation *(bhāvanā)*.

The three types of nimitta are:

1) The *parikamma-nimitta* (preparatory sign)
2) The *uggaha-nimitta* (taken-up sign)
3) The *paṭibhāga-nimitta* (counterpart sign)

The three types of concentration are:

1) Preparatory concentration *(parikamma·samādhi)*: it is sometimes called momentary concentration *(khaṇika·samādhi)*.
2) Access concentration *(upacāra·samādhi)*
3) Absorption concentration *(appanā·samādhi)*: it is also called jhāna concentration: the eight attainments.[172]

The three types of meditation are:

1) Preparatory meditation *(parikamma·bhāvanā)*
2) Access meditation *(upacāra·bhāvanā)*
3) Absorption meditation *(appanā·bhāvanā)*

The object of preparatory concentration can be the *parikamma-nimitta*, the *uggaha-nimitta*, and occasionally the *paṭibhāga-nimitta*. Preparatory meditation is the same as preparatory concentration.

Real access concentration, and real access meditation are very close to absorption concentration (jhāna); this is why they are called 'access'. But sometimes deep and strong concentration before absorption concentration, with the *paṭibhāga-nimitta* as object, is as a metaphor also called 'access concentration' or 'access meditation'.[173] When preparatory concentration, or momentary concentration, is fully developed it leads to access concentration. When access concentration is fully developed, it leads to absorption concentration (jhāna).

We already discussed the nimitta in previous talks. There are, as mentioned, three types of nimitta: the *parikamma-nimitta*, the *uggaha-nimitta*, and the *paṭibhāga-nimitta*.

---

172 eight attainments: the four material jhānas, and four immaterial jhānas.

173 In this connection, see also Q&A 4.6, p.149.

1) The *parikamma-nimitta* (preparatory sign): the natural breath is a nimitta. The touching point is also a nimitta. Here the nimitta is the object of concentration. The commentary says the nostril nimitta *(nāsika·nimitta)*, and upper-lip nimitta *(mukha·nimitta)* are the *parikamma-nimitta* for beginners. When the concentration is a little stronger, a smoky grey usually appears around the nostrils. This smoky grey is also the *parikamma-nimitta*. It may have another colour too. The concentration and meditation at the *parikamma-nimitta* stage are preparatory.
2) The *uggaha-nimitta* (taken-up sign): when the preparatory concentration increases in strength and power, the smoky grey usually changes to white: white like cotton wool. But it may become another colour, owing to a change in perception.[174] When the perception changes, the colour and shape of the nimitta may also change. If the colour and shape change very often, the concentration will gradually decrease. This is because whenever yogi's perception changes, his object thereby also changes, which means he has different objects. So the yogi should ignore the colour and shape of the nimitta. He should concentrate on it only as an *ān·āpāna-nimitta*. The concentration and meditation on the *uggaha-nimitta* are also preparatory.
3) The *paṭibhāga-nimitta* (counterpart sign): when the concentration has become even stronger and more powerful, the *uggaha-nimitta* changes to the *paṭibhāga-nimitta*. Usually the *paṭibhāga-nimitta* is clear, bright and radiant, like the morning star. In this case too, if the perception changes, the nimitta may also change. If, when the concentration is strong and powerful, the yogi wants the nimitta to be long it will become long; if he wants it to be short it will become short; if he wants it to be ruby red, it will become ruby red. The *Visuddhi·Magga* says one should not do so.[175] If one does, then even though the concentration is deep, it will gradually decrease. This is because one has different perceptions, and thereby different objects. So a yogi should not play with the nimitta. If he plays with it he cannot attain jhāna.

The beginning stage of concentration and meditation on the *paṭibhāga-nimitta* are also preparatory. But close to jhāna they are access concentration, and access meditation. When absorption arises, the nimitta is still

---

[174] For further details on the relationship between the nimitta and perception, see p.38.

[175] VsM.iii.47 *'Cattālīsa·Kammaṭṭhāna·Vaṇṇanā'* ('Forty Meditations-Subjects Description') PP.iii.113

the *paṭibhāga-nimitta*, but the concentration is now absorption concentration, and the meditation is absorption meditation.

Question 3.2 What is the difference between access concentration and absorption concentration?

Answer 3.2 When the *paṭibhāga-nimitta* appears, the concentration is powerful. But at this stage, which is the stage of access concentration, the jhāna factors are not fully developed, and bhavaṅgas (life-continuum consciousnesses) still occur; one falls into bhavaṅga. The yogi will say that everything stopped, or may think it is Nibbāna, and say: 'I knew nothing then.' If one practises in this way, one can eventually stay in bhavaṅga for a long time.

In any kind of practice, be it good or bad, one will achieve one's aim, if one practises again and again. 'Practice makes perfect.' In this case too, if one practises again and again, in the same way, one may fall into bhavaṅga for a long time. Why does one say one knew nothing? Because the object of the bhavaṅga is the object of the near-death consciousness in the past life. That object may be kamma, a kamma sign *(kamma·nimitta)* or a destination sign *(gati·nimitta)*. But one cannot see this unless one has discerned dependent origination. It is only once one has discerned dependent origination that one sees that the bhavaṅga took one of those objects.[176]

If one thinks it is Nibbāna, this idea is a very big 'rock' blocking the way to Nibbāna. If one does not remove this big 'rock', one cannot attain Nibbāna. Why does this idea occur? Many yogis think that a disciple *(sāvaka)* cannot know mentality-materiality as taught by The Buddha. So they think it is not necessary to develop sufficiently deep concentration in order to discern mentality-materiality and their causes as taught by The Buddha. Thus their concentration is only weak, and bhavaṅgas still occur, because the jhāna factors too are weak. Their concentration cannot be maintained for long. If one purposely practises to fall into bhavaṅga, one will achieve one's aim, but it is not Nibbāna. To attain Nibbāna one must practise the seven stages of purification step by step; without knowing ultimate mentality, ultimate materiality, and their causes, one cannot attain Nibbāna.

The problem of thinking that the attainment of knowing nothing is Nibbāna needs perhaps to be explained further.

Nibbāna is *vi·saṅkhāra*: that is, 'without formations'. Formations *(saṅkhārā)* are mentality-materiality and their causes, and Nibbāna is without either of them. The mind that knows Nibbāna is called *vi·saṅkhāra·gata-*

---

[176] For details, see Table 1d 'Death and Rebirth', p.188.

·*citta*. But it is not itself *vi·saṅkhāra*: the act of seeing Nibbāna requires the formation of consciousness.

The consciousness that is formed when, for example, a Buddha or Arahant enters the Fruition Attainment, and sees Nibbāna, is the Arahant Fruition-Consciousness *(Arahatta·Phala·Citta)*, together with its associated mental factors. If the Arahant Fruition-Consciousness is entered upon from the first jhāna, and is thus a first-jhāna Arahant Fruition-Consciousness, there are thirty-seven mental formations. This principle applies in all the other Path and Fruition Knowledges. Together with their associated mental factors, they all take Nibbāna as object; and Nibbāna has the characteristic of peaceful bliss.

Whenever a Noble One *(Ariya)* enters the Fruition Attainment, she or he knows Nibbāna, and with the Fruition Knowledge enjoys the peaceful bliss that is Nibbāna.

It is therefore, impossible to enter one of the Fruition attainments and say about it: 'Everything stopped: I knew nothing then.' Before entering a Fruition Attainment, one determines how long it will last, for example one or two hours. And for the duration of that period, Nibbāna is known continuously as the peaceful bliss it is *(santi·sukha)*.

It is therefore clear that when one knows nothing, it is not because one has attained Nibbāna; it is because one's concentration is still weak.

When the *ān·āpāna paṭibhāga-nimitta* appears, the yogi's mind may fall into bhavaṅga, because the jhāna factors are not yet strong. Just like, when learning to walk, a small child who is too weak to stand by himself, will fall down again and again. In the same way, at the access concentration stage, the jhāna factors are still not fully developed, and one may fall into bhavaṅga: it is not Nibbāna.

To avoid falling into bhavaṅga, and to develop concentration further, you need the help of the five controlling faculties: faith *(saddhā)*, effort *(vīriya)*, mindfulness *(sati)*, concentration *(samādhi)*, and wisdom *(paññā)*, to push the mind and fix it on the *paṭibhāga-nimitta*. It takes effort to make the mind know the *paṭibhāga-nimitta* again and again, mindfulness to not forget it, and wisdom to know it.

At the absorption-jhāna stage, the jhāna factors are fully developed. Just like a strong and powerful man can stand up straight the whole day, a yogi can, taking the *paṭibhāga-nimitta* as object, stay in absorption jhāna for a long time without falling into bhavaṅga. Complete and uninterrupted absorption may continue for one, two, three hours, or more. At that time one does not hear a sound. One's mind does not go to other objects. Apart from the *paṭibhāga-nimitta*, one knows nothing.

Question 3.3 Under what conditions, or in what state, can we say that a meditation experience is access concentration or absorption concentration?

Answer 3.3 If many bhavaṅgas occur during concentration, one can say that it is access concentration. But the nimitta must be the *paṭibhāga-nimitta.* Only if one is able to stay in complete absorption for a long time, without interruption, with also the *paṭibhāga-nimitta* as object, can one say it is absorption concentration.

How does a yogi know his mind is falling into bhavaṅga? When he notices that he has very often been unaware of the *paṭibhāga-nimitta*, he knows there were bhavaṅgas. His mind may also for brief moments have thought of an object other than the *paṭibhāga-nimitta.* This does not happen in absorption concentration. In absorption concentration there is only complete absorption without interruption.

Question 3.4 Is there access concentration, as well as absorption concentration at each of the four jhānas? What are their characteristics?

Answer 3.4 Let us take the example of the *ān·āpāna* jhānas, which take the *ān·āpāna paṭibhāga-nimitta* as object. There are four levels of access concentration, and four levels of absorption concentration. At each level there is access jhāna first, and then absorption jhāna. Both take the same *ān·āpāna paṭibhāga-nimitta* as object. So it is the level of concentration that is different.

In the first, second, and third access-jhāna, there are five jhāna factors. But in the fourth access-jhāna, there is no bliss *(sukha)*, only application *(vitakka)*, sustainment *(vicāra)*, equanimity *(upekkhā)* and one-pointedness *(ek-·aggatā)*. Although they take the same nimitta as object, the jhāna factors become increasingly powerful at each access-jhāna.

The jhāna factors at the first access-jhāna suppress physical pain *(kāyika-·dukkha·vedanā)*; at the second, mental suffering *(domanassa·vedanā)*; at the third, physical pleasant feeling *(kāyika·sukha·vedanā)*; and at the fourth, mental pleasant feeling or happiness *(somanassa·vedanā)*. This is how we distinguish between the different levels of access concentration, especially the fourth. At that level, the breath is the subtlest, and has nearly stopped. It stops completely at the fourth absorption-jhāna.

We distinguish between the absorption-jhānas also by looking at the jhāna factors. In the first absorption jhāna, five jhāna factors are present: application, sustainment, joy, bliss and one-pointedness; in the second, three: joy, bliss and one-pointedness; in the third, two: bliss and one-pointedness; and in the fourth, also two: equanimity and one-pointedness. By looking at the jhāna factors, we can say, 'This is the first absorption jhāna', 'This is the second absorption jhāna', etc. Also, here the concentration increases level by level. Fourth-jhāna concentration is the highest. How is it the highest? You should try for yourself. Many yogis report that the fourth jhāna is the best and the quietest.

Question 3.5 Under what conditions does a yogi drop or regress from absorption to access concentration? Under what conditions does a yogi in access concentration attain absorption concentration?

Answer 3.5 If the yogi does not respect his meditation practice, but respects objects other than the *paṭibhāga-nimitta*, many hindrances *(nīvaraṇa)* will arise. Many thoughts of greed and hatred will arise. They arise due to unwise attention *(ayoniso manasikāra)*. Those objects reduce the concentration, because wholesome dhammas and unwholesome dhammas are always in opposition. When wholesome dhammas are strong and powerful, unwholesome dhammas are far away, and when (because of unwise attention) unwholesome dhammas are strong and powerful, wholesome dhammas are far away. Wholesome and unwholesome dhammas cannot arise simultaneously in one consciousness moment or mental process.

Here we need to understand wise attention *(yoniso manasikāra)* and unwise attention *(ayoniso manasikāra)*. When a yogi practises *ān·āpāna·sati* (mindfulness-of-breathing), and concentrates on the natural breath, his attention is wise attention. When the *uggaha-nimitta* or *paṭibhāga-nimitta* appears, and the yogi concentrates on it, his attention is still wise attention. If, in vipassanā meditation, a yogi sees: 'This is materiality', 'This is mentality', 'This is cause', 'This is effect', 'This is impermanence', 'This is suffering', or 'This is non-self', his attention is also wise attention.

But if he sees: 'This is a man, a woman, a son, a daughter, a father, a mother, a deity, a brahmā, an animal, etc.'; 'This is gold, money, etc.' then his attention is unwise attention. Generally speaking, we can say that because of wise attention many wholesome dhammas arise, and because of unwise attention many unwholesome dhammas arise. If, while you are practising meditation, unwise attention arises, then hindrances or defilements will certainly follow; they are unwholesome dhammas. Those unwholesome dhammas reduce the concentration, or cause it to regress and drop.

If you look at your meditation object with wise attention, again and again, then wholesome dhammas will arise and increase. Jhāna wholesome dhammas, for example, are among those wholesome dhammas. So, if you concentrate on the nimitta, such as the *ān·āpāna paṭibhāga-nimitta*, again and again, it is wise attention. If you develop this wise attention to full strength, then from access concentration you will attain absorption concentration.

Question 3.6 When a person dies, a *kamma-nimitta* may arise because of past wholesome or unwholesome kamma. Is this phenomenon similar to that which occurs during meditation, when images of past events, which the yogi had forgotten, appear?

Answer 3.6 There may be some similarity, but only in some cases. It may be similar to the arising of a *kamma-nimitta* in those whose death took place quickly.

Question 3.7 While meditating, images of events from more than thirty years back, which the yogi had forgotten, appear. Is this due to lack of mindfulness, which lets the mind leave the object?

Answer 3.7 It could be. But it could also be because of attention *(manasikāra)*. Many yogis do not know about attention. Only once they have practised meditation on mentality do they understand it. Mental processes occur very quickly, so they do not understand that these images appear because of attention. But no formation occurs by itself, without a cause. This is because all formations are conditioned.

Question 3.8 If, when dying, a person has strong mindfulness, can he prevent a kamma sign *(kamma·nimitta)* of previous unwholesome or wholesome kamma from arising?[177]

Answer 3.8 Strong, powerful mindfulness can prevent such nimittas from arising; but what is strong, powerful mindfulness? If a yogi enters jhāna, and keeps it completely stable right up to the time of death, you can say that the mindfulness of that jhāna is strong and powerful. That type of mindfulness can prevent an unwholesome sign or sensual-sphere wholesome sign from arising. It takes only the jhāna object, for example, an *ān·āpāna paṭibhāga-nimitta* or white-kasiṇa *paṭibhāga-nimitta*.

Another type of strong, powerful mindfulness is the mindfulness associated with vipassanā knowledge. If a yogi's vipassanā knowledge is the Formations-Equanimity Knowledge *(Saṅkhār·Upekkhā·Ñāṇa)*, and if he practises vipassanā up to the near-death moment, then his near-death impulsion is vipassanā knowledge associated with strong and powerful mindfulness. That type of mindfulness can also prevent unwholesome signs from appearing, as well as prevent other wholesome signs from replacing his vipassanā sign. The vipassanā sign is the impermanent, suffering, or non-self nature of a chosen formation. He may die with such a sign as the object of his near-death impulsion *(maraṇ·āsanna·javana)*. It can produce a

[177] For details in this regard, see Table 1d 'Death and Rebirth', p.188.

deva rebirth-linking consciousness *(paṭisandhi·citta)*, so that he is spontaneously reborn as a deva.

Concerning the benefits that this type of yogi may get in his future life as a deva, The Buddha says in the *'Sotānugata'* sutta of the *Aṅguttara Nikāya*, *'Catukka Nipāta'*:[178]

So muṭṭhassati[179] *kālaṁ kurumāno aññataraṁ devanikāyaṁ upapajjati. Tassa tattha sukhino dhammapadā plavanti. Dandho bhikkhave satuppādo, atha so satto khippameva visesagāmī hoti.*

Bhikkhus, an ordinary person *(puthu·jjana)* **who has heard the Teachings, often repeated them, reflected upon them, and thoroughly penetrated them with vipassanā knowledge, if he dies, he may be reborn in one of the deva realms, where all formations appear clearly in his mind. He may be slow to reflect on the Dhamma or to do vipassanā, but he attains Nibbāna very quickly.**

Why do formations appear clearly in his mind? Because the near-death impulsion consciousness of the previous human life, and the bhavaṅga consciousness of the following deva life take the same object, in this case the impermanent, suffering, or non-self nature of formations. The host, the bhavaṅga that is, already knows the vipassanā object, which is why vipassanā knowledge can easily be developed. So according to that sutta, strong mindfulness associated with vipassanā knowledge can prevent unwholesome signs from appearing, as well as other wholesome signs that may replace his vipassanā sign. You should try to possess this type of mindfulness before death takes place.

An example of this is the *'Sakka·Pañha'* sutta, about three bhikkhus who practised samatha and vipassanā.[180] They had good morality and good concentration, but their minds inclined towards life as male *gandhabbas*.[181] When they died they went to the deva realm. They were reborn as very beautiful and radiant *gandhabbas*, who looked sixteen years old. During their lives as bhikkhus, the three bhikkhus had gone to a laywoman's house every day for almsfood, and had taught her Dhamma. She had become a Stream-Enterer, and when she died, she was reborn as Gopaka, the son of Sakka. The three *gandhabbas* performed for the son of Sakka, and he saw that they were very beautiful and radiant. He thought: 'They are very beautiful and radiant. What was their kamma?'

---

178 A.IV.IV.v.1 *'Sotānugata·Suttaṁ'* ('The One-Who-Has-Heard Sutta'), mentioned also p.147.

179 *Muṭṭhasati* means 'muddled mindfulness', but in this context, The Buddha means that he is reborn as an ordinary person*(puthujjana)* and not a Noble One*(Ariya)*.

180 D.ii.8 *'Sakka·Pañha·Suttaṁ'* ('The Sakka's Questions Sutta')

181 Musicians and dancers in the deva realm.

He saw they were the three bhikkhus who had come to his house when he was a laywoman. He knew that their virtue, concentration and wisdom had been very good. So he reminded them of their past life. He said: 'When you listened to the teachings and practised the Dhamma, what were your eyes and ears directed at?' Two of the gandhabbas remembered their past lives and were ashamed. They developed samatha and vipassanā again, quickly attained the Non-Returning Path and Fruition, and died. They were reborn in the realm of *Brahma·Parohitā* (Brahma's Ministers),[182] and attained Arahantship there. The third bhikkhu was not ashamed, and remained a *gandhabba.*

So, it is not necessary to contact a life insurance company. This type of mindfulness is the best insurance.

Question 3.9 Is it necessary when discerning the twelve characteristics in four-elements meditation, to start with hardness, roughness, and heaviness in that sequence? Can one choose to start with any one of the characteristics?

Answer 3.9 In the beginning we can start with a characteristic that is easy to discern. But once we can discern all the characteristics easily and clearly, we must follow the sequence given by The Buddha: earth element *(pathavī-·dhātu)*, water element *(āpo·dhātu)*, fire element *(tejo·dhātu)*, and wind element *(vāyo·dhātu)*. This is because that sequence produces strong, powerful concentration. When we see the rūpa-kalāpas, and are able to easily discern the four elements in each one, the sequence is not important; what is very important then is to discern them simultaneously.

Why? The life span of a rūpa-kalāpa is very short. It may be less than a billionth of a second. When discerning the four elements in a rūpa-kalāpa there is not enough time to recite 'earth, water, fire, wind', so we must discern them simultaneously.

Question 3.10 Practising four-elements meditation enables one to balance the four elements in the body. One may at some time get sick because the four elements are out of balance. When one is sick, can one practise four-elements meditation with strong mindfulness to cure the sickness?

Answer 3.10 There are many types of affliction. Some afflictions are due to previous kamma, such as The Buddha's back pain. Some afflictions are due to unbalanced elements. The afflictions born of previous kamma cannot be cured by balancing the four elements. But some of the afflictions that occur because of unbalanced elements may disappear when the yogi tries to balance them.

---

[182] DA-II-8 *'Sakka·Pañha·Suttaṁ'* ('The Sakka's Questions Sutta')

There are also afflictions that occur because of food, temperature *(utu)* or the mind *(citta)*. If an affliction arises because of the mind, and we can cure the mind, the affliction may disappear; if the affliction arises because of temperature, fire element, as with cancer, malaria, etc., it can be cured only by taking medicine, not by balancing the elements. This is the same for afflictions born of unsuitable food.

Question 3.11 Before we attain the fourth jhāna, and eradicate[183] ignorance *(avijjā)*, many unwholesome thoughts still arise due to bad habits. For example, in our daily life (outside a meditation retreat) we know that greed or hatred arises. Can we use foulness meditation *(asubha)* or loving-kindness meditation *(mettā·bhāvanā)* to remove them? Or should we ignore them and just concentrate on our meditation subject, and let them disappear automatically?

Answer 3.11 Unwholesome kamma has ignorance *(avijjā)* as a latent cause, and unwise attention *(ayoniso manasikāra)* as the proximate cause. Unwise attention is very harmful. If you are able to replace unwise attention with wise attention, the greed or hatred will disappear for a while, or maybe forever if the wise attention is very strong and powerful. We already discussed wise and unwise attention in a previous question.

You can use foulness meditation or loving-kindness meditation to remove greed and hatred. These meditations are also wise attention. But vipassanā is the best weapon to destroy defilements. It is the best wise attention.

Question 3.12 How does the bhavaṅga function in the sensual sphere planes, fine-material sphere planes, immaterial sphere planes and supramundane sphere planes? Would the Sayadaw please explain with examples?[184]

---

[183] The fourth jhāna does not eradicate ignorance; it only suppresses ignorance. See further Q&As 7.7, 7.8 and 7.9 p.232*ff.*

[184] bhavaṅga: This does not correspond to the subconscious/unconscious as hypothesized in Freudian psychology: two consciousnesses cannot arise at the same time. The life-continuum consciousness is a flow of resultant consciousnesses, maintained by the kamma that matured at the time of death in the previous life. It maintains the continuum of mentality between mental processes. It functions also as the mind door *(mano·dvāra)*. Once the kamma that produces this life comes to an end, the life-continuum consciousness of this life stops. In the non-Arahant, a new life-continuum consciousness, with a new object, arises after the first consciousness of the new life, i.e. after the rebirth-linking consciousness there arise sixteen life-continuum consciousnesses. Being produced by the same kamma as the kamma that produces the rebirth-linking consciousness, the new life-continuum consciousness takes the same object (see Table 1d, 'Death and Rebirth', p.188). Hence, the life-continuum is not a 'subconscious undercurrent' operating 'below' the mental processes of the six doors. As can be seen in table '1c: The Five-Door Process', (p.168), prior to the arising of a five-door process, the flow of life-continuum consciousnesses is

(Please see further next page.)

Answer 3.12 The function of the bhavaṅga is the same on the first three types of plane.[185] It arises so the consciousness moments in a life do not stop; it maintains the mentality, which is the life-continuum. This is because the kamma that produces this life has not yet been exhausted. Since there is materiality-mentality *(nāma·rūpa)* in the sensual and fine-material sphere planes, and mentality in the immaterial sphere planes, there is also a bhavaṅga there.

In the sensual sphere planes *(kām·āvacara·bhūmi)*, the bhavaṅga may have as object a kamma, kamma sign *(kamma·nimitta)* or rebirth sign *(gati·nimitta)*. For example, one being's bhavaṅga may have as object the Kyaikhtiyo Pagoda, while another's may have as object the Shwedagon Pagoda:[186] these objects are concepts.

In the fine-material sphere plane *(rūp·āvacara·bhūmi)*, the bhavaṅga has as object only a kamma sign: no kamma and no rebirth sign. The bhavaṅga of one on a fine-material sphere plane is called the fine-material sphere resultant jhāna *(rūp·āvacara·vipāka·jhāna)*, because it is the result of the jhāna-attainment at death in the foregoing life. Since the object of the bhavaṅga is thus the same as the object of the jhāna attainment, the object of the bhavaṅga will depend upon the jhāna. For example, the bhavaṅga of one who has reached a fine material sphere plane due to *ān·āpāna* jhāna will have as object the *ān·āpāna paṭibhāga-nimitta*, while the one who is there due to mettā-jhāna will have as object all beings in the infinite universe: both these objects are concepts.

In the immaterial sphere planes *(a·rūp·āvacara·bhūmi)*, the bhavaṅga has as object only kamma or a kamma sign: no rebirth sign. For example, on the plane of the base of boundless space one's bhavaṅga will have as object boundless space, and on the plane of the base of nothingness, it will have as object the absence of the base-of-boundless-space consciousness: both these objects are concepts.

On the plane of the base of boundless consciousness, one's bhavaṅga will have as object the consciousness of the base of boundless space, and on the plane of the base of neither perception nor non-perception, it will

---

arrested. And it is resumed once the mental process is complete (see also table '1b: The Mind-Door Process', p.164). The life-continuum cognizes always the same object, which is independent of the objects that enter the six doors: that is why it is called process-separate *(vīthi-mutta)*. See also explanation, p.159.

[185] The three spheres: 1) The sensuous sphere *(kām·āvacara)*, which includes the human world, the animal-, ghost-, and asura worlds, the hells and the deva-worlds. 2) The fine-material sphere *(rūp·āvacara)*, which includes the Brahma worlds, where the materiality is very subtle. 3) The immaterial sphere *(a·rūp·āvacara)*, where there is only mentality.

[186] The two most famous pagodas in Myanmar.

have as object the consciousness of the Base of Nothingness: being consciousnesses, these objects are kamma.

When we say 'sensual sphere planes', 'fine-material sphere planes' and 'immaterial sphere planes', we are referring to planes of existence that exist, places that exist. But when we say 'supramundane plane' *(lokuttara·bhūmi)*, the word 'plane' is only a metaphor. It is, in fact, not a place at all. When we say 'supramundane plane' we mean only the four Paths, four Fruitions, and Nibbāna; not a place. Hence, there is no bhavaṅga in the supramundane plane. There is none in the four Path and four Fruition consciousnesses, and since there is no mentality-materiality *(nāma·rūpa)* in Nibbāna, there is no mentality for the bhavaṅga to maintain, which means there cannot be any bhavaṅga in Nibbāna.

Question 3.13 What is the difference between mundane jhānas *(lokiya·jhāna)* and supramundane jhānas *(lokuttara·jhāna)*?

Answer 3.13 The mundane jhānas are the four fine-material sphere jhānas and four immaterial-sphere jhānas *(a·rūp·āvacara·jhāna)*, that is, the eight attainments *(samāpatti)*. The supramundane jhānas are the jhāna factors associated with the Path and Fruition Knowledges. When you discern the mental formations of, for example, the mundane fine-material sphere first jhāna as impermanence, suffering or non-self, and if you see Nibbāna, your Path Knowledge is the first jhāna. This is a supramundane jhāna.

Why? In the mundane fine-material sphere first jhāna, which was the object of vipassanā, there are the five jhāna factors: application, sustainment, joy, bliss and one-pointedness. In the supramundane first jhāna there are the same five. This is how the Path and Fruition can be the first jhāna Path, and first jhāna Fruition. The other jhānas can in the same way be (the conditions for their respective) supramundane (jhānas).

How You Discern Materiality

INTRODUCTION

Today, we shall discuss materiality meditation *(rūpa·kammaṭṭhāna)*. That is four-elements meditation *(catu·dhātu·vavatthāna)*, which is discerning the different types of ultimate materiality *(paramattha·rūpa)*. Materiality is the first of the five clinging-aggregates, and the remaining four (feeling *(vedanā)*, perception *(saññā)*, mental formations *(saṅkhārā)*, and consciousness *(viññāṇa)*) can together be called mentality *(nāma)*. In our five-constituent existence *(pañca·vokāra·bhava)*, mentality depends on materiality, which means that consciousnesses arise dependent on their respective material base. For eye-, ear-, nose-, tongue- and body materiality, the base *(vatthu)* and the door *(dvāra)* are the same thing. Thus, an eye consciousness arises dependent on the materiality that is the eye door/eye base; an ear consciousness arises dependent on the materiality that is the ear door/ear base, etc. But a mind consciousness arises dependent on the mind door (bhavaṅga), which is mentality: and in our five-constituent existence, mentality arises dependent on a material base that is located in the blood in the heart: it is for that reason called the heart base *(hadaya·vatthu)*.[187]

To see this, you need to see the individual types of materiality, which means you need first to penetrate to the sub-atomic particles called rūpa-kalāpas. You need to see that materiality is nothing except these rūpa-kalāpas. But they are not ultimate reality.[188] To penetrate to ultimate reality, you need to see that the individual type of rūpa-kalāpa consists of elements *(dhātu)*:[189] only then can you see what materiality really is, and can see how it is related to mentality. That is the aim of four-elements meditation.

But, before explaining the meditation, let us discuss briefly the different types of rūpa-kalāpa and their elements, and then explain about the origin

---

[187] For the necessity of discerning the different types of materiality etc. see also The Buddha's explanation in M.I.iv.3 *'Mahā·Gopālaka·Suttaṁ'* ('The Great Cowherd Sutta'), quoted p.11. For the difference between *āyatana* and *vatthu*, see footnote 23, p.6.

[188] For the difference between rūpa-kalāpas and ultimate materiality, see also Q&A 7.6, p.231.

[189] *dhātu*: element, substance that cannot be analysed further. See, for example, M.III.ii.5 *'Bahu·Dhātuka·Suttaṁ'* ('The Many-Element Sutta'). The *Visuddhi·Magga* explains that the elements 'cause the individual characteristic to be carried' *(attano sabhāvaṁ dhārentīti dhātuyo)* (VsM.xv.518 *'Dhātu·Vitthāra·Kathā'* ('Elements Details Discussion') PP.xv.21).

of materiality, in order that it may be easier for you to understand the profound meditation that is four-elements meditation *(catu·dhātu·vavatthāna)*.[190]

THREE TYPES OF RŪPA-KALĀPA

As mentioned, materiality is nothing except rūpa-kalāpas, and there are basically three types of rūpa-kalāpa:

1) Octad-kalāpas *(aṭṭhaka)*: they comprise a basic eight types of materiality.
2) Nonad-kalāpas *(navaka)*: they comprise the basic eight plus a ninth.
3) Decad-kalāpas *(dasaka)*: they comprise the nine plus a tenth.

Generally speaking, the materiality of our body is composed of these three types of rūpa-kalāpa mixed together in different ways.

THE MATERIALITY OF THE THREE TYPES OF RŪPA-KALĀPA

The first type of rūpa-kalāpa comprises the four elements *(catu·dhātu)*, which are the four 'great essentials' *(mahā·bhūtā)*, and four types of derived materiality *(upādā·rūpa)*;[191] in total eight types of materiality:

1) Earth element .... *(pathavī·dhātu)*	3) Fire element .... *(tejo·dhātu)*
2) Water element .... *(āpo·dhātu)*	4) Wind element .... *(vāyo·dhātu)*

And then:

5) Colour .... *(vaṇṇa)*	7) Flavour .... *(rasa)*
6) Odour .... *(gandha)*	8) Nutritive Essence .... *(ojā)*

Because it has eight types of materiality, this type of rūpa-kalāpa is called an octad-kalāpa *(aṭṭhaka·kalāpa)*, and because nutritive essence is the eighth, it is also called a nutritive-essence octad-kalāpa *(oj·aṭṭhamaka·kalāpa)*.[192] They are found throughout the body, and are untranslucent materiality *(na·pasāda·rūpa)*.[193]

The second type of rūpa-kalāpa comprises these basic eight types of materiality, and a ninth, life faculty *(jīvit·indriya)*.[194] Because it has nine

---

190 See also Q&A 2.2 p.72.

191 derived materiality: so called because it derives from, depends on the four great essentials.

192 The Pali for the different types of rūpa-kalāpa is *kalāpa that has x as the yth*.

193 translucent/translucency: see dictionary definition, footnote 504, p.276.

194 There are also rūpa-kalāpas of derived materiality that need to be discerned but are here not discussed, for example, rūpa-kalāpas with sound/bodily intimation as the ninth/twelfth; verbal intimation as the tenth/thirteenth; lightness as the eleventh. For these

(Please see further next page.)

types of materiality, this type of rūpa-kalāpa is called a nonad-kalāpa *(navaka·kalāpa)*, and because it has life faculty as the ninth, it is also called a life nonad-kalāpa *(jīvita·navaka·kalāpa)*. They are found throughout the body and are also untranslucent.[195]

The third type of rūpa-kalāpa comprises the basic eight types of materiality, life faculty as the ninth, and a tenth. Because it has ten types of materiality, this type of rūpa-kalāpa is called a decad-kalāpa *(dasaka)*. There are three types of decad-kalāpa:

1) Eye- *(cakkhu-)*, ear- *(sota-)*, nose- *(ghāna-)*, tongue- *(jivhā-)*, and body *(kāya-)* decad-kalāpas *(·dasaka·kalāpa)*: their tenth type of materiality is eye-, ear-, nose-, tongue-, and body translucent-materiality *(pasāda·rūpa)*.
2) Heart decad-kalāpas *(hadāya·dasaka·kalāpa)*: their tenth type of materiality is heart materiality *(hadāya·rūpa)*.
3) Sex decad-kalāpas *(bhāva·dasaka·kalāpa)*: their tenth type of materiality is sex materiality *(bhāva·rūpa)*.

1) Eye-, ear-, nose-, tongue-, and body decad-kalāpas are found in the respective organ. Their tenth, translucent materiality *(pasāda·rūpa)*, is the respective sense base. The five material sense bases are also the five material sense doors, i.e., the five material sense bases *(vatthu)* (eye-, ear-, nose-, tongue- and body base) are also the five material sense doors *(dvāra)*[196] (eye-, ear-, nose-, tongue- and body door).
2) Heart decad-kalāpas are found in the blood in the heart. Their tenth type of materiality is also the sense base: the heart base *(hadaya·vatthu)*. But it is not the mind door (the bhavaṅga), because the mind door is mentality, although it depends on the heart decad-kalāpa's tenth type of materiality.

   Whenever an object strikes upon one of the five sense doors, it strikes the sixth sense door (the mind door, bhavaṅga) at the same time.[197] For example, when a colour object[198] strikes upon the eye

and other elements, see VsM.xiv *'Rūpa·Kkhandha·Kathā'* ('Materiality Aggregate Discussion'), or the Most Venerable Pa-Auk Tawya Sayadaw's little book *Mindfulness-of-Breathing and Four-Elements-Meditation* (WAVE Publications, Kuala Lumpur, Malaysia).

195 The fire element of rūpa-kalāpas that have life faculty sustains concomitant octad-kalāpas, which is why, although they are without life faculty, they are 'coexistent with consciousness*(sa·viññāṇaka)*'. Without the heat of the life faculty, the materiality rots, such as happens when a person dies: the animate body becomes an inanimate corpse.

196 The term *dvāra* (door) describes the fact that objects need an entrance through which to be known by a consciousness.

197 See also S.V.IV.v.2 *'Uṇṇābha·Brāhmaṇa·Suttaṁ'* ('The Uṇṇābha-Brahmin Sutta') quoted in 'Introduction', p.6.

198 Strictly speaking a visual/chromatic object, and a sound object is an auditory object etc.

(Please see further next page.)

door (the translucent, tenth type of materiality of an eye decad-kalāpa),[199] it strikes at the same time upon the mind door (bhavaṅga). And the mind door is based on the tenth type of materiality of a heart decad-kalāpa.[200] The colour object is picked up first by a mind consciousness, second by an eye consciousness, and further by mind consciousnesses. This same principle applies for when a sound object strikes upon the ear door, which is the translucent, tenth type of materiality in an ear decad-kalāpa, and for an odour object, etc. Apart from the objects that also strike the five sense doors, there are also objects that strike the mind door (bhavaṅga) alone: they are the six types of dhamma object.[201]

3) Sex decad-kalāpas are found throughout the body. Their tenth type of materiality is sex materiality *(bhāva)*, which is of two types:[202]
   i) Male sex-materiality *(purisa·bhāva)*: it provides the physical characteristics of males, by which we know: 'This is a male.' It is found in only males.
   ii) Female sex-materiality *(itthi·bhāva)*: it provides the physical characteristics of females, by which we know: 'This is a female.' It is found in only females.

It is because their tenth type of materiality is translucent that eye-, ear-, nose-, tongue-, and body decad-kalāpas are translucent. All other types of rūpa-kalāpa are without translucent materiality, which is why they are untranslucent, as, for example, the sex- and heart decad-kalāpas we just discussed.

THE FOUR ORIGINS OF MATERIALITY

Having now discussed the basic structures of ultimate materiality, we can go on to a general discussion about the origin of materiality, which you will also need to discern when doing four-elements meditation. Mate-

---

See footnote 26, p.7.

[199] Eye decad-kalāpa: (8) the basic eight elements [1-earth 2-water 3- fire 4-wind 5-colour 6-odour 7-flavour 8-nutritive essence] + (9) life faculty + (10) eye translucency.

[200] Heart decad-kalāpa: (8) the basic eight elements [1-earth 2-water 3- fire 4-wind 5-colour 6-odour 7-flavour 8-nutritive essence] + (9) life faculty + (10) heart element. See also table '2d: The Basic Types of Materiality of the Heart', p.140.

[201] See 'Introduction' p.7.

[202] Also referred to as *puris·indriya* and *itth·indriya* (*indriya* = faculty).

riality has one of four origins: kamma, consciousness, temperature and nutriment, which means we have four types of materiality:[203]

1) Kamma-born materiality *(kammaja·rūpa)*
2) Consciousness-born materiality *(cittaja·rūpa)*
3) Temperature-born materiality *(utuja·rūpa)*
4) Nutriment-born materiality *(āhāraja·rūpa)*

As mentioned, the materiality of our body is nothing except rūpa-kalāpas, and all rūpa-kalāpas have at least the basic eight types of materiality: earth, water, fire, wind, colour, odour, flavour and nutritive essence. The eighth, nutritive essence, maintains materiality, which is why when there is no longer nutritive essence, the materiality falls apart.

Let us now look further at each of the four origins of materiality.

KAMMA-BORN MATERIALITY

Kamma-born materiality *(kammaja·rūpa)* comprises life nonad-kalāpas, and decad-kalāpas: eye-, ear-, nose-, tongue-, body-, heart- and sex decad-kalāpas. Their nutritive essence *(ojā)* is kamma-born *(kammaja·ojā)*.

It is in kamma-born materiality that we see something of the realities of the Second Noble Truth, the Noble Truth of the Origin of Suffering. Kamma-born materiality is materiality with the life faculty, which arises at rebirth, the First Noble Truth. And, as explained by The Buddha in the *'Mahā·Sati·Paṭṭhāna'* sutta,[204] rebirth (suffering) takes place because of craving *(taṇhā)*, and craving arises in anything that is agreeable and pleasant: sights through the eye, striking upon the translucent materiality of eye decad-kalāpas (the eye door) and the bhavaṅga (mind door); sounds through the ear, striking upon the translucent materiality of ear decad-kalāpas (the ear door) and the bhavaṅga (mind door) etc. The translucent materiality that is the five sense doors/bases, and the materiality that is the heart base exist because of craving for pleasant and agreeable sights, sounds, odours, flavours, tangibles and dhamma objects.

As the Buddha also explains, the direct cause for rebirth is kamma, but for there to be a result, it requires craving. And although the kamma that

---

[203] In the *Visuddhi·Magga*, the order of the four origins of materiality is: 1) kamma, 2) consciousness, 3) nutriment, 4) temperature. The order here is that taught by the Most Venerable Pa-Auk Tawya Sayadaw.

[204] D.ii.9 ('The Great Mindfulness-Foundation Sutta') *'Samudaya·Sacca·Niddeso'* ('Origin-Noble-Truth Description'), and VsM.xiv *'Rūpa·Kkhandha·Kathā'* ('Materiality Aggregate Discussion').

produces the materiality at a human rebirth[205] of a human life is wholesome, rebirth itself has taken place because of clinging, which is conditioned by craving, which is conditioned by ignorance: not understanding the Four Noble Truths.

Kamma-born materiality is being produced all the time. It is the foundation of all other materiality. Each consciousness moment *(citta·kkhaṇa)* (of the seventeen that are materiality's life-span) has three stages (three sub-moments): arising *(uppāda)*, standing *(ṭhiti)*, and dissolution *(bhaṅga)*.

At each stage, new kamma-born materiality is arising. This means that during one five-door process, countless kamma-born rūpa-kalāpas are produced at each of the fifty-one sub-moments (17 consciousness moments x 3 stages). Their temperature produces temperature-born rūpa-kalāpas, and their nutritive-essence produces new nutriment-born rūpa-kalāpas, and the temperature and nutritive-essence of those rūpa-kalāpas produce also more etc.[206]

CONSCIOUSNESS-BORN MATERIALITY

Consciousness-born materiality *(cittaja·rūpa)* comprises octad-kalāpas. Their nutritive *(ojā)* essence is consciousness-born, and is produced only by consciousnesses that arise dependent on the heart base, not consciousnesses of the five sense doors/bases. And, apart from the rebirth-linking consciousness, all consciousnesses that arise dependent on the heart base produce consciousness-born materiality.

An example is anger and worry. Anger and worry are both hatred *(dosa)*, and a consciousness of hatred produces consciousness-born materiality with predominant fire element. That is why, when we are angry or worried, we get hot.

Another example is bodily movement: moving the limbs and body forwards and backwards, up and down. For example, when we walk, the mind is directed at the leg and foot. That intention produces consciousness-born materiality in the leg and foot, and throughout the body: it has predominant. wind element. Just as wind carries objects along, so too the wind element carries the limbs and body along. The movement is a long series of different consciousness-born rūpa-kalāpas being produced in different places. The consciousness-born rūpa-kalāpas that arise at the raising of the foot are different from the consciousness-born rūpa-kalāpas

---

[205] At a human rebirth, in the womb, the very first materiality is only heart-, body- and sex decad-kalāpas, all kamma-born.

[206] For details, see table '1c: The Five-Door Process', p.168.

that arise at the lowering of the foot. Each rūpa-kalāpa arises and passes away in the same place, and new rūpa-kalāpas arise elsewhere and perish there.

A third example is samatha, vipassanā, Path and Fruition consciousnesses. Such consciousnesses are very pure, very powerful and superior, because there are no *upakkilesa* (imperfections). That means these consciousnesses produce very many generations of pure and superior consciousness-born materiality of which the earth-, wind- and fire element are very soft and subtle. When those soft and subtle rūpa-kalāpas touch the body door (the tenth type of materiality in the body decad-kalāpas) the yogi experiences great bodily comfort, with no heaviness (the earth element). Since, as mentioned before, the fire element of all rūpa-kalāpas produces temperature-born rūpa-kalāpas, the fire element in those superior consciousness-born rūpa-kalāpas produces many temperature-born rūpa-kalāpas inside and outside the body.

The radiance, brilliance and brightness that arise with those superior consciousnesses is produced by the brilliance of the colour materiality of the consciousness- and temperature-born materiality.[207] This accounts also for the clear and bright skin and faculties of yogis who develop these superior consciousnesses.[208] The materiality born of, for example, the Venerable Anuruddha's divine-eye consciousnesses *(dibba·cakkhu abhiññāṇa)* spread throughout a thousand world-systems: they were lit up by the superior consciousness-born materiality and became visible to him.[209] You too, if you develop sufficiently concentrated and pure consciousness, may be able to see other realms of existence etc.

TEMPERATURE-BORN MATERIALITY

Temperature-born materiality *(utuja·rūpa)* comprises octad-kalāpas. Their nutritive essence is temperature-born *(utuja·ojā)*, which comes from the fire element *(tejo·dhātu)*. the third element of all rūpa-kalāpas.[210] The fire element of all rūpa-kalāpas produces temperature-born rūpa-kalāpas, which themselves have fire element that produces temperature-born rūpa-kalā-

[207] For The Buddha's description of this light, see 'Introduction', p.13. For a more detailed explanation of this light, see also Q&A 4.10, p.156.

[208] Frequently referred to in the Texts, e.g. the ascetic who meets the newly enlightened Buddha says: 'Friend, your faculties are clear, the colour of your skin is pure and bright.' (M.I.iii.6 *'Ariya·Pariyesanā·Suttaṁ'* ('The Noble Search Sutta'))

[209] AA.VIII.I.iii.10 *'Anuruddha·Mahā·Vitakka·Suttaṁ'* ('The Anuruddha Great-Application Sutta')

[210] *tejo* (fire) and *utu* (temperature) refer to the same phenomenon.

pas, which themselves have fire element etc.[211] That is how, according to its power, the fire element produces materiality through a number of generations.

All inanimate materiality is born of and maintained by temperature. A good example is plants. Their materiality is temperature-born materiality and is born of the fire element originally in the seed. Their growth is nothing except the continued production of temperature-born materiality through many generations. It takes place with the assistance of the fire element from the soil, sun (hot), and water (cold).

The fire element in, for example, stones, metals, minerals and hardwood is very powerful, and produces very, very many generations of materiality. That is why that materiality can last long. But the fire element in, for example, softwood, tender plants, flesh, food and water is very weak, not very many generations of materiality are produced, which is why the materiality soon falls apart. When materiality falls apart, it is because the fire element no longer produces new materiality but instead consumes itself: the materiality rots, falls apart, and dissolves.

When materiality is consumed by fire, such as when wood is burning, it is because the fire element of the external materiality (the flames that strike the wood) supports the fire element of the internal materiality (the wood), and an huge amount of fire element bursts forth, which means the fire element becomes predominant and the materiality is consumed.

NUTRIMENT-BORN MATERIALITY

Nutriment-born materiality *(āhāraja·rūpa)* also comprises octad-kalāpas. Their nutritive essence is nutriment-born nutritive essence *(āhāraja·ojā)*. It is born of the food and drink that we consume. The food in the bowl, the food in the alimentary canal (the food in the mouth, the newly eaten undigested food in the stomach, semi-digested- and fully digested food in the intestines, the faeces), pus, blood and urine are the same: nothing but inanimate temperature-born nutritive-essence octad-kalāpas.

The digestive heat is the fire element of life nonad-kalāpas, which are (as mentioned[212]) born of kamma. When the digestive heat meets with the nutritive essence of the temperature-born nutritive-essence octad-kalāpas *(utuja·oj·aṭṭhamaka·kalāpa)* of the undigested and semi-digested food, further nutritive-essence octad-kalāpas are produced: they are nutriment-born nutritive-essence octad-kalāpas, with nutriment-born nutritive-essence

[211] See footnote 247, p.133.

[212] See 'Kamma-Born Materiality', p.111.

(ahāraja·ojā) as the eighth. Again, when that nutritive-essence meets the (kamma-born) digestive heat, it reproduces further through many generations of nutritive-essence octad-kalāpas. And it supports also the nutritive-essence in kamma-, consciousness-, and temperature-born rūpa-kalāpas, and the existing nutriment-born rūpa-kalāpas.

The nutriment of food taken in one day may reproduce in this way for up to seven days, although the number of generations produced depends on the quality of the food. Divine nutriment, which is of the deva realm and is most superior, may reproduce this way for up to one or two months.

Since life nonad-kalāpas are found throughout the body, the process of digestion found in the alimentary canal is found to a weaker degree throughout the body. That is why, for example, when medicinal oil is applied to the skin, or an injection of medicine is made under the skin, the medicine spreads throughout the body (is 'digested'). But if very much oil is applied, the weakness of the digestion may mean it takes long to digest.

That concludes the brief discussion of the origins of materiality. There is much more that could be explained, but this should be sufficient for you better to understand four-elements meditation, which will now be discussed.

If you want to attain Nibbāna, you need to know and see all these things, because you need to see materiality as it really is, not only as a concept.[213] You need first to see that materiality *(rūpa)* consists of rūpa-kalāpas, after which you need to penetrate the delusion of compactness to see the individual types of materiality that comprise the individual rūpa-kalāpa: that is seeing ultimate materiality. Then you need to analyse the materiality: see the different types of materiality, their origin, and how they function. To be able to do that, you start with four-elements meditation, which is to know and see the four great essentials *(mahā·bhūtā)*: earth-, water-, fire- and wind element.

THE BEGINNING OF VIPASSANĀ

Although you are here not practising vipassanā proper, we may say that this is the beginning of vipassanā, because at the end of four-elements meditation you will have developed the ability to discern ultimate materiality, which is necessary for vipassanā. We can say that you are now collecting the material necessary to do the work of vipassanā.

[213] For The Buddha's words on the need to see the ultimate realities of materiality, see 'Introduction', p.11 (M.I.iv.3 *'Mahā·Gopālaka·Suttaṁ'* ('The Great Cowherd Sutta')).

That is why it is necessary for all yogis to develop four-elements meditation. Whether one's path to vipassanā is first to develop a samatha subject of meditation (such as *ān·āpāna·sati* (mindfulness-of-breathing) up to jhāna), or one's path begins with four-elements meditation (that leads only up to access concentration), one needs to complete four-elements meditation before one can do vipassanā. Both paths are taught at the Pa-Auk monasteries in Myanmar. If one has first developed a samatha subject of meditation, one should please enter the fourth jhāna at every sitting, until the light is bright, brilliant and radiant. Having emerged from the jhāna, one should then begin four-elements meditation.

HOW YOU DEVELOP FOUR-ELEMENTS MEDITATION

In the Pali texts, there are two ways to develop four-elements meditation: in brief and in detail. The brief is for those of quick understanding, and the detailed for those who have difficulty with the brief one. The Buddha taught the brief method in the *'Mahā·Sati·Paṭṭhāna'* sutta:[214]

A bhikkhu reviews this very body, however it be placed or disposed, as consisting of just elements, thus: 'There are in this body just

[1] **the earth element** .... *(pathavī·dhātu)*,	[3] **the fire element** .... *(tejo·dhātu)*,
[2] **the water element** .... *(āpo·dhātu)*,	[4] **the wind element** .... *(vāyo·dhātu)*.'

The *Visuddhi·Magga* explains further:[215]

So firstly, one of quick understanding who wants to develop this meditation should go into solitary retreat. Then he should advert to his entire material body, and discern the elements in brief in this way, 'In this body,

[1] **what is hardness or roughness is the earth element;**

[2] **what is flowing or cohesion is the water element;**

[3] **what is maturing or heat is the fire element;**

[4] **what is pushing or supporting is the wind element,'**[216]

and he should advert and give attention to it, and review it again and again as 'earth element, water element, fire element, wind element,' that is to say, as mere elements, not a being, and soulless.

As he makes effort in this way, it is not long before concentration arises in him, which is reinforced by understanding that illuminates the classification of the elements, and which is only access and does not reach absorption because it has states with individual essences as its object.

---

[214] D.ii.9 'The Great Mindfulness-Foundation Sutta' (Also M.I.i.10)

[215] VsM.xi.306 *'Catu-Dhātu·Vavatthāna·Bhāvanā'* ('Four-Elements Definition Meditation') PP.xi.41-43

[216] See also footnote 219, p.121.

Or alternatively, there are these four [bodily] parts mentioned by the Elder Sāriputta, for the purpose of showing the absence of any living being in the four great primary elements thus: 'When a space is enclosed with bones, sinews, flesh, and skin, there comes to be the term 'materiality *(rūpa)*'. And he should resolve each of these, separating them out by the hand of knowledge, and then discern them in the way already stated thus: 'In these what is hardness... as its objects.'

As taught at Pa-Auk Tawya Monastery (in accordance with the *Dhamma·Saṅgaṇī*),[217] you should discern the four elements in the whole body as twelve characteristics:

earth		water	fire	wind
1) hardness	4) softness	7) flowing	9) heat	11) supporting
2) roughness	5) smoothness	8) cohesion	10) cold	12) pushing
3) heaviness	6) lightness			

To develop this meditation, you must learn how to discern each of the twelve characteristics, one at a time. Usually, the beginner is first taught the characteristics easier to discern, and later the more difficult ones. They are usually taught in this order: pushing, hardness, roughness, heaviness, supporting, softness, smoothness, lightness, heat, coldness, cohesion, flowing. Each characteristic must be discerned in first one place in the body, and then throughout the body.

HOW YOU SEE THE TWELVE CHARACTERISTICS

1) **Pushing**: to discern pushing, begin by being aware, through the sense of touch, of pushing in the centre of your head as you breathe in and out. When you discern it, concentrate on it until it becomes clear to your mind. Then move your awareness to a part of the body nearby, and try to find pushing there. This way you will slowly be able to discern pushing first in the head, then the neck, the trunk of the body, the arms, and the legs and feet. Do it again and again, many times, until wherever you place your awareness in the body you see pushing easily.If the pushing of the breath in the centre of the head is not easy to discern, then try to feel the pushing as the chest expands, or the abdomen moves when breathing. If that is not clear, try to feel the pulse, or any other obvious form of pushing. Wherever there is movement, there is pushing.

Wherever you begin, you must slowly develop your understanding, so that you discern pushing throughout the body, from head to foot. In some

[217] The first book of the *Abhidhamma*.

places it will be obvious, in other places less so, but it is present throughout the body. When you are satisfied that you can see pushing, try to find hardness.

2) **Hardness**: to discern hardness, bite your teeth together and feel how hard they are. Relax your bite, and feel their hardness. When you can feel this, try to discern hardness throughout the body systematically from head to foot, in the same way as you did to discern pushing. Do not deliberately tense the body.

When you can discern hardness throughout the body, again try to find pushing throughout the body. Alternate between these two, pushing and hardness, again and again, discerning pushing throughout the body, and then hardness throughout the body, from head to foot. Repeat this many times until you are satisfied that you can do it.

3) **Roughness**: to discern roughness, rub your tongue over the edge of your teeth, or brush your hand over your robe, or the skin of your arm, and feel roughness. Now try to discern roughness throughout the body systematically as before. If you cannot feel roughness, try looking at pushing and hardness again, and you may discern it with them.

When you can discern roughness, go back to discern the three, pushing, hardness, roughness, one at a time, again and again, throughout the body, until you are satisfied.

4) **Heaviness**: to discern heaviness, place one hand on top of the other in your lap, and feel the heaviness of the top hand, or feel the heaviness of the head by bending it forward. Practise systematically until you discern heaviness throughout the body.

When you can discern heaviness clearly, try to find the four, pushing, hardness, roughness, and heaviness, in turn, throughout the body until you are satisfied.

5) **Supporting**: to discern supporting, relax your back, so your body bends forward. Then straighten it, and keep it straight. The force that keeps the body straight is supporting. Practise systematically until you discern supporting throughout the body. If it is not clear, try to discern it together with hardness, as this can make it easier.

Then, when you can discern supporting easily try to find the five, pushing, hardness, roughness, heaviness, and supporting throughout the body.

6) **Softness**: to discern softness, press your tongue against the inside of your lower lip to feel its softness. Then relax your body, and practise systematically until you can discern softness easily throughout the body.

Now try to find the six, pushing, hardness, roughness, heaviness, supporting, and softness throughout the body.

7) **Smoothness**: to discern smoothness, wet your lips and rub your tongue over them from side to side. Practise until you can discern smoothness throughout the body.

Then try to find all seven characteristics throughout the body.

8) **Lightness**: to discern lightness, wag a finger up and down, and feel its lightness. If you cannot feel it, try to find heaviness again. When you can feel the heaviness of the whole body, then again wag a finger up and down and feel its lightness. Practise until you can discern lightness throughout the body.

And then try to find all eight characteristics.

9) **Heat**: it is usually very easy to discern heat (or warmth) throughout the body. Begin by being aware, through the sense of touch, of heat in any place where it is clear to you.

And then try to find all nine characteristics.

10) **Cold**: to discern cold, feel the coldness of the breath as it enters the nostrils, and then discern it systematically throughout the body.

You can now discern ten characteristics.

The first ten characteristics are all known directly through the sense of touch, but the last two characteristics, flowing and cohesion, are inferred from the other ten characteristics. That is a good reason to teach them last.

11) **Cohesion**: to discern cohesion, be aware of how the body is held together by the skin, flesh, and sinews. The blood is held inside by the skin, like water in a balloon. Without cohesion the body would fall into separate pieces and particles. The force of gravity that keeps the body stuck to the earth is also cohesion. If this is not clear, discern all ten qualities again and again, one at a time throughout the body. When you have become skilled in that, you will find that the quality of cohesion also becomes clear. If it is still not clear, discern just the qualities of pushing and hardness again and again. Then you should feel as if your whole body was wound up in rope. Discern this as cohesion, and develop it as you developed the other characteristics.

12) **Flowing**: to discern flowing, be aware of the saliva flowing in the mouth, the blood flowing through the blood vessels, the air flowing into the lungs, or heat flowing throughout the body. If this is not clear, look at it together with coldness, heat, or pushing, and you may discern flowing.

When you can discern all twelve characteristics clearly throughout the body, from head to foot, you should discern them again and again in this order. When satisfied you should rearrange the order to the one first mentioned in the beginning: hardness, roughness, heaviness, softness, smoothness, lightness, flowing, cohesion, heat, coldness, supporting, and pushing. In that order try to discern each characteristic one at a time from head to foot. You should try to develop this until you can do it quite quickly, at least three rounds a minute.

While practising in this way, the elements will for some yogis become unbalanced, some elements may become excessive and even unbearable. Particularly hardness, heat, and pushing can become excessive. If this occurs, you should concentrate more on the opposite quality, and continue to develop concentration in that way.

For example, if flowing is in excess concentrate more on cohesion, or if supporting is in excess concentrate more on pushing. The opposites are: hardness and softness, roughness and smoothness, heaviness and lightness, flowing and cohesion, heat and coldness, and supporting and pushing.

It is for the sake of balancing the elements that twelve characteristics were taught in the first place. When the elements are balanced, it is easier to attain concentration.

Having now become skilled in the discernment of the twelve characteristics in the whole body, with the twelve characteristics having become clear, you should discern the first six at one glance as the earth element, the next two at one glance as the water element, the next two as the fire element, and the last two as the wind element. You should thus continue to discern earth, water, fire, and wind, in order to traquillize the mind and attain concentration. You should do this again and again hundreds, thousands, or millions of times.

A good method for keeping the mind tranquil and concentrated is to no longer move your awareness from one part of the body to another. Instead, take an overview of the body. It is usually best to take the overview as if you were looking from behind your shoulders. It can also be done as if looking from above your head down, although this may lead to tension and imbalance of the elements.

THE TEN WAYS TO DEVELOP YOUR CONCENTRATION

The sub-commentary to the *Visuddhi·Magga* says now to develop your concentration in ten ways.[218] You should discern the four elements

[218] VsMṬ.xi.308 *'Catu·Dhātu·Vavatthāna·Bhāvanā'* ('Four-Elements Definition Meditation')

1) **In sequence** *(anupubbato)*: that is the sequence given by The Buddha: earth, water, fire, and wind.
2) **Not too fast** *(nāti·sīghato)*: if you discern the four elements too fast, you will not see them clearly.
3) **Not too slow** *(nāti·saṇikato)*: if you discern the four elements too slowly, you will not reach the end.
4) **Warding off distractions** *(vikkhepa·paṭibāhanato)*: you should keep the mind with only the object of meditation, the four elements, and not let it wander.
5) **Going beyond concepts** *(paññatti·samatikkamanato)*: you should not just mentally note, 'earth, water, fire, wind', but be aware of the actual realities the concepts represent: hardness, roughness, heaviness, softness, smoothness, lightness, flowing, cohesion, heat, coldness, supporting, and pushing.
6) **Discarding what is unclear** *(anupaṭṭhāna·muñcanato)*: once you can discern all twelve characteristics, you may temporarily leave out characteristics that are unclear, but not if it leads to pain or tension, because of an imbalance in the elements. You need also to keep at least one characteristic for each of the four elements. You cannot work on just three, two, or one element. And it is best if all twelve characteristics are clear, with none left out.
7) **Discerning the characteristics** *(lakkhaṇato)*: when you begin to meditate, and the characteristics of each element are not yet clear, you can also concentrate on the function and manifestation of the elements.[219] When your concentration gets better, however, you should concentrate on only the natural characteristics *(sabhāva·lakkhaṇa)*: the hardness and roughness of the earth element, the flowing and cohesion of the water element, the heat and coldness of the fire element, and the supporting of the wind element.

At this point you will see only elements, and not see them as a person or self.

---

219 EARTH Characteristic (natural): hardness(1), softness(2), roughness(3), smoothness(4), heaviness(5), lightness(6); Function: act as foundation (for all other types of materiality); Manifestation: receive (all other types of materiality within the same rūpa-kalāpa) WATER Ch: fluidity/flow/trickle(7); Fct: expand/dilate; Mf: bind/cohere [here Ch and Mf are sometimes seen as the same thing](8) FIRE Ch: heat(9)/cold(10); Fct: warm/age/digest/consume/mature; Mf: soften (as in cooking raw materials into edible food) WIND Ch: support(11) Fct: move/push(12) Mf: carry. <See also M.II.ii.2 *'Mahā·Rāhul·Ovāda·Suttaṁ'* (The Great Advice-to-Rāhula Sutta'), and VsM.xi.350 *'Catu·Dhātu·Vavatthāna·Bhāvanā'* ('Four-Elements Definition Meditation') PP.xi.93.>

The sub-commentary further recommends that you develop your concentration according to three suttas:

8) The *'Adhi·Citta'* sutta ('The Higher-Mind Sutta')
9) The *'Sīti·Bhāva'* sutta ('The Becoming-Cool Sutta')
10) The *'Bojjh·Aṅga'* sutta ('The Enlightenment-Factors Sutta')[220]

In those three suttas, The Buddha advises balancing the five faculties *(indriya)*: faith, effort, mindfulness, concentration, and understanding; and balancing the seven enlightenment-factors *(bojjhaṅga)*: mindfulness, investigation of phenomena, effort, joy, tranquillity, concentration and equanimity. We discussed them in our first talk.[221]

HOW YOU SEE ULTIMATE MATERIALITY

SEEING THE BODY TRANSLUCENT- ELEMENT AS ONE BLOCK

As you continue to develop concentration on the four elements, and approach access concentration *(upacāra·samādhi)*, you will see different kinds of light. To some yogis it is a smoky grey light. If you continue to concentrate on the four elements in that grey light, it will become whiter like cotton wool, and then bright white, like clouds, and your whole body will appear as a white form. As you continue to concentrate on the four elements in the white form, it will eventually become translucent like a block of ice or glass.

This translucent materiality is the five translucencies *(pasāda)*:[222] the body-, eye-, ear-, nose-, and tongue translucencies. The body translucency is found throughout the body, in all six sense bases, which is why your whole body appears translucent. You see the translucencies as one translucent form or block, because you have not yet seen through the three kinds of compactness *(ghana)*: compactness of continuity, of group and of function.[223]

HOW YOU SEE THE RŪPA-KALĀPAS

If you continue to discern the four elements in the translucent form (or block) it will sparkle and emit light. When you can concentrate on the

---

[220] 8) A.III.II.v.11 (Also called *'Nimitta·Suttaṁ'* ('The Sign Sutta')); 9) A.VI.IX.1 *'Sīti·Bhāva·Suttaṁ'* ('The Becoming Cool Sutta'); 10) S.V.II.vi.3 'The Enlightenment Factors Sutta' also called *'Aggi·Suttaṁ'* ('The Fire Sutta').

[221] Balancing the five faculties, see p.39 *ff,* and the enlightenment factors, see p.42 *ff.*

[222] Some also translate *pasāda* as the abstract 'sensitivity.'

[223] Regarding compactness of materiality and mentality, see also Q&A 1.3, p.49.

four elements in this form (or block) continuously for at least half an hour, you have reached access concentration. With the light, discern the space element in the translucent form, by looking for small spaces in it. You will now find that the translucent form breaks down into small particles; they are called rūpa-kalāpas.[224] Having reached this stage, which is consciousness purification *(citta·visuddhi)*, you can proceed to develop view purification *(diṭṭhi·visuddhi)*, by analysing the rūpa-kalāpas. That is the beginning of vipassanā meditation.

(BENEFITS OF CONCENTRATION)

Before explaining how to develop vipassanā meditation, let us look at a practical benefit that is to be gained from both the access concentration that a pure-vipassanā yogi has here reached, and the jhāna concentration of a samatha yogi. There is much to discern in vipassanā meditation, and tiredness will usually occur. When this happens, it is good to take a rest. There is a simile in the commentary to the *'Dv·Edhā·Vitakka'* sutta[225] of the *Majjhima·Nikāya*, which explains how a yogi can rest in jhāna. It says that during a battle, sometimes the warriors feel tired. The enemy may be strong, and many arrows flying. So the warriors retreat to their fortress. Inside the fortress they are safe from the enemy's arrows and can rest. Then, when they feel strong and powerful again, they leave the fortress and return to the battle-field. Jhāna is like a fortress, and can be used as a resting-place during vipassanā meditation. Pure-vipassanā yogis, who have no jhāna, and have started directly with four-elements meditation, can instead use their access concentration as a fortress to rest in. In both cases, the yogi can then return to the battle-field of vipassanā clear and refreshed. There is thus great benefit in having a resting-place.

Let us then go back to discussing how you develop vipassanā meditation, and start with the analysis of rūpa-kalāpas.

TRANSLUCENT AND UNTRANSLUCENT RŪPA-KALĀPAS

Rūpa-kalāpas fall into two groups: translucent rūpa-kalāpas and untranslucent ones. Rūpa-kalāpas that include one of the five translucencies (eye-, ear-, nose-, tongue- or body translucency) are the translucent rūpa-kalāpas. All other rūpa-kalāpas are untranslucent.

---

[224] *Rūpa* (materiality) + *kalāpa* (group/cluster)

[225] MA.I.ii.9 *'Dv·Edhā·Vitakka·Suttaṁ'* ('The Two Kinds of Application Sutta')

HOW YOU ANALYSE THE RŪPA-KALĀPAS

HOW YOU SEE THE FOUR ELEMENTS

You should first discern the four elements, earth, water, fire, and wind, of individual translucent- and untranslucent rūpa-kalāpas. You will find that the rūpa-kalāpas arise and perish very, very quickly, and will be unable to analyse them, because you still see them as small particles with size. Since you have not yet seen through the three kinds of compactness, you are still in the realm of concepts *(paññatti)*, and have not arrived at ultimate truth *(param·attha sacca)*.[226]

It is because you have not seen through the concepts of group and shape that the particles, the small lumps, remain. If you do not go any further, but try to do vipassanā by contemplating the arising and perishing of those small lumps, which are the rūpa-kalāpas, you will be trying to do vipassanā on concepts.[227] So you must analyse the rūpa-kalāpas further, until you can see the elements in single ones: in order to reach ultimate reality.

If, because they arise and perish very, very quickly, you are unable to discern the four elements in single rūpa-kalāpas, then ignore their arising and perishing: just as when meeting someone you do not want to meet, you would pretend not to see or notice him. You should in the same way take no notice of the arising and perishing of the rūpa-kalāpas, and concentrate on only the four elements in single ones. It is possible for you to do this because of the power of your concentration.

If you are still unsuccessful, you should concentrate on the earth element alternately in the whole body at once and in a single rūpa-kalāpa. And do the same with the water-, fire-, and wind element. You need to discern the four elements in a single translucent rūpa-kalāpa and a single untranslucent one.

This is the procedure that we teach at Pa-Auk: you discern the elements one-by-one. The Texts explain that one should discern all the elements at once, but they were composed by skilled yogis and also meant for skilled yogis. Because discerning the elements of materiality is very profound, the power of vipassanā of beginners is usually not yet strong and powerful enough for them to see all the elements at once. So we teach them to discern the elements one-by-one, base-by-base, from the easiest to the

---

[226] Compactness of continuity *(santati·ghana)*, of group *(samūha·ghana)*, and of function *(kicca-ghana)*. For details about compactness of materiality and mentality, see Q&A 1.3 p.49.

[227] For a discussion of vipassanā on concepts, see 'Introduction' p.8*ff*.

more difficult. Then, when they have become very skilled in the practice, they can see all four elements (eight characteristics) in a rūpa-kalāpa at once.[228]

When you have seen the four elements in a single translucent- and a single untranslucent rūpa-kalāpa, it is the end of your samatha practice, the end of consciousness purification *(citta·visuddhi)*, and the beginning of your vipassanā practice, the beginning of view purification *(diṭṭhi·visuddhi)*: you have begun the discernment of ultimate mentality-materiality *(nāma·rūpa·pariggaha)* and the analysis of ultimate mentality-materiality *(nāma·rūpa·pariccheda)*. That is how four-elements meditation comprises both samatha and vipassanā.

When you have succeeded, discern the four elements in a number of translucent and untranslucent rūpa-kalāpas of the six sense bases: the eye-, ear-, nose-, tongue-, body- and heart base in turn.

As mentioned before, translucent and untranslucent rūpa-kalāpas all comprise a basic eight types of materiality. You will now have discerned the first four, and should go on to discern the remaining four: colour, odour, flavour, and nutritive essence. But before proceeding, let us first discuss the general procedure for discerning these four elements.

The Dispeller of Delusion, an Abhidhamma commentary, says:[229]

Sabbopi panesa pabhedo mano·dvārika·javaneyeva labbhati.

All phenomena are known by the mind-door impulsion *(javana)*[230] **alone.**[231]

The earth, water, fire and wind elements of a rūpa-kalāpa you knew with mind consciousnesses alone. And you can know, for example, also the colour, odour, and flavour of a rūpa-kalāpa that way. But although it is easy to see colour with a mind consciousness alone, it is difficult to see odour and flavour that way, because it is a life-long habit to use the nose and tongue. Therefore, until your meditation has become strong and powerful, you use a nose- or tongue consciousness to help you.

---

[228] Although the yogi has discerned twelve characteristics, he can discern only eight characteristics in one given rūpa kalāpa: 1) hardness, 2) roughness, 3) heaviness (or 1) softness, 2) smoothness, 3) lightness), 4) flowing, 5) cohesion, 6) heat (or coldness), 7) supporting, 8) pushing. There are not opposing characteristics within one rūpa kalāpa.

[229] VbhA.xvi.1 (766) *'Ekaka·Niddesa·Vaṇṇana'* ('One-Description Commentary')

[230] The actual knowing of an object is performed by seven *javana* consciousnesses in the mind-door process, this regardless of the door through which the object has arrived. See also 'Introduction' p.8, and table '1b: The Mind-Door Process', p.164.

[231] For The Buddha's explanation of how the mind faculty knows the objects of the other five faculties, see quotation, p.6.

Having now explained the two ways for discerning an object, we can then look at how you discern the colour, odour, flavour and nutritive-essence in rūpa-kalāpas.

HOW YOU SEE COLOUR

Colour *(vaṇṇa)*, the fifth type of materiality to be discerned, is the object of sight *(rūp·ārammaṇa)*, and is found in all rūpa-kalāpas. It is very easily known with a mind consciousness alone, because by seeing the rūpa-kalāpas you have already seen colour. Colour is always the colour of something, and that something is the four elements.[232]

HOW YOU SEE ODOUR

Odour *(gandha)*, the sixth type of materiality to be discerned, is the object of smell *(gandh·ārammaṇa)*, and is also found in all rūpa-kalāpas. Because it is a lifelong habit to use the nose to smell with, you will in the beginning need a nose consciousness to help you know odour with a mind consciousness.

To do this, you need first to discern the materiality that the two types of consciousness depend on, namely the nose translucency and heart materiality. The nose translucency is the tenth type of materiality of a nose decad-kalāpa, and heart materiality is the tenth type of materiality of a heart decad-kalāpa.

To find the nose translucency, first discern the four elements in the nose, but be sure to look at a decad-kalāpa in the nose that is of the nose base and not of the body base. Only nose decad-kalāpas have the nose translucency.

Next, to find heart materiality, you need to discern the bright, luminous mind door (the bhavaṅga).[233] It should be easy to do because you have already discerned the four elements in the translucent and untranslucent rūpa-kalāpas of the six sense bases.

Having now discerned the nose translucency (the nose door) and the bhavaṅga (the mind door), you can proceed to discern the odour of a rūpa-kalāpa near the nose decad-kalāpa where you discerned the translu-

---

[232] The Most Venerable Pa-Auk Tawya Sayadaw explains that just as we see the translucency of a glass by looking at the glass, so do we see the translucency of a rūpa-kalāpa by discerning the four elements: they are the 'glass' that possesses the translucency.

[233] To speak of the bhavaṅga's luminosity is to use a metaphor, because it is in fact the luminosity of the rūpa-kalāpas produced by the bhavaṅga: consciousness-born rūpa-kalāpas, the temperature of which produces further bright rūpa-kalāpas. A samatha-vipassanā mind produces particularly bright rūpa-kalāpas because there are no *upakkilesa* (imperfections). For details, see 'Consciousness-Born Materiality' p.112.

cency. You will see that the odour impinges on the nose- and mind door at the same time.

HOW YOU SEE FLAVOUR

Flavour *(rasa)* is the seventh type of materiality to discern, is the object of taste *(gandhārammaṇa)*, and is also found in all rūpa-kalāpas. As with the nose, you will in the beginning need a tongue consciousness to help you know flavour with a mind consciousness. And here too, you need first to discern the materiality that the two types of consciousness depend on: the tongue translucency and heart materiality. Having done that, you then discern the flavour of a rūpa-kalāpa. You can take a rūpa-kalāpa from the saliva on your tongue.

HOW YOU SEE NUTRITIVE ESSENCE

Nutritive essence *(ojā)* is the eighth type of materiality to discern. It is also found in all rūpa-kalāpas, and is, as mentioned earlier, of four types:[234]

1) Kamma-born nutritive-essence *(kammaja·ojā)*
2) Consciousness[235]-born nutritive-essence *(cittaja·ojā)*
3) Temperature-born nutritive-essence *(utuja·ojā)*
4) Nutriment-born nutritive-essence *(āhāraja·ojā)*

Examine any rūpa-kalāpa, and you will find nutritive essence from which rūpa-kalāpas are seen to multiply forth again and again.

Having now discerned the eight basic types of materiality that are found in all rūpa-kalāpas, you should try to discern the remaining three basic types of materiality found in specific rūpa-kalāpas: the life faculty-, sex-, and heart materiality.

HOW YOU SEE LIFE FACULTY- AND SEX MATERIALITY

Life faculty *(jīvit·indriya)* materiality sustains only kamma-born materiality, which means it is found only there. Since, as explained earlier,[236] all translucent rūpa-kalāpas are kamma-born, it is easiest for you to discern the life faculty first in a translucent rūpa-kalāpa. Discern an eye decad-

---

[234] For an explanation of kamma-, consciousness-, temperature- and nutriment-born materiality, see p.110*ff.*

[235] According to usage in the Pali Texts, *citta* is synonymous with *viññāna* (consciousness): see also S.II.I.vii.1 *'A·Ssutavā·Suttaṁ'* ('The_Unlearned Sutta'). Out of respect for the authority of the Pali Texts, the Most Venerable Pa-Auk Tawya Sayadaw remains faithful also to the terminology used in the particular Pali Text, which is why he will often use more than one Pali term for the same thing: depending on which text he is referring to.

[236] See 'Kamma-Born Materiality' p.111.

kalāpa,[237] and see that the life faculty sustains the materiality of its own rūpa-kalāpa only, not the materiality of others.

Then you need also try to discern life faculty in an untranslucent rūpa-kalāpa. The body has three types of untranslucent rūpa-kalāpa with life-faculty materiality:

1) Heart decad-kalāpas[238] *(hadaya·dasaka·kalāpa)*: only in the heart.
2) Sex decad-kalāpas[238] *(bhāva·dasaka·kalāpa)*: throughout the body.
3) Life nonad-kalāpas[238] *(jīvita·navaka·kalāpa)*: throughout the body.

It is easiest first to discern the life faculty of either a life nonad-kalāpa or a sex decad-kalāpa. To tell the two rūpa-kalāpas apart, you try to find sex materiality *(bhāva·rūpa)*.

Just now you discerned the life faculty in a translucent rūpa-kalāpa of the eye, so look again in the eye and discern an untranslucent rūpa-kalāpa with the life faculty. Since life nonad-kalāpas and sex decad-kalāpas are found in all six sense-organs, it will be either one. If it has the sex materiality, it is a sex decad-kalāpa, if not it is a life nonad-kalāpa. In that case, discern another untranslucent rūpa-kalāpa until you discern the sex materiality, and then try to find it in a rūpa-kalāpa of also the ear, nose, tongue, body and heart.

HOW YOU SEE HEART MATERIALITY

To discern an untranslucent rūpa-kalāpa of the heart, you concentrate again on the bright, luminous mind door, the bhavaṅga. To see it very clearly, wiggle your finger, and see the consciousness that wants to wiggle the finger. Then try to discern how the bhavaṅga arises dependent on the heart base: the untranslucent, heart decad-kalāpas. You should be able to find them in the lower part of the bhavaṅga.[238]

With this, you have completed the discernment of all the types of materiality in rūpa-kalāpas: earth, water, fire, wind, colour, odour, flavour, nutritive essence, life faculty and sex materiality. And you have discerned them in the appropriate translucent and untranslucent rūpa-kalāpas in all six sense-organs. The next stage in discerning materiality is to analyse the materiality of each of the six sense-organs: the eye, ear, nose, tongue,

---

[237] Eye decad-kalāpa: (8) the basic eight elements [1-earth 2-water 3- fire 4-wind 5-colour 6-odour 7-flavour 8-nutritive essence] + (9) life faculty + (10) eye translucency

[238] Heart decad-kalāpa: (8) the basic eight elements [1-earth 2-water 3- fire 4-wind 5-colour 6-odour 7-flavour 8-nutritive essence] + (9) life faculty + (10) heart element. Sex decad-kalāpa: (8) the basic eight elements + (9) life faculty + (10) sex materiality. Life nonad-kalāpa: (8) the basic eight elements + (9) life faculty. See also Tables 2b-2c, p.138*ff*.

body and heart, and see the different types of rūpa-kalāpa there.[239] You start by analysing just the two types of translucency.

HOW YOU ANALYSE EACH SENSE ORGAN

HOW YOU ANALYSE THE TRANSLUCENCIES

Each organ has several kinds of rūpa-kalāpa mixed together. The eye, ear, nose, and tongue have, for example, two types of translucent materiality mixed together like rice- and wheat flour: the translucent rūpa-kalāpas of the respective organ and translucent rūpa-kalāpas of the body. The two types of translucent rūpa-kalāpas of, for example, the eye are:

1) The eye decad-kalāpa *(cakkhu·dasaka·kalāpa)*: its tenth type of materiality is the eye translucency.
2) The body decad-kalāpa *(kāya·dasaka·kalāpa)*: its tenth type of materiality is the body translucency.

Body decad-kalāpas are found throughout the six sense-organs (eye, ear, nose-, tongue, body and heart), mixed with the respective types of decad-kalāpas there: in the eye mixed with the eye decad-kalāpas, in the ear mixed with the ear decad-kalāpas *(sota·dasaka·kalāpa)* etc. To see this, you need to analyse the translucent rūpa-kalāpas in the five sense-organs, and identify the translucency respective to each (the eye-, ear-, nose- and tongue translucency) as well as the body translucency there. You begin with the eye.

1) The eye translucency *(cakkhu·pasāda)*: it is sensitive to colour, whereas the body translucency is sensitive to touch (tangible objects). This difference allows you to know which is which. First discern the four elements in the eye to discern a translucent rūpa-kalāpa, and discern that rūpa-kalāpa's translucency. Then look at the colour of a group of rūpa-kalāpas some distance away from the eye. If it impinges on the translucency, the translucency is an eye-translucency (of an eye decad-kalāpa). Otherwise it is a body translucency (of a body decad-kalāpa).
2) The body translucency *(kāya·pasāda)*: it is sensitive to touch, to tangible objects. Tangible objects are the earth, fire, and wind elements. Again discern a translucency in the eye. Then look at the earth-, fire-,

[239] These six sense-organs are referred to also as the six 'sense bases', but since the bases have already been explained as being in fact only the tenth element in the appropriate rūpa-kalāpas, it has been considered safer to say 'sense-organ' here, referring to the actual physical entity, the eye-ball etc.

or wind element of a group of rūpa-kalāpas nearby. If it impinges on the translucency, the translucency is a body translucency (of a body decad-kalāpa).

Now you will have discerned both the eye-translucency in the eye, and the body-translucency in the eye. You then follow the same procedure for the remaining organs. You begin with the ear.

1) The ear translucency *(sota·pasāda)*: it is sensitive to sound. Discern a translucency in the ear. Then listen. If a sound impinges on the translucency, the translucency is an ear translucency (of an ear decad-kalāpa). Then discern the body translucency as you did it in the eye.
2) The nose translucency *(ghāna·pasāda)*: it is sensitive to odour. Discern a translucency in the nose. Then smell the odour of a group of rūpa-kalāpas nearby. If it impinges on the translucency, the translucency is a nose translucency (of a nose decad-kalāpa). Discern the body decad-kalāpa as you did it in the eye and ear.
3) The tongue translucency *(jivhā·pasāda)*: it is sensitive to taste. Discern a translucency in the tongue. Then taste the flavour of a group of rūpa-kalāpas nearby. If it impinges on the translucency, the translucency is a tongue translucency (of a tongue decad-kalāpa). Discern the body decad-kalāpa as you did it in the eye, ear and nose.

Once you have analysed the two types of translucency in each of the five sense-organs, you need also to see that the body translucency (in body decad-kalāpas) is found in also the heart. Having done that, you will have analysed all five types of translucent materiality.

HOW YOU ANALYSE SEX MATERIALITY

Sex decad-kalāpas too are found throughout the six sense-organs, and are also mixed with the translucent rūpa-kalāpas. You discerned sex decad-kalāpas when you discerned life faculty. Now you discern them in all six sense-organs.

THE FIFTY-FOUR TYPES OF MATERIALITY OF THE EYE

So far, we have discussed three basic types of rūpa-kalāpa:

1) The decad-kalāpas of each of the six sense-organs
(the eye, ear, nose, tongue, body and heart).
2) The life nonad-kalāpas.
3) The octad-kalāpas.

The eye, ear, nose, tongue, and heart comprise, as we have now seen, seven types of rūpa-kalāpa, with altogether sixty-three types of materiality.[240] But when analysing the materiality of each sense-organ, the Pali Texts say you should look at only six types of rūpa-kalāpa (not the life nonad-kalāpas): you should concentrate on only fifty-four types of materiality (63 – 9 = 54).[241] The life nonad-kalāpas you discern in another way later. And since one of the six types of rūpa-kalāpa is (as you just saw) the body decad-kalāpa, when you analyse the materiality of the body itself (outside the eye, ear, nose, tongue, and heart), you can analyse only five types of rūpa-kalāpa, only forty-four types of materiality.

Let us then look at the said fifty-four types of materiality of, for example, the eye. The six types of rūpa-kalāpa in the eye are first the three types of rūpa-kalāpa you just discerned and analysed, altogether thirty types of materiality:

1) The eye decad-kalāpa[242] *(cakkhu·dasaka·kalāpa)*: it is sensitive to colour, is translucent, and born of kamma.
2) The body decad-kalāpa[242] *(kāya·dasaka·kalāpa)*: it is sensitive to tangible objects (earth, fire, and wind elements), is translucent, and born of kamma.
3) The sex decad-kalāpa[242] *(bhāva·dasaka·kalāpa)*: it is untranslucent, and born of kamma.

And then there are three more types of rūpa-kalāpa, with eight types of materiality each, altogether twenty-four (3 x 8 = 24). They are the three types of nutritive-essence octad-kalāpa, which are untranslucent:

---

240 Taking the eye as example: 1) eye decad-kalāpas (ten types of materiality), 2) body decad-kalāpas (ten types), 3) sex decad-kalāpas (ten types), 4) life nonad-kalāpas (nine types), 5) consciousness-born octad-kalāpas (eight types), 6) temperature-born octad-kalāpas (eight types), 7) nutriment-born octad-kalāpas (eight types) (10 + 10 + 10 + 9 + 8 + 8 + 8 = 63). The same equation applies for the ear, nose, tongue, and heart. Since the body has only its own type of decad-kalāpa and sex decad-kalāas, it has in all only fifty-three types of materiality (10 + 10 + 9 + 8 + 8 + 8 = 53).

241 The life nonad-kalāpas are included in only the analysis of what is called the forty-two parts of the body (VsM.xviii.664 'Mentality-Materiality Definition Discussion' PP.xviii.-6). Only then (following the Texts) does the Most Venerable Pa-Auk Tawya Sayadaw instruct the yogi to discern the life nonad-kalāpas. Nevertheless, the yogi can, if he so wishes, include them at this point.

242 Eye decad-kalāpa: (8) the basic eight elements [1-earth 2-water 3- fire 4-wind 5-colour 6-odour 7-flavour 8-nutritive essence] + (9) life faculty + (10) eye translucency. Body decad-kalāpa: (8) the basic eight elements + (9) life faculty + (10) body translucency. Sex decad-kalāpa: (8) the basic eight elements + (9) life faculty + (10) sex materiality. Nutritive-essence octad-kalāpas: (8) the basic eight elements, which includes nutritive essence as the eighth. See also table '2b: The Basic Types of Materiality of the Eye', p.138.

1) The consciousness-born nutritive-essence octad-kalāpa *(cittaja·oj·aṭṭhamaka·kalāpa)*
2) The temperature-born nutritive-essence octad-kalāpa *(utuja·oj·aṭṭhamaka·kalāpa)*
3) The nutriment-born nutritive-essence octad-kalāpa *(āhāraja·oj·aṭṭhamaka·kalāpa)*

The first three types of rūpa-kalāpa (the decad-kalāpas) are kamma-born, whereas the last three types of rūpa-kalāpa (the octad kalāpas) are either temperature-, consciousness-, or nutriment-born. As discussed in the beginning of this talk, there are four origins of materiality.[243] Since you have by now discerned the kamma-born rūpa-kalāpas, we will discuss how to discern which type of octad kalāpa is which.

HOW YOU SEE CONSCIOUSNESS-BORN MATERIALITY

As also mentioned in the introduction,[244] every single consciousness that arises dependent on heart materiality (apart from the rebirth-linking consciousness) produces a great number of consciousness-born nutritive-essence octad-kalāpas *(cittaja·oj·aṭṭhamaka·kalāpa)*. They are untranslucent and spread throughout the body.

That is why, if you concentrate on the bhavaṅga, you will see many consciousnesses dependent on heart materiality producing rūpa-kalāpas. If it is not clear, concentrate again on the bhavaṅga, and again wiggle one of your fingers. You will then see a large number of rūpa-kalāpas being produced because the mind wants to wiggle the finger. And you will see that such rūpa kalāpas can arise anywhere in the body.

HOW YOU SEE TEMPERATURE–BORN MATERIALITY

As mentioned in the introduction,[245] the fire element *(tejo)* is also called 'temperature' *(utu)*, and is found in all rūpa-kalāpas. The fire element of all rūpa-kalāpas produces temperature-born nutritive-essence octad-kalāpas *(utuja oj·aṭṭhamaka·kalāpa)*. They themselves contain the fire element, which produces further temperature-born nutritive-essence octad-kalāpas. You need to see that this process takes place in all the types of rūpa-kalāpa in each sense-organ.

---

[243] For a brief discussion of the four origins of materiality (kamma, consciousness, temperature and nutriment) see p.110*ff.*

[244] For a brief discussion (with examples) of consciousness-born materiality, see p.112.

[245] For a brief discussion (with examples) of temperature-born materiality, see p.113*ff.*

First discern the fire element in, for example, an eye decad-kalāpa. Then see that it produces temperature-born nutritive-essence octad-kalāpas: that is the first generation. Then discern the fire element in a rūpa-kalāpa of that first generation of temperature-born nutritive-essence octad-kalāpas, and see that it too reproduces: that is the second generation. In this way, see that the fire element in the eye decad-kalāpa (which is itself kamma-born)[246] reproduces through four or five generations, depending on the strength of the food and the power of the kamma.[247]

You need to see that this process takes place for each type of rūpa-kalāpa in each sense-organ, and need yourself to see how many generations of temperature-born nutritive-essence octad-kalāpas each type of rūpa-kalāpa produces.

HOW YOU SEE NUTRIMENT-BORN MATERIALITY

As mentioned before,[248] four parts of the body, namely, undigested food, digested food (faeces), pus, and urine, are nothing but inanimate temperature-born nutritive-essence octad-kalāpas *(utuja oj·aṭṭhamaka·kalāpa)*. And the body's digestive heat (which is most powerful in the alimentary canal) is just the fire element of life nonad-kalāpas *(jīvita·navaka·kalāpa)*, which are kamma-born.[249]

When the nutritive essence of the temperature-born nutritive-essence octad-kalāpas meets with the digestive heat, further materiality is produced, namely, nutriment-born nutritive-essence octad-kalāpas *(āhāraja oj·aṭṭhamaka·kalāpa)*. They have themselves nutritive-essence (nutriment-born nutritive essence *(āhāraja ojā)*) which reproduces in the same way through many generations. Nutriment taken in one day reproduces like this for up to a week, during which time it also supports the nutritive essence in kamma-, consciousness-, and temperature-born rūpa-kalāpas, as well as preceding nutriment-born rūpa-kalāpas.[250] Divine nutriment reproduces for up to one or two months.

To see these things you meditate when eating. At that time the nutriment-born rūpa-kalāpas can be seen to spread throughout the body, from

---

[246] For a brief discussion (with examples) of kamma-born materiality, see p.111*ff.*

[247] The fire element *(tejo)* of a kamma-born *(kamma·ja)* rūpa-kalāpa produces temperature-born *(utuja)* rūpa-kalāpas through five generations:

kammaja → [1st *utuja*] → [2nd *utuja*] → [3rd *utuja*] → [4th *utuja*] → [5th *utuja*]

[248] For a brief discussion (with examples) of nutriment-born materiality, see p.114*ff.*

[249] For a brief discussion (with examples) of kamma-born materiality, see p.111*ff.*

[250] preceding nutriment-born rūpa-kalāpas: see p.134.

the entire alimentary canal: the mouth, the throat, the stomach, and the intestines. First you discern the four elements in the newly eaten food in those places, and see the rūpa-kalāpas there. Continue to look until you see that when the digestive heat (the fire element of the life nonad-kalāpas) meets the nutritive essence of the newly eaten food (temperature-born nutritive-essence octad-kalāpas), many generations of nutriment-born nutritive-essence octad-kalāpas are produced, which spread throughout the body. See that they are untranslucent, and contain the eight types of materiality. You can also see these things after you have eaten, in which case you analyse the undigested food in the stomach and intestines.

Next, you need to discern these nutriment-born nutritive-essence octad-kalāpas as they spread out through the body, and reach, for example, the eye. Discern the eight types of materiality in them there, and see that their nutritive essence is nutriment-born nutritive essence. Then see what happens when it meets the kamma-born nutritive essence of the eye decad-kalāpas: together with the digestive heat, it causes the nutritive essence of the eye decad-kalāpas *(cakkhu·dasaka·kalāpa)* to produce four or five generations of nutriment-born nutritive-essence octad kalāpas.[251] The number of generations produced depends on the strength of both the nutritive essences.

Again, in those four or five generations of rūpa-kalāpas, there is temperature. Try again to discern that at its standing phase it too reproduces through many generations.

Try also to discern that when the nutriment-born nutritive essence meets the nutritive essence of the eye's kamma-born body- and sex decad-kalāpas, four or five generations of nutriment-born nutritive-essence octad kalāpas are produced. In also these many generations, the temperature reproduces through many generations.

Furthermore, when the nutriment-born nutritive essence meets the nutritive essence of the eye's consciousness-born nutritive-essence octad-kalāpa *(cittaja oj·aṭṭhamaka·kalāpa)* two or three generations of nutriment-born nutritive-essence octad-kalāpas are produced, and in also these generations, the temperature reproduces through many generations.

And again, there are two types of nutriment-born nutritive-essence octad-kalāpa: preceding and succeeding.

When the preceding nutriment-born nutritive-essence meets the succeeding nutritive-essence of nutriment-born nutritive-essence octad-kalāpas and the digestive heat, ten to twelve generations of nutriment-born

[251] The nutriment-born nutritive-essence and digestive heat are the supporting cause, and the nutritive-essence of the eye decad-kalāpas is the generating cause.

nutritive-essence octad-kalāpas are produced: the temperature also there reproduces through many generations.

In every case, the nutritive essence of any rūpa-kalāpa (born of either kamma, consciousness, temperature or nutriment) reproduces only when it is supported by digestive heat.

Having discerned all the types of nutritive-essence octad kalāpa in the eye, how they reproduce, and how the materiality of the rūpa-kalāpas that they produce also reproduce, you will have discerned all fifty-four types of materiality in the eye. You should then do the same for all the types of materiality in the remaining five sense-organs: the ear, nose, tongue, body and heart.

SUMMARY

Today, we have discussed very briefly how to analyse rūpa-kalāpas, but the actual practice involves much more. For example, the so-called detailed method, involves analysing what are called the forty-two parts of the body mentioned in the *'Dhātu·Vibhaṅga'* sutta of the *Majjhima·Nikāya*: twenty earth-, twelve water-, four fire-, and six wind-element parts.[252] If you wish to know how to develop this, you should approach a proper teacher. By practising systematically, you will gradually become proficient in the discernment of rūpa-kalāpas, which are born of the four causes: kamma, consciousness, temperature, and nutriment.

With the complete discernment of materiality, you will have finished the first part of the first vipassanā knowledge, the Mentality-Materiality Definition Knowledge *(Nāma·Rūpa·Pariccheda·Ñāṇa)*.

Let us then summarize the discernment of materiality *(rūpa·kammaṭṭhāna)*:

- To see the rūpa-kalāpas, you must develop concentration up to access concentration by concentrating on the four elements: earth, water, fire, and wind.
- When you can see the rūpa-kalāpas, you must analyse them to see all the different types of materiality in single rūpa-kalāpas, for example: in one eye decad-kalāpa, you must see earth, water, fire, wind, colour, odour, flavour, nutritive-essence, life faculty, and eye translucency.

---

[252] M.III.iv.10 *'Dhātuvibhaṅga·Suttaṁ'* 'Elements Analysis Sutta'. The four fire-element parts are: 1) warming heat, 2) maturing/ageing heat, 3) burning heat, 4) digestive heat. The six wind-element parts are: 1) up-going wind, 2) down-going wind, 3) abdominal wind, 4) intestinal wind, 5) wind in the limbs, 6) in&out-breath.

- With the brief method you must discern the different types of materiality in one sense-organ, and then do the same for the remaining five sense-organs.
- With the detailed method you must discern all the types of materiality in all forty-two parts of the body.

When you have completed the discernment of materiality *(rūpa·kamma-ṭṭhāna)*, you will be skilful enough to see all the elements of all six sense-organs at a glance, and see also all forty-two parts of the body at a glance. This was what you were aiming at as you progressed through the meditation, going from element to element, and then from sense-organ to sense-organ: from the easier to the more difficult.

It is like looking at ten banisters that support a hand-rail. We may look at them individually, as one, two, three, four etc. up to ten, and we may look at all ten at once, at a glance. When you are able to see all types of element at a glance, they become your object for vipassanā: you see all the elements as impermanence, suffering and non-self.[253] But if, even after completing the discernment of materiality, you are still unable to see them all at a glance, you take them individually, one-by-one, do it again and again, and try to see them all at a glance.[254]

This completes our discussion of the materiality meditation-subject *(rūpa·kammaṭṭhāna)*. In the next talk we shall discuss the mentality meditation subject *(nāma·kammaṭṭhāna)*.

---

[253] For details, see 'Knowledge of Comprehension', p.209.

[254] There are two ways of discerning: As a group *(kalāpa sammāsana)* and consecutively *(anupada)*. See VsM.xx.606 *'Magg·Ā·Magga·Ñāṇa·Dassana·Visuddhi·Niddesa'* ('Description of Path&Non-Path Knowledge&Vision Purification') PP.xx.704. See also e.g. M.III.ii.1 *'Anupada·Suttaṁ'* ('The Consecutive Sutta'), mentioned at Q&A 4.6, p.149*ff.*

Table **2a**: THE TWENTY-EIGHT TYPES OF MATERIALITY

FOUR GREAT ESSENTIALS *(mahā·bhūta)*:[255]	
Concrete Materiality *(nipphanna·rūpa)*	
1) Earth element	*(pathavī·dhātu)*
2) Water element	*(āpo·dhātu)*
3) Fire element	*(tejo·dhātu)*
4) Wind element	*(vāyo·dhātu)*

TWENTY-FOUR TYPES OF DERIVED MATERIALITY *(upādāya·rūpa)*

Concrete Materiality *(nipphanna·rūpa)*			
Field Materiality *(gocara·rūpa)*: (objective materiality)		Translucent Materiality *(pasāda·rūpa)*:[256] (subjective materiality)	
1) Colour	*(vaṇṇa)*	1) Eye translucency	*(cakkhu·pasāda)*
2) Sound	*(sadda)*	2) Ear translucency	*(sota·pasāda)*
3) Odour	*(gandha)*	3) Nose translucency	*(ghāna·pasāda)*
4) Flavour	*(rasa)*	4) Tongue translucency	*(jivhā·pasāda)*
(Tangible *(phoṭṭhabba)*)[256]		5) Body translucency	*(kāya·pasāda)*
1) Nutritive Essence[256]	*(ojā)*	Sex Materiality *(bhāva-rūpa)*:[256]	
1) Life faculty[256]	*(jīvit·indriya)*	1) Male scx-materiality	*(purisa·bhāva·rūpa)*
1) Heart materiality[256]	*(hadaya·rūpa)*	2) Female sex-materiality	*(itthi·bhāva·rūpa)*
Unconcrete Materiality *(anipphanna·rūpa)*			
1) Space element[257]	*(ākāsa·dhātu)*	6) Wieldiness[257]	*(kammaññatā)*
2) Bodily Intimation	*(kāya·viññatti)*	7) Generation[257]	*(upacaya)*
3) Verbal Intimation	*(vacī·viññatti)*	8) Continuity[257]	*(santati)*
4) Lightness[257]	*(lahutā)*	9) Ageing	*(jaratā)*
5) Softness	*(mudutā)*	10) Impermanence[257]	*(aniccatā)*

---

[255] At the end of discerning materiality, the yogi will have examined all types of concrete materiality (four great essentials & first fourteen types of derived materiality), and nine of the ten types of unconcrete materiality (see 'generation').

[256] TANGIBLE: the object of body consciousness is not an element of its own, but three of the four great essentials: earth-, fire-, and wind element. NUTRITIVE ESSENCE is also called nutriment materiality *(āhāra·rūpa)*. LIFE FACULTY also life materiality *(jīvita·rūpa)*. HEART MATERIALITY also heart base *(hadaya·vatthu)*. TRANSLUCENT/TRANSLUCENCY: see dictionary definition, footnote 504, p.276. SEX MATERIALITY also sex faculty *(indriya)*. Other names may also be found.

[257] SPACE ELEMENT: delimitation, boundary of rūpa-kalāpas, separating one from the other. LIGHTNESS/ SOFTNESS/ WIELDINESS: exist only in consciousness-, temperature-, and nutriment-born materiality. GENERATION: generation of the fœtus's physical faculties: discerned only when discerning dependent origination (see 'How You Discern Your Past', p.184); CONTINUITY: generation of materiality thereafter; IMPERMANENCE: the dissolution *(bhaṅga)* of materiality.

Table 2b: The Basic Types of Materiality of the Eye[a]

(3 types of decad-kalāpa [3 x 10 = 30]+ nonad kalāpas [9] + 3 types of octad-kalāpa[3 x 8= 24] = 63)

type	EYE DECAD-KALĀPA[b]	BODY DECAD-KALĀPA	SEX DECAD-KALĀPA
quality	*translucent*	*translucent*	*untranslucent*
origin	*kamma*	*kamma*	*kamma*
function	*base/door for sights*[c]	*door to tangibles (earth, fire, and wind)*	*determines sex*
1	earth	earth	earth
2	water	water	water
3	fire	fire	fire
4	wind	wind	wind
5	colour	colour	colour
6	odour	odour	odour
7	flavour	flavour	flavour
8	nutritive essence	nutritive essence	nutritive essence
9	life faculty	life faculty	life faculty
10	eye translucency [d]	body translucency	sex materiality

[a] With due changes, read the same for the ear, nose and tongue. For the body and heart, see Tables 2c and 2d just following.

[b] For the ear, nose and tongue, read EAR DECAD-KALĀPA, NOSE DECAD-KALĀPA and TONGUE DECAD-KALĀPA respectively.

[c] For the ear-, nose- and tongue door, read sound, odour, and flavour respectively.

[d] For the ear-, nose- and tongue door, read ear-, nose- and tongue translucency respectively.

+

type	LIFE NONAD-KALĀPA	OCTAD–KALĀPA		
quality	*untranslucent*	*untranslucent*	*untranslucent*	*untranslucent*
origin	*kamma*	*consciousness*	*temperature*	*nutriment*
1	earth	earth	earth	earth
2	water	water	water	water
3	fire	fire	fire	fire
4	wind	wind	wind	wind
5	colour	colour	colour	colour
6	odour	odour	odour	odour
7	flavour	flavour	flavour	flavour
8	nutritive essence	nutritive essence	nutritive essence	nutritive essence
9	life faculty			

The life nonad-, and octad-kalāpas are the same throughout the six sense-organs.

Table 2c: The Basic Types of Materiality of the Body

(2 types of decad-kalāpa [2 x 10 = 20] + nonad kalāpas [9] + 3 types of octad-kalāpa [3 x 8= 24] = 53)

type	BODY DECAD-KALĀPA	SEX DECAD-KALĀPA
quality	*translucent*	*untranslucent*
origin	*kamma*	*kamma*
function	*base/door for tangibles (earth, fire, and wind)*	*determines sex*
1	earth	earth
2	water	water
3	fire	fire
4	wind	wind
5	colour	colour
6	odour	odour
7	flavour	flavour
8	nutritive essence	nutritive essence
9	life faculty	life faculty
10	body translucency	sex materiality

These two types of decad-kalāpa are found in all six sense-organs.

+

type	LIFE NONAD-KALĀPA	OCTAD-KALĀPA		
quality	*untranslucent*	*untranslucent*	*untranslucent*	*untranslucent*
origin	*kamma*	*consciousness*	*temperature*	*nutriment*
1	earth	earth	earth	earth
2	water	water	water	water
3	fire	fire	fire	fire
4	wind	wind	wind	wind
5	colour	colour	colour	colour
6	odour	odour	odour	odour
7	flavour	flavour	flavour	flavour
8	nutritive essence	nutritive essence	nutritive essence	nutritive essence
9	life faculty			

The life nonad-, and octad-kalāpas are the same throughout the six sense-organs.

Table 2d: The Basic Types of Materiality of the Heart

(3 types of decad-kalāpa [3 x 10 = 30] + nonad kalāpas [9] + 3 types of octad-kalāpa [3 x 8= 24] = 63)

type	HEART DECAD-KALĀPA[a]	BODY DECAD-KALĀPA	SEX DECAD-KALĀPA
quality	*untranslucent*	*translucent*	*untranslucent*
origin	*kamma*	*kamma*	*kamma*
function	*base for the mind- and mind-consciousness element* [b]	*base/door for tangibles (earth, fire, and wind)*	*determines sex*
1	earth	earth	earth
2	water	water	water
3	fire	fire	fire
4	wind	wind	wind
5	colour	colour	colour
6	odour	odour	odour
7	flavour	flavour	flavour
8	nutritive essence	nutritive essence	nutritive essence
9	life faculty	life faculty	life faculty
10	heart materiality	body translucency	sex materiality

[a] Eye-, ear-, nose-, tongue- and body consciousnesses arise dependent upon the translucent, tenth type of materiality (the door) of respectively the eye-, ear-, nose-, tongue- and body decad-kalāpas, whereas all other consciousnesses (which comprise the mind element and mind-consciousness element) arise dependent upon the heart materiality of heart decad-kalāpas. See also p.109*ff.*

[b] Mind element *(mano·dhātu)*: the five-door adverting- and un/wholesome receiving consciousness; mind-consciousness element *(mano·viññāṇa·dhātu)*: the investigation-, impulsion-, registration, and process-separate consciousness (see table '1c: The Five-Door Process', p.168). +

type	LIFE NONAD-KALĀPA	OCTAD–KALĀPA		
quality	*untranslucent*	*untranslucent*	*untranslucent*	*untranslucent*
origin	*kamma*	*consciousness*	*temperature*	*nutriment*
1	earth	earth	earth	earth
2	water	water	water	water
3	fire	fire	fire	fire
4	wind	wind	wind	wind
5	colour	colour	colour	colour
6	odour	odour	odour	odour
7	flavour	flavour	flavour	flavour
8	nutritive essence	nutritive essence	nutritive essence	nutritive essence
9	life faculty			

The life-nonad-, and octad kalāpas are the same throughout the six sense-organs.

Question 4.1 Is a Bodhisatta, including Arimetteyya Bodhisatta, an ordinary person *(puthu·jjana)*? If Arimetteyya Bodhisatta is an ordinary person like us, then at the time for him to come down to become Metteyya Buddha, what is the difference between the conditions for him to become a Buddha and for us?[258]

Answer 4.1 The difference is that his *pāramī* have matured, as they had for our Sakyamuni Buddha as the Bodhisatta Prince Siddhattha. Such Bodhisattas will for many lives have been cultivating their *pāramī*. There are ten *pāramī*:

1) Generosity	*(dāna)*	6) Patience	*(khantī)*
2) Virtue	*(sīla)*	7) Truthfulness	*(sacca)*
3) Renunciation	*(nekkhamma)*	8) Resolution	*(adhiṭṭhāna)*
4) Wisdom	*(paññā)*	9) Loving-kindness	*(mettā)*
5) Energy	*(vīriya)*	10) Equanimity	*(upekkhā)*

When these ten *pāramī* are mature, they push the Bodhisatta to renounce the world, even though he is enjoying sensual pleasures. In his last life, a Bodhisatta marries and has a son; this is a law of nature. We forget the names of Metteyya Bodhisatta's wife and son. According to the Theravāda *Tipiṭaka*, it is his last life, because no Arahant, including The Buddha, is reborn after his Parinibbāna. His Parinibbāna is the end of his round of rebirths. He will not be reborn anywhere.[259]

Take our Sakyamuni Bodhisatta: in his last life, before his enlightenment, he was a ordinary person. How? When he was sixteen years old, he became Prince Siddhattha and married princess Yasodharā. They had a son. He enjoyed sensual pleasures for more than thirteen years. He did not have five hundred female deities on his left, and five hundred female deities on his right, but was surrounded by twenty thousand princesses. This is *kāma·sukhallik·anuyogo*: devotion to sensual pleasures.

After he had renounced those sensual pleasures, he practised self-mortification in the Uruvela forest. After six years of that futile practice, he abandoned it, practised the middle way, and before long attained enlightenment. After His enlightenment, in His first sermon, the *'Dhamma·Cakka·Pavattana'* sutta, He declared:[260]

Kāmesu kāma·sukhallik·anuyogo hīno, gammo, puthujjaniko, an·ariyo, an·at-

[258] The Most Venerable Pa-Auk Tawya Sayadaw's audience was almost only Buddhists of the Mahāyana tradition, for whom the goal is not Arahantship but Buddhahood.

[259] See also The Buddha's words quoted Q&A, 5.4, p.178.

[260] S.V.XII.ii.1 'The Dhamma-Wheel Setting-in-Motion Sutta'

tha·saṁhito.

This enjoyment of sensual pleasures is inferior *(hīno)*, **the practice of villagers** *(gammo)*, **the practice of ordinary persons** *(puthujjaniko)*. **It is the practice of unenlightened ones** *(an.ariyo)*. **It is unbeneficial** *(an·attha·saṁhito)*.

This means that the enjoyment of sensual pleasures is not the practice of enlightened ones. And sensual pleasures are unbeneficial because although they provide mundane benefit such as human happiness, deva happiness and brahma happiness, they do not provide the supramundane benefit that is Nibbāna happiness, which can be enjoyed only by Path- and Fruition Knowledge.

So, in His first sermon The Buddha declared that anyone who enjoys sensual pleasures is a ordinary person. When he was still a Bodhisatta, he too had enjoyed sensual pleasures, that is, with Yasodharā in the palace. At that time, he too was a ordinary person, because enjoyment of sensual pleasures is the practice of a ordinary person.

This is not only for our Bodhisatta, but for every Bodhisatta. There may be many Bodhisattas here among the present audience. You should consider this carefully: are the Bodhisattas here ordinary persons *(puthu·jjana)* or Noble Ones *(Ariya)*? We think you may know the answer.

Question 4.2 After finishing the meditation course, can a yogi attain Path *(Magga·Ñāṇa)* and Fruition Knowledges *(Phala·Ñāṇa)* and? If not, why not?

Answer 4.2 Maybe he can; it depends on his *pāramī*. Take, for example, the case of Bāhiya Dārucīriya.[261] He practised samatha-vipassanā up to the Formations-Equanimity Knowledge *(Saṅkhār·Upekkhā·Ñāṇa)* in the time of Kassapa Buddha's dispensation. He had about twenty thousand years of practice, but did not attain any Path and Fruition Knowledges, because he had received a definite prophecy from Padumuttara Buddha. It was that he was to be the *khipp·ābhiñña*, the quickest to attain Arahantship in Sakyamuni's dispensation. Hence, his *pāramī* would mature only then.[262] In the same way, other disciples *(sāvaka)*, who attained the Four Analytical Knowledges *(Paṭisambhidā·Ñāṇa)* in this Sakyamuni Buddha's dispensation, had also practised samatha-vipassanā up to the Formations-Equanimity Knowledge in the dispensation of previous Buddhas; this is a law of nature. The four analytical knowledges they attained are:

1) The Analytical Knowledge of Meaning *(Attha·Paṭisambhidā·Ñāṇa)*: this is the vipassanā knowledge of effect, the Noble Truth of Suffering.

---

[261] Ap.II.liv.6 (&A.) *'Bāhiya·Tthera·Apadāna'* ('The Elder Bāhiya's Heroic Deed')

[262] AA.I.XIV.iii.216 *'Bāhiya·Dārucīriya·Tthera·Vatthu'* ('The Case of the Elder Bāhiya Dārucīriya')

2) The Analytical Knowledge of Dhamma *(Dhamma·Paṭisambhidā·Ñāṇa)*: this is the vipassanā knowledge of cause: the Noble Truth of the Cause for Suffering.
3) The Analytical Knowledge of Enunciation of Language *(Nirutti·Paṭisambhidā·Ñāṇa)*: this is knowledge of grammar, especially Pali grammar.
4) The Analytical Knowledge of the Kinds of Knowledge *(Paṭibhāna·Paṭisambhidā·Ñāṇa)*: this is the vipassanā knowledge that knows the previous three analytical knowledges.

There are five causes *(pāramī)* for attaining these four analytical knowledges:[263]

1) Achievement *(adhigama)*: this is the attainment of the Arahant Path and Fruition, or any other Path and Fruition.
2) Mastery of scriptures *(pariyatti)*: this is learning the Dhamma scriptures.
3) Hearing *(savana)*: this is listening to Dhamma explanations attentively and respectfully.
4) Inquiry *(paripuccha)*: this is discussing the difficult passages and explanations in the texts and commentaries.
5) Prior effort *(pubbayoga)*: this is the practice of samatha-vipassanā up to the Formations-Equanimity Knowledge *(Saṅkhār·Upekkhā·Ñāṇa)* during the dispensations of former Buddhas.

If those who practise in this dispensation do not attain Nibbāna, it is because their *pāramī* have not yet matured. The reason may also be that they have received a definite prophecy from a previous Buddha, or have made an aspiration to escape from the round of rebirths *(saṁsāra)* in a future dispensation such as Arimetteyya Buddha's. For example, there were two thousand bhikkhunīs, all ordinary Arahants, who attained Parinibbāna on the same day as Yasodharā. They had, during Dīpaṅkara Buddha's time, made an aspiration to escape from the round of rebirths *(saṁsāra)* in the dispensation of Sakyamuni Buddha, which would be four incalculables and one hundred thousand aeons later. To become an ordinary Arahant does not require that one cultivate one's *pāramī* for that long, but these two thousand bhikkhunis had remained in the round of rebirths for that long period because of their aspiration only, not because of a definite prophecy.

Question 4.3 A yogi who has finished the meditation course, but not yet attained the Path Knowledge *(Magga·Ñāṇa)* and Fruition Knowledge *(Phala-*

263 VsM.xiv.429 *'Paññā·Pabheda·Kathā'* ('How Many Kinds of Understanding Are There? [title in PP]' PP.xiv.28)

·Ñāṇa), if his concentration drops, will his vipassanā knowledge also drop? Can he be reborn in a woeful state *(apāya)*?

Answer 4.3 Maybe his vipassanā knowledge will also drop, but it is very rare. If he does not practise for a long time, his samatha-vipassanā may slowly weaken. The potency of kamma, however, remains.

There is an example of this in the Pali Texts.[264] It takes place in Sri Lanka. Some thirty bhikkhus and novices *(sāmaṇeras)* had paid homage at the Great Shrine at Kalyāṇī, and as they were coming down the forest track on to the main road, they saw a man coming in the opposite direction. He had been working in a charcoal burner's field beside the road; his body was smeared with ashes, and the single yellow loin-cloth he wore hitched up was also smeared with ashes, so that he seemed like a charcoal stump. Having done his day's work, he had picked up a bundle of half-burnt wood and was coming along a by-path with his hair hanging down his back; and he stood facing the bhikkhus.

The novices, when they saw him, joked with each other, saying, 'That is your father, that is your grandfather, your uncle!' and laughed as they went along. Then they asked 'What is your name, lay follower?' On being asked his name, the man was remorseful and, putting down his bundle of wood and arranging his clothes, he did obeisance to the Mahāthera in order to detain him for a while.

The bhikkhus waited, but the novices came up and laughed even in front of the Mahāthera. The man said to the Mahāthera: 'Bhante, you laugh on seeing me. You think you fulfill the bhikkhu's life just on account of your robes. But you have not attained so much as mental one-pointedness.

'I was once a recluse like you, and I was mighty with the psychic powers and powerful in this dispensation. I treated the air like the earth and the earth like the air; I treated the far like the near and the near like the far. I penetrated in a moment the one hundred thousand worlds systems. You see my hands now? Now they are like the hands of a monkey'.

Then pointing to a tree, he said further, 'Sitting under that tree I would touch with these very hands the moon and the sun. I would sit with the moon and the sun as the ground on which to rub these very feet. Such were my psychic powers, but they vanished through negligence. Do not be negligent. Through negligence people reach ruin such as this. But those who live strenuously make an end of birth, old age and death.

[264] VbhA.viii.1 *'Suttanta·Bhājanīya·Vaṇṇanā'* ('Sutta-Classification Description')

Therefore, take me as an example, and do not neglect practising samatha-vipassanā wholesome dhammas. Be strenuous, Venerable Sirs.'

Thus, he admonished and warned them. Impelled by the urgency of his words, standing in that place, thirty Bhikkhus practised samatha-vipassanā and attained Arahantship. So samatha-vipassanā may drop temporarily because of negligence *(pamāda)*, but the potency of kamma remains.

There are four types of person who attain Nibbāna. The first type is a Paccekabuddha, which we shall not discuss. The remaining three types are: 1) a Bodhisatta, 2) a chief disciple *(agga·sāvaka)* or great disciple *(mahā·sāvaka)*, and 3) an ordinary disciple *(pakati·sāvaka)*.

1) Our Bodhisatta had the eight attainments *(samāpatti)* and five mundane psychic powers during Dīpaṅkara Buddha's time. He had in past lives also practised samatha-vipassanā up to the Formations-Equanimity Knowledge *(Saṅkhār·Upekkhā·Ñāṇa)*. Had he really wanted to attain Nibbāna, he could have attained it quickly, by listening to a short stanza by Dīpaṅkara Buddha about the Four Noble Truths. But he did not want only to attain Nibbāna, so he made an aspiration to be a Buddha in the future, after which he received a definite prophecy from Dīpaṅkara Buddha.

   During the four incalculables *(a·saṅkhyeyya)* and one hundred thousand aeons *(kappa)* which followed, that is from Dīpaṅkara Buddha's time to Kassapa Buddha's time, our Bodhisatta was ordained as a bhikkhu in nine lives, each time under the guidance of a Buddha. In each life as a bhikkhu, our Bodhisatta's training included seven practices:[265]

   i) Study of the Three Piṭakas by recitation[266] *(tipiṭakaṁ Buddha·vacanaṁ uggaṁhitvā)*
   ii) Purification in the four types of morality[267] *(catu pārisuddhi sīle supatiṭṭhāya)*
   iii) The thirteen ascetic practices *(terasa dhutaṅgāni samādāya)*

---

[265] MA.II.iv.1 *'Ghaṭikāra·Suttaṁ'* ('The Ghaṭikāra Sutta'). This text lists only 1, 2, 3 and 4, with a fifth being: *gata-paccāgata-vattaṁ pūrayamānā samaṇadhammaṁ karontā* (practising the 'going &going-back duty recluse practice'), which refers to full-time meditation (samatha and vipassanā), also when going out for alms, and going back to the dwelling from alms. From sources that explain the Bodhisatta's practice, this fifth one may be understood specifically to be 5,6 & 7. In other contexts, however, *samaṇa dhamma* (ascetic practices) refers to all these seven practices.

[266] This is *gantha·dhura* (book burden/obligation), which is also called *pariyatti* (learning), and 2-7 are *vipassanā·dhura* (Vipassanā burden/obligation), which is also called *paṭipatti* (practice). See p.278.

[267] For the four types of morality purification, see Q&A 2.3, p.77.

iv) Always the forest-dweller ascetic practice[268] *(araññaṁ pavisitvā)*
v) The eight attainments *(aṭṭha samāpattiyo)*
vi) The five mundane psychic powers *(pañca abhiññā)*
vii) Vipassanā meditation up to *(vipassanaṁ vaḍḍhatvā)* the Conformity Knowledge[269] *(yāva anuloma·ñānāṁ)*

These *pāramī* must be fulfilled for the attainment of Omniscient Knowledge *(Sabbaññuta·Ñāṇa)*. But before his *pāramī* had matured, that is, from the time of his definite prophecy till his birth as Prince Siddhattha, our Bodhisatta was sometimes reborn in the animal kingdom because of previous unwholesome kamma. The lives as a bhikkhu and the lives as an animal, however, were very far apart. This is the nature of a Bodhisatta.

2) Some <u>Chief Disciples</u> will also have received a definite prophecy; for example, the Venerables Sāriputta and Mahāmoggallāna had received one from Anomadassī Buddha. Also great disciples will sometimes have received a definite prophecy; the Venerable Kassapa and The Venerable Ānanda had received one from Padumuttara Buddha. In our Buddha's time, all these disciples became Arahants possessed of the Four Analytical Knowledges.[270] This type of Arahants will also have been skilful in samatha-vipassanā up to the Formations-Equanimity Knowledge *(Saṅkhār·Upekkhā·Ñāṇa)*, in times of many previous Buddhas; this is a law of nature. Even so, from the time of their definite prophecy till the time of our Buddha, some of them were sometimes reborn in one of the four woeful states, because of unwholesome kamma, sometimes together with our Bodhisatta. This is the nature of a chief or great disciple.[271]

3) As for <u>ordinary disciples</u>, if they have practised samatha-vipassanā thoroughly up to the Cause-Apprehending Knowledge *(Paccaya-Pariggaha·Ñāṇa)* or the Arise&Perish Knowledge *(Udaya·Bbaya·Ñāṇa)*, or the Formations-Equanimity Knowledge *(Saṅkhār·Upekkhā·Ñāṇa)*, they will not be reborn in one of the four woeful realms *(apāya)* after death, even though they may not have attained Path and Fruition in this life. This is explained in the *Visuddhi·Magga* as:

---

268 Although the forest-dweller practice is included in the thirteen ascetic practices, the Commentary mentions it separately for emphasis.

269 This is the Formations-Equanimity Knowledge *(Saṅkhār·Upekkhā·Ñāṇa)*.

270 For the Four Analytical Knowledges, see Q&A 4.2, p.142.

271 VsM.xiv.429 *'Paññā·Pabheda·Kathā'* ('How Many Kinds of Understanding Are There? [title in PP]' PP.xiv.28)

...laddhassāso laddhapatiṭṭho niyatagatiko cūḷa·sotāpanno nāma hoti
...he has found relief in the Buddha's Dispensation, he has found a secure place, he has a sure, good destination, so he is called a Lesser Stream-Enterer *(Cūḷa Sot·Āpanna)*.

Lesser Stream-Enterers may thus be reborn in the deva realm, and then there are four things that can happen. In the *'Sotānugata'* sutta, The Buddha taught which four:[272]

1) If, as soon as he attains rebirth in the deva realm, the Lesser Stream-Enterer reflects on the Dhamma, it will be clear to his vipassanā knowledge, and he can attain Nibbāna quickly.
2) If he does not attain Nibbāna by reflecting on the Dhamma with vipassanā knowledge, he can attain Nibbāna by listening to a bhikkhu who has psychic powers, and has come to the deva realm to teach the Dhamma.
3) If he does not get the opportunity to listen to the Dhamma from a bhikkhu, he may get the opportunity to listen to it from Dhamma-teaching devas *(Dhamma·kathika·deva)*, like Sanaṅkumāra Brahmā, etc. and attain Nibbāna by listening to them.
4) If he does not get the chance to listen to the Dhamma from Dhamma-teaching devas, he may get the chance to meet friends who were fellow yogis in his past human life in a dispensation. Those fellow yogis may say, for example: 'Oh friend, please remember this and that Dhamma which we practised in the human world.' He may then remember the Dhamma, and if he practises vipassanā, he can attain Nibbāna very quickly.

An example of a Lesser Stream-Enterer who was reborn in the deva realm, and who attained Nibbāna very quickly afterwards, is the Venerable Samaṇa-Devaputta.[273] He was a bhikkhu who practised samatha-vipassanā earnestly. He died while practising, and was reborn in the deva realm. He did not know he had died, and continued meditating in his mansion in the deva realm. When the female devas in his mansion saw him, they realized he must have been a bhikkhu in his previous life, so they put a mirror in front of him and made a noise. He opened his eyes, and saw his image in the mirror. He was very disappointed, because he did not want to be a deva; he wanted only Nibbāna.

---

[272] A.IV.IV.v.1 *'Sotānugata·Suttaṁ'* ('The One Who Has Heard Sutta'), mentioned also p.102.

[273] The case of Samaṇa-Devaputta is described in the commentary to S.I.I.vi.6 *'Accharā·Suttaṁ'* ('The Nymph Sutta').

So immediately he went down to The Buddha to listen to the Dhamma. The Buddha was teaching Dhamma about the Four Noble Truths. After listening to the Dhamma, Samaṇa-devaputta attained the Stream-Entry Path Knowledge *(Sot·Āpatti·Magga·Ñāṇa)* and Stream-Entry Fruition Knowledge *(Sot·Āpatti·Phala·Ñāṇa)*.[274]

Thus, when an ordinary disciple practises samatha and vipassanā very hard, and even attains the Cause-Apprehending Knowledge, the Arise&-Perish Knowledge, or the Formations-Equanimity Knowledge, although he may not attain a Path and Fruition in this life, the practice he has done does mean that he will very likely attain them in one of his future lives. At the time of death, a yogi may not have strong samatha or vipassanā, but because of the powerful samatha-vipassanā meditation wholesome kamma, a good nimitta appears at his mind door. Death may take place with that good nimitta as object, and because of this wholesome kamma, he will definitely reach a good place, and can there attain Nibbāna.

If, however, he practises vipassanā up to the moments of the near-death impulsion *(maraṇ·āsanna·javana)*, he will be of the first type of person mentioned in the *'Sotānugata'* sutta, which we just discussed.

Question 4.4 Can a yogi who has finished the course, but not yet attained Nibbāna, attain the Knowledge Standing on Phenomena *(Dhamma·Ṭṭhiti·Ñāṇa)*? If so, can it regress?

Answer 4.4 Yes, he can attain that knowledge.

Pubbe kho Susīma dhamma·ṭṭhitiñāṇaṁ pacchā Nibbāne ñāṇaṁ.

The Knowledge Standing on Phenomena *(Dhammaṭṭhiti·Ñāṇa)* **comes first, the** [Path] **Knowledge that takes Nibbāna as object comes next.**

This was The Buddha's explanation to Susīma.[275] Susīma was a wanderer *(paribbājaka)*, who ordained to 'steal' the Dhamma. But The Buddha saw that he would attain Nibbāna within a few days, so He accepted him.

Susīma had heard that many Arahants went to The Buddha and reported that they had attained Arahantship. So Susīma asked them whether they had the eight attainments and five psychic powers. They answered 'No'. 'If you do not have the eight attainments and five psychic powers, how did you attain Arahantship?' Then they answered '*Paññā·vimuttā kho mayaṁ āvuso Susīma*': 'Oh, friend Susīma, we are free from defilements, and attained Arahantship by the pure-vipassanā vehicle *(suddha-vipassanā yānika)*.' He did not understand, so he asked The Buddha the same question. The Buddha said:

---

[274] S.I.I.v.6 *'Accharā·Suttaṁ'* ('The Deva Sutta') & SA.ibid.

[275] S.II.I.vii.10 *'Susīma·Suttaṁ'* ('The Susīma Sutta')

Pubbe kho Susīma dhamma·ṭṭhitiñāṇaṁ pacchā Nibbāne ñāṇaṁ.

The Knowledge Standing on Phenomena comes first; the [Path] **Knowledge that takes Nibbāna as object comes next.**

What does this mean? The Path Knowledge is not the result of the eight attainments and five psychic powers; it is the result of vipassanā knowledges. So the Path Knowledge can occur only after the vipassanā knowledges have occurred. In the *'Susīma'* sutta, all vipassanā knowledges are referred to as the Knowledge Standing on Phenomena. The Knowledge Standing on Phenomena is the vipassanā knowledge of the impermanent, suffering and non-self nature of all formations, conditioned things *(saṅkhāra·dhamma)*, that is, mentality, materiality, and their causes. This is how the Knowledge Standing on Phenomena comes first, and the Path Knowledge that takes Nibbāna as object comes next.

Afterwards, The Buddha gave a Teaching on the Three Rounds[276] *(tepari-vaṭṭa Dhamma-desanā)*, which is like the *'An·Atta·Lakkhaṇa'* sutta ('Non-self-Characteristic Sutta').[277] When the teaching was finished, Susīma attained Arahantship, even though he did not have the eight attainments or five psychic powers. He too became a pure-vipassanā-vehicle person. At that time he understood clearly the meaning of The Buddha's discourse.

If a yogi attains the Knowledge Standing on Phenomena, then although he does not attain Nibbāna in this life, his vipassanā knowledge will not decrease. His vipassanā kammic potency is still powerful. If he is an ordinary disciple, he may attain Nibbāna in his next life.

Question 4.5 Can one attain supramundane states[278] with only access concentration?[279]

Answer 4.5 Yes, one can. At access concentration there is also bright, brilliant and radiant light. With that light, one can discern the rūpa-kalāpas, materiality, ultimate mentality, and their causes. One can then continue with vipassanā meditation stage by stage.

Question 4.6 Can one with only momentary concentration *(khaṇika·samādhi)*, practise mindfulness of feeling *(vedān·ānupassanā sati·paṭṭhāna)* to attain supramundane states?[279]

Answer 4.6 Here we need to define momentary concentration. What is momentary concentration? There are two types of momentary concentration:

---

[276] Here, the three rounds refer to the three characteristics: impermanence, suffering, and non-self.

[277] S.III.I.II.i.7, quoted 'Introduction' p.26.

[278] This would be a Path&Fruition attainment.

[279] For a discussion of the different types of concentration, see also Q&A 3.1, p.95.

1) Momentary concentration in samatha meditation
2) Momentary concentration in vipassanā meditation

In samatha meditation there are three types of concentration:

1) Momentary concentration (a type of preparatory concentration)
2) Access concentration
3) Absorption concentration

The momentary concentration in samatha refers in particular to the concentration that takes a *paṭibhāga-nimitta* as object, like the *ān·āpāna paṭibhāga-nimitta*. It is the concentration before access concentration. This is for a samatha vehicle person *(samatha·yānika)*.

There is another type of momentary concentration for a pure-vipassanā vehicle yogi *(suddha·vipassanā·yānika)*. A pure-vipassanā-vehicle yogi must usually begin with four-elements meditation in order to attain access concentration or momentary concentration, and see the rūpa-kalāpas, and the four elements in one kalāpa. The *Visuddhi·Magga* says that is access concentration. But the sub-commentary to the *Visuddhi·Magga* says it is only a metaphor, not real access concentration, because real access concentration is close to jhāna concentration.[280]

Jhāna cannot, however, be attained with four-elements meditation. When one is able to see the four elements in individual rūpa-kalāpas there is deep concentration, and there is bright, brilliant and radiant light. Even so, one cannot attain jhāna using them as object. There are two reasons for this:

1) To see the four elements in individual rūpa-kalāpas is to see ultimate materiality *(paramattha·rūpa)*, and to see ultimate materiality is deep and profound. One cannot attain jhāna with ultimate reality as object.[281]
2) Even though one's concentration while analysing the rūpa-kalāpas is deep, it cannot become as deep as jhāna concentration. Why? Because the rūpa-kalāpas perish as soon as they arise. That means the

---

[280] Access concentration is the three impulsion consciousnesses that follow the mind-door adverting consciousness and precede the Change-of-Lineage to the jhāna process. See table '1a: The Absorption-Process', p.44, and notes.

[281] VsM.xi.308 *'Catu·Dhātu Vavatthāna Bhāvanā'* ('Four-Elements Definition Meditation') PP.xi.42 explains that since four-elements meditation has as object phenomena with natural characteristics *(sa·bhāva·dhamm·ārammaṇattā)*, one reaches only access-concentration: not absorption (jhāna). VsT then explains that this it is called access-concentration only according to popular speech *(ruḷhī·vasena)*. VsM.viii.177 *'Maraṇa·Ssati·Kathā'* ('Discussion of Death-Mindfulness') PP.viii.40 explains, however, that because of the preceding practice leading up to the supramundane- and second- and fourth immaterial attainments, then even though their object is also a phenomenon with natural characteristics, their concentration is nonetheless absorption concentration, jhāna. See also footnote 385, p.204.

object is always changing. One cannot attain jhāna with an object that is always changing.

Thus, since four-elements meditation does not produce jhāna, we may understand that the access concentration which takes the four elements in individual rūpa kalāpas as object is not real access concentration, but momentary concentration. Then let us discuss the momentary concentration in vipassanā. It is discussed in the section on *ān·āpāna·sati* (mindfulness-of-breathing) of the *Visuddhi·Magga*.[282]

Here you should know that vipassanā momentary concentration is seeing thoroughly the impermanent, suffering, and non-self nature of ultimate mentality-materiality and their causes. Without seeing ultimate mentality-materiality and their causes, how can there be vipassanā momentary concentration? It is impossible.

When a samatha-vehicle yogi wants to practise vipassanā, he enters the first jhāna, for example, the first *ān·āpāna* jhāna. This is samatha. He emerges from it, and discerns the thirty-four mental formations of the first jhāna, and then impermanence, suffering or non-self by seeing the arising and perishing nature of those jhāna formations *(jhāna dhamma)*. He does the same with the second jhāna, etc.

At the time of discerning there is still concentration. He concentrates on the impermanent, suffering, or non-self nature of those jhāna formations. His concentration is at that time deep and profound, and does not go to other objects. This is momentary concentration, because the object is momentary; as soon as it arises, it passes away.

In the same way, when a yogi is practising vipassanā to see either the impermanent, suffering, or non-self nature of ultimate mentality-materiality and their causes, then usually his mind does not leave the object. His mind has sunk into one of the characteristics. This is also called momentary concentration.

If a yogi can see ultimate mentality-materiality and their causes thoroughly and clearly, without having done any samatha meditation, it is of course not necessary for him to practise samatha meditation. If not, he should cultivate one of the samatha meditation subjects, and develop sufficient concentration so as to be able to see ultimate mentality-materiality and their causes.

---

[282] VsM.viii.235 *'Ān·Āpāna·Sati·Kathā'* ('Mindfulness-of-Breathing Discussion') PP.viii.232

But in the *'Samādhi'* sutta of the *'Khandha Saṁyutta'* The Buddha says:[283]

Samādhiṁ, bhikkhave, bhāvetha. Samāhito, bhikkhave, bhikkhu yathā·bhūtaṁ pajānāti.

Develop concentration, bhikkhus *(Samādhiṁ, bhikkhave, bhāvetha)*. **Concentrated, bhikkhus, a bhikkhu according to reality understands** *(yathā·bhūtaṁ pajānāti)*.

So, you should cultivate concentration to know the five aggregates, their causes and cessation; you should cultivate concentration to know their nature of impermanence, suffering, and non-self. Their cessation you will be able to see at the time of the Arahant Path and Parinibbāna.

Also in the *'Samādhi'* sutta of the *Sacca Saṁyutta*, The Buddha says one should cultivate concentration to know the Four Noble Truths.[284]

Now, if a yogi wants to contemplate only feeling, he should be aware of the following facts explained by The Buddha:

Sabbaṁ, bhikkhave, an·abhijānaṁ a·parijānaṁ a·virājayaṁ a·ppajahaṁ a·bhabbo dukkha·kkhayāya ...
Sabbañca kho, bhikkhave, abhijānaṁ parijānaṁ virājayaṁ pajahaṁ bhabbo dukkha·kkhayāya.

The all, bhikkhus, not knowing directly *(sabbaṃ an·abhijānaṃ)*, **not fully understanding** *(a·parijānaṃ)*, **not having dispassion for** *(a·virājayaṃ)*, **not abandoning** *(a·ppajahaṃ)*, **it is impossible to destroy suffering** *(abhabbo dukkha·kkhayāya)*.

But, bhikkhus, the all knowing directly, fully understanding, having dispassion for, and abandoning, it is possible to destroy suffering *(bhabbo dukkha·kkhayāya)*.

This is from the first *'Aparijānana'* sutta in the *'Saḷāyatana·Vagga'* of the *Saṁyutta·Nikāya*.[285] What is the all? It is all mentality and materiality and their causes.[286] Unless one knows the all with the three types of full understanding *(pariññā)*, one cannot attain Nibbāna. Only those who know the all with those three types of full knowledge can attain Nibbāna.

---

[283] *'Samādhi·Suttaṁ'* ('The Concentration Sutta') of the *'Khandha Saṁyutta'* ('Section on the Aggregates') S.III.I, quoted, p.23.

[284] *'Samādhi·Suttaṁ'* ('The Concentration Sutta') of the *'Sacca Saṁyutta'* ('Section on the Truths') S.V.XII quoted, p.12. See also related quotation, footnote 45, p.14.

[285] S.IV.I.iii.4 *'Paṭhama-Aparijānana·Suttaṁ'* ('The First Non-Understanding Sutta')

[286] In the sutta, The Buddha explains the all as: the eye-, ear-, nose-, tongue-, body-, and mind base; the sight-, sound-, odour-, flavour-, tangible- and dhamma base; the six types of consciousness *(viññāṇa)* that arise when those bases meet: eye-, ear, nose-, tongue-, body-, and mind consciousness respectively; the six types of contact *(phassa)* that arise with the six types of consciousness: eye-, ear-, nose-, tongue-, body-, and mind contact respectively; and the feelings *(vedanā)* that arise with the six types of contact: pleasant feelings, painful feelings, and neither painful nor pleasant feelings, that arise because of eye-, ear-, nose-, tongue-, body-, and mind contact.

In the same way, The Buddha says in the *'Kūṭāgāra'* sutta of the *'Sacca·Vagga'* that, without knowing the Four Noble Truths with vipassanā knowledge and Path Knowledge, one cannot reach the end of the round of rebirths *(saṁsāra)*.[287] So if a yogi wants to attain Nibbāna, he must try to know all mentality, materiality, and their causes with the three types of full understanding.

What are the three types of full understanding? They are:

1) Full Understanding as the Known *(ñāta·pariññā)*: this is the Mentality-Materiality Definition Knowledge *(Nāma·Rūpa·Pariccheda·Ñāṇa)*, and Cause-Apprehending Knowledge *(Paccaya·Pariggaha·Ñāṇa)*. They are the vipassanā knowledges that know all ultimate mentality-materiality and their causes.
2) Full Understanding as Investigation *(tīraṇa·pariññā)*: this is the Comprehension Knowledge *(Sammasana·Ñāṇa)*, and Arise&Perish Knowledge *(Udaya·bbaya·Ñāṇa)*. These two vipassanā knowledges comprehend clearly the impermanent, suffering, and non-self nature of ultimate mentality-materiality and their causes.
3) Full Understanding as Abandoning *(pahāna·pariññā)*: this is the higher vipassanā knowledges from the Dissolution Knowledge *(Bhaṅga·Ñāṇa)* to the Path Knowledge *(Magga·Ñāṇa)*.

The teaching in those two suttas, the *'Paṭhama Aparijānana'* sutta, and *'Kūṭāgāra'* sutta, is very important. So, if a yogi wants to practise vipassanā beginning with mindfulness of feeling, he should remember the following:

- He must have discerned ultimate materiality.
- Discerning feeling alone is not enough: he must also discern the mental formations associated with feeling in the six-door processes.

Nevertheless, it is in fact possible to become enlightened by discerning only one dhamma, but that is only so long as all the other dhammas have been discerned before: either in this life or in a past life. Take for, example, the Venerable Sāriputta. When he heard the Venerable Assaji utter one sentence of Dhamma, he became a Stream-Enterer. Then he became a bhikkhu and practised meditation. In the *'Anupada'* sutta,[288] The Buddha describes how the Venerable Sāriputta was very skilled in discerning the individual mental formations of his jhāna attainments consecutive-

---

[287] S.V.XII.v.4 'The Peaked House Sutta', quoted 'Introduction' p.2.

[288] M.III.ii.1 *'Anupada·Suttaṁ'* ('The Consecutive Sutta')

ly.[289] But even though the Venerable Sāriputta meditated hard, he did not attain Arahantship.

Then one day, The Buddha taught the *'Dīghanakha'* sutta to the Venerable Sāriputta's nephew, explaining one dhamma: feeling *(vedanā)*.[290] At this time, the Venerable Sāriputta was standing behind The Buddha fanning Him, and listening to the teaching. At the end of the teaching, the Venerable Sāriputta attained Arahantship, and his nephew attained Stream-Entry. He attained Arahantship by contemplating only one dhamma, but that was because he had meditated on all five aggregates beforehand.[291]

We shall repeat: The Buddha said that if a bhikkhu does not know all mentality-materiality and their causes with the three types of full-understanding, he cannot attain Nibbāna. It is, therefore, not enough if a yogi tries to discern feeling alone, such as unpleasant feeling, and does not discern ultimate mentality-materiality thoroughly. Here 'it is not enough' means he will not attain Nibbāna.

Question 4.7 The Buddha was a great Arahant. What was the difference between Him, and disciples like the Venerables Sāriputta and Mahāmoggallāna who were also Arahants?

Answer 4.7 A Buddha's Arahant Path is always associated with Omniscient Knowledge *(Sabbaññuta·Ñāṇa)*, but the Arahant Path of disciples is not. The Arahant Path of disciples comprises the enlightenment *(bodhi)* of the three types of disciples:

1) Chief Disciple Enlightenment *(agga·sāvaka bodhi)*
2) Great Disciple Enlightenment *(mahā·sāvaka bodhi)*
3) Ordinary Disciple Enlightenment *(pakati·sāvaka bodhi)*

The Arahant Path of disciples is sometimes associated with the Four Analytical Knowledges *(Paṭisambhidā·Ñāṇa)*;[292] sometimes with the Six Direct Knowledges *(Abhiññā)*;[293] sometimes with the three Direct Knowledges *(te·vijja)*;[294] or is sometimes a pure Arahant Path: either Both Ways Liber-

---

[289] For details about how to discern the individual mental formations of one's jhāna attainments, see 'How You Discern Jhāna Mental-Processes', p.161.

[290] M.II.iii.4 *'Dīghanakha·Suttaṁ'* ('The Dīghanakha Sutta')

[291] For details regarding the past practice of those who attain, see Q&A 4.3, p.143, and Q&A 5.2, p.176.

[292] For the Four Analytical Knowledges, see Q&A 4.2, p.142.

[293] 1) various kinds of supernormal power *(iddhi·vidhā)*, 2) divine ear *(dibba·sota)*, 3) knowledge of the minds of others *(parassa ceto·pariya·ñāṇa)*, 4) divine eye *(dibba·cakkhu)*, 5) recollection of past lives *(pubbe·nivās·ānussati)*, 6) destruction of the taints *(āsava·kkhaya)*.

[294] Nos. 4, 5, and 6 of the Direct Knowledges just mentioned.

ated *(Ubato·bhāga·Vimutta)*,[295] or Wisdom Liberated *(Paññā·Vvimutta)*).[296] But it is never associated with Omniscient Knowledge *(Sabbaññuta·Ñāṇa)*. Thus, for example, the Venerables Sāriputta's and Mahāmoggallāna's Arahant Paths were not associated with Omniscient Knowledge. A Buddha's Arahant Path, on the other hand, is not only associated with Omniscient Knowledge, but also all the other knowledges, as well as all special qualities of a Buddha.

Another thing is that Buddhas have (because of their matured *pāramī*) attained the Path, Fruition, and Omniscient Knowledges by themselves without a teacher. But a disciple can only attain the Path and Fruition Knowledges by listening to Dhamma related to the Four Noble Truths from a Buddha, or a Buddha's disciple. They cannot practise by themselves, without a teacher. These are the differences.

Question 4.8 What is the 'intermediate life' *(antara·bhava)*?

Answer 4.8 According to the Theravāda Piṭaka there is no such thing as an intermediate life *(antara·bhava)*. Between a decease consciousness *(cuti citta)* and its subsequent rebirth-linking consciousness *(paṭisandhi·citta)*, there are no consciousness moments, or anything resembling an intermediate life.[297] If a person were to reach the deva world after death, then between his decease consciousness and the deva's rebirth-linking consciousness, there would be no consciousness moment or anything like an intermediate life. As soon as death takes place, the deva rebirth-linking consciousness arises. In the same way, if a person were to reach hell after death, then between his decease consciousness and the rebirth-linking consciousness in hell, there would be no such thing as an intermediate life. He would go to hell directly after death.

The idea of an intermediate life usually arises when someone dies, inhabits the *peta* world for a short time, and is then reborn as a human being again. He may think his *peta* life was something like an intermediate life, even though it was, in fact, nothing like an intermediate life. What really happened is this: after the human decease consciousness had passed, the *peta* rebirth-linking consciousness arose; after the *peta* decease consciousness had passed, a human rebirth-linking consciousness arose again. The person suffered in the *peta* world because of his unwholesome kamma. The kammic potency of that unwholesome kamma

[295] Both Ways Liberated *(ubhato·bhāga·vimutta)*: this refers to those who escape first from the material sphere with the attainment of the immaterial jhānas, and second, escape also from the immaterial sphere with the attainment of Arahantship.

[296] Wisdom Liberated *(paññā·vimutta)*: this refers to pure-vipassanā Arahants.

[297] For details in this regard, see Table 1d 'Death and Rebirth', (and footnote 360) p.188.

finished after only a short time, and he took a human rebirth-linking consciousness again, because of wholesome kamma that had matured.

The short life in the *peta* world is mistaken for an intermediate life by those who cannot see the reality of the round of rebirths or dependent origination. If they could discern dependent origination with vipassanā knowledge, then this misbelief would disappear. So we should like to suggest that you discern dependent origination with your own vipassanā knowledge. Then the question about an intermediate life will disappear from your mind.

Question 4.9 Are the methods for *ān·āpāna·sati* (mindfulness-of-breathing) and four-elements meditation the same? Why must we practise four-elements meditation only after *ān·āpāna·sati*?

Answer 4.9 No, the methods are not the same. In vipassanā you must discern materiality and mentality, and their causes, which is why there are two types of meditation: discernment of materiality and discernment of mentality.

When The Buddha taught discernment of materiality, he always taught four-elements meditation, either in brief or in detail. So if you want to discern materiality, you must practise according to The Buddha's instructions. It is better to practise four-elements meditation with deep concentration like the fourth *ān·āpāna* jhāna, because it helps us see ultimate materiality, ultimate mentality, and their causes clearly.

But if you do not want to practise samatha meditation like *ān·āpāna·sati*, you can practise the four-elements meditation directly: no problem. We discussed this in a previous question.

Question 4.10 Could the Sayadaw please explain the light experienced in meditation scientifically?

Answer 4.10 What is the light seen in meditation? Every consciousness *(citta)*, except rebirth-linking consciousnesses, which arises dependent upon the heart base *(hadaya·vatthu)*, produces consciousness-born materiality *(cittaja·rūpa)*: consciousness-born nutritive-essence octad-kalāpas *(cittaja·oj·aṭṭhamaka·kalāpa)*.[298] One consciousness produces many consciousness-born rūpa-kalāpas. Of the heart-base-dependent consciousnesses, samatha-meditation consciousnesses *(samatha·bhāvanā-citta)* and vipassanā-meditation consciousnesses *(vipassanā·bhāvanā-citta)* are very strong and powerful; they produce very many rūpa-kalāpas. When we analyse those rūpa-kalāpas, we see the eight types of materiality. They are: the earth, water, fire, and wind elements, colour, odour, flavour, and nutritive essence. The materiality of

[298] See further 'Consciousness-Born Materiality', p.112.

colour is bright. The more powerful the samatha and vipassanā-meditation consciousnesses are, the brighter is the colour. Since, rūpa-kalāpās arise simultaneously as well as successively, the colour of one rūpa-kalāpa and the colour of another rūpa-kalāpa arise closely together like in an electric bulb: that is why light appears.

Again, in each rūpa-kalāpa born of samatha and vipassanā-meditation consciousnesses, there is the fire element, which also produces many new rūpa-kalāpas. They are called temperature-born materiality, because they are produced by the fire element, which is temperature *(utu)*. This occurs externally as well as internally. When we analyse these rūpa-kalāpas we see the same eight types of materiality: earth-, water-, fire-, and wind element, colour, odour, flavour, and nutritive essence. Colour is again one of them. Because of the power of the samatha and vipassanā-meditation consciousnesses that colour too is bright. So the brightness of one colour and the brightness of another colour arise closely together, like in an electric bulb.

The light of consciousness-born materiality and temperature-born materiality appear simultaneously. Consciousness-born colour materiality arises internally only, but temperature-born colour materiality arises both internally and externally and spreads in all directions up to the whole world system or universe *(cakkavāḷa)* or farther, depending on the power of the samatha and vipassanā-meditation consciousnesses. A Buddha's Mentality-Materiality Definition Knowledge produces light in up to ten thousand world systems. The Venerable Anuruddha's divine-eye consciousness *(dibba·cakkhu·citta)* produced light in up to one thousand world systems. Other disciples' vipassanā knowledge produces light going up to one league *(yojana)*, two leagues, etc. in every direction depending on the power of their samatha and vipassanā-meditation consciousnesses.

Usually many yogis realize that this light is a group of rūpa-kalāpas when they have reached the Arise&Perish Knowledge. While practising samatha meditation, they do not yet understand that it is a group of rūpa-kalāpas, because the rūpa-kalāpas are very subtle. It is not easy to understand and see the rūpa-kalāpas when practising only samatha meditation. If you want to know with certainty, you should try to acquire the Arise&-Perish Knowledge. That is the most scientific way to understand the light experienced in meditation.

Question 4.11 Can those who have discerned the thirty-two parts of the body see them in someone else, with their eyes open?

Answer 4.11 It depends. Beginners can with their eyes open see only the external parts. They can see the internal parts only with their vipassanā knowledge eyes. If you want to know this scientifically, please try to see it yourself with your vipassanā knowledge.

A Mahāthera, however, may, because of previous practice, be able to see another's skeleton with his eyes open, like the Venerable Mahā-Tissa, who was an expert in skeleton meditation. He always practised internal skeleton meditation as repulsiveness up to the first jhāna, and then vipassanā. He discerned mentality-materiality, their causes, and nature of impermanence, suffering, and non-self. This was his usual practice.

One day he went for alms *(piṇḍapāta)*, from Anuradhapura to Mahāgāma village. On the way, he met a woman who tried to attract his attention with loud laughter. When he heard the sound, he looked her way, saw only her teeth, and then used them for skeleton meditation. Because of his previous constant practice he saw her as a skeleton, and not as a woman. He saw only a skeleton. Then he concentrated on his own skeleton, attained the first jhāna, and practised vipassanā quickly. He attained the Arahant Path standing in the road.

The woman had quarrelled with her husband, and had left home to go to her parents' house. Her husband followed her, and also met Mahā Tissa Mahāthera. He asked him, 'Bhante, did you see a woman go this way?' The Mahāthera answered, 'Oh, lay-supporter *(dāyaka)*, I saw neither man nor woman, I saw only a skeleton going this way.' This story is mentioned in the *Visuddhi·Magga* in the 'Morality Chapter'.[299]

This is an example of how someone who has, like Mahā Tissa Mahāthera, practised skeleton meditation thoroughly may be able to see another's skeleton with his eyes open.

---

[299] VsM.i.15 *'Indriya·Saṁvara·Sīlaṁ'* ('Sense Restraint Morality') PP.i.55

Talk 5

How You Discern Mentality

INTRODUCTION

In our last talk, we discussed how to develop four-elements meditation, and also how to analyse the particles of materiality called 'rūpa-kalāpas'. In this talk, we shall discuss briefly about how to discern mentality *(nāma-·kammaṭṭhāna)*, which is the next stage in vipassanā meditation.[300]

Let me begin by explaining briefly the basic facts of the mind necessary to understand the discernment of mentality.

As is explained in the Abhidhamma, the mind consists of a consciousness *(citta)* that knows its object, and associated mental factors *(cetasika)* that arise with that consciousness. There are fifty-two such associated mental factors, for example: contact *(phassa)*, feeling *(vedanā)*, perception *(saññā)*, volition *(cetanā)*, one-pointedness *(ek·aggatā)*, life faculty *(jīvit·indriya)*, and attention *(manasikāra)*.[301]

There are a total of eighty-nine types of consciousness,[302] and they can be classified according to whether they are wholesome, unwholesome, or indeterminate, or according to their sphere of existence, the sensual sphere *(kām·āvacara)*, fine-material sphere *(rūp·āvacara)*, immaterial sphere *(arūp·āvacara)*, or according to whether they are mundane *(lokiya)* or supramundane *(lokuttarā)*.[303] We may, however, speak of just two basic types of consciousness:

1) The consciousness of the mental process *(citta·vīthi)*.
2) The 'process-separate' *(vīthi·mutta)* consciousness outside the mental process: at rebirth and death, and of the bhavaṅga.[304]

---

[300] Vipassanā refers sometimes to all sixteen knowledges, including the Mentality-Materiality Definition Knowledge and Cause-Apprehending Knowledge (knowledge of materiality and mentality); sometimes vipassanā refers only to knowledge of materiality and mentality as impermanent, suffering and non-self, beginning with the Comprehension Knowledge: for the sixteen knowledges, see Q&A 1.5, p.53.

[301] Mentality consists thus of 1 consciousness + 52 mental factors = 53 types of mentality.

[302] For the eighty-nine types of consciousness, see p.10.

[303] The three spheres: 1) The sensuous sphere *(kām·āvacara)*: deva, human, animal worlds, and hells. 2) The fine-material sphere *(rūp·āvacara)*: Brahma worlds, with only subtle materiality. 3) The immaterial sphere *(arūp·āvacara)*: only mentality, no materiality.

[304] For details regarding these consciousnesses, see Table 1d 'Death and Rebirth', p.188, and notes; for the bhavaṅga, see also Q&A 3.12, p.104, and footnote 184, p.104.

There are six types of mental process. The first five are the eye door-, ear door-, nose door-, tongue door-, and body-door processes, whose respective objects are visible forms, sounds, smells, tastes, and tangibles. They are together called the 'five-door process' *(pañca·dvāra vīthi)*.[305] The sixth type of process has all objects[306] as its objects, and is called the 'mind-door process' *(mano·dvāra·vīthi)*.[307] Each mental process comprises a series of different types of consciousness. The consciousnesses in any one mental process occur according to the natural law of consciousness *(citta·niyāma)*. If you want to discern mentality, you must see them as they occur in the order of that natural law.

To do so, you must first have developed concentration with either *ān·āpāna·sati* (mindfulness-of-breathing), another samatha meditation subject, or four-elements meditation. A pure-vipassanā-vehicle yogi must also have finished the discernment of materiality *(rūpa·kammaṭṭhāna)*, before he starts on discernment of mentality *(nāma·kammaṭṭhāna)*. A samatha-vehicle yogi, however, can choose: he can first discern materiality, or first discern the mentality of the jhānas he has attained (fine-material[308]/immaterial mentality[309]). Although to discern sensual realm mentality, he too needs first to have finished the discernment of materiality.[310]

THE FOUR STAGES TO DISCERNING MENTALITY

Mentality is discerned in four stages:

1) Discerning all the types of consciousness *(citta)* that occur internally.
2) Discerning each and every mental formation *(nāma·dhamma)* in all the types of consciousness one is able to discern.
3) Discerning the sequences of consciousnesses, that is, the mental processes *(vīthi)* that occur at the six sense doors *(dvārā)*.
4) Discerning external mentality *(bahiddha·nāma)* generally.[311]

---

[305] See also table '1c: The Five-Door Process', p.168.

[306] For the mind faculty's taking of all objects, see quotation p.6 ('The Uṇṇābha Brahmin Sutta').

[307] See also table '1b: The Mind-Door Process', p.164.

[308] These are the four jhānas.

[309] These are the immaterial jhānas, but not the Base of Neither-Perception-Nor-Non-Perception. (VsM.xviii.663 *'Diṭṭhi·Visuddhi·Niddesa'* ('Description of View Purification') PP.xviii.3-4).

[310] VsMṬ.xviii.664 *'Diṭṭhi·Visuddhi·Niddesa'* ('Description of View Purification')

[311] M.I.i.10 *'Satipaṭṭhāna·Suttaṁ'* ('The Mindfulness Foundations Sutta') explains: 'In this way he abides contemplating mind as mind internally, or he abides contemplating mind as

(Please see further next page.)

HOW YOU DISCERN JHĀNA MENTAL PROCESSES

If you have attained jhāna with, for example, *ān·āpāna·sati* (mindfulness-of-breathing), the best place to start to discern mentality is the jhāna consciousnesses and associated mental factors.

There are two reasons for this. The first reason is that when developing jhāna, you discerned the five jhāna factors, which means you have some experience in discerning those associated mental factors. The second reason is that the jhāna impulsion-consciousnesses *(jhāna·javana-citta)* occur many times in succession, and are therefore prominent, and easy to discern. This is in contrast to a sensual-sphere process *(kām·āvacara·vīthi)*, in which impulsion *(javana)* occurs only seven times before a new mental process occurs.[312]

So, to discern the mentality of jhāna you begin by re-establishing the first jhāna with, for example, *ān·āpāna·sati*, till the light is bright, brilliant, and radiant. Emerge from it and discern the bhavaṅga (mind door), and the *ān·āpāna paṭibhāga-nimitta* together. When the nimitta appears in the bhavaṅga, discern the mental formations that are the five jhāna factors according to their natural characteristic. The five jhāna factors are:

1) Application *(vitakka)*: directing and placing the mind on the *ān·āpāna paṭibhāga-nimitta.*
2) Sustainment *(vicāra)*: maintaining the mind on the *ān·āpāna paṭibhāga-nimitta.*
3) Joy *(pīti)*: liking for the *ān·āpāna paṭibhāga-nimitta.*
4) Bliss *(sukha)*: happiness about the *ān·āpāna paṭibhāga-nimitta.*
5) One-pointedness *(ek·aggatā)*: one-pointedness of mind on the *ān·āpāna paṭibhāga-nimitta.*

Practise until you can discern all five jhāna factors all at once in each first-jhāna impulsion consciousness *(javana·citta)*. And then proceed to discern all thirty-four mental formations. You begin with either consciousness *(viññāṇa)*, contact *(phassa)*, or feeling *(vedanā)*; whichever is most prominent. Then add one mental formation at a time: discern first one type, then add one, so you discern two types of mental formation; add one more, so you see three; add one more, so you see four etc. until eventu-

---

mind externally.' This is not the psychic power of penetrating the mind of others *(ceto·pariya·ñāṇa)*, but vipassanā power. Hence, it is usually not possible to discern external mentality in detail. See also quotation 'The Aggregates Sutta' p.4.

312 Jhāna-processes are mental processes of the fine-material sphere *(rūp·āvacara)* or immaterial sphere *(arūp·āvacara)*.

ally you see all thirty-four types of mental formation in each first-jhāna impulsion consciousness. They are:

1) consciousness ... *(citta)*	
MENTAL FACTORS *(cetasika)*	
Seven Universals *(sabba·citta·sādhāraṇa)*	**Six Occasionals** *(pakiṇṇaka)*
1) contact ... *(phassa)*	1) application ... *(vitakka)*
2) feeling[313] ... *(vedanā)*	2) sustainment ... *(vicāra)*
3) perception ... *(saññā)*	3) decision ... *(adhimokkha)*
4) volition ... *(cetanā)*	4) energy ... *(viriya)*
5) one-pointedness[314] ... *(ek·aggatā)*	5) joy ... *(pīti)*
6) life faculty ... *(jīvit·indriya)*	6) desire ... *(chanda)*
7) attention ... *(manasikāra)*	
Nineteen Beautiful Universals *(sobhana·sādhāraṇa)*[315]	
1) faith ... *(saddhā)*	11) lightness of consciousness ... *(citta·lahutā)*
2) mindfulness ... *(sati)*	12) flexibility of [mental] body ... *(kāya·mudutā)*
3) conscience ... *(hiri)*	13) flexibility of consciousness ... *(citta·mudutā)*
4) shame ... *(ottapa)*	14) wieldiness of [mental] body ... *(kāya·kammaññatā)*
5) non-greed ... *(a·lobha)*	15) wieldiness of consciousness ... *(citta·kammaññatā)*
6) non-hatred ... *(a·dosa)*	16) proficiency of [mental] body ... *(kāya·pāguññatā)*
7) ever-evenness ... *(tatra·majjhattatā)*	17) proficiency of consciousness ... *(citta·pāguññatā)*
8) tranquillity of [mental] body[316] ... *(kāya·passaddhi)*	18) rectitude of [mental] body ... *(kāy·ujukatā)*
9) tranquillity of consciousness ... *(citta·passaddhi)*	19) rectitude of consciousness ... *(citt·ujukatā)*
10) lightness of [mental] body ... *(kāya·lahutā)*	
1) **Non-Delusion** *(a·moha)*: wisdom faculty ... *(paññ·indriya)*	

After this, discern all the types of mental formation in the sequence of six types of consciousness that comprises a mind-door process *(mano·dvāra·vīthi)* of the first jhāna. The six types of consciousness are first:[317]

---

313 The five underlined factors are the jhāna factors.

314 one-pointedness: a synonym for concentration *(samādhi)*.

315 There are twenty-five beautiful mental factors in all, but these nineteen are present in any wholesome consciousness.

316 tranquillity of body/ consciousness: body = three mental aggregates (feeling, perception, and formations); consciousness = the consciousness aggregate. There are six such modes, attributes, of wholesome mentality: 1) tranquillity (opposite restlessness); 2) lightness (opposite sloth&torpor); 3) flexibility (opposite the mental rigidity of views and conceit); 4) wieldiness (opposite the remaining hindrances); 5) proficiency (opposite faithlessness, etc.), 6) rectitude (opposite deceit, dishonesty, etc.). When there is tranquillity, etc. of the mental body, there comes to be also tranquillity, etc. of the material body. That is why The Buddha divided these mental attributes into two.

1) A mind-door adverting consciousness *(mano·dvār·āvajjana)*: 12 mental formations
2) A preparatory consciousness *(parikamma)*: 34 mental formations
3) An access consciousness *(upacāra)*: 34 mental formations
4) A conformity consciousness *(anuloma)*: 34 mental formations
5) A change-of-lineage consciousness *(gotrabhu)*: 34 mental formations
6) An uninterrupted sequence of jhāna impulsion-consciousnesses *(jhāna·javana·citta)*: 34 mental formations, which you have by now already discerned.

To discern all these mental formations, you must again re-establish the first jhāna, such as the first *ān·āpāna* jhāna, emerge from it, and again discern the bhavaṅga and *paṭibhāga-nimitta* together. When the nimitta appears in the bhavaṅga, discern the jhāna mind-door process that just occured. You discern each of the different consciousnesses in the first-jhāna mind-door process, and their twelve or thirty-four types of mental formation.

After this, and to give you an understanding of mentality as a whole, discern the characteristic common to all mentality *(nāma)*, to all mental formations, which is the characteristic of bending towards *(namana)* and adhering to the object, in this case, the *ān·āpāna paṭibhāga-nimitta.*

You need, in the same way, to discern and analyse the mentality of also the second, third, and fourth *ān·āpāna* jhānas, as well as any other jhānas of other meditation subjects that you have attained; for example, foulness-, white kasiṇa-, and loving-kindness jhāna.

If, however, you have only access concentration, with four-elements meditation, you must begin your discernment of mentality there: you cannot discern the mentality of a jhāna consciousness without jhāna. In that case, you must with four-elements meditation re-establish access concentration, where the translucent form of your body sparkles and emits light. After resting there for some time, turn to vipassanā with a refreshed and clear mind, and discern the mentality of that access concentration.

Having now discerned the different mental processes in all your previous samatha practice, be it access or jhāna concentration, you then move on to discern the different mental formations of a sensual-sphere process *(kām·āvacara vīthi)*.

---

[317] See table '1a: The Jhāna-Attainment Process', p.44.

1b: **The Mind-Door Process** *(mano·dvāra vīthi)* (with colour object as example)[1]

- One consciousness lasts one consciousness-moment *(citta·kkhaṇa)*, with three stages: arising *(uppāda)* ↑, standing *(ṭhiti)* |, dissolution *(bhaṅga)* ↓.
- In between each mental process arises a number of life-continuum consciousnesses (see table '1d: 'Death and Rebirth').
- Before the mind-door process, there is a five-door process or other mind-door process.

CONSCIOUSNESS MOMENT *Citta·Kkhaṇa*	(Before the mental process)		
	⇒⇒⇒⇒⇒⇒	⇒	⇒
OBJECT *Ārammaṇa*	Previous life's near-death object.		
CONSCIOUSNESS *Citta*	Life-Continuum *Bhavaṅga* ↑|↓	Trembling Life-Continuum *Bhavaṅga·Calana* ↑|↓	Arrest Life-Continuum *Bhavaṅg·Upaccheda* ↑|↓
	Resultant *Vipāka*		

CONSCIOUSNESS MOMENT *Citta·Kkhaṇa*	1⇒	2⇒	3⇒	4⇒	5⇒	6⇒	7⇒	8⇒	9⇒	10⇒	(After the mental process) ⇒⇒⇒⇒⇒⇒⇒
OBJECT *Ārammaṇa*	Colour Object *Rūp·Ārammaṇa*										Previous life's near-death object.
CONSCIOUSNESS *Citta*	Mind-Door Adverting *Mano·Dvār·Āvajjana* ↑|↓	1st Impulsion *Javana* ↑|↓	2nd Impulsion *Javana* ↑|↓	3rd Impulsion *Javana* ↑|↓	4th Impulsion *Javana* ↑|↓	5th Impulsion *Javana* ↑|↓	6th Impulsion *Javana* ↑|↓	7th Impulsion *Javana* ↑|↓	1st Registration *Tad·Ārammaṇa* ↑|↓	2nd Registration *Tad·Ārammaṇa* ↑|↓	Life-Continuum *Bhavaṅga* ↑|↓
	Functional *Kiriya*	**Kamma**							Resultant *Vipāka*	Resultant *Vipāka*	Resultant *Vipāka*

[1] DhSA *'Kām·Āvacara·Kusala·Pada·Bhājanīyaṁ'* ('Sensual-Sphere Wholesome Section Classification' E.I.ii.97-99 & AbS.iv.17 *'Mano·Dvāra·Vīthi'* (Mind-Door Process') (CMA.iv.12)

Further Notes for Table 1b 'The Mind-Door Process'

- Cognition follows a fixed procedure, according to the natural law of consciousness *(citta·niyāmā)*. For example, visual cognition:[318]

1st) Eye-door process that 'picks-up' the object; cognizes colour. (See table '1c: The Five-Door Process', p.168.)
2nd) Mind-door process that perceives the colour; knows the past colour, the object of the eye-door process.
3rd) Mind-door process that knows which colour it is; knows the colour's name.
4th) Mind-door process that knows the object's 'meaning'; sees the whole image, a concept determined by past experience (perception *(saññā)*).
5th) Mind-door process that judges and feels. This is the beginning of true cognition. In the preceding mental processes, the volition of the impulsions is only weak, which means the kamma can produce a result only in that life's continuance *(pavatti)*: it cannot produce a rebirth-linking consciousness *(paṭisandhi·citta)*.

It is from the fifth mind-door process onwards that the concept is known: 'a man', 'a woman', 'a pot', 'a sarong', 'gold', 'silver' etc. And it is from that mental process onwards that there is mental proliferation *(papañca)*, and the accomplishment of kamma: accomplished by the mental factor volition *(cetanā)* of each impulsion consciousness, which takes the same object.

With wise attention *(yoniso manasikāra)*, wholesome kamma is accomplished with, for example, respect for and worship of one's teacher, a Buddha-statue or a bhikkhu; knowing one's samatha meditation subject, and with vipassanā knowledge seeing formations as impermanence *(anicca)*, suffering *(dukkha)*, non-self *(an·atta)*, or foulness *(asubha)*.

With unwise attention *(ayoniso manasikāra)*, unwholesome kamma is accomplished when one sees self, husband, wife, children, property, etc. as existing according to reality: as permanence *(nicca)*, happiness *(sukha)*, self *(atta)*, or beauty *(subha)*.

With this same object and perception arise countless mental processes (series of mental formations *(saṅkhārā)*), reinforcing the cognition, until again the mind adverts to a new object.

HOW YOU DISCERN SENSUAL SPHERE PROCESSES

WISE AND UNWISE ATTENTION

A jhāna-attainment process (which is a mind-door process of either the fine-material sphere or immaterial sphere) is always wholesome: it can never be unwholesome. But a sensual-sphere process (either a five-door-, or a mind-door process) is either wholesome or unwholesome: it depends on wise attention *(yoniso manasikāra)* or unwise attention *(ayoniso manasikāra)*.

318 For further details, see Q&As 3.5, 3.11, 7.9, 7.11, 7.12, and Abs.

Attention determines whether a sensual-sphere process is wholesome or unwholesome.

If you look at an object and know it as materiality, mentality, cause or effect, impermanence, suffering, non-self, or repulsiveness, then your attention is wise attention, and the impulsion consciousness is wholesome.

If you look at an object and see it as a concept, such as a person, man, woman, being, gold, silver, or see it as permanence, happiness, or self, then your attention is unwise attention, and the impulsion consciousness is unwholesome.

In exceptional cases, however, an impulsion consciousness connected with a concept may be wholesome, for example, when practising loving-kindness and making offerings. You will see the difference when you discern those mental processes.

HOW YOU DISCERN MIND-DOOR PROCESSES

To discern sensual-sphere processes, you should begin by discerning a mind-door process, because there the types of consciousness are fewer. You may start with a wholesome mind-door process. A wholesome mind-door process of the sensual sphere consists of a sequence of three types of consciousness:

1) A mind-door adverting consciousness *(mano·dvār·āvajjana)*: 12 mental formations
2) Seven impulsion consciousnesses *(javana·citta)*: if unwholesome, 16/18/19/20/21/22 mental formations, if wholesome 32/33/34/35 mental formations.
3) Two registration consciousnesses *(tadārammaṇa·citta)*: 34/33/32/12/11 mental formations

First, you discern the bhavaṅga (mind door), and then the eye translucency *(cakkhu·pasāda)* in a rūpa-kalāpa in the eye. When it appears in the bhavaṅga, you cognize it with wise attention as: 'This is eye-translucency', 'This is materiality', 'This is impermanent', 'This is suffering', 'This is non-self', or 'This is repulsive'. And there will occur a sensual-sphere mind-door process.

Then, to discern the different types of mental formation of that mind-door process's consciousnesses, you do as you did with the jhāna mind-door process: begin with either consciousness, feeling, or contact: whichever is most prominent. Then add one mental formation at a time: discern first one type, then add one, so you discern two types of mental formation; add one more, so you see three; add one more, so you see four etc.

until eventually you see all thirty-four, thirty-three or thirty-two types of mental formation of each consciousness of a sensual-sphere wholesome mind-door process. You should do this again and again until you are satisfied.

You need to thus discern the mind-door processes that take place when you look at each type of materiality that you examined when you discerned materiality *(rūpa·kammaṭṭhāna)*.[319]

HOW YOU DISCERN FIVE-DOOR PROCESSES

Once you have finished discerning the mind-door processes, you should go on to discern the five-door processes, starting with the eye-door process.

To discern the mental formations of each consciousness in an eye-door process, you cause an eye-door process to occur. First, you first discern the eye-translucency (eye door), then the bhavaṅga (mind door), and then both at once. Then concentrate on the colour of a nearby group of rūpa-kalāpas as it appears in both doors, and cognize it with wise attention as 'This is colour', etc. And there will occur a first an eye-door process, and then (in accordance with the natural law of consciousness *(citta·niyāma)*) many mind-door processes, all with the same object.

The eye-door process consists of a sequence of seven types of consciousness.

1) A five-door adverting consciousness *(pañca·dvār·āvajjana)*: 11 mental formations
2) An eye consciousness *(cakkhu·viññāṇa)*: 8 mental formations
3) A receiving consciousness *(sampaṭicchana)*: 11 mental formations
4) An investigating consciousness *(santīraṇa)*: 11/12 mental formations
5) A determining consciousness *(voṭṭhapana)*: 12 mental formations
6) Seven impulsion consciousnesses *(javana·citta)*: if unwholesome, 16/18/19/20/21/22 mental formations, if wholesome 32/33/34/35 mental formations
7) Two registration consciousnesses *(tadārammaṇa·citta)*: 11/12/32/33/34 mental formations

---

319 When discerning materiality, all types of materiality need to be discerned, but when practising vipassanā (discerning their impermanence, suffering, and non-self nature), only concrete materiality is examined. Table '2a: The Twenty-Eight Types of Materiality' p.137 lists all the different types of materiality, and Talk 4 'How You Discern Materiality' explains how to discern them.

1c: **The Five-Door Process** *(pañca·dvāra·vīthi)* (eye/ear/nose/tongue/body-door process: example is eye-door process.)[1]

CONSCIOUSNESS MOMENT *Citta·Kkhaṇa*	(Before the mental process) ⇒⇒…⇒⇒	1⇒	2⇒	3⇒	4⇒	5⇒	6⇒	7⇒	8⇒
OBJECT *Ārammaṇa*	Previous life's near-death object.				Colour Object *Rūp·Ārammaṇa*				
CONSCIOUSNESS *Citta*	Life-Continuum *Bhavaṅga* ↑|↓	Past Life-Continuum *Atīta·Bhavaṅga* ↑|↓	Trembling Life-Continuum *Bhavaṅga·Calana* ↑|↓	Arrest Life-Continuum *Bhavaṅg·Upaccheda* ↑|↓	Five-Door Adverting *Pañca·Dvār·Āvajjana* ↑|↓	Eye Consciousness *Cakkhu·Viññāṇa* ↑|↓	Receiving *Sampaṭi·Cchana* ↑|↓	Investigation *Santīraṇa* ↑|↓	Determining *Voṭṭhapana* ↑|↓
	Resultant *Vipāka*				Functional *Kiriya*	Resultant *Vipāka*			Functional *Kiriya*

CONSCIOUSNESS MOMENT *Citta·Kkhaṇa*	9⇒	10⇒	11⇒	12⇒	13⇒	14⇒	15⇒	16⇒	17⇒	(After the mental process) ⇒⇒⇒…⇒⇒⇒
OBJECT *Ārammaṇa*	Colour Object *Rūp·Ārammaṇa*									Previous life's near-death object.
CONSCIOUSNESS *Citta*	1st Impulsion *Javana* ↑|↓	2nd Impulsion *Javana* ↑|↓	3rd Impulsion *Javana* ↑|↓	4th Impulsion *Javana* ↑|↓	5th Impulsion *Javana* ↑|↓	6th Impulsion *Javana* ↑|↓	7th Impulsion *Javana* ↑|↓	1st Registration *Tad·Ārammaṇa* ↑|↓	2nd Registration *Tad·Ārammaṇa* ↑|↓	Life-Continuum *Bhavaṅga* ↑|↓
	Kamma							Resultant *Vipāka*		Resultant *Vipāka*

[1] VsM.i.15 *'Indriya·Saṁvara·Sīlaṁ'* ('Faculty-Restraint Morality') PP.i.57; VsM.xiv.455 *'Viññāṇa·Kkhandha·Kathā'* ('Discussion of the Consciousness-Aggregate) PP.xiv.114-123; DhSA.i.1 *'Kām·Āvacara·Kusala·Pada·Bhājanīyaṁ'* ('Sensual-Sphere Wholesome Section Classification') E.I.ii.96; DhSA.I.iii *'Vipāk·Uddhāra·Kathā'* ('Discussion of the Result-Apprehension') E.I.x.ii.359-360; & AbS.iv.10 *'Pañca·Dvāra·Vīthi'* (Five-Door Process') CMA.iv.6.

Further Notes for Table 1c 'The Five-Door Process'

- One consciousness lasts one consciousness moment *(citta·kkhaṇa)*, with three stages: arising *(uppāda)* ↑, standing *(ṭhiti)* |, dissolution *(bhaṅga)*↓
- The material object that is cognized by a five-door process lasts 17 consciousness moments.
- All five-door processes (eye-, ear-, nose-, tongue-, body door) follow the same procedure, according to the natural law of consciousness *(citta·niyāma)*.
  Thus, the five-door process only 'picks up' the object (the eye-door process only cognizes that there is colour), does not yet 'know' the object (colour). The 'knowing' of the colour and the object takes place at the fourth and subsequent mental processes.[320]

After this follows a sequence of bhavaṅga consciousnesses, and then the three types of consciousness of the mind-door process, as described before:

1) A mind-door adverting consciousness
2) Seven impulsion consciousnesses
3) Two registration consciousnesses

To discern the different types of mental formation of the consciousnesses of those processes (the eye-door and subsequent mind-door processes that take the same object), you do as before: begin with either consciousness, feeling, or contact: whichever is most prominent.[321] Then, as before, add one at a time, until you see all the different types of mental formation of each consciousness.

As you did for the eye door, you then discern the mental processes of the other four doors: the ear, nose, tongue, and body.

By this stage, you will have developed the ability to discern mentality associated with wholesome consciousnesses, and now need to discern mentality associated with also unwholesome consciousnesses. To do this, you simply take the same objects as you did for the wholesome consciousnesses, and instead pay unwise attention to them.

This is merely a brief explanation, but the examples given here should be sufficient for you at least to understand what is involved in discerning mentality internally.

In summary, you have so far completed the first three stages of discerning mentality:

---

[320] See table '1b: The Mind-Door Process', p.164.

[321] For details, see tables 1b & 1c, p.164*ff*.

1) You have discerned all the types of consciousness *(citta)* that occur internally.[322]
2) You have discerned each and every mental formation *(nāma·dhammā)* in all the types of consciousness.
3) You have discerned the sequences of consciousnesses, that is, the mental processes *(vīthi)* that occur at the six sense doors.

As mentioned earlier, there is also a fourth stage to discerning mentality. The fourth stage is to discern mentality also externally.

HOW YOU DISCERN EXTERNAL MENTALITY

To discern mentality externally, you need always first to discern materiality externally.

FIRST YOU DISCERN MATERIALITY INTERNALLY/EXTERNAL

You begin by discerning the four elements internally, and then externally in the clothes you are wearing. You will see that your clothes break down into rūpa-kalāpas, and that you are able to discern the eight types of materiality in each. They are temperature-born nutritive-essence octad-kalāpas *(utuja oj·aṭṭhamaka·kalāpa)*, and the temperature they arise from is the temperature in rūpa-kalāpas.[323]

You should alternate between the internal and external materiality three or four times, and then with the light of concentration discern external materiality a little farther away, such as the floor. You will also there be able to discern the eight types of materiality in each rūpa-kalāpa, and should again alternate between the internal and external three or four times.

In this way, gradually expand your field of discernment to the materiality in the building in which you are sitting, the area around it, including the trees, other buildings, etc., until you discern all inanimate materiality externally. While doing this, you will see also materiality co-existent with consciousness (translucent materiality, etc.) in the inanimate objects: it is the insects and other small animals in the trees, buildings, etc.

Once you have discerned all inanimate materiality externally, you now go on to discern the materiality of other living beings, external materiality that is coexistent with consciousness*(sa·viññāṇaka)*. You discern only their materiality, and see that they are not a man, a woman, a person, or a be-

---

[322] It is understood that the supramundane types of consciousness are as yet out of reach.

[323] For details regarding temperature-born nutritive-essence octad-kalāpas etc., see p.113.

ing: only materiality. Discern all external materiality at once, then all the different types of materiality both internally and externally.

To do this, you should first see the six basic types of rūpa-kalāpa[324] in your own eye, and then in an external eye, another being's eye. As when you analysed materiality, discern the fifty-four types of materiality, but now do it both internally and externally.[325] Do the same for the remaining five sense bases, and remaining types of materiality.

DISCERNING MENTALITY INTERNALLY AND EXTERNALLY

Having now discerned materiality completely, you proceed to discern mentality internally and externally.

You discern mentality internally by again starting with the mind door, and then five-door processes, discerning all their wholesome and unwholesome mental formations.

To do this externally, you do as you did internally, but discern the eye door and bhavaṅga (mind door) of other beings in general. Then, when the colour of a group of rūpa-kalāpas appears in both doors, discern also here the eye-door process that occurs, and the many mind-door processes that occur, all with the same object.

You should do this again and again, internally and externally, and again for each of the other four sense doors, until you are satisfied. If you have jhāna, you should also discern external jhāna mind-door processes. That may be in another meditator, although jhāna concentration is now very, very rare in the human world. But you will find beings in jhāna in the deva- and Brahma-worlds.

Following the same procedure as before, you should gradually extend your range of discernment until you can see materiality throughout the infinite universe, and can see mentality throughout the infinite universe. Then you should discern them together throughout the infinite universe.

Lastly, you define all that mentality and materiality with wisdom to see no beings, men, or women: only mentality and materiality throughout the infinite universe. That concludes the discernment of mentality *(nāma·kamma-ṭṭhāna)*.

Having reached this stage in your meditation, you will have developed concentration, and will have used it to discern all twenty-eight kinds of

---

[324] Six basic types of rūpa-kalāpa: 1) eye decad-kalāpas; 2) body decad-kalāpas; 3) sex decad-kalāpas; 4) consciousness-born octad-kalāpas; 5) temperature-born octad-kalāpas; 6) nutriment-born octad-kalāpas. See also p.131*f.*

[325] Although you have in fact discerned sixty-three types of materiality, you do here discern only fifty-four. Why you do this is explained in detail, p.131*f.*

materiality,[326] and all fifty-three kinds of mentality throughout the infinite universe:[327] you will have completed the first vipassanā knowledge, the Mentality-Materiality Definition Knowledge *(Nāma·Rūpa·Pariccheda·Ñāṇa)*.

Our next talk will be about the next stage of vipassanā: the discernment of dependent origination *(paṭicca·samuppāda)*.

[326] For the twenty-eight types of materiality, see p.137.

[327] For the fifty-three types of mentality, see footnote 301, p.159.

QUESTIONS AND ANSWERS 5

Question 5.1 The eight attainments *(samāpatti)*[328] make it possible to attain the Mentality-Materiality Definition Knowledge *(Nāma-Rūpa·Pariccheda·Ñāṇa)*, and to see their subtle arising and perishing, so as to become disgusted with them, and attain the Path Knowledge *(Magga·Ñāṇa)*. Are there, apart from this, other benefits to the eight attainments?

Answer 5.1 There are five benefits to jhāna concentration:[329]

The first benefit of jhāna concentration is a present blissful abiding *(diṭṭha·dhamma·sukha·vihāra)*: enjoying jhāna happiness in this very life. This refers to Arahants. Even though pure vipassanā Arahants naturally possess the supramundane jhānas *(lokuttāra·jhāna)*, they may still want to develop the mundane jhānas *(lokiya·jhāna)*, because they want to enjoy the blissful abiding of jhāna. Since they are Arahants, with all defilements removed by Path Knowledge (which means also their hindrances have been removed), it is very easy for them to develop jhāna. Another reason why they will usually develop jhāna is that they want to attain cessation *(nirodh·ānisaṁsa)*: it requires mastery of the eight attainments.

A bhikkhu's duty is to learn the scriptures *(pariyatti)*, to practise samatha-vipassanā meditation *(paṭipatti)*, and to attain the four Paths and four Fruitions *(paṭivedha)*. That is what Arahants have done, so there is no more work for them to do. They practise jhāna concentration for no reason other than the enjoyment of jhāna bliss *(jhāna·sukha)* in this very life.

The second benefit of jhāna concentration is the benefit of vipassanā *(vipassan·ānisaṁsa)*.[330] Jhāna concentration is a support for vipassanā knowledge, because with jhāna, one can see ultimate mentality-materiality and their causes clearly, and can discern their impermanent, suffering, and non-self nature.

When a yogi has practised vipassanā thoroughly, especially up to the Path Knowledge *(Magga·Ñāṇa)* and Fruition Knowledge *(Phala·Ñāṇa)*, or the Formations-Equanimity Knowledge *(Saṅkhār·Upekkhā·Ñāṇa)*, jhānas are usu-

---

[328] The four mundane jhānas, and four immaterial jhānas.

[329] Vis.xi.362 *'Samādhi-Ānisaṁsa·Kathā'* ('Discussion of the Concentration-Benefits') PP.xi.120*ff.*

[330] This is called vipassanā-basis jhāna *(vipassanā·pādaka·jjhāna)*. VsM.ibid. explains: 'When ordinary people and Trainees [non-Arahant Noble Ones] develop it [concentration], thinking "After emerging we shall exercise vipassanā with concentrated consciousness," the development of absorption concentration provides them with the benefit of vipassanā by serving as the proximate cause for vipassanā, and so too does access concentration.' This is followed by a quotation from S.III.I.i.5 *'Samādhi·Suttaṁ'* ('The Concentration Sutta'): see p.23. See also quotation, footnote 37, p.12.

ally stable. They make the vipassanā knowledge clear, bright, strong and powerful. That strong and powerful vipassanā knowledge, in its turn, also protects the jhānas from falling down.

Then again, when a yogi has been practising vipassanā for a long time, tiredness may occur. Then he should go into jhāna for long, to rest the mind. Refreshed he can then switch back to vipassanā. When it happens again he can again rest in jhāna.[331]

So, because of concentration, vipassanā is clear, bright, strong and powerful, and well protected. vipassanā in its turn destroys the defilements that hinder concentration, and keeps it stable. samatha protects vipassanā and vice-versa.

Furthermore, the concentration of the eight attainments is not only a support for the discernment of mentality-materiality and their causes, because those eight attainments are themselves mentality, and included in the discernment of mentality.[332] One enters into, for example, the first jhāna, emerges, and then contemplates the formations *(saṅkhāra)* associated with that jhāna as impermanence, suffering, and non-self. Then one enters the second jhāna, and does the same. And one can do this with all eight attainments, up to the fourth immaterial jhāna. It is called samatha and vipassanā yoked together *(yuganaddha)*, like two bullocks pulling one cart: pulling one towards Path, Fruition and Nibbāna.[333] If one practises vipassanā up to the Formations-Equanimity Knowledge *(Saṅkhār·Upekkhā·Ñāṇa)*, one can also keep one's discernment of the jhāna formations to only one of the jhānas. With such strong and powerful samatha yoked with strong and powerful vipassanā, one may attain Path and Fruition, up to Arahantship.

The <u>third benefit</u> of jhāna concentration is psychic powers *(abhiññ·āni-saṁsa)*: If one wants to master the mundane psychic powers, like the recollection of past lives *(pubbe·nivās·ānussati abhiññā)*, the divine eye *(dibba·cakkhu)*, the divine ear *(dibba·sota)*, knowing the consciousness of others *(para·citta vijānana)*, and the supernormal powers *(iddhi·vidha)*, flying, walking on water, etc., one must develop the ten kasiṇas and eight attainments *(samāpatti)* in fourteen ways.[334]

The <u>fourth benefit</u> of jhāna concentration is what is called 'a specific existence' *(bhava·visesāvah·ānisaṁsa)*. That is, if one wants rebirth in a brahma

---

[331] For a more detailed explanation, see p.123.

[332] See p.161*ff*.

[333] This is explained in A.IV.IV.iv.10 *'Yuganaddha·Suttaṃ'* ('The Yoked Sutta').

[334] For details, see VsM.xii *'Iddhi·Vidha·Niddesa'* ('Description of Direct Knowledge').

realm at death, one must develop concentration such as the ten kasiṇa-, *ān·āpānā*-, or loving-kindness jhāna. But to be sure of rebirth in a brahma realm means the jhāna must be maintained up to the moment of death.

The fifth benefit of jhāna concentration is cessation *(nirodh·ānisaṁsa)*: the attainment of cessation *(nirodha·samāpatti)*, which is the temporary cessation of consciousness *(citta)*, associated mental factors *(cetasika)* and consciousness-born materiality *(cittaja·rūpa)*. 'Temporary' means usually for a day up to seven days, depending on one's prior determination *(adhiṭṭhāna)*.

Only Non-Returners *(Anāgāmi)* and Arahants can attain cessation. And for Arahants, apart from when they are asleep, and apart from when they pay attention to concepts, they never stop seeing the arising and perishing, or just the perishing of mentality-materiality and their causes: all day, all night, for days, months, and years.[335] Sometimes they get disenchanted and 'bored', and just do not want to see those 'phenomena of perishing' *(bhaṅga·dhamma)* anymore. But, because their life span is not over, it is not yet time for their Parinibbāna. Therefore, to stop seeing those phenomena of perishing, they enter cessation.

Why do they never stop seeing those phenomena? Because, with Arahantship, they have destroyed all defilements (including the hindrances), and have therefore concentration. The concentrated mind sees ultimate phenomena *(paramattha·dhamma)* as they really are, so it sees always ultimate mentality-materiality as they really are, which are the 'phenomena of perishing'. When one enters cessation, let's say for seven days, one does not see the phenomena of perishing, because (for as long as the attainment lasts) the consciousness and associated mental factors that would have known those phenomena have ceased.

Although Arahants are able to abide in Nibbāna-attainment, they may still prefer to abide in cessation, because although the Nibbāna-attainment takes the Unformed as object, there remains the mental formation of feeling. But in the attainment of cessation the only formation that remains is the material formation of kamma-, temperature- and nutriment-born materiality: no consciousness-born materiality, and no consciousness.

To enter cessation, one must establish the first jhāna, emerge from it, and discern the first-jhāna dhammas as impermanence, suffering, or non-self. One must do the same progressively up to the base of boundless consciousness, which is the second immaterial jhāna *(viññāṇañc·āyatana·jhāna)*.

---

[335] For related details, see 'How You Develop the Arise&Perish Knowledge' p.216*ff.* Details regarding the path to Arahantship, and thence the Arahant's 'permanent dwelling' (seeing only the continuous rising and perishing of formations) are described by The Buddha in S.III.I.vi.5 *'Satta·Ṭṭhāna·Suttaṁ'* ('The Seven Cases Sutta').

Then one must enter the base of nothingness, the third immaterial jhāna *(ākiñcaññ·āyatana·jhāna)*, emerge from it and make four determinations:

1) To reflect on the limit of one's life-span, and then within that to determine a period for the attainment of cessation (for example, seven days), at the end of which one will emerge from the attainment.
2) To emerge from the attainment of cessation should one be wanted by a Buddha.
3) To emerge from the attainment of cessation should one be wanted by the Saṅgha.
4) That the property in one's immediate surroundings not be destroyed by, for example, fire or water. One's robes and the seat one is sitting on is protected by the attainment itself. But the furniture in the room one is in, or the room itself or the building will be protected only if one makes this fourth determination.

Then one enters the base of neither perception nor non-perception, the fourth immaterial jhāna *(neva·saññā·n·āsaññ·āyatana·jhāna)*. After only one or two consciousness moments in that attainment, one enters cessation for the determined period, for example, seven days. One does not see anything while in the attainment, because all consciousness and associated mental factors have ceased.[336]

Question 5.2 Which is easiest and quickest for the attainment of Nibbāna: using theory to perceive impermanence, suffering, and non-self, or using concentration to discern ultimate phenomena *(paramattha·dhamma)*?

Answer 5.2 What is impermanence? Impermanence is the five aggregates.[337] This definition is mentioned in many commentaries. If a yogi sees the five aggregates clearly, he can see impermanence, suffering, and non-self: no problem. But without seeing the five aggregates, how can he see impermanence, suffering and non-self? If he tries to do so without seeing the five aggregates, his vipassanā will be only reciting vipassanā; not true vipassanā. Only true vipassanā produces the Path and Fruition Knowledges.

What are the five aggregates? They are the materiality aggregate, the feeling aggregate, the perception aggregate, the formations aggregate and the consciousness aggregate, of past, future, present, internal and external, gross and subtle, inferior and superior, far and near. The materiality

---

336 VsM.xxiii.879 *'Nirodha·Samāpatti·Kathā'* ('Cessation-Attainment Discussion') PP.xxii.43

337 *Aniccanti khandapañcakaṁ... Pañcakkhandhā aniccanti.* (VbhA.ii.1 *'Suttanta-·bhājanīya·Vaṇṇanā'* ('Sutta-Classification Description')). Quoted also Q&A 2.3, p.77.

aggregate is the twenty-eight types of materiality *(rūpa)*. The feeling-, perception- and formations aggregate are the fifty-two associated mental factors *(cetasika)*. The consciousness aggregate is the eighty-nine types of consciousness *(citta)*. The twenty-eight types of materiality are what is called materiality, and the fifty-two associated mental factors and eighty-nine types of consciousness are what is called mentality. So, the five aggregates and mentality-materiality are one and the same thing.

These are all ultimate mentality-materiality. If a yogi sees these ultimate mentality-materiality, he can practise vipassanā, and see the impermanent, suffering, and non-self nature of these mentality-materiality. But if he cannot see ultimate mentality-materiality, how can he practise vipassanā, since they and their causes are the necessary objects of vipassanā knowledge? This is true vipassanā. Only true vipassanā produces the Path and Fruition Knowledges.

In the *'Mahā·Sati·Paṭṭhāna'* sutta,[338] The Buddha taught that to attain Nibbāna there is only one way *(ek·āyana)*: no other way. What is the way? The Buddha said to practise concentration first, because a concentrated mind can give rise to the seeing of ultimate mentality-materiality and their causes. Again, a concentrated mind can give rise to the seeing of impermanence, suffering, and non-self nature of ultimate mentality-materiality and their causes.[339] But we cannot say which is the quickest way to attain Nibbāna: it depends on one's *pāramī*.

For example, the Venerable Sāriputta needed about two weeks' hard work to attain the Arahant Path and Fruition, whereas the Venerable Mahāmoggallāna needed only seven days. And, Bāhiya Dārucīriya needed only to listen to a very short discourse: *Diṭṭhe diṭṭhamattaṁ....* **'In the seen, the seen merely will be....**[340] The speed with which they each attained Arahantship was because of their individual *pāramī*.

The Venerable Sāriputta and the Venerable Mahāmoggallāna had developed their *pāramī* for one incalculable *(a·saṅkhyeyya)* and a hundred thousand aeons *(kappa)*, and Bāhiya Dārucīriya for about one hundred thousand aeons. The Venerable Sāriputta and the Venerable Mahāmoggallāna's Arahant Paths were associated with the Chief Disciple's Enlightenment Knowledge *(Agga·Sāvaka·Bodhi·Ñāṇa)*, whereas Bāhiya Dārucīriya's Arahant-Path was associated with only the Great Disciple's Enlightenment Know-

---

338 D.ii.9 'The Great Mindfulness-Foundation Sutta'

339 See quotation, footnote 45, p.14.

340 U.i.10 *'Bāhiya·Suttaṁ'* ('The Bāhiya Sutta')

ledge *(Mahā·Sāvaka·Bodhi·Ñāṇa)*. The Chief Disciple's Enlightenment Knowledge is higher than the Great Disciple's Enlightenment Knowledge.[341]

Since there is only one way to attain Nibbāna, these disciples did not attain Arahantship because of a wish: they attained Arahantship through present effort supported by their past effort, their *pāramī*.

Question 5.3 The round of rebirths *(saṁsāra)* is without beginning or end. Beings are also infinite in number, so those who have been our mother are infinite too. How can we develop loving-kindness by contemplating that all beings have been our mother? Can we attain loving-kindness jhāna *(mettā jhāna)* by contemplating that all beings have been our mother?

Answer 5.3 Loving-kindness meditation does not concern the past and future. It concerns only the present. Only an object of the present can produce loving-kindness jhāna *(mettā·jhāna)*, not one of the past or future: we cannot attain jhāna by extending loving-kindness to the dead. In the endless round of rebirths *(saṁsāra)*, there may very well be no one who has not been our father or mother, but loving-kindness meditation is not concerned with the endless round of rebirths. It is not necessary to consider that this was our mother, this our father.

In the *'Karaṇīya·Mettā'* sutta, The Buddha said:

Mātā yathā niyaṁputtamāyusā ekaputtamanurakkhe; evampi sabbabhūtesu, mānasaṁ bhāvaye aparimāṇaṁ.

This means that just as a mother with an only son would give up even her life for him, so a bhikkhu should extend loving-kindness to all beings. This is The Buddha's instruction. But the attitude of a mother cannot alone lead to jhāna. If we extend loving-kindness with the thought, 'May this person be well and happy' it will produce jhāna.

Question 5.4 (The following questions are all covered by the same answer.)

- Was there a Bodhisatta during The Buddha's time? If so, did he attain a Path or was he just an ordinary person *(puthu·jjana)*?
- Why can a Noble One *(Ariya)* not become a Bodhisatta?
- Can a disciple *(sāvaka)* change to become a Bodhisatta? If not, why not?
- When by following the Sayadaw's teaching one is able to attain the Path and Fruition Knowledges of Stream-Entry *(Sot·Āpatti·Magga·Ñāṇa/ Sot·Āpatti·Phala·Ñāṇa)*, can one choose to not do so, because of a desire and vow to practise the Bodhisatta path?

---

[341] For the four types of person who attains Nibbāna, see Q&A 4.3, p.143; for the four types of Arahant path, see Q&A 4.7, p.154.

Answer 5.4 One can change one's mind before attaining a Path or Fruition, but not afterwards. In many suttas, The Buddha taught that the Path occurs according to a law of nature *(sammatta·niyāma)*. The law of nature says:

1) The Stream-Entry Path *(Sot·Āpatti·Magga)* produces the Stream-Entry Fruition *(Sot·Āpatti·Phala)*, after which one can progress to the Once-Returner *(Sakad·Āgāmi)* stage, but one cannot regress to the ordinary person *(puthu·jjana)* stage.
2) A Once-Returner can progress to the Non-Returner *(An·Āgāmi)* stage, but cannot regress to the Stream-Enterer or ordinary person stages.
3) A Non-Returner can progress to Arahantship, but cannot regress to the Once-Returner, Stream-Enterer or ordinary person stages.
4) An Arahant attains Parinibbāna at death, and cannot regress to the lower noble stages, the ordinary person stage, or any other stage.

Arahantship is the end. This is a law of nature *(sammatta·niyāma)*. Referring to Arahantship, The Buddha said many times:[342]

Ayamantimā jāti, natthidāni punabbhavoti.
This is the last rebirth, now there is no new rebirth.

This means that one cannot change one's mind, and decide to become a Bodhisatta after having attained a Path or Fruition. Moreover, one cannot change one's mind after having received a definite prophecy from a Buddha or Arahant. But one may wish to wait, and become an Arahant some time in the future, and then change one's mind, and attain Arahantship in this life.

The *Visuddhi·Magga* gives an example of a Mahāthera, the Venerable Mahāsaṅgharakkhita, who did this.[343] He was expert in the four foundations of mindfulness, had practised samatha-vipassanā up to the Formations-Equanimity Knowledge, and had never performed a bodily or verbal action without mindfulness. And he had developed sufficient samatha-vipassanā *pāramī* to be able to attain Arahantship if he wanted to. But, because he wanted to see Arimetteyya Buddha, he had decided to wait, and become an Arahant only in that dispensation. According to the law of nature we just mentioned, he would not be able to see Arimetteyya Buddha, if he attained Arahantship now.

But, at the time near his death, a large number of people gathered, because they thought he was an Arahant, and thought he was going to attain Parinibbāna, although he was in fact still a ordinary person. When his disciple told him many people had gathered, because they thought he was

---

[342] For example, D.iii.6 *'Pāsādika·Suttaṁ'* ('The Pleasing Sutta')

[343] VsM.i.20 *'Paṭhama·Sīla·Pañcakaṁ'* ('First Morality Pentad') PP.i.135

going to attain Parinibbāna, the Mahāthera said, 'Oh, I had wanted to see Arimetteyya Buddha. But if there is a large assembly, then let me meditate.' And he practised vipassanā. Now that he had changed his mind, and because he had in his past lives not received a definite prophecy, he very soon attained Arahantship.

During The Buddha's time there was no mention of a definite prophecy to a Bodhisatta except for Arimetteyya Bodhisatta, who was a bhikkhu named Ajita. The Tipiṭaka does not say either when the next Buddha after Arimetteyya Buddha will arise, so we cannot say how many Bodhisattas there were during The Buddha's time.

Question 5.5 Is it possible to practise the path to liberation *(vimutti·magga)* and the path of Bodhisatta [path to Buddhahood][344] at the same time? If so, what is the method?

Answer 5.5 Liberation *(vimutti)* means escape from defilements or the round of rebirths. When a Bodhisatta becomes a Buddha, he escapes from the round of rebirths at his Parinibbāna. If you, as a disciple *(sāvaka)*, try to attain Arahantship and succeed, you will also escape from the round of rebirth at your Parinibbāna. A person cannot become a Buddha as well as a disciple. He must choose either one or the other, but they both escape from the round of rebirths when they attain Arahantship. The way to attain the Arahant Path is the final path to liberation *(vimutti·magga)*.

Question 5.6 Is this method [of meditation] for liberation only, or is it also for the Bodhisatta path?

Answer 5.6 It is for both. In a previous talk, we mentioned that Sakyamuni Buddha was a bhikkhu in nine of his past lives as a Bodhisatta.[345] If we look at his practice in those nine lives, we see the three trainings: morality *(sīla)*, concentration *(samādhi)*, and wisdom *(paññā)*. The Bodhisatta was able to practise the eight attainments, five mundane psychic powers, and vipassanā up to the Formations-Equanimity Knowledge.

Now you too are developing samatha-vipassanā meditation based on morality. When you have practised the three trainings up to the Formations-Equanimity Knowledge, you can choose either way. If you want liberation you can choose to go to Nibbāna; if you want to become a Bodhisatta you can choose the Bodhisatta way: no problem.

---

[344] The Most Venerable Pa-Auk Sayadaw's audience was almost only Buddhists of the Mahāyana tradition, for whom the path is not towards Arahantship (liberation) but the Bodhisatta path towards Buddhahood (saving all beings).

[345] See Q&A 4.3, p.143.

Question 5.7 Do all the good and bad kammas of an Arahant mature prior to his Parinibbāna?

Answer 5.7 Not all. Some good and bad kamma may mature and produce their results. If they do not mature they do not produce a result, and are lapsed kamma *(ahosi·kamma)*, kamma that no longer produce any result. For example, the unwholesome kamma of one of the Venerable Mahāmoggallāna's past lives produced its results just before his Parinibbāna. In one of his past lives he had tried unsuccessfully to kill his blind parents. Due to that unwholesome kamma, he suffered in hell for many thousands of years, and when he escaped from hell, he was killed in about two hundred lives. In each of those lives his skull was crushed. In his last life too, every bone in his body was crushed, including his skull. Why? The unwholesome kamma had matured. Unless unwholesome and wholesome kammas have matured, they do not produce any results. They are kamma by name only.

Question 5.8 After His enlightenment, did The Buddha say, 'Originally all beings have the Tathāgata's wisdom and other qualities'?

Answer 5.8 Now you have accepted that Sakyamuni Buddha attained enlightenment. You should consider whether the Tathāgata's qualities of enlightenment are present in all beings, especially in yourself. Do you possess any of the Tathāgata's qualities?

Question 5.9 Is the Arahant's perception of voidness *(suññatā)* in his own five aggregates the same as his perception of voidness in outside inanimate things? Is Nibbāna the same as entering voidness?

Answer 5.9 The perception of voidness in one's five aggregates and in outside inanimate things is the same.

Nibbāna was given the name voidness *(suññatā)* because of the Path. When a yogi knows formations *(saṅkhāra·dhamma)* as non-self, and if at that time he sees Nibbāna, his Path Knowledge is called the void liberation *(suññatā·vimokkha)*. Just like the Path is called the void liberation, so is the object of the Path, which is Nibbāna, also called voidness. Here the void liberation means the escape from defilements by seeing the non-self nature of formations.[346]

Question 5.10 Are all suttas taught by The Buddha only?

Answer 5.10 Most of the suttas in the Tipiṭaka are taught by The Buddha. A few suttas are said to be taught by disciples like the Venerable Sāriputta, the Venerable Mahākaccāyana, and the Venerable Ānanda. But the suttas

---

346 Further to Nibbāna as the perception of voidness, see also p.27, and the three entrances to Nibbāna, p.58.

taught by disciples have the same meaning as had they been taught by The Buddha. This is evident when The Buddha in some of the suttas gives his approval by uttering, **It is good** *(sādhu)*, for example, in the *'Mahākaccāyana·Bhadd·Eka·Ratta'* sutta, of the *Majjhima·Nikāya*, which was taught by the Venerable Mahākaccāyana.[347]

Question 5.11 Since we cannot see The Buddha while in concentration, can we see Him by psychic powers to discuss Dhamma with Him?[348]

Answer 5.11 No, you cannot. One of the psychic powers is called recollection of past lives *(pubbe·nivas·ānussati)*. If a yogi possesses this psychic power, and met a Buddha in one of his past lives, he can see that as a past experience only, not as a new experience. If Dhamma was discussed, there will be only old questions and answers; there cannot be new questions and answers.

---

347 M.III.iv.3 *'Mahākaccāyana-Bhadd·Eka·Ratta·Suttaṁ'* ('The Mahākaccāyana One-Excellent-Night Sutta')

348 See further the end of 'How You Develop Buddha Recollection', p.91.

How You See the Links of Dependent Origination

INTRODUCTION

In our last talk, we discussed how to discern mentality *(nāma)*, and in the talk before that, how to discern materiality *(rūpa)*. If you are able to discern mentality and materiality in the way then described, you will also be able to discern their causes. This means discerning dependent origination *(paṭicca·samuppāda)*. Dependent origination is about how causes and effects operate over the three periods of past, present, and future.

The Buddha taught four methods to discern dependent origination, according to the character of his listeners, and there is a fifth method taught by the Venerable Sāriputta, recorded in the *Paṭisambhidā·Magga*.[349] It would take some time to explain the many methods in detail, so we shall look at only the two methods we at the Pa-Auk monasteries teach most often to yogis. They are what we call the Venerable Sāriputta's fifth method, and then what we call the first method, taught by The Buddha, in for example, the *'Mahānidāna'* sutta in the *Dīgha·Nikāya* and the *'Nidāna·Vagga'* in the *Saṁyutta·Nikāya*.[350]

Both methods involve discerning the five aggregates *(khandha)* of the present, of the past, and of the future[351], discerning which of them is cause and which is effect. When you can do this, you can also learn how to discern dependent origination in the other ways taught in the suttas and commentaries.

---

[349] PsM.I.i.4 *'Dhamma·Ṭṭhiti·Ñāṇa·Niddeso'* ('Standing-on-Phenomena Knowledge Description'). See also VsM.xvii.653 *'Paññā·Bhūmi·Niddesa'* ('Description of the Wisdom-Ground') PP.xvii.284*ff.*

[350] *'Mahā·Nidāna·Suttaṁ'* ('The Great Causation Sutta' D.ii.2); *'Nidāna·Vagga'* ('Causation Section' S.II)

[351] The Most Venerable Pa-Auk Tawya Sayadaw is here speaking of vipassanā power, which enables you to see only the five clinging-aggregates. (SA.III.I.viii.7 *'Khajjanīya·Suttaṁ'* ('The Being Consumed Sutta'). He is not speaking of the psychic power, Recollection of Past Lives *(pubbe·nivās·ānussati·abhiññā)*, which enables you to see: 1) The aggregates *(khandhā)* associated with supramundane states *(lokuttara·dhamma)*, which are the aggregates (four/five in the Brahmā world; five in the deva/human world) of beings who have attained one of the four Path Consciousnesses and four Fruition Consciousnesses; 2) The clinging-aggregates *(upādāna·kkhandhā)*; 3) Clan, appearance, food, pleasure and pain etc; 4) Concepts such as names and race.

THE FIFTH METHOD

THE THREE ROUNDS OF DEPENDENT ORIGINATION

Dependent origination *(paṭicca·samuppāda)* consists of twelve factors.[352] They can be said to comprise three rounds *(vaṭṭa)*, two rounds of causes (five causes), and one round of results (five results):[353]

1) The defilements round *(kilesā·vatta)*:
   - i) ignorance *(avijjā)*
   - ii) craving *(taṇhā)*
   - iii) clinging *(upādāna)*
2) The kamma round *(kamma·vaṭṭa)*:
   - i) volitional formations *(saṅkhārā)*
   - ii) kamma-process existence *(kamma·bhava)*
3) The results round *(vipāka·vaṭṭa)*:
   - i) consciousness *(viññāṇa)*
   - ii) mentality-materiality *(nāma·rūpa)*
   - iii) six sense bases *(sal·āyatana)*
   - iv) contact *(phassa)*
   - v) feeling *(vedanā)*

The defilements round is the cause for the kamma round, which is the cause for the results round, which is, in other words, birth, ageing and death (the eleventh and twelfth factors). The discernment of dependent origination involves seeing this sequence of rounds, and starts with discernment of the past.

HOW YOU DISCERN YOUR PAST

To discern the past, you begin by making an offering of either candles, flowers, or incense at a pagoda, or to a Buddha image. You should make a wish for the rebirth you desire, for example, to become a monk, nun, man, woman, or deva.

Afterwards, you should go and sit in meditation, and enter the fourth jhāna, until the light is bright, brilliant and radiant. Then internal and ex-

---

352 1) ignorance, 2) volitional formations, 3) consciousness, 4) mentality-materiality, 5) six sense bases, 6) contact, 7) feeling, 8) craving, 9) clinging, 10) existence, 11) birth, 12) ageing and death, sorrow, lamentation, pain, suffering and despair. See e.g. *'Mahā·Nidāna·Suttaṁ'* ('The Great Causation Sutta' D.ii.2), or *'Titthāyatana·Suttaṁ'* ('The Sectarian Doctrines Sutta' A.III.II.ii.1) quoted 'Introduction' p.21.

353 See footnote 349, p.183, and table '3a: Dependent Origination from Life to Life', p.192.

ternal mentality-materiality *(nāma·rūpa)* again and again. This is necessary, because if you cannot discern external mentality-materiality, you will have great difficulty discerning past mentality-materiality. That is because the discernment of past mentality-materiality is similar to the discernment of external mentality-materiality.

Then you should discern the mentality-materiality that occurred when you made the offering at the pagoda or Buddha image, as if they were external objects. When doing this, an image of yourself at the time of offering will appear: you should discern the four elements in that image.

When the image breaks into rūpa-kalāpas, discern all the different types of materiality of the six doors, especially the fifty-four types of materiality of the heart base.[354] You will then be able to discern the bhavaṅga consciousnesses, and the many mind-door processes that arise in-between. You should look among those many mind-door processes, searching backwards and forwards, until you find the defilements round *(kilesa·vaṭṭa)* mind-door process with twenty mental formations in each impulsion consciousness-moment, and kamma round *(kamma·vaṭṭa)* mind-door process *(mano·dvāra vīthi)* with thirty-four mental formations in each impulsion consciousness-moment.

Let us illustrate with a practical example: the case of making an offering of candles, flowers, or incense to a Buddha image, and making a wish to be reborn to become a monk. In this case,

1) ignorance is to deludedly think that 'a monk' truly exists;
2) craving is the desire and longing for life as a monk; and
3) clinging is the attachment to life as a monk.

These three, ignorance, craving, and clinging, are all found in the consciousnesses that make up the defilements round *(kilesa·vaṭṭa)*.

If you had instead made a wish to be reborn to become a woman, then

1) ignorance would be to deludedly think that a woman truly exists;
2) craving would be the desire and longing for life as a woman; and
3) clinging would be the attachment to life as a woman.

In the examples, volitional formations *(saṅkhāra)* are the wholesome volition *(kusala cetanā)* of the offering, and kamma is their kammic potency. Both are found in the consciousnesses that make up the kamma round *(kamma·vaṭṭa)* of dependent origination.

When you are thus able to discern the mentality-materiality of the defilements round and kamma round of the recent past, you should go back to the more distant past, to some time previous to the offering, and in the

354 For how you do this, see Talk 4, 'How You Discern Materiality'.

same way discern the mentality-materiality. Then go back a little further again, and repeat the process.

In this way, you discern the mentality-materiality of one day ago, one week ago, one month ago, one year ago, two years ago, three years ago and so on. Eventually you will be able to discern right back to the mentality-materiality of the rebirth-linking consciousness *(paṭisandhi citta)* that arose at the conception of your present life.[355]

When looking for the causes of conception, you go back even further, and see either the mentality-materiality of the time near death in your previous life, or the object of the near-death impulsion consciousness *(maraṇāsanna javana-citta)*.[356]

There are three possible objects for the near-death impulsion consciousness:

1) Kamma: the mental formations of a kamma you performed earlier in this life or a previous life: for example, you may recollect the hatred associated with slaughtering animals, happiness associated with offering food to bhikkhus, or tranquillity associated with meditation.
2) Kamma Sign *(kamma·nimitta)*: an image associated with a kamma you performed earlier in this life or a previous life. A butcher may see a butcher's knife or hear the screams of animals about to be slaughtered, a doctor may see patients, a devotee of the Triple Gem may see a bhikkhu, a pagoda, a Buddha image, flowers, an object offered, and a meditator may see the *paṭibhāga-nimitta* of his meditation subject.
3) Destination sign *(gati·nimitta)*: a vision of your destination, where you are about to be reborn. For rebirth in hell, you may see fire; for a human, your future mother's womb (usually like a red carpet), for an animal rebirth, forests or fields; for a deva-rebirth, deva-mansions.

The object appears because of the kammic potency that produced the rebirth-linking consciousness *(paṭisandhi·citta)*.[357] When you discern this, you will be able to discern also the volitional formations and kamma that produced the resultant *(vipāka)* aggregates of this life,[358] and the preceding ig-

---

[355] In the five-constituent existence, mentality-materiality arises dependent on consciousness, and vice-versa. See p.5.

[356] See also table '1d: Death and Rebirth', p.188.

[357] See also Q&A 3.12, p.104.

[358] There are also so-called non-resultant *(a·vipāka)* aggregates: they are the product *(phala)* of a cause *(hetu)*, as in, for example, consciousness-born materiality, which is not the product of kamma.

norance, craving, and clinging. And you will discern also the other mental formations of that kamma round and defilements round.

EXAMPLES

WHAT A FEMALE YOGI DISCERNED

To make this clearer, let us give an example of what one yogi was able to discern. When she discerned the mentality-materiality at the time near death, she saw the kamma of a woman offering fruit to a Buddhist monk. Then, beginning with the four elements, she examined further the mentality-materiality of that woman. She found that the woman was a very poor and uneducated villager, who had reflected on her state of suffering, and had made an offering to the monk, with the wish for life as an educated woman in a large town.

In this case,

1) deludedly to think that an educated woman in a large town truly exists is ignorance *(avijjā)*;
2) the desire and longing for life as an educated woman is craving *(taṇhā)*;
3) the attachment to life as an educated woman is clinging *(upādāna)*;
4) the wholesome act of offering fruit to a Buddhist monk is volitional formations *(saṅkhārā)*, and
5) the kamma is their kammic potency.

In this life the yogi is an educated woman in a large town in Myanmar. She was able (with Right View) to discern directly how the kammic potency of offering fruit in her past life produced the resultant five aggregates of this life. The ability to discern causes and effects in this way is called the Cause-Apprehending Knowledge *(Paccaya·Pariggaha·Ñāṇa)*.

Table 1d: **Death and Rebirth**[1]

	PREVIOUS LIFE						PRESENT LIFE	
CONSCIOUSNESS MOMENT *Citta·Kkhaṇa*	Final consciousnesses of near-death process *(maraṇ·āsanna·vīthi)*.						First consciousness	Sixteen Life-Continuum consciousnesses.
	⇒	⇒	⇒	⇒	⇒	⇒	1⇒	2⇒ - - - - -17⇒
OBJECT *Ārammaṇa*	Near-death object (kamma/ kamma sign/ destination sign)					Previous life's near-death object	Previous life's near-death object	
CONSCIOUSNESS *Citta*	1st Impulsion *Javana* ↑|↓	2nd Impulsion *Javana* ↑|↓	3rd Impulsion *Javana* ↑|↓	4th Impulsion *Javana* ↑|↓	5th Impulsion *Javana* ↑|↓	**DECEASE** *Cuti* ↑ | ↓	Rebirth-Linking *Paṭisandhi* ↑|↓	Life-Continuum *Bhavaṅga* ↑|↓

CONSCIOUSNESS MOMENT *Citta·Kkhaṇa*	PRESENT LIFE'S FIRST COGNITIVE PROCESS (a mind-door process)								(After the cognitive process)
	1⇒	2⇒	3⇒	4⇒	5⇒	6⇒	7⇒	8⇒	⇒⇒⇒⇒⇒⇒⇒
OBJECT *Ārammaṇa*	New aggregates (For a deva, a human being, an animal, a ghost, and a being in hell, it is five aggregates.)								Previous life's near-death object.
CONSCIOUSNESS *Citta*	Mind-Door Adverting *Mano·Dvār·Āvajjana* ↑|↓	1st Impulsion *Javana* ↑|↓	2nd Impulsion *Javana* ↑|↓	3rd Impulsion *Javana* ↑|↓	4th Impulsion *Javana* ↑|↓	5th Impulsion *Javana* ↑|↓	6th Impulsion *Javana* ↑|↓	7th Impulsion *Javana* ↑|↓	Life-Continuum *Bhavaṅga* ↑|↓

[1] VsM.xiv.455 *'Viññāṇa·Kkhandha·Kathā'* ('Discussion of the Consciousness-Aggregate') PP.xiv.111-114 & VsM.xvii.622-627 *'Saṅkhāra·Paccayā·Viññāṇa·Pada·Vitthāra·Kathā'* ('Detailed Discussion of the "Because of Formations, Consciousness" Phase') PP.xvii.133-145.

Further Notes for Table 1d

- One consciousness lasts one consciousness moment *(citta·kkhaṇa)*, with three stages: arising *(uppāda)* ↑, standing *(ṭhiti)* |, dissolution *(bhaṅga)* ↓.
- Cognition follows a fixed procedure, according to the natural law of consciousness *(citta·niyāmā)*. Thus:

Final Mental Process in One Life: the object of the final mental process is one of three: kamma, kamma sign, or destination sign (explained above, p.186).

This object serves as the object of the next life's process-separate consciousnesses *(vīthi·mutta)* in the next life.[359] They arise independently of sense-door processes. They are:

1) The first consciousness of the next life, the rebirth-linking consciousness *(paṭisandhi·citta)*
2) The next life's life-continuum consciousnesses *(bhavaṅga·citta)*
3) The last consciousness of the next life, the decease consciousness *(cuti·citta)*: the decease consciousness of one life takes always that same life's kamma, kamma sign or destination sign as object.

The final mental process of a life has always only five impulsions. Their volition does not alone produce the rebirth-linking consciousness, but functions as a bridge to cross into the new life. They may be followed by registration consciousnesses. And there may arise also life-continuum consciousness before the decease consciousness: they may arise for a shorter or longer time, even up to days or weeks. With the cessation of the decease consciousness, the life faculty is cut off, and there remains only a corpse: dead materiality.

First Mental Process in One Life: Immediately after the rebirth-linking consciousness (the first consciousness of a life),[360] follow sixteen life-continuum consciousnesses with the same object.[361] And then always a mind-door process, which has the new aggregates as object.

---

[359] process-separate: lit. 'process-freed', also called door-separated *(dvāra·vimutta)* lit.'door-freed'. See also explanation, p.159, and footnote 184, p.104.

[360] As may be seen on the chart, rebirth in one of the three realms of existence follows immediately after death in one of those realms. Nonetheless, there are those who speak of an intermediate existence *(antarā·bhava)*. It is hypothesized to be an existence between the arising of the decease consciousness and the subsequent rebirth-linking consciousness <where one has been neither reborn nor not reborn>. This wrong view is discussed in KV.viii.2 *'Antarā·Bhava·Kathā'* ('Discussion of Intermeditate Existence'). There, it is explained that such a hypothesis amounts to declaring a realm of existence apart from the three stated by The Buddha. Such a wrong view arises owing to a misinformed reading of the different kinds of Non-Returner. It arises also because of misunderstanding a brief existence as ghost *(peta)*. It is discussed at Q&A 4.8, p.155.

[361] An exception is death of the impercipient being *(a·sañña·satta)*. The previous life's near-death object is a kasiṇa object, with strong revulsion for mentality. And there is rebirth of only materiality: no mentality, rebirth-, or decease consciousness, or near-death mental process. The object of the next life's rebirth-linking consciousness is then a kamma,

(Please see further next page.)

WHAT A MALE YOGI DISCERNED

Here is a slightly different example. When a male yogi discerned the mentality-materiality at the time near death, he discerned four competing kammas. One was the kamma of teaching Buddhist texts, another teaching dhamma, another practising meditation, and finally one teaching meditation. When he investigated which of the four kammas had produced the resultant five aggregates of this life, he found it was the kamma of practising meditation. When he investigated further (to discern which meditation subject had been practised) he saw it was vipassanā meditation, seeing the three characteristics, impermanence *(anicca)*, suffering *(dukkha)*, and non-self *(an·atta)* in mentality-materiality. With further investigation, he saw that before and after each meditation sitting, he had made the wish to be reborn as a human male, to become a monk, and be a monk who disseminates The Buddha's teachings.

In this case,

1) deludedly to think that a man, a monk, or a monk who disseminates The Buddha's Teachings truly exists is ignorance *(avijjā)*;
2) the desire and longing for life as a man, a monk, or a monk who disseminates The Buddha's Teachings is craving *(taṇhā)*;
3) the attachment to life as a man, a monk, or a monk who disseminates The Buddha's Teachings is clinging *(upādāna)*;
4) the wholesome act of practising vipassanā meditation is volitional formations *(saṅkhārā)*;
5) the kamma is their kammic potency.

HOW YOU DISCERN MORE PAST LIVES

When you are able to discern your immediate past life in this way, and are able to see the five causes in the past life (ignorance, craving, clinging, volitional formations, and kamma), and their five results in the present life (the rebirth-linking consciousness *(paṭisandhi·citta)*, mentality-materiality, the six sense bases, contact, and feeling), you need in the same way to discern progressively back to the second, third, fourth, and as many lives back as you can.

---

kamma-, or destination sign from the infinite past. *'Pañca·Ppakaraṇa Anu·Ṭīka'* ('Sub-Sub-commentary of Five Expositions') *'Paccaya·Paccanīy·Ānuloma·Vaṇṇanā'* §190 explains that this principle applies both to impercipient existence (which is always followed by sensual-sphere existence), and immaterial existence (which may be followed by another immaterial existence on the same or a higher plane), or by sensual-sphere existence.

Should you discern a past- or future life in the brahma realm, you will see only three sense bases (eye-, ear- and heart base), in contrast to the six sense bases that you see in the human-, and deva realms.

HOW YOU DISCERN YOUR FUTURE

Once the power of this vipassanā knowledge has been developed (by discerning the causes and effects through those past lives), you can, in the same way, discern the causes and effects in future lives. The future you will see, and which may still change, is the result of both past and present causes, one of which is the meditation you are doing.[362] To discern the future, you begin by discerning the present mentality-materiality, and then look into the future until the time of death in this life. Then either the kamma, kamma sign, or rebirth sign will appear, because of the potency of a particular kamma you performed in this life. You will then be able to discern the rebirth-linking mentality-materiality *(paṭisandhi·nāma·rūpa)* that will be produced in the future life.[363]

You must discern as many lives into the future as it takes till ignorance ceases without remainder. This happens with the attainment of the Arahant Path *(Arahatta·Magga)*, that is, your own attainment of Arahantship. You should then continue discerning into the future, until you see that the five aggregates, mentality-materiality, cease without remainder, that is, at the end of the Arahant life, at your own Parinibbāna. You will thus have seen that with the cessation of ignorance, mentality-materiality cease. You will have seen the complete cessation of phenomena *(dhamma)*, that is, no further rebirth.

---

362 For how the future can change, see further p.24*f.*

363 Rebirth *(jāti)* is the manifestation of the aggregates, which is also mentality-materiality. For details, see VsM.xvii.641 *'Paññā Bhūmi Niddesa'* ('Description of the Wisdom-Ground') PP.xvii.218*f.*

3a: Dependent Origination from Life to Life[364]

(one life) NON-ARAHANT		(next life) NON-ARAHANT		(last life) FROM ARAHANTSHIP		✖
⏩ results ⏩[365]	causes ⏩[366]	⏩ results ⏩	causes ⏩	⏩ results ⏭	causes ✖[367]	results ✖
	IGNORANCE		ignorance		IGNORANCE ✖	
consciousness	FORMATION ⏩	CONSCIOUSNESS	formation ⏩	consciousness	FORMATION ✖	CONSCIOUSNESS ✖
mentality–materiality		MENTALITY–MATERIALITY		mentality–materiality		MENTALITY–MATERIALITY ✖
six bases		SIX BASES		six bases		SIX BASES ✖
contact		CONTACT		contact		CONTACT ✖
feeling ⏩	craving	FEELING ⏩	CRAVING	feeling ⏭	craving ✖	FEELING ✖
	clinging		CLINGING		clinging ✖	
BIRTH	existence ⏩	birth	EXISTENCE ⏩	BIRTH	existence ✖	birth ✖
AGEING&DEATH ⏩		ageing&death ⏩		AGEING&DEATH ⏭		ageing&death ✖

Discerning, in this way, the five aggregates of the past, present, and future, and also discerning their causal relation, is what we call the fifth method; taught by the Venerable Sāriputta. Having completed it, you can now learn what we call the first method, the one taught by The Buddha.

---

364 The Buddha teaches in two ways: according to custom *(vohāra·desanā)*, and according to ultimate truth *(param·attha·desanā)*. Of the twelve factors of dependent origination, birth/ ageing&death are according to custom. They correspond to the five factors consciousness/ mentality-materiality/ six bases/ contact/ feeling, which are according to ultimate truth. The process going from life to life is explained by The Buddha in, for example, A.III.II.-iii.6 *'Paṭhama·Bhava·Suttaṁ'* ('The First Existence Sutta'): 'Sensual-element [sensual-sphere kamma-] result, and, Ānanda, kamma not existing, would any sensual existence be manifest?… Fine-material element [fine-material sphere, kamma-] result… and kamma not existing, would any fine-material existence be manifest?… Immaterial element [immaterial-sphere kamma] result… and kamma not existing, would any immaterial existence be manifest?' ('Surely not, Venerable Sir.') 'In this way, Ānanda, kamma is the field, consciousness is the seed, craving the moisture. For ignorance-hindered beings fettered by craving in the inferior element [sensual] … in the middle element [fine-material]… in the superior element [immaterial], there is consciousness established *(viññāṇam patiṭṭhitaṁ)*. Thus, in the future, there is re-existence of rebirth.'

365 Results in the life of both a non-Arahant and Arahant: kamma formation in a past life results in the arising of a rebirth consciousness, and subsequent consciousnesses in that life, and the simultaneous arising of mentality-materiality, the six bases, contact, and feeling. In D.ii.2 *'Mahā Nidāna·Suttaṁ'* ('The Great Causation Sutta'), The Buddha explains that in one life one can go only as far back as the arising of mentality-materiality and consciousness at rebirth: 'Thus far the round [of rebirth] goes as much as can be discerned in this life, namely to mentality-materiality together with consciousness.'

366 Causes in non-Arahant's life: the non-Arahant is possessed of ignorance. Hence, when there is feeling, there is craving, and clinging, owing to which there is existence of the kammic potency, the formation of kamma. This means there is at death the arising of a rebirth consciousness.

367 Causes in Arahant's life: because there is no ignorance, there is no craving, and no

(Please see further next page.)

THE FIRST METHOD

The first method[368] of discerning dependent origination *(paṭicca·samuppāda)* goes over three lives, and in forward order. It begins with the causes in the past life, that is, ignorance and volitional formations. They cause the results in the present life: the resultant consciousnesses (beginning with the rebirth-linking consciousness),[369] mentality-materiality, the six sense bases, contact, and feeling. There are then the causes in this life, craving, clinging, and existence, which cause the results of birth, ageing, death, and all forms of suffering in the future life.

You have to try to find ignorance, craving and clinging in the defilement round, see how it causes the kamma round, and how the kammic potency of the kamma round in turn causes the five aggregates at conception, and in the course of existence.

That concludes our brief explanation of how to discern dependent origination according to the fifth- and first methods. There are many more details that you can learn by practising with a proper teacher.

When you have fully discerned the causal relationship between mentality-materiality of the past, present, and future, you will have completed the second vipassanā knowledge, the Cause-Apprehending Knowledge *(Paccaya·Pariggaha·Ñāṇa)*.

---

clinging, which means there is no further existence of the kammic potency, no formation of kamma. This means there is at death no arising of a rebirth consciousness. Until then, the five results are still in operation.

368 See *'Mahā·Nidāna·Suttaṁ'* ('The Great Causation Sutta' D.ii.2); *'Nidāna·Vagga'* ('Causation Section' S.II).

369 As an example of this, the Most Venerable Pa-Auk Tawya Sayadaw mentions The Buddha's back-pain (pain-associated body consciousness *(dukkha·sahagata kāya·viññāṇa)*), which arose from past unwholesome kamma: see p.241.

Question 6.1 How should a yogi who practises *ān·āpāna·sati* (mindfulness-of-breathing), but who cannot see a nimitta, check himself physically and mentally, so that he can improve and enter jhāna? In other words, what are the conditions needed to have a nimitta?

Answer 6.1 Constant practice is necessary in all types of meditation. In *ān·āpāna·sati* you should be mindful of the breath in every bodily posture, and be so with respect. Walking, standing or sitting, take no objects apart from the breath: you should watch only the breath. Try to stop thinking; try to stop talking. If you try continuously in this way, your concentration will slowly improve. Only deep, strong and powerful concentration can produce a nimitta. Without a nimitta, especially the *paṭibhāga-nimitta*, one cannot attain jhāna, because the *ān·āpāna* jhāna's object is the *ān·āpāna paṭibhāga-nimitta.*

Question 6.2 Does the sitting posture affect the ability for beginners to concentrate, and enter jhāna? There are many yogis who sit on a small stool to meditate; can they enter jhāna?

Answer 6.2 The sitting posture is best for beginners. But those who have enough *pāramī* in *ān·āpāna·sati* (mindfulness-of-breathing) can enter jhāna in any posture. A skilled yogi too can enter jhāna in any posture. So they can go into jhāna sitting on a stool or chair.

The Venerable Sāriputta and the Venerable Subhūti are examples of this. The Venerable Sāriputta was expert in the attainment of cessation *(nirodha·samāpatti)*.[370] When he went for alms in the village, he always entered the attainment of cessation at every house, before accepting their offerings. He accepted the offerings only after having emerged from the attainment of cessation. That was his nature. The Venerable Subhūti was expert in loving-kindness meditation. He entered the loving-kindness jhāna also at every house before accepting the offerings. After emerging from the loving-kindness jhāna he accepted the offerings. Why did they do this? They wanted the donor to get the maximum benefit. They knew that if they did this, immeasurable and superior wholesome kamma would occur in the donor's mental process. They had such loving-kindness for the donors to want to do this. Thus they were able to enter an attainment while in the standing posture. You should think about *ān·āpāna* jhāna in the same way.

Question 6.3 What is the object of the fourth *ān·āpāna* jhāna? If there is no breath in the fourth jhāna, how can there be a nimitta?

---

[370] For details regarding this attainment, see Q&A 5.1, p.173.

Answer 6.3 There is still a *paṭibhāga-nimitta* in the fourth *ān·āpāna* jhāna, although there is no in&out-breath. That *ān·āpāna paṭibhāga-nimitta* arose from the ordinary, natural breath. This is why the object is still the in&out-breath *(assāsa-passāsa)*. It is explained in the *Visuddhi·Magga* sub-commentary.[371]

Question 6.4 Can one enter an immaterial jhāna-attainment *(arūpa·jhāna·samā-patti)*, or practise loving-kindness meditation directly from *ān·āpāna·sati* (mindfulness-of-breathing)?

Answer 6.4 One cannot enter an immaterial jhāna-attainment directly from the fourth *ān·āpāna* jhāna. Why not? Immaterial jhānas, especially the base of boundless-space jhāna *(ākāsānañc·āyatana jhāna)*, are attained by removing a kasiṇa object. After removing the kasiṇa object and concentrating on the space *(ākāsa)* left behind, the object of the base of boundless-space jhāna will appear. When one sees the space, one must extend it gradually, and when it extends in every direction, the kasiṇa object will have disappeared. One must extend the space further out to the boundless universe. That is the object of the base of boundless-space jhāna, which in its turn is the object of the base of boundless consciousness jhāna *(viññāṇañc·āyatana jhāna)*. The absence of the base of boundless-space jhāna is the object of the base of nothingness jhāna *(ākiñcaññ·āyatana jhāna)*, which is finally the object of the base of neither perception nor non-perception jhāna *(neva·saññā·nā·saññ·āyatana jhāna)*. So the four immaterial jhānas are based on a fourth kasiṇa jhāna, and its object. Without removing the kasiṇa one cannot go to the immaterial jhānas. So if a yogi practises *ān·āpāna·sati* up to the fourth jhāna, and then wants to go to immaterial jhānas, he should first practise the one of the kasiṇas (except the space kasiṇa)[372] up to the fourth jhāna. Only then can he go on to the immaterial jhāna.[373]

If he wants to practise loving-kindness meditation *(mettā·bhāvanā)* from the fourth *ān·āpāna* jhāna he can do so; no problem. He must see the person who is the object of loving-kindness with the light of the fourth *ān·āpāna* jhāna. If his light is not strong enough it may be a little bit problematic. But that is exceptional. If after the fourth kasiṇa jhāna, especially the fourth white kasiṇa jhāna, he practises loving-kindness he may succeed

---

[371] In this case, the *ān·āpāna-nimitta* which arises depending on the ordinary, natural breath is also said to be as *assāsa-passāsa* (in-and-out breath). *(Assāsa-passāsa nissāya uppannanimittampettha assāsa-passāsa sāmaññameva vuttaṁ.)* (VsMṬ.viii.215 *'Ān·Āpāna·Sati·Kathā'* 'Mindfulness-of-Breathing Discussion').

[372] See in this connection footnote 138, p.67.

[373] For details regarding how you develop the immaterial jhānas, see p.66*ff*.

quickly. That is why we teach white kasiṇa meditation before loving-kindness meditation.[374]

Question 6.5 How can one decide when to die, that is, choose the time of one's death?

Answer 6.5 If you have practised *ān·āpāna·sati* (mindfulness-of-breathing) up to the Arahant Path, you can know the exact time of your Parinibbāna. The *Visuddhi·Magga* mentions a Mahāthera who attained Parinibbāna while walking.[375] First he drew a line on his walking path, and then told his fellow-bhikkhus that he would attain Parinibbāna when reaching that line, and it happened exactly as he had said. Those who are not Arahants can also know their life span if they have practised dependent origination *(paṭicca·samuppāda)*, the relationship between causes and effects of the past, present and future, but not exactly like the Mahāthera just mentioned. They do not know the exact time, maybe only the period in which they will die.

But these people do not die and attain Parinibbāna according to their own wish: it is according to the law of kamma. There is a stanza uttered by the Venerable Sāriputta:[376]

N·ābhinandāmi jīvitaṁ, n·ābhinandāmi maraṇaṁ; kālañ·ca paṭikaṅkhāmi, nibbisaṁ bhatako yathā.

I do not delight in life, I do not delight in death; I await the time [of Parinibbāna], **like a government servant** [waits for] **his wages.**

To die when one has desired to do so is called 'death by desire' *(adhimutti·maraṇa)*. This can usually be done by matured Bodhisattas only. Why do they do so? When they are reborn in the celestial realms, where there is no opportunity to develop their *pāramī*, they do not want to waste time, so sometimes they decide to die, and take rebirth in the human world, to develop their *pāramī*.

Question 6.6 If one day we were to die in an accident, for example in an air crash, could our mind at that time 'leave' so that we would not have any bodily pain? How? Can one, depending on the power of one's meditation, be without fear at that time, and be liberated? What degree of concentration is required?'

Answer 6.6 The degree of concentration required is that of the psychic power of supernormal powers *(iddhividha·abhiññā)*. With those powers you

---

[374] For details in this regard, see Q&A 2.2., p.72.

[375] VsM.viii.238 *'Ān·Āpāna·Sati·Kathā'* 'Mindfulness-of-Breathing Discussion' PP.viii.244

[376] TG.XVII.2 (v.1002) *'Sāriputta·Tthera·Gāthā'* ('The Elder Sāriputta's Verses')

can escape from danger, but not if you have a matured unwholesome kamma ready to produce its result. You should remember the case of Venerable Mahāmoggallāna. He was expert in psychic powers, but on the day when his unwholesome kamma matured he could not enter jhāna. This was not because of defilements or hindrances: it was only because of his matured unwholesome kamma. That is why the bandits were able to crush his bones to the size of rice grains.[377] Thinking he was dead, the bandits left, and only then could he enter jhāna again, and regain his psychic powers. He made a determination *(adhiṭṭhāna)* that his body should become whole again, and then went to request The Buddha for permission to attain Parinibbāna. Then he returned to his Kalasīla Monastery, and attained Parinibbāna there. His matured unwholesome kamma first produced its result, after which it lost its power, and only then could he regain his psychic powers.

Thus, if you have no unwholesome kamma about to mature, and have psychic powers, you can escape from an air crash. But ordinary jhāna concentration and vipassanā knowledge, cannot save you from such danger. We can in fact say that the reason why one meets with this type of accident in the first place may be that one's unwholesome kamma is about to mature.

The mind cannot leave the body, because the mind arises dependent upon one of the six bases. The six bases are the eye base, the ear base, the nose base, the tongue base, the body base and the heart base. These six bases are your body. A mind cannot arise in this human world without a base. That is why the mind cannot leave the body.[378]

We can, however, suggest that if you have jhāna, you should at the time of danger quickly enter jhāna. That means you need to have fully developed the mastery of entering jhāna. If you enter jhāna at the time of danger, then that wholesome kamma may save you, but we cannot say for sure. If you are in jhāna at the moment of death, you may go up to one of the brahma realms.

If you are skilled at vipassanā, then you should practise it at the time of danger. You should discern the impermanent *(anicca)*, suffering *(dukkha)*, and non-self *(an·atta)* nature of formations *(saṅkhāra·dhamma)*. If you can practise vipassanā thoroughly before death takes place, you may attain one of the Paths *(Magga)* and Fruitions *(Phala)*, and reach a happy realm after death. But if you attain Arahantship, you attain Parinibbāna. Should you, how-

---

377 For details, see Q&A 5.7, p.181.

378 For the dependence between mind and body (mentality-materiality), see also p.5.

ever, not have psychic powers, nor jhāna, nor be able to practise vipassanā, you may still escape, due to good kamma alone. If you have good enough kamma, which ensures a long life, there may also be a chance to escape from this danger, just like Mahājanaka Bodhisatta. He was the only person to survive a shipwreck. After swimming for seven days and seven nights, he was eventually saved by a deva.

Question 6.7 After attaining the Path and Fruition, a Noble One *(Ariya)* does not regress to become an ordinary person *(puthu·jjana)*, this is a natural fixed law *(sammatta niyāma)*. Similarly, one who has received a definite prophecy cannot abandon his Bodhisatta practice. This too is a natural fixed law. But The Buddha declared that everything is impermanent[379]. Are these fixed laws in accordance with the law of impermanence?

Answer 6.7 Here you should understand what is fixed and what is permanent. The law of kamma says unwholesome kammas *(akusala·kamma)* produce bad results, and wholesome kammas *(kusala·kamma)* produce good results. This is the natural law of kamma *(kamma·niyāma)*. Does that mean that the wholesome and unwholesome kammas are permanent *(nicca)*? Please think about it.

If the wholesome kammas are permanent then consider this: Now you are listening to Dhamma concerning The Buddha's Abhidhamma. This is called wholesome kamma of listening to Dhamma *(Dhamma·sāvana kusala·kamma)*. Is it permanent? Please think about it.

If it were permanent, then during your whole life you would have only this kamma, no other. Do you understand? Wholesome kammas produce good results and unwholesome kammas produce bad results. This is a natural law, but it does not mean that the kammas are permanent. Wholesome volition *(kusala·cetanā)* and unwholesome volition *(akusala·cetanā)* are kamma. As soon as they arise they perish; they are impermanent. That is their nature. But the potency of kamma, the capacity to produce the results of kammas, still exists in the mentality-materiality process.

Suppose there is a mango tree. Now there is no fruit on the tree, but it is certain that one day it will bear fruit. This is a natural law. You could say the capacity to produce fruit exists in the tree. What is that capacity? If we study the leaves, branches, bark and stems we cannot see it, but that does not mean it does not exist, because one day that tree will produce fruit. In the same way we do not say wholesome and unwholesome kammas are permanent. We say the potency of kamma exists in the mentality-

---

379 The Buddha did not say: 'Everything is impermanent'; He said: 'All formations are impermanent.' (DhP.xx.5 *'Magga·Vagga'* ('Path Chapter'))

materiality process as a capacity, and that one day, when the potency matures, it produces its result.

Let us now discuss the natural fixed law *(sammatta niyāma)*. We say Path and Fruition dhammas are dhammas of a fixed natural law, but we do not say they are permanent *(nicca)*. They are also impermanent *(anicca)*, but the potency of Path Knowledge exists in the mentality-materiality process of those who have attained a Path, Fruition, and Nibbāna. That potency exists because of a natural fixed law, and has a natural result. For example, the potency of the Stream-Entry Path *(Sot·Āpatti·Magga)* results in the Stream-Entry Fruition *(Sot·Āpatti·Phala)*, and is a contributing cause for higher and higher Fruitions. But it cannot result in lower Fruitions. This is also a law of nature.

Here you should think about this: to attain Arahantship is not easy. You have to practise with great effort: strong and powerful perseverance is necessary. For example, in his last life our Sakyamuni Bodhisatta practised very hard (for over six years) to attain Arahantship associated with Omniscient Knowledge *(Sabbaññuta·Ñāṇa)*. You can imagine how hard it was. So if after attaining Arahantship with enormous difficulty, he became an ordinary person *(puthu·jjana)* again, what would be the fruit of the practice? You should think about this carefully.

In this connection, let us look at when a Bodhisatta can receive a definite prophecy.[380]

Manussattaṁ liṅga·sampatti, hetu satthāra·dassanaṁ;
pabbājjā guṇa·sampatti, adhikāro ca chandatā;
Aṭṭha·dhamma·samodhānā abhinīhāro samijjhati.

He can receive a definite prophecy when the following eight conditions are fulfilled:

1) *Manussattaṁ*: he is a human being.
2) *Liṅga·Sampatti*: he is a male.
3) *Hetu* (cause or root): he has sufficient *pāramī* to attain Arahantship while listening to a Buddha utter a short stanza related to the Four Noble Truths. That means, he must have practised vipassanā thoroughly up to the Formations-Equanimity Knowledge *(Saṅkhār·Upekkhā·Ñāṇa)*.
4) *Satthāra·dassanaṁ* (sight of the Master): he meets a Buddha.
5) *Pabbājjā* (going forth): he has gone forth as a hermit or bhikkhu, and has strong and firm faith in the law of kamma.

---

[380] *Buddha·Vaṁsa*.ii.59 *'Sumedha·Patthanā·Kathā'* (*Chronicle of Buddhas*: 'Sumedha's Aspirations Discussion'

6) *Guṇa·sampatti* (achievement of qualities): he has acquired the eight attainments *(samāpatti)* and five mundane psychic powers *(abhiññāṇa)*.
7) *Adhikāro* (aspiration): he has sufficient *pāramī* to receive a definite prophecy from a Buddha. That means he must in previous lives have practised the *pāramī* necessary for attaining Omniscient Knowledge *(Sabbaññuta·Ñāṇa)*. In other words, he must have sowed the seeds of knowledge *(vijjā)* and conduct *(caraṇa)* for Omniscient Knowledge in a previous Buddha's dispensation. According to the *'Yasodharā Apadāna'*, the future prince Siddhattha had made the wish to attain (and the future princess Yasodharā had made the wish for him to attain) Omniscient Knowledge in the presence of many billions of Buddhas, and had developed all the *pāramī* under their guidance. And one way in which he developed his *pāramī* was to make a bridge of himself for Dīpaṅkara Buddha and a hundred thousand bhikkhus to cross, knowing that this act would cost him his life.
8) *Chandata* (desire): he has a sufficiently strong desire to attain Omniscient Knowledge. How strong is that desire? Suppose the whole world system were burning charcoal. If someone told him that he would attain Omniscient Knowledge by crossing the burning charcoal from one end to the other, he would go across the burning charcoal without hesitation. Here we ask you: Would you go across that burning charcoal? If not the whole world system, then if just from Taiwan to Pa-Auk it were all burning charcoal, would you go across it? If it were certain that one could attain Omniscient Knowledge that way, the Bodhisatta would go across that burning charcoal. That is the strength of his desire for Omniscient Knowledge.

If these eight factors are present in a Bodhisatta he will certainly receive a definite prophecy from a Buddha. They were present in our Sakyamuni Bodhisatta, when he was the hermit Sumedha, at the time of Dīpaṅkara Buddha. That is why he received a definite prophecy from Dīpaṅkara Buddha with the words:[381]

You shall attain Omniscient Knowledge after four incalculables *(a·saṅkhyeyya)* **and a hundred thousand aeons** *(kappa)*, **and shall bear the name of Gotama.**

Now, what does it mean that the prophecy is 'definite'? It is definite because it cannot be changed. That does not mean it is permanent. Dīpaṅkara Buddha's mentality-materiality were impermanent. Sumedha's mentality-materiality were also impermanent. This is a fact, but the potency of kamma, especially the kammic potency of his *pāramī*, could not perish

---

381 ibid.

so long as he has not attained Omniscient Knowledge. Dīpaṅkara Buddha's words, that is the definite prophecy, also could not be changed, and could not be false. If those words were changed so that the definite prophecy was not true, then there would be another problem, namely that a Buddha would have uttered false speech. A Buddha gives a definite prophecy only when he sees that the previously mentioned eight conditions have been fulfilled. For example, if a skilful farmer saw a banana tree that was under the right conditions, he would be able to tell you that the tree was going to bear fruit in four months. Why? Because he was skilled in agriculture, and he saw flowers and small leaves growing out from the tree. In the same way, when someone has fulfilled the eight conditions, a Buddha can see that he will attain the Fruition of Omniscient Knowledge, which is why he makes a definite prophecy.

At the time of Dīpaṅkara Buddha, our Sakyamuni Bodhisatta was the hermit Sumedha, an ordinary person *(puthu·jjana)*. As Prince Siddhattha, before attaining enlightenment he was still a ordinary person. Only after his enlightenment did he become Sakyamuni Buddha. After attaining the Arahant Path associated with Omniscient Knowledge, he could not change his Arahant Path; this is a natural fixed law *(sammatta·niyāma)*. Here fixed law means that the result of that Arahant Path cannot change. This does not mean that the Arahant Path is permanent. It means that its result comes because of a potency of kamma that cannot change. What does this mean exactly? It means that it is certain the Arahant Path will produce Arahant Fruition, and certain that it will destroy all the defilements, all the unwholesome kamma and all the wholesome kamma, which would otherwise have produced their result after the Parinibbāna. This law of kamma is called a natural fixed law and cannot be changed. So a natural fixed law and a definite prophecy are not contrary to the law of impermanence.

Here again, a further comment is necessary. Making an aspiration or wish alone is not enough to attain Omniscient Knowledge. When Bodhisattas receive a definite prophecy, the eight conditions must already be fulfilled. Moreover, a definite prophecy alone cannot produce Buddhahood. Even after the definite prophecy, they must continue to develop the ten *pāramī* on the three levels:

1) The ten basic *pāramī* *(pāramī)*:[382] that is offering their sons, daughters, wives and external property.

---

[382] For a list of the ten *pāramī*, see Q&A 4.1, p.141.

2) The ten medium *pāramī* *(upa·pāramī)*: that is offering their limbs and organs, such as eyes and hands.
3) The ten superior *pāramī* *(paramattha·pāramī)*: that is offering their life.

Altogether there are thirty *pāramī*. If we summarize them, we have just:

1) Offering *(dāna)*
2) Morality *(sīla)*
3) Meditation *(bhāvanā)*: samatha and vipassanā.

They are superior wholesome kammas. Bodhisattas must perfect them by giving up animate and inanimate property, their limbs, and their lives. If you believe you are a Bodhisatta, can you and will you perfect these *pāramī*? If you can, and if you also have received a definite prophecy from a Buddha, then you shall one day attain Omniscient Knowledge. But according to the Theravāda teachings, only one Buddha can appear at one given time. And for how long must they perfect their *pāramī*? After he had received his definite prophecy, our Sakyamuni Bodhisatta developed the *pāramī* for four incalculables and a hundred thousand aeons. This is the shortest time. But we cannot say exactly how long it takes prior to the definite prophecy. So you should remember: making an aspiration or wish alone is not enough to become a Buddha.

Question 6.8 When an ordinary disciple has practised samatha-vipassanā up to the Cause-Apprehending Knowledge, the Arise&Perish Knowledge, or the Formations-Equanimity Knowledge, he will not be reborn in any of the four woeful realms. Even if he loses his samatha-vipassanā due to negligence, the kamma of having practised samatha-vipassanā still exists. The *'Sotānugata'* sutta says also that he will attain Nibbāna quickly.[383] So, why did the Sayadaw, in the Question&Answer session of June 2nd, say that a Bodhisatta who has received a definite prophecy from a Buddha can (even if he has practised meditation up to the Formations-Equanimity Knowledge) be reborn in a woeful state?[384] In which sutta is this mentioned?

Answer 6.8 This is because the Bodhisatta way and ordinary disciple way are not the same. You can find this in The *Buddha·Vaṁsa* and *Cariya·Piṭaka* Pali Texts.

How are the two ways different? Although a Bodhisatta has received a definite prophecy from a Buddha, his *pāramī* have at that time not yet matured for him to attain Omniscient Knowledge. He must cultivate his

---

383 A.IV.IV.v.1 *'Sotānugata·Suttaṁ'* ('The One Who Has Heard Sutta'). Mentioned p.102 and 147.

384 See Q&A 4.3, p.143.

pāramī further. For example, after receiving the definite prophecy from Dīpaṅkara Buddha, our Sakyamuni Bodhisatta had to continue cultivating his *pāramī* for four incalculables and a hundred thousand aeons. Between the definite prophecy and the penultimate life, a Bodhisatta is sometimes reborn in the animal kingdom, because of previous unwholesome kamma. At this time he is still unable to totally destroy that unwholesome kammic potency. So when those unwholesome kammas mature, he cannot escape their results. This is a law of nature.

But ordinary disciples, who have attained the Cause-Apprehending Knowledge, the Arise&Perish Knowledge, or the Formations-Equanimity Knowledge, have *pāramī* mature enough to attain the Path Knowledge and Fruition Knowledge. For this reason, they attain Path and Fruition, that is, see Nibbāna, in this life or in their subsequent future life. This is also a law of nature.

Question 6.9 An Arahant can also give a definite prophecy; what is the definition of definite prophecy here? In which sutta or other source can this information be found?

Answer 6.9 For that please refer to The *Buddha·Vaṁsa·Pāḷi* (*Chronicle of Buddhas*) and *Apadāna·Pāḷi* (*Valorous Deeds*). But only Arahants who possess particularly the Knowledge of the Future *(Anāgataṁsa·Ñāṇa)*, a power secondary to the divine eye *(dibba·cakkhu)*, can give a definite prophecy. And they can see only a limited number of lives into the future, and not many incalculables *(a·saṅkhyeyya)*, or aeons *(kappa)*, as can a Buddha.

Question 6.10 Can one practise vipassanā while in the base of neither perception nor non-perception attainment *(neva·saññā·n·āsaññ·āyatana samāpatti)*? In which sutta or other source can the answer be found?

Answer 6.10 One cannot practise vipassanā while in any jhāna attainment, and the base of neither perception nor non-perception is a jhāna. Why? Because in developing vipassanā, we usually do not use the same objects as we use for developing jhāna.[385] Also, jhāna we develop by concentrating on one and the same object (e.g. the *ān·āpāna-*, or kasiṇa-nimitta), whereas vipassanā we develop by examining different objects. For example, the object of the *ān·āpāna* jhānas is the *ān·āpāna paṭibhāga-nimitta*: a concept, not ultimate reality. But the object of vipassanā is not a concept; it is ultimate mentality-materiality and their causes, including the jhāna dhammas (e.g. the thirty-four mental formations of the first jhāna,

[385] Exceptions are, for example, the second and fourth immaterial jhānas, when you concentrate on the preceding immaterial jhāna's consciousness, which is not a concept but an ultimate reality: see footnote 281, p.150. See also 'The Four Immaterial Jhānas', p.66.

the thirty-two mental formations of the second jhāna, the thirty-one mental formations of the third, fourth and immaterial jhanās).[386]

Only after having emerged from the jhāna can one practise vipassanā meditation on, for example, the jhāna consciousness and its associated mental factors, in this case the thirty-one mental formations. It is mentioned in the *'Anupada'* sutta in the *Majjhima·Nikāya.*[387] There The Buddha describes in detail the Venerable Sāriputta's meditation in the fifteen days after he had attained Stream-Entry.

The Venerable Sāriputta entered, for example, the first jhāna. He emerged from it, and discerned the thirty-four first-jhāna mental formations, one by one, as impermanence, suffering, and non-self, by seeing their arising-, static- and perishing stages. He discerned in this manner up to the base of nothingness jhāna. This is vipassanā of consecutive dhammas *(anupada·dhamma·vipassanā)*, in which the mental formations are discerned one by one. But when he reached the base of neither perception nor non-perception, he could discern only the mental formations as a group. This is vipassanā of Comprehension in Groups *(Kalāpa·Sammasana·Vipassanā)*. Only a Buddha can discern the mental formations of the base of neither perception nor non-perception one by one. Because they are extremely subtle, even a Chief Disciple like the Venerable Sāriputta cannot discern them one by one.[388]

Question 6.11 Can a person who is mentally abnormal, hears voices, has schizophrenia, a brain disease, stroke or malfunction of the brain and nerves, practise this type of meditation? If he can, what kinds of precaution should he take?

Answer 6.11 Such people can practise this type of meditation, but usually they do not succeed, because they cannot concentrate long enough. By 'long enough' is meant that when one's concentration is strong and powerful, it must be maintained for many hours, and many sittings. Usually, such people's concentration is inconstant. This is a problem. They may succeed, if they can maintain their concentration over many successive sittings, over many days or many months.

There is a famous example: the case of Paṭācārā. Her husband, two children, parents, and brothers all died on the same day. She went mad with grief, and wandered about with no clothes on. One day she came to

---

[386] For how you discern jhāna-processes, see p.161.

[387] M.III.ii.1 *'Anupada·Suttaṁ'* ('The Consecutive Sutta'), mentioned also in connection with vipassanā into only feeling, Q&A 4.6, p.149.

[388] ibid.A.

the Jetavana monastery in Sāvatthi where The Buddha was teaching Dhamma. Her *pāramī* of previous lives were ready to mature. Due to this, as well as to the loving-kindness and compassion of The Buddha, she was able to listen to the Dhamma with respect.

Slowly her mind became quiet, and she understood the Dhamma. Very soon she became a Stream-Enterer *(Sot·Āpanna)*. She ordained as a bhikkhunī, and continued her meditation. She could maintain her concentration and vipassanā knowledge, and one day her meditation matured. She became an Arahant with the five mundane psychic powers, and Four Analytical Knowledges.[389] Of the bhikkhunīs who were expert in the monastic rule, she was first. She observed the rule very strictly, and learnt it by heart, including the commentaries.

She had been developing her *pāramī* from Padumuttara Buddha's dispensation till Kassapa Buddha's dispensation, and particularly during Kassapa Buddha's dispensation. At that time she was the daughter of a King Kikī. She practised *komāri·brahma·cariya* for twenty thousand years. *Komāri·brahma·cariya* is to observe the five precepts, but in place of the ordinary precept of abstinence from sexual misconduct, complete chastity is observed. She cultivated the three trainings, morality *(sīla)*, concentration *(samādhi)*, and wisdom *(paññā)*, as a lay devotee, for twenty-thousand years. Those *pāramī* matured in Gotama Buddha's dispensation. So, although she had gone mad, she was able to regain her mind, practise the three trainings well, and became an Arahant.

When they practise meditation, such people need *kalyāna·mitta*, which is good teachers, good friends, and spiritual friends. Proper medicine and proper food also helps. From our experience, we know that most of them cannot maintain their concentration for a long time. Usually they do not succeed.

Question 6.12 If a person, who does not have good human relations, succeeds in attaining the fourth jhāna, will this improve his skill in communicating with others? Can attaining jhāna correct such problems?

Answer 6.12 These problems occur usually because of hatred *(dosa)*. It is one of the hindrances. As long as a person is unable to change this attitude, he cannot attain jhāna. But if he can remove this attitude, he can attain not only jhāna, but also the Paths and Fruitions up to Arahantship. A famous example is the Venerable Channa Thera. He was born on the same day as our Bodhisatta, in the palace of King Suddhodana in Kapilavatthu. He was the son of one of King Suddhodana's female slaves. He became one

---

[389] For the Four Analytical Knowledges, see Q&A 4.2, p.142.

of the Bodhisatta prince Siddhattha's playmates, when they were young. This gave later rise to much conceit in him. He thought things like: 'This is my King; The Buddha was my playmate; the Dhamma is our Dhamma; when he renounced the world, I followed him up to the bank of the Anomā River. No one else did. Sāriputta and Mahāmoggallāna etc.are flowers that blossomed later, etc.' Because of this, he always used harsh language. He did not show respect to Mahātheras like the Venerable Sāriputta, the Venerable Mahāmoggallāna and others. So no one had friendly relations with him. He could not attain jhāna or Path and Fruition in The Buddha's lifetime, because he was unable to remove his conceit and hatred.

On the night of The Buddha's Parinibbāna, The Buddha told the Venerable Ānanda to mete out the noble punishment *(brahma·daṇḍa)* on the Venerable Channa. It means that no one was to talk to the Venerable Channa, even if he wanted to. When nobody talked with the Venerable Channa, his conceit and hatred disappeared. This act of the Saṅgha *(saṅgha·kamma)* took place in the Ghositārāma monastery in Kosambī, five months after The Buddha's Parinibbāna. The Venerable left Ghositārāma, and went to the Isipatana monastery in the deer park near Benares. He worked hard on meditation but was, in spite of great effort, not successful. So one day, he went to the Venerable Ānanda and asked him to help him. Why was he not successful? He discerned the impermanent, suffering, and non-self nature of the five aggregates, without discerning dependent origination *(paṭicca·samuppāda)*. So the Venerable Ānanda taught him how to discern dependent origination, and taught him the *'Kaccānagotta'* sutta.[390] After listening to the Venerable Ānanda's Dhamma talk, the Venerable Channa attained Stream-Entry. He continued his practice and very soon became an Arahant. So if a person can change his bad character, and practise samatha-vipassanā in the right way, he can attain jhāna, Path and Fruition.

[390] S.II.I.ii.5 *'Kaccānagotta·Suttaṁ'* ('The Kaccānagotta Sutta') & S.III.1.ix.8 *'Channa·Suttaṁ'* ('The Channa Sutta')

How You Develop the Vipassanā Knowledges to See Nibbāna

Introduction

In the last talk, we discussed briefly how to discern dependent origination according to the fifth and first methods. Today, we shall discuss briefly how to develop the vipassanā knowledges to see Nibbāna.

There are sixteen vipassanā knowledges *(Ñāṇa)* that need to be developed progressively in order to see Nibbāna.

The first vipassanā knowledge is the Mentality-Materiality Definition Knowledge *(Nāma·Rūpa·Pariccheda·Ñāṇa)*. This knowledge was explained when we discussed how to discern mentality and materiality.

The second vipassanā knowledge is the Cause-Apprehending Knowledge *(Paccaya·Pariggaha·Ñāṇa)*. This knowledge was explained in our last talk, when we discussed how to discern the causal relationship between mentality-materiality of the past, present, and future, which is to discern dependent origination.

After you have developed those two knowledges, you need to complete them, by again discerning all mentality, all materiality, and all the factors of dependent origination, according to their individual characteristic,[391] function, manifestation, and proximate cause. It is not really possible to explain this in a brief way, so it is best to learn the details at the time of actually practising.

Now let us look briefly at the remaining knowledges.

How You Develop the Comprehension Knowledge

The third vipassanā knowledge is the Comprehension Knowledge *(Sammasana·Ñāṇa)*, which is to comprehend formations by categories: to see the three characteristics, impermanence *(anicca)*, suffering *(dukkha)*, and non-self *(an·atta)* in formations according to different categories:[392]

- Two categories, as mentality and materiality

[391] individual characteristic: see footnote 103, p.33.

[392] VsMṬ.xiv *'Paññā·Kathā'* ('Understanding Discussion') & VsM.xx.694 *'Magg·Ā·Magga·Ñāṇa·Dassana·Visuddhi·Niddesa'* ('Description of Path&Non-Path Knowledge&Vision Purification') PP.xx.9

- Five categories, as the five aggregates[393]
- Twelve categories, as the twelve bases[394]
- Twelve categories, as the twelve factors of dependent origination[395]
- Eighteen categories, as the eighteen elements[396]

For example, in the case of the five categories, The Buddha teaches in the *'An·Atta·Lakkhaṇa'* sutta[397] to discern the five aggregates (all materiality, feeling, perception, formations, and consciousness) with right understanding in three ways, as: 'This is not mine' *(netaṁ mama)*, 'This I am not' *(nesohamasmi)*, and 'This is not my self' *(na meso attā)*.[398]

And in the *'Khandha'* sutta, He explains each of the five aggregates as **past, future, and present; internal and external; gross and subtle; inferior and superior; far and near.**[399]

To develop this knowledge, you first re-establish the fourth jhāna, with the light bright, brilliant, and radiant. If you, as a pure-vipassanā individual, have developed only the four-elements meditation, you re-establish concentration until the light is bright and strong. In either case, you take materiality as your first category. That is, you discern the concrete materiality[400] of each of the six sense doors,[401] see its arising and perishing, and know it as impermanence *(anicca)*. You need to do this internally and externally, alternately, again and again. While doing this externally, you should gradually extend your range of perception from near to far, to the infinite universe.

---

[393] five aggregates: materiality, feeling, perception, formations, consciousness, see quotation p.3.
[394] twelve bases: eye/sights, ear/sounds, nose/odours, tongue/flavours, body/touches, mind/dhammas. See quotation, p.5*ff.*
[395] twelve factors of dependent origination: 1) ignorance, 2) volitional formations, 3) consciousness, 4) mentality-materiality, 5) six sense bases, 6) contact, 7) feeling, 8) craving, 9) clinging, 10) existence, 11) birth, 12) ageing&death, sorrow, lamentation, pain, suffering and despair. See quotation p.21.
[396] eighteen elements: the twelve bases and their respective six types of consciousness: eye-, ear-, nose-, tongue-, body-, and mind consciousness (12 + 6 = 18): see p.5.
[397] S.III.I.II.i.7 *'An·Atta·Lakkhaṇa·Suttaṁ'* ('The Non-Self Characteristic Sutta'), quoted 'Introduction' p.25.
[398] The commentary to the M.III.v.2 *'Chann·Ovāda·Suttaṁ'* ('The Advice to Channa Sutta') explains that 'This is not mine' is a reflection on impermanence; 'This I am not' is a reflection on suffering; 'This is not my self' is a reflection on non-self.
[399] *'Khandha·Suttaṁ'* ('The Aggregates Sutta') S.III.I.v.6, quoted 'Introduction' p.4.
[400] For a list of concrete materiality, see table '2a: The Twenty-Eight Types of Materiality' p.137.
[401] For how you do this, see p.136.

Then, following the same procedure, see the pain and suffering one has to constantly experience because of that materiality's arising and perishing, and know it as suffering *(dukkha)*. Lastly, see the materiality as devoid of a permanent self, and know it as non-self *(an·atta)*.

The next category in which you need to see impermanence, suffering and non-self is mentality. First discern all the mentality at the six sense doors that you discerned before: that is, the consciousness and associated mental factors in each consciousness moment of each sense-door process *(vīthi)*, and the bhavaṅga consciousnesses that occur between them. You follow the same procedure as with materiality.

Having seen these two categories (the materiality and mentality of the six sense doors of the present), you need now to see the impermanence, suffering and non-self of the materiality and mentality of this life that you discerned, from the rebirth-linking consciousness up to the decease consciousness. Here again, you see the three characteristics one at a time, again and again, both internally and externally.

After doing this life, you need to see the impermanence, suffering, and non-self of the past, present and future lives that you discerned when discerning dependent origination. Here too, you see the three characteristics one at a time, internally and externally, again and again, in all the materiality and mentality that you discerned of the past, present, and future.

And then you need also to see the impermanence, suffering and non-self of the factors of dependent origination for the past, present and future, according to the first method of dependent origination:[402] one at a time, again and again, internally and externally.

At this stage, you may find that you develop the higher vipassanā knowledges quickly, stage by stage, up to the attainment of Arahantship. If not, there are several exercises to increase your vipassanā.

HOW YOU INCREASE YOUR VIPASSANĀ KNOWLEDGE

THE FORTY PERCEPTIONS

The first exercise is to see the impermanent, suffering, and non-self of mentality and materiality, internally and externally, in the past, present, and future according to forty different contemplations *(cattārīsākāra·anupassanā)*.[403] In Pali they all end with the suffix '*to*', so we call them the forty '*to*'.

---

402 For the first method of dependent origination, see p.193.

403 VsM.xx.697 *'Maggā·Magga·Ñāṇa·Dassana·Visuddhi·Niddesa'* ('Description of

(Please see further next page.)

There are ten different perceptions of impermanence:

1) Impermanence ..... *(aniccato)*
2) Disintegrating ..... *(palokato)*
3) Fickle ..... *(calato)*
4) Perishable ..... *(pabhaṅguto)*
5) Unenduring ..... *(a·ddhuvato)*
6) Of a changeable nature ..... *(vipariṇāma·dhammato)*
7) Coreless ..... *(a·sārakato)*
8) Extinguishable ..... *(vibhavato)*
9) Of a mortal nature ..... *(maraṇa·dhammato)*
10) Formed ..... *(saṅkhatato)*

There are twenty-five perceptions of suffering:

1) Suffering ..... *(dukkhato)*
2) A disease ..... *(rogato)*
3) A misery ..... *(aghato)*
4) A tumour ..... *(gaṇḍato)*
5) A dart ..... *(sallato)*
6) An affliction ..... *(ābādhato)*
7) A disaster ..... *(upaddavato)*
8) A fearsome thing ..... *(bhayato)*
9) A plague ..... *(ītito)*
10) A menace ..... *(upasaggato)*
11) No protection ..... *(a·tāṇato)*
12) No shelter ..... *(a·leṇato)*
13) No refuge ..... *(a·saraṇato)*
14) Murderous ..... *(vadhakato)*
15) The root of calamity ..... *(aghamūlato)*
16) A danger ..... *(ādīnavato)*
17) Tainted ..... *(sāsavato)*
18) Mara's bait ..... *(mārāmisato)*
19) Of a born nature ..... *(jāti·dhammato)*
20) Of an ageing nature ..... *(jarā·dhammato)*
21) Of an ailing nature ..... *(byādhi·dhammato)*
22) Of a sorrowful nature ..... *(soka·dhammato)*
23) Of a lamentable nature ..... *(parideva·dhammato)*
24) Of a despairing nature ..... *(upayāsa·dhammato)*
25) Of a defiled nature ..... *(saṁkilesika·dhammato)*

There are five perceptions of non-self:

1) Non-self ..... *(an·attato)*
2) Void ..... *(suññato)*
3) Alien ..... *(parato)*
4) Empty ..... *(rittato)*
5) Vain ..... *(tucchato)*

While seeing the forty '*to*' in mentality and materiality, internally and externally, in the past, present, and future, some people's vipassanā progresses to the attainment of Arahantship.

If not, there are then the exercises called the seven ways for materiality *(rūpa·sattaka)*, and the seven ways for mentality *(arūpa·sattaka)*.[404]

Path&Non-Path Knowledge&Vision Purification') PP.xx.18

[404] VsM.xx.706*ff* '*Rūpa·Sattaka·Sammasana·Kathā*', ('Material Septad-Group Discussion') PP.xx.46*ff*; ibid.717*ff* '*Arūpa·Sattaka·Sammasana·Kathā*', ('Immaterial Septad-Group Discussion' ibid.76*ff*)

THE SEVEN WAYS FOR MATERIALITY

The materiality you discern in the seven ways for materiality the four types according to origin (kamma-, temperature-, consciousness-, and nutriment-born materiality).[405]

1) In the first of the seven ways for materiality, you see the impermnence, suffering and non-self of the materiality of this entire lifetime, from rebirth-linking to death, both internally and externally.
2) In the second way for materiality you see the impermanence, suffering and non-self of the materiality of different periods in this lifetime, both internally and externally. You consider this lifetime to be a hundred years, and divide it into three periods of thirty-three years. Then see that the materiality in one period arises and ceases there, and does not pass on to the next period, which means it is impermanent, suffering and non-self.

   You then divide this lifetime into progressively smaller periods, and do the same. Divide the hundred years of this lifetime into: ten periods of ten years, twenty periods of five years, twenty-five periods of four years, thirty-three periods of three years, fifty periods of two years, and one hundred periods of one year; then three hundred periods of four months, six hundred periods of two months, and two thousand four hundred periods of half-a-month; and finally divide each day into two periods, and then six periods. In each case see that the materiality in one period arises and ceases there, and does not pass on to the next period, which means it is impermanent, suffering and non-self.

   You reduce the periods further to the duration of each movement of the body: the periods of going forth and going back, looking ahead and looking aside, and bending a limb and stretching a limb. Then you divide each footstep into six periods: lifting, raising, moving forward, lowering, placing and pressing. Again see the impermanence, suffering and non-self in the materiality of each period in this hundred-year lifetime.
3) In the third way for materiality you see the impermanence, suffering and non-self of nutriment-born materiality.[406] That is, you see them in the materiality of the periods when hungry, and when satisfied,

[405] For details on these four types of materiality, see p.110*ff.*

[406] This means that you discern all the four types of materiality that have arisen owing to the support of nutriment-born materiality. This principle applies also to the discernment of kamma-, consciousness-, and temperature-born materiality.

and see that it does not pass on from a period of hunger to a period of satiety (and vice-versa), every day in this hundred-year lifetime.

4) In the fourth way for materiality you see the impermanence, suffering and non-self of temperature-born materiality. That is, you see them in the materiality of the periods when hot, and when cold, and see that it does not pass on from a period of feeling hot to a period of feeling cold (and vice-versa), every day in this hundred-year lifetime.
5) In the fifth way for materiality you see the impermanence, suffering and non-self of kamma-born materiality. That is, you see that the materiality of each of the six sense doors arises and ceases there, and does not pass on to another door, every day in this hundred-year lifetime.
6) In the sixth way for materiality you see the impermanence, suffering and non-self of the consciousness-born materiality. That is, you see them in the materiality of the periods when happy and pleased, and when unhappy and sad, every day in this hundred-year lifetime.
7) In the seventh way for materiality you see the impermanence, suffering and non-self of present inanimate materiality. Materiality is inanimate when it is without kamma-born materiality such as the life faculty and the five translucencies. That is, for example, iron, steel, copper, gold, silver, plastic, pearls, gemstones, shells, marble, coral, soil, rocks, concrete and plants. Such materiality is found only externally.

These are the seven ways for materiality.

THE SEVEN WAYS FOR MENTALITY

In the seven ways for mentality, you see the impermanence, suffering and non-self of the vipassanā-minds (the mentality) that saw those three characteristics in the seven ways for materiality. This means your object is in each case an vipassanā-mind, which you see with a subsequent vipassanā-mind.[407]

1) In the first of the seven ways for mentality you see the impermanence, suffering and non-self of the materiality of the seven ways for

[407] vipassanā-mind: vipassanā mind-door process: one mind-door adverting consciousness and seven impulsions, sometimes followed by two registering consciousnesses. In the mind-door adverting consciousness there are twelve mental formations, and in each impulsion consciousness, there are thirty-four, thirty-three or thirty-two mental formations. See also table '1b: The Mind-Door Process', p.164.

materiality, but see the materiality as a group *(kalāpa)*. You then see the impermanence, suffering and non-self of the mentality that saw this. That means, you see the grouped materiality as impermanence, and then see the impermanence, suffering and non-self of that vipassanā-mind itself with in each case a subsequent vipassanā-mind. You do the same with the grouped materiality seen as suffering and non-self.

2) In the second way for mentality you see the impermanence, suffering and non-self of the mentality for each of the seven ways for materiality. That means, you see again the materiality in each of the seven ways for materiality as impermanence, and then see the impermanence, suffering and non-self of that vipassanā-mind itself with in each case a subsequent vipassanā-mind. You do the same with the materiality seen as suffering and non-self.
3) In the third way for mentality you see again the impermanence, suffering and non-self of the mentality for each of the seven ways for materiality, but do so four times in succession. That means, you see again the materiality in each of the seven ways for materiality as impermanence, and then see the impermanence, suffering and non-self of that first vipassanā-mind with a second vipassanā-mind, and the second with a third etc., until you with a fifth vipassanā-mind see the impermanence, suffering and non-self of the fourth vipassanā-mind.
4) In the fourth way for mentality you do as before, but continue until you with an eleventh vipassanā-mind see the impermanence, suffering and non-self of the tenth vipassanā-mind.
5) In the fifth way for mentality you see the impermanence, suffering and non-self of mentality for the removal of views *(diṭṭhi)*. Here again, you see the vipassanā-minds of the seven ways for materiality. Then, once the perceptions of impermanence and suffering have become strong and powerful, you intensify the perception of non-self. With the support of the other two perceptions, the intensified perception of non-self removes views, especially the view of self.
6) In the sixth way for mentality you see the impermanence, suffering and non-self of mentality for the removal of conceit *(māna)*. Again you see the vipassanā-minds of the seven ways for materiality. Then, once the perceptions of suffering and non-self have become strong and powerful, you intensify the perception of impermanence. With the support of the other two perceptions, the intensified perception of impermanence removes conceit.
7) In the seventh way for mentality you see the impermanence, suffering and non-self of mentality for the removal of attachment *(nikanti)*.

Again you see the vipassanā-minds of the seven ways for materiality. Then, once the perceptions of impermanence and non-self have become strong and powerful, you intensify the perception of suffering. Witht the support of the other two perceptions, the intensified perception of suffering removes attachment.

These are the seven ways for mentality. It is best, although not strictly necessary, to have done these exercises for the materiality and mentality of the present, past and future, internally and externally.

With the exercises completed, materiality and mentality will have become very clear to you.

Now the explanation of how to develop the knowledge of formations in categories is complete, so let us discuss how to develop the Arise&Perish Knowledge.

HOW YOU DEVELOP THE ARISE&PERISH KNOWLEDGE[408]

INTRODUCTION

The Arise&Perish Knowledge *(Udaya·Bbaya·Ñāṇa)* is to know the arising and perishing of formations: mentality-materiality, the five aggregates, the twelve bases, the eighteen elements, the Noble Truths, and dependent origination, internally and externally, in the present, past and future.[409] This knowledge consists, in fact, of two knowledges:

1) Knowledge of the causal *(paccayato)*: that is the causal arising and perishing of formations.
2) Knowledge of the momentary *(khaṇato)*: that is the momentary arising & perishing of formations.

To see the causal arising and perishing of formations, you see it, for example, according to the fifth method of dependent origination, as described in our previous talk.[410]

To see the momentary arising and perishing of formations you see how the five aggregates arise and perish in every consciousness moment of the mental processes that you have discerned, from rebirth to death of every life you have discerned.

---

[408] 'Perishing' is here used for *vaya*, 'cessation' for *nirodha*, although the two Pali terms are (as are the English) synonymous.

[409] VsM.xx.723 *'Maggā·Magga·Ñāṇa·Dassana·Visuddhi·Niddesa'* ('Description of Path-&Non-Path Knowledge&Vision Purification') PP.xx.93

[410] For the 'fifth method', see p.184*ff.*

There are two methods for developing the Arise&Perish Knowledge: the brief method (seeing only the momentary nature of formations), and the detailed method (seeing both the causal and momentary nature of formations). I shall explain only the detailed method.

The detailed method is developed in three stages. You see:

1) Only the arising *(udaya)*: that is the causal and momentary arising of formations.
2) Only the perishing *(vaya)*: that is the causal and momentary perishing of formations.
3) Both the arising & perishing *(udaya·bbaya)*: that is both the causal and momentary arising and perishing of formations.

HOW YOU DEVELOP THE ARISE&PERISH KNOWLEDGE ACCORDING TO THE FIFTH METHOD OF DEPENDENT ORIGINATION

THE CONTEMPLATION OF THE NATURE OF ARISING

To begin the detailed method for developing the Arise&Perish Knowledge, you should see again and again the causal and momentary arising of formations. This is the Contemplation of the Nature of Arising *(Samudaya·Dhamm·Ānupassi)*.

For example, you see the causal arising of materiality according to the fifth method of dependent origination, as just mentioned. This means you look back again to the near-death moments of your past life, to see the five past causes that caused the arising *(udaya)* in this life of kamma-born materiality.[411] One by one, you see how the arising (1) of ignorance, (2) of craving, (3) of clinging, (4) of volitional formations, and (5) of kamma, each caused the arising in this life of kamma-born materiality.

Afterwards, you see the momentary arising of kamma-born materiality in every consciousness moment of the mental processes that you have discerned, from rebirth to death.

This means you see the five aggregates at the arising *(udaya)* of the process-separate consciousnesses *(vīthi·mutta·citta)*,[412] and at the arising of each consciousness moment in all the intervening six sense-door processes

---

[411] For a brief explanation of materiality produced by kamma (with examples), see p.111*f.*

[412] process-separate consciousnesses *(vīthi·mutta·citta)*: the rebirth-linking consciousness *(paṭisandhi·citta)*, bhavaṅga consciousness and decease consciousness *(cuti·citta)*. For a brief explanation of process-separate consciousnesses etc., Table 1d 'Death and Rebirth', p.188, p.159, and footnote 184, p.104.

(vīthi) that you have discerned. You see this in every past life that you have discerned, and in all the future lives up to your Parinibbāna.[413]

You need then to see, one after the other, also the causal arising of temperature-, of consciousness-, and of nutriment-born materiality.[414] You see how:

- Consciousness caused the arising of consciousness-born materiality.
- Temperature caused the arising of temperature-born materiality.
- Nutriment caused the arising of nutriment-born materiality.

In each case, you see also the momentary arising of the particular type of materiality.

After this you have to see, in the same way, the causal and momentary arising of mentality, and see the arising of materiality and mentality in all the mental processes that you have discerned, in all the past and future lives that you have discerned. It would, however, take some time to list the details, so we shall pass them over, and in each instance explain the details for only materiality.

THE CONTEMPLATION OF THE NATURE OF PERISHING

After seeing the causal and momentary arising *(udaya)* of materiality and mentality, you now see again and again only their perishing *(vaya)*. This is the Contemplation of the Nature of Perishing *(vaya·dhamm·ānupassi)*.

The perishing of ignorance, craving, clinging, volitional formations, and the kammic potency[415] takes place when you attain Arahantship, and the cessation of the five aggregates takes place at your Parinibbāna. Whereas the causal arising is the individual type of ignorance, craving, clinging, volitional formation and kammic potency that you discern at each life where it takes place, the cessation is always in the same life: when the five aggregates at Parinibbāna no longer arise. But actual Nibbāna and the Arahant Path is not evident to us, because we have not yet realized the Four Path Knowledges *(Magga·Ñāṇa)* and Four Fruition Knowledges *(Phala-·Ñāṇa)*: we understand that our Parinibbāna has taken place, because there is no more arising of the aggregates.

---

413 In some cases, the yogi begins with this life alone, and then looks at past and future lives.

414 For a brief explanation of materiality produced by consciousness, by temperature, and by nutriment (with examples), see p.112*ff*.

415 There is, though, still the kammic potency from past volitional formations (before Arahantship) that manifests as pleasure and pain. There is no kammic potency in the present volitional formations, however, to produce new such results. See also, p.22.

For example, you see the causal cessation *(nirodha)* of materiality, again according to the fifth method of dependent origination.[416] That is when you look forward to the time when you become an Arahant, and see that when you attain the Arahant Path *(Arahatta·Magga)* and Arahant Fruition *(Arahatta·Phala)*, all defilements cease, and that at the end of that life all formations cease: it is directly seeing your Parinibbāna, after which no new materiality or mentality arises or passes away. Should you attain Arahantship in this very life, it will be in the future: should you attain Arahantship in one of your future lives, it will also be in the future. One by one, you see that the cessation *(nirodha)* (1) of ignorance, (2) of craving, (3) of clinging, (4) of volitional formations, and (5) of kamma respectively, each cause the cessation of kamma-born materiality.

Having in that way seen the causal cessation of kamma-born materiality, you now see only its momentary perishing.

Afterwards, you see the momentary perishing of kamma-born materiality in every consciousness moment of the mental processes that you have discerned, from rebirth to death, in every past and future life that you have discerned.[417] This means you again see the five aggregates at the arising *(udaya)* of the process-separate consciousnesses *(vīthi·mutta·citta)*, and at the arising of each consciousness moment in all the intervening six sense-door processes *(vīthi)* that you have discerned.[418]

You need then to see, one after the other, the causal cessation of consciousness-, of temperature-, and of nutriment-born materiality. You see how:

- The cessation of consciousness causes the cessation of consciousness-born materiality.
- The cessation of temperature causes the cessation of temperature-born materiality.
- The cessation of nutriment causes the cessation of nutriment-born materiality.

In each case, you see also the momentary perishing of the particular type of materiality.

After this you have to see the causal cessation and momentary perishing of mentality.

---

[416] For causal cessation according to the fifth method of dependent origination, see p.191.

[417] Sometimes the Most Venerable Pa-Auk Tawya Sayadaw instructs the yogi to start by looking at this life, and then to look at past lives and the future.

[418] For a brief explanation of process-separate consciousnesses etc., see Table 1d 'Death and Rebirth', p.188, p.159, and footnote 184, p.104.

THE CONTEMPLATION OF THE NATURE OF ARISING & PERISHING

Once you have seen both the causal and momentary cessation of materiality and mentality, you now see again and again both their arising and perishing. This is the Contemplation of the Nature of Arising & Perishing (*samudaya·vaya·dhamm·ānupassi*). It involves seeing first their causal arising and perishing, and then their momentary arising and perishing. You see each one in three ways successively:

1) The arising of the cause and its result.
2) The perishing of the cause and its result.
3) The impermanence of the cause and its result.

For example, you see one by one how:

1) The arising of each cause (1- ignorance, 2- craving, 3- clinging, 4- volitional formations, 5- kamma) causes the arising of kamma-born materiality.
2) The cessation of each same cause, causes the cessation of kamma-born materiality.
3) Each cause and the materiality it produced is impermanent.

Likewise, you see one by one how:

1) Consciousness causes the arising of consciousness-born materiality.
2) The cessation of consciousness causes the cessation of consciousness-born materiality.
3) Consciousness is impermanent, and consciousness-born materiality is impermanent.

And you see the same for temperature-, and nutriment-born materiality.

This is how you see both the causal and momentary arising and perishing of materiality. After that, you have to see the causal and momentary arising and perishing of mentality.

So, in the way just outlined, you see the causal and momentary arising and perishing of also the five aggregates, and see the three characteristics of impermanence, suffering, and non-self in them. You should do this for the five internal aggregates, the five external aggregates, and the five aggregates of the past, present, and future.

HOW YOU DEVELOP THE ARISE&PERISH KNOWLEDGE
ACCORDING TO THE FIRST METHOD OF DEPENDENT ORIGINATION

Next, you need to develop this vipassanā with also the first method of dependent origination.[419] In that case, to see the casual arising of formations, you see the factors of dependent origination one-by-one in forward order, and see that:[420]

[1] **Because of ignorance** *(avijjā)*, **formations** [arise] *(saṅkhārā)*;
[2] **because of formations, consciousness** *(viññāṇa)*;
[3] **because of consciousness, mentality-materiality** *(nāma·rūpa)*;
[4] **because of mentality-materiality, the six bases** *(saḷ·āyatana)*;
[5] **because of the six bases, contact** *(phassa)*;
[6] **because of contact, feeling** *(vedanā)*;
[7] **because of feeling, craving** *(taṇhā)*;
[8] **because of craving, clinging** *(upādāna)*;
[9] **because of clinging, existence** *(bhava)*;
[10] **because of existence, birth** *(jāti)*;
[11] **because of birth,**
[12] **ageing&death** *(jarā·maraṇa)*, **sorrow** *(soka)*, **lamentation** *(parideva)*, **pain** *(dukkha)*, **grief** *(domanassa)* **and despair** *(upāyāsā)* **arise.**

Such is the origin of this whole mass of suffering.

To see the causal cessation of formations at Arahantship, and the resultant Parinibbāna, you see the factors of dependent-cessation one-by-one in forward order, to see that:[421]

[1] **With ignorance's remainderless fading away and cessation, volitional formations cease;**
[2] **with volitional formations' cessation, consciousness ceases;**
[3] **with consciousness's cessation, mentality-materiality ceases;**
[4] **with mentality-materiality's cessation, the six sense bases cease;**
[5] **with the six sense bases' cessation, contact ceases;**
[6] **with contact's cessation, feeling ceases;**
[7] **with feeling's cessation, craving ceases;**
[8] **with craving's cessation, clinging ceases;**
[9] **with clinging's cessation, existence ceases;**
[10] **with existence's cessation, birth ceases;**
[11] **with birth's cessation,**
[12] **ageing&death, sorrow, lamentation, pain, grief and despair cease.**

Such is the cessation of this whole mass of suffering.

---

[419] See also p.193.

[420] M.I.iv.8 *'Mahā·Taṇhā·Saṅkhaya·Suttaṁ'* ('The Great Craving-Destruction Sutta')

[421] ibid.

As before, you see both the causal and momentary arising and perishing of formations. You see the factors of dependent origination and cessation one-by-one in forward order. For example, in the case of ignorance, you see:

1) Ignorance causes volitional formations.
2) With the remainderless fading away and cessation of ignorance, volitional formations cease.
3) Ignorance is impermanent, volitional formations are impermanent.

You see each of the factors of dependent origination in the same way, internally and externally, in the past, present, and future.

This is a very brief explanation of how you develop the Arise&Perish Knowledge of formations.

HOW YOU OVERCOME THE TEN IMPERFECTIONS

It is at this stage that, as you apply these methods, and your vipassanā becomes stronger, the ten imperfections *(dasa upakkilesa)* may arise. The ten imperfections are:[422]

1) Light	*(obhāsa)*	1) Confidence	*(adhimokkha)*
2) Knowledge	*(ñāṇa)*	2) Exertion	*(paggaha)*
3) Joy	*(pīti)*	3) Foundation [mindfulness]	*(upaṭṭhāna)*
4) Tranquillity	*(passaddhi)*	4) Equanimity	*(upekkhā)*
5) Happiness	*(sukha)*	5) Attachment	*(nikanti)*

With the exception of light and attachment, the imperfections are wholesome states, and are as such not imperfections. But they can become the objects for unwholesome state (you may become attached to them), which is why they are called imperfections. Should you experience any of the ten vipassanā imperfections, you need to ovecome the attachment and desire that may arise, by seeing it as impermanence, suffering, and non-self: that way, you can continue to make progress.

---

[422] VsM.xx.634 *'Vipassan·Upakkilesa·Kathā'* ('Vipassanā Imperfection Discussion') PP.xx.107 explains how the yogi may experience light such as never experienced before; knowledge of mentality-materiality sharp as never experienced before, joy, tireless tranquillity, very refined happiness, very strong confidence and decision, very well balanced and continuous exertion, very well established mindfulness, and very stable equanimity, all such as never experienced before. Because of inexperience, the yogi may very easily think these things are equivalent to a Path&Fruit, may become attached to them, and develop wrong view and conceit. That is how those things can become what we call insight contaminations *(vipassan·upakkilesa)*. They are very dangerous, because they lead the yogi off the right path onto the wrong path.

HOW YOU DEVELOP THE DISSOLUTION KNOWLEDGE

After you have developed the Arise&Perish Knowledge, your vipassanā concerning formations is steadfast and pure. Then you have to develop the Dissolution Knowledge *(Bhaṅga·Ñāṇa)*. To do this, you concentrate on only the momentary perishing *(vaya)* and dissolution *(bhaṅga)* of formations. You see neither the arising *(uppāda)* of formations, nor the standing *(ṭhiti)* of formations, nor the signs *(nimitta)* of individual formations, nor the causal occurrence *(pavatta)* of formations. Using the power of your vipassanā knowledge, you see only the dissolution of formations, and perceive them as impermanence, suffering and non-self.

1) You see the destruction, fall, and dissolution of formations, to see their impermanence.
2) You see the continuous dissolution of formations as fearful, to see the suffering in them.
3) You see the absence of any permanent essence in formations, to see non-self.

You have to see the impermanence, suffering and non-self in not only the dissolution of mentality-materiality, but also in the dissolution of those vipassanā-minds that saw this. That means, you see the dissolution of materiality and know it is impermanent. That is your first vipassanā mind. Then, with a second vipassanā-mind you see the dissolution of the first vipassanā-mind, and thus know it too is impermanent. You do the same for mentality, and then again for materiality and mentality to know them as suffering and non-self. You repeat these exercises again and again, alternating between internal and external, materiality and mentality, causal formations and resultant formations: past, present and future.

As you continue to discern the perishing and ceasing of formations in this way, your strong and powerful vipassanā will progress through the next six vipassanā knowledges.

YOU KNOW THE FIRST ELEVEN KNOWLEDGES

At this stage, you will have developed the first eleven of the sixteen knowledges. The first five knowledges that you have already developed are:

1) Mentality-Materiality Definition Knowledge *(Nāma·Rūpa·Pariccheda·Ñāṇa)*[423]

---

[423] See Talk 4 'How You Discern Materiality' (p.107*ff*), and Talk 5 'How You Discern

(Please see further next page.)

2) Cause-Apprehending Knowledge *(Paccaya·Pariggaha·Ñāṇa)*[424]
3) Comprehension Knowledge *(Sammasana·Ñāṇa)*[425]
4) Arise&Perish Knowledge *(Udaya·bbaya·Ñāṇa)*[426]
5) Dissolution Knowledge *(Bhaṅga·Ñāṇa)*[427]

And the next six knowledges that you will progress through are:

6) Fearsomeness Knowledge *(Bhaya·Ñāṇa)*
7) Danger Knowledge *(Ādīnava·Ñāṇa)*
8) Disenchantment Knowledge *(Nibbidā·Ñāṇa)*
9) Liberation-Longing Knowledge *(Muñcitukamyatā·Ñāṇa)*
10) Reflection Knowledge *(Paṭisaṅkhā·Ñāṇa)*
11) Formations-Equanimity Knowledge *(Saṅkhār·Upekkhā·Ñāṇa)*

Since you developed the first five vipassanā knowledges thoroughly, these six knowledges develop quickly. There are a few instructions for them, but we do not have time to explain.

YOU KNOW AND SEE NIBBĀNA

After realizing these knowledges, as you continue to see the perishing and vanishing of each formation, with a wish for release from them, you will find that eventually all formations cease. Your mind knows and sees Nibbāna directly: it is fully aware of the (unformed) Nibbāna as object. This takes place with the arising of the Path-process *(Magga·vīthi)*.

With the arising of the Path-process *(Magga·vīthi)*, you go through the remaining five knowledges. They are:

12) Conformity Knowledge *(Anuloma·Ñāṇa)*
13) Change-of-Lineage Knowledge *(Gotrabhu·Ñāṇa)*
14) Path Knowledge *(Magga·Ñāṇa)*
15) Fruition Knowledge *(Phala·Ñāṇa)*
16) Reviewing Knowledge *(Paccavekkhaṇa·Ñāṇa)*

These last five knowledges arise with the arising of the Path Process. It consists of a sequence of seven types of consciousness:

Mentality', p.159*ff.*

[424] See Talk 6 'How You See the Links of Dependent Origination', p.183*ff.*

[425] See 'How You Develop the Comprehension Knowledge', p.209*ff.*

[426] See 'How You Develop the Arise&Perish Knowledge', p.216*ff.*

[427] See 'How You Develop the Dissolution Knowledge', p.223*f.*

1) A mind-door adverting consciousness arises that sees formations as impermanence, suffering or non-self, depending on how the Formations-Equanimity Knowledge[428] arose.

Afterwards, there arise three preparatory impulsion consciousnesses *(javana)* which see formations in the same way.

2) Preparation *(parikamma)*[429]
3) Access *(upacāra)*
4) Conformity *(anuloma)*

These three impulsion consciousnesses comprise, in fact, the twelfth knowledge: the Conformity Knowledge *(Anuloma·Ñāṇa)*. Conformity to what? To what came before, and to what will come after. Thus they may be said to function as preparation for, access to and conformity with the Change of Lineage. Their repetition prepares the way for transition from the eight insight knowledges that came before (from the Arise&Perish Knowledge to the Formations-Equanimity Knowledge) with the formed as object to the thirty-seven dhammas of the Path&Fruition Knowledges with the Unformed as object.[430]

The Conformity Knowledge is the last knowledge that has formations as its object.

5) A fourth impulsion consciousness arises, with Nibbāna as object. This is the thirteenth knowledge: Change-of-Lineage Knowledge *(Gotrabhu·Ñāṇa)*.

Although this consciousness knows the (unformed) Nibbāna, it does not destroy the defilements: its function is to change the lineage from ordinary person to Noble.

6) A fifth impulsion consciousness arises, with Nibbāna as object. This is the fourteenth knowledge, which destroys the appropriate defilements:[431] Path Knowledge *(Magga·Ñāṇa)*.

---

[428] Knowledge No. 11

[429] In some cases, if the yogi's vipassanā is very strong, this consciousness does not arise, and the first impulsion consciousness is 'access' *(upacāra)*, which in this case is number three. See also table '1b: The Mind-Door Process', p.164.

[430] These are the thirty-seven requisites of enlightenment *(Bodhi·Pakkhiya·Dhamma)*: the four foundations of mindfulness, the four Right Efforts, the four roads to power, the five faculties, the five powers, the seven enlightenment factors, and the Noble Eightfold Path. For a brief explanation, see p.245*ff*, and VsM.xxii.817-826 *'Ñāṇa·Dassana·Visuddhi·Niddesa'* ('Description of Knowledge&Vision Purification') PP.xxii.32-43.

[431] For example, Stream-Entry destroys the first three fetters *(saṁyojana)* (1- personality view *(sakkāya·diṭṭhi)*, 2- doubt about The Buddha, Dhamma and Saṅgha, 3- clinging to rule-&-rite), and cuts of lust, hatred and delusion powerful enough to lead to a rebirth lower

(Please see further next page.)

7) A sixth and seventh[432] impulsion consciousness arises, with Nibbāna as object. They are the fifteenth knowledge: Fruition Knowledge *(Phala·Ñāṇa)*.

YOU REVIEW YOUR KNOWLEDGE

After this follows the last and sixteenth knowledge, the Reviewing Knowledge *(Paccavekkhaṇa·Ñāṇa)*. It is five separate reviewings:

1) Reviewing the Path Knowledge.
2) Reviewing the Fruition Knowledge.
3) Reviewing the defilements that have been destroyed.
4) Reviewing the defilements that have yet to be destroyed.[433]
5) Reviewing Nibbāna.

Then you will have attained true knowledge of the Four Noble Truths, and will for yourself have realized Nibbāna. With this realization, your mind will have become purified and free from wrong views. If you continue in this way, you will be able to attain Arahantship and Parinibbāna. There are many more details about this development of vipassanā, but we have had to leave them out, so as to make this explanation as brief as possible. The best way to learn about this practice is by undertaking a meditation course with a competent teacher, because then you can learn in a systematic way, step by step.[434]

than a human one. Complete destruction of the defilements is achieved only at Arahantship.

432 If no 'preliminary work' *(parikamma)* consciousness arose, these consciousnesses will be a fifth, sixth and seventh (three) to complete the necessary seven impulsion consciousnesses. See also table '1b: The Mind-Door Process', p.164.

433 Nos. 1, 2, and 5 arise automatically. Nos. 3, and 4 you need to do deliberately, and require that you know how to do it.

434 For contact addresses, see Appendix 2, p.287.

Question 7.1 What is the difference between perception *(saññā)* and the perception aggregate *(saññā·kkhandha)*, and between feeling *(vedāna)* and the feeling aggregate *(vedānā·kkhandha)*?

Answer 7.1 The eleven categories of perception *(saññā)* together are called the perception aggregate *(saññā·kkhandha)*. The eleven categories of feeling *(vedānā)* together are called the feeling aggregate *(vedānā·kkhandha)*. What are the eleven? Past, present, future, internal, external, gross, subtle, inferior, superior, near, and far. All five aggregates should be understood in the same way. Please refer to the *'Khandha'* sutta[435] of the *'Khandha·Vagga'* in the *Saṁyutta·Nikāya* for the explanation.

Question 7.2 To which associated mental factors do memory, inference and creativity belong? They are part of the five aggregates, but how do they become suffering *(dukkha)*?

Answer 7.2 What is memory? If you remember samatha meditation- objects, such as a kasiṇa- or *ān·āpāna nimitta* is Right Mindfulness *(Sammā·Sati)*. If you can see past, present, and future ultimate mentality-materiality *(paramattha·nāma·rūpa)* and their causes, and see them as impermanence *(anicca)*, suffering *(dukkha)*, and non-self *(an·atta)*, this is also Right Mindfulness *(Sammā·Sati)*; the mindfulness associated with vipassanā knowledge. This mindfulness is associated with thirty-three mental formations, which together are the four mentality aggregates *(nāma·kkhandha)*. Remembering The Buddha, the Dhamma, the Saṅgha, and offerings made in the past is also Right Mindfulness *(Sammā·Sati)*. When the remembering of actions produces wholesome dhammas *(kusala·dhammā)*, it is also Right Mindfulness, but not when it produces unwholesome dhammas *(akusala·dhammā)*. These are unwholesome perceptions *(akusala·saññā)*, perceptions associated with unwholesome dhammas; they are also the four mentality aggregates.

The wholesome and unwholesome mentality aggregates are impermanent. As soon as they arise, they perish; they are subject to constant arising and perishing, which is why they are suffering.

Question 7.3 Which associated mental factor does 'Taking an object' involve?

Answer 7.3 All consciousnesses *(citta)* and associated mental factors *(cetasika)* take an object. Without an object they cannot occur. Consciousness and associated mental factors are the subject. The subject, *ārammaṇika-·dhamma*, cannot arise without an object *(ārammaṇa)*. *Ārammaṇika* is the dhamma or phenomenon that takes an object. In other words, the dhamma

---

435 *'Khandha·Suttaṁ'* ('The Aggregates Sutta') quoted p.4.

that knows an object. If there is no object to be known, then there is no dhamma that knows. Different groups of consciousness and associated mental factors take different objects. There are eighty-nine types of consciousness *(citta)*, and fifty-two types of associated mental factor *(cetasika)*; they all take their respective object. For example, the Path and Fruition consciousnesses and associated mental factors *(Magga·citta·cetasika)* and *(Phala·citta·cetasika)* take only one object, Nibbāna; an *ān·āpāna* jhāna consciousness and associated mental factors take only one object, the *ān·āpāna paṭibhāga-nimitta*; the earth-kasiṇa jhāna takes only the earth-kasiṇa *paṭibhāga-nimitta* as object. They are supramundane and fine-material sphere consciousnesses. But a sensual-sphere consciousness *(kām·āvacara·citta)* takes different objects, good or bad. If you want to know in detail, you should study the Abhidhamma; more exactly the *Ārammaṇa* section of the *Abhidhammattha·Saṅgaha*.[436]

Question 7.4 Does work for the Saṅgha affect one's meditation? Does it depend on the individual, or can one achieve a certain degree of concentration, after which work has no effect?

Answer 7.4 In many suttas The Buddha criticizes bhikkhus who practise the following:

- Pleasure in working *(kammā·rāmatā)*
- Pleasure in talking *(bhassā·rāmatā)*
- Pleasure in sleeping *(niddā·rāmatā)*
- Pleasure in company *(saṅghaṇikā·rāmatā)*
- Not controlling the faculties *(indriyesu a·guttadvāratā)*
- Not knowing the proper amount of food to take *(bhojāne a·mattaññutā)*
- Not devoted to vigilance *(jāgariye an·anuyuttā)*: to practise samatha-vipassanā with only moderate sleep.
- Laziness *(kusita* [or] *kosajja)*: not practising samatha-vipassanā diligently.

So if there is any work you have to do for the Saṅgha or yourself, try to do it as quickly as possible, and then return to your meditation with a peaceful mind.

If you enjoy working too much, it is a hindrance to meditation, because strong and powerful mindfulness on the meditation object can then not be attained: enjoying work does not produce good concentration.

Question 7.5 Can a person who develops the jhānas with evil intent benefit from attaining them? And how about a person who has, for example, spent the money of a Saṅgha[437] for his personal use and does not think it

[436] e.g. *A Comprehensive Manual of Abhidhamma*, Ed. Bhikkhu Bodhi, BPS

[437] The Buddha made it a serious offence against the monastic rule *(Vinaya)* for a monk to

(Please see further next page.)

is wrong. When he attains jhāna up to the fourth jhāna, does his mind or view change?

Answer 7.5 In this case you should distinguish between a layman and a bhikkhu. If a bhikkhu has committed an offence *(āpatti)*, it is a hindrance to attain jhāna. For example, if he has appropriated an allowable requisite of a Saṅgha for his personal use, it is not easy for him to attain jhāna, unless he corrects that offence *(āpatti)*.[438] That means he must pay it back with requisites of equal value to the allowable requisites he used. Then he should confess his offence in front of the Saṅgha, or to another bhikkhu. That means he should do a confession of offence *(āpatti·paṭidesanā)*. After correcting his fault, if he practises samatha-vipassanā, he can attain jhāna, Path, and Fruition. If, without correcting his fault he really did attain jhāna, then maybe he is not a real bhikkhu, and so the offence was in fact not an offence.

For lay-people, purification of conduct is also necessary, and it is better if they purify their conduct before meditating, that is, if they undertake either the five or eight precepts. That way, while meditating, their conduct is pure, and they can attain jhāna, although they were evil before meditation. For example, in the *Dhamma·Pada Commentary*, there is a story about the servant Khujjuttarā.[439] She was a servant of King Udena's wife Queen Sāmāvatī. Every day King Udena gave her eight coins to buy flowers for the queen, and every day Khujjuttarā put four of the coins into her pocket, and bought flowers with only the other four. One day, The Buddha came with the Saṅgha for almsfood at the florist's house. Khujjuttarā helped the florist give the almsfood. After the meal The Buddha gave a Dhamma-talk, during which Khujjuttarā developed shame at having stolen the money, and decided not to steal any more. Her decision is an example of morality purified while listening to the Dhamma. With meditation, Khujjuttarā became a Stream-Enterer *(Sot·Āpanna)*. On that day

---

accept, receive, possess, or handle money under any form. This prohibition is observed and taught by the Most Venerable Pa-Auk Tawya Sayadaw.

438 This question involves two offences. One is the use of property belonging to the Saṅgha (money cannot be handled by the Saṅgha, but may be held in custody and handled by a layperson, although he may not be appointed to do so by the Saṅgha). The other offence is using and handling money. The first offence cannot be rectified by again committing the offence of using money. The first offence can be rectified only by allowable means, which is to compensate the Saṅgha with allowable requisites (money is not an allowable requisite) that have been obtained in an allowable way (not purchased by a bhikkhu). Hence, in his answer, the Most Venerable Sayadaw discusses rectification of the offence only in terms of 'allowable requisites'.

439 DhPA.I.ii.1 *'Sāmāvatī·Vatthu'* ('The Sāmāvatī Case')

she did not put four coins in her pocket, but bought flowers for all eight coins. When she gave the flowers to Queen Sāmāvatī, the queen was surprised because there were more flowers than usual. Then Khujjuttarā confessed.

Consider also the case of the Venerable Aṅgulimāla. Before he became a bhikkhu, he was a notorious murderer. But as a bhikkhu, he purified his conduct and strove hard in meditation. So he was able to attain Arahantship.

Consider also this fact: in the round of rebirths everybody has done good and bad actions. There is no one who is free from bad actions.[440] But if they purify their conduct while meditating, then previous bad actions cannot prevent them from attaining jhāna. That is, however, only as long as those previous bad actions are not any of the five unintervenable kammas *(an·antariya·kamma)*.[441]

The five unintervenable kammas are:

1) Killing one's mother,
2) Killing one's father,
3) Killing an Arahant,
4) With evil intention shedding the blood of a Buddha,
5) Causing a schism in the Saṅgha.

If any of these evil actions has been done one cannot attain jhāna, Path, and Fruition, just like King Ajātasattu. King Ajātasattu had enough *pāramī* to become a Stream-Enterer *(Sot·Āpanna)* after listening to the '*Sāmañña·Phala*' sutta.[442] But because he had killed his own father, King Bimbisāra, it did not happen.

You asked whether after attaining jhāna, such people's mind or view changes. Jhāna can remove the hindrances for a long time. 'A long time' means, if they enter jhāna for about an hour, then within that hour the hindrances do not occur. When they emerge from jhāna, the hindrances may recur because of unwise attention. So we cannot say for certain whether such a person's mind will change with jhāna. We can say only that so long as he is in jhāna, the hindrances do not occur.[443]

---

440 In other words, if bad actions in the past made it impossible for one to attain jhāna, no one would be able to attain jhāna.

441 See e.g. A.V.ix.3 '*Parikuppa·Suttaṁ*' ('The "Festering" Sutta').These five kammas are called 'immediate', because they will definitely ripen in the present life, and give rise to rebirth in the big hell of Avīci, or one of its minor hells, as was the case for King Ajātasattu.

442 D.2 'The Fruits of Asceticism Sutta'

443 Regarding jhāna and vipassanā and views, see also Q&As 7.7 and 7.9, p.232.

There are exceptions, as for example, with the Venerable Mahāthera Mahānāga.[444] Although he had practised samatha and vipassanā meditation for more than sixty years, he was still an ordinary person *(puthu·jjana)*. Even so, because of his strong, powerful samatha and vipassanā practices, no defilements appeared in those sixty years. Due to this, he thought he was an Arahant. But one of his disciples, the Arahant Dhammadinna, knew he was still a ordinary person, and helped him realize indirectly that this was so. When Mahānāga Mahāthera discovered that he was still a ordinary person, he practised vipassanā, and within a few minutes attained Arahantship. But this is a most exceptional case.

You should remember another thing too: he was expert in the scriptures *(pariyatti)* as well as practice *(paṭipatti)*. He was also a meditation teacher *(kammaṭṭhān·ācariya)*, and there were many Arahants who, like Dhammadinna, were his disciples. Although he was expert in samatha and vipassanā, sometimes misunderstandings occured in his mind because of a similarity in experiences. So if you think to yourself, 'I have attained the first jhāna, etc.', you should examine your experience thoroughly over many days and many months. Why? If it is real jhāna and real vipassanā, then they are beneficial to you, as they can help you attain real Nibbāna, which is the 'Pureland'[445] of Theravāda Buddhism. But artificial jhāna and artificial vipassanā cannot give rise to this benefit. Do you want the real benefit or the artificial benefit? You should ask yourself this question.

So we should like to suggest, that you do not say to others, 'I have attained the first jhāna, etc.' too soon, because there may be someone who does not believe you. It could be that your experience is genuine, but it could also be false like with Mahānāga Mahāthera. You should be aware of this problem.

Question 7.6 What is the difference between rūpa-kalāpas and ultimate materiality *(paramattha·rūpa)*?[446]

---

444 VsM.xx.733 *'Vipassan·Upakkilesa·Kathā'* ('Vipassanā Imperfection Discussion' PP.xx.110-113)

445 Pureland: The so-called 'Western Land', 'Land of Ultimate Bliss' in Mahāyāna teaching, where a Buddha called Amitabbha Buddha is waiting. Rebirth there is obtained by reciting his name. The aim in the Mahāyāna tradition is, on the whole, rebirth in Pureland, as all who go there will become Buddhas, and then go and save all beings of all world systems. The Most Venerable Pa-Auk Tawya Sayadaw speaks here of 'the "Pureland" of Theravāda Buddhism' only as a metaphor for Nibbāna that will suit his Mahāyāna audience: he is not suggesting that Nibbāna is a place, or in any way to be compared with the 'Western Land' etc. See 'supramundane plane' *(lokuttara·bhūmi)* explained Q&A 3.12, p.104.

446 For details between rūpa-kalāpas and ultimate materiality, see further p.124.

Answer 7.6 Rūpa-kalāpas are small particles. When a yogi analyses those little particles, he sees ultimate materiality *(paramattha·rūpa)*. In a rūpa-kalāpa, there are at least eight types of materiality: earth, water, fire, wind, colour, odour, flavour, and nutritive essence. These eight types of materiality are ultimate materiality. In some rūpa-kalāpas there is a ninth too: life-faculty materiality *(jīvita·rūpa)*; and in others a tenth: sex-materiality *(bhāva·rūpa)* or translucent materiality *(pasāda·rūpa)*. These eight, nine or ten types of materiality are all ultimate materiality.

Question 7.7 When a yogi is able to see rūpa-kalāpas or ultimate materiality, will his mind *(citta)* and views *(diṭṭhi)* change?
Answer 7.7 When he with vipassanā knowledge sees ultimate materiality in each rūpa-kalāpa, his mind and views change, but only temporarily, because vipassanā knowledge removes wrong views and other defilements only temporarily. It is the Noble Path *(Ariya·Magga)* that stage by stage destroys wrong views and other defilements totally.[447]

Question 7.8 How does concentration purify consciousness (*(citta·visuddhi)*)? What kinds of defilement *(kilesa)* are removed by concentration?
Answer 7.8 Concentration practice is directly opposite the five hindrances. Access- and first-jhāna concentration remove the five hindrances for a long time. Second-jhāna concentration removes application *(vitakka)* and sustainment *(vicāra)*. Third-jhāna concentration removes *(pīti)*. Fourth-jhāna concentration removes bliss *(sukha)*. That is how consciousness is purified by concentration, and that is called consciousness purification *(citta·visuddhi)*.[448]

Question 7.9 How does vipassanā purify views (*(diṭṭhi·visuddhi)*)? What kinds of defilement *(kilesa)* are removed by vipassanā?
Answer 7.9 Before seeing ultimate mentality-materiality, their causes, and nature of impermanence, suffering, and non-self, a yogi may have wrong views or wrong perceptions, such as, 'This is a man, a woman, a mother, a father, a self, etc.' But when he sees ultimate mentality-materiality, their causes, and nature of impermanence, suffering, and non-self clearly, this wrong view is removed temporarily. Why is it removed? He sees that there are only ultimate mentality-materiality and their causes. He sees also that as soon as they arise, they perish, which is their nature of impermanence. They are always subject to arising and perishing, which is their nature of suffering. There is no self in these mentality-materiality and causes, which is their nature of non-self. This is vipassanā knowledge

---

[447] Regarding jhāna and vipassanā and views, see also Q&A 7.5, and Q&A 7.9.

[448] For details regarding the different jhānas, see 'How You Attain Jhāna', p.43*ff*.

(vipassanā·ñāṇa). It is Right View *(Sammā·Diṭṭhi)*, and removes wrong views *(micchā·diṭṭhi)*. Vipassanā knowledge also removes defilements such as attachment and conceit, which are 'partners' to wrong view. So while a yogi is practising vipassanā, Right View is present. But it is only temporary, because when he stops meditating, wrong view recurs because of unwise attention *(ayoniso manasikāra)*. He again perceives: 'this is a man, a woman, a mother, a father, a self, etc.,' and the associated defilements such as attachment, conceit, and anger, will also recur. But, when he goes back to vipassanā meditation, this wrong view again disappears. So vipassanā knowledge removes wrong views and other defilements only temporarily. When he reaches the Path and Fruition, however, his Path Knowledge *(Magga·Ñāṇa)* will destroy those wrong views and other defilements completely, stage by stage.[449]

Question 7.10 What is the difference between *citta* and *diṭṭhi*?
Answer 7.10 *Citta* means consciousness or mind, but in *citta·visuddhi* (consciousness purification), it refers especially to a consciousness: an access-concentration consciousness *(upacāra·samādhi·citta)* or absorption-jhāna consciousness *(appanā·jhāna citta)*.[450] *Diṭṭhi* means wrong view, and is an associated mental factor *(cetasika)*. It arises together with the four consciousnesses rooted in greed. A consciousness rooted in greed *(lobha·mūla·citta)* is associated with either wrong view or conceit.

One wrong view is the perception of self *(atta·saññā)*. There are two types of perception of self.

1) The world's general perception of self *(loka·samañña·attavāda)*: this is wrong view because of convention: the perception that there is a man, woman, father, mother, etc.
2) Wrong view of self *(atta·diṭṭhi)*: this is wrong view because of craving *(taṇhā)*: the perception of an indestructible self *(atta)*, which may include the perception that the indestructible self is created by a creator *(paramatta)*.

In the thirty-one realms there is no self, only mentality-materiality and their causes. They are always impermanent, suffering, and non-self. Outside the thirty-one realms there is no self either. This vipassanā knowledge is Vipassanā Right View *(Vipassanā·Sammā·Diṭṭhi)*. It destroys wrong view *(micchā diṭṭhi)* temporarily, including wrong view of self. But the Path Knowledge *(Magga·Ñāṇa)*, which is Path Right View *(Magga·Sammā·Diṭṭhi)*, de-

[449] Regarding jhāna and vipassanā and views, see also Q&A 7.5, and Q&A 7.7.
[450] Regarding the different kinds of concentration etc., see Q&A 3.1, p.95.

stroys wrong view completely. So what we have is in fact three types of view:

1) Wrong view *(micchā·diṭṭhi)*
2) Vipassanā Right View *(Vipassanā·Sammā·Diṭṭhi)*, which is mundane *(lokiya)*.
3) Path Right View *(Magga·Sammā·Diṭṭhi)*, which is supramundane *(lokuttara)*.

In the *'Brahmajāla'* sutta, all sixty-two types of wrong view that exist are discussed.[451] They all go under wrong view of self, which is also called 'personality wrong view' *(sakkāya·diṭṭhi)*. Personality *(sakkāya)* is the five aggregates, so personality wrong view is to see the five aggregates as self. There are also many types of Right View, such as the Right Views called 'Right Views about the Four Noble Truths' *(Catu·Sacca·Sammā·Diṭṭhi)*:

- Jhāna Right View *(Jhāna·Sammā·Diṭṭhi)*: jhāna knowledge associated with the jhāna factors.
- Mentality-Materiality Apprehending *(Nāma·Rūpa·Pariggaha)* Right View *(Sammā·Diṭṭhi)*: the Mentality-Materiality Definition Knowledge.
- Kamma-Ownership Right View *(Kamma·Ssakatā·Sammā·Diṭṭhi)*: the Cause-Apprehending Knowledge.
- Vipassanā Right View *(Vipassanā·Sammā·Diṭṭhi)*: vipassanā knowledge of the impermanent, suffering, and non-self nature of mentality-materiality and their causes.
- Path Right View *(Magga·Sammā·Diṭṭhi)*: knowledge of Nibbāna.
- Fruition Right View *(Phala·Sammā·Diṭṭhi)*: knowledge of Nibbāna.

Question 7.11 How should a yogi practise wise attention *(yoniso manasikāra)* in his daily life, and how in his samatha-vipassanā practice? [452]

Answer 7.11 The best wise attention is vipassanā. If you practise up to the vipassanā level, you will have the truly best wise attention. If you then practise vipassanā in your daily life, it will produce good results, such as Path and Fruition that see Nibbāna. But if you cannot practise up to the vipassanā level, you should consider the fact that all formations are impermanent *(sabbe saṅkhārā aniccā)*. This is also wise attention, but very weak, and only second-hand.

You can also practise the four sublime abidings *(brahma·vihāra)*, and especially the sublime abiding of equanimity *(upekkhā·brahma·vihāra)*. That is superior wise attention, because to practise the sublime abiding of equanimity is to see beings with regard to the law of kamma: '*Sabbe sattā kamma·ssakā*': 'All beings are the owners of their kamma'. You can also some-

---

[451] D.i.1 *'Brahma·Jāla·Suttaṁ'* ('The Supreme Net Sutta')

[452] For details regarding wise/unwise attention, see also 'Wise and Unwise Attention', p.165.

times reflect on the effects of unwise attention. Unwise attention causes many unwholesome kammas to come one by one. These unwholesome kammas will produce much suffering in the four woeful realms *(apāya)*. To know this is wise attention. You should practise it in your daily life.

Question 7.12 What is the difference between attention *(manasikāra)* and practising the seven enlightenment factors *(bojjh·aṅga)*?

Answer 7.12 When you practise the seven enlightenment factors, they are usually at the head of thirty-four mental formations that include attention. Sometimes the thirty-four mental formations are called 'vipassanā knowledge', because the thirty-fourth mental-formation, wisdom *(paññā)* is the main factor.

In this connection, you should know the three types of attention:

1) Attention as the basic cause for the object *(ārammaṇa paṭipādaka manasikāra)*: that is the associated mental factor of attention. Its function is to make the object clear to the yogi's mind.
2) Attention as the basic cause for the mental process *(vīthi paṭipādaka manasikāra)*: that is the five-door adverting consciousness *(pañca·dvār·āvajjana)* in the five-door process *(pañca·dvāra·vīthi)*. Its function is to enable all five-door processes to take their respective object.
3) Attention as the basic cause for the impulsion *(javana·paṭipādaka manasikāra)*: that is the mind-door adverting consciousness *(mano·dvār·āvajjana)* in the mind-door process *(mano·dvāra vīthi)*, and determining consciousness *(voṭṭhapana)* in the five-door process. It is either wise attention or unwise attention. Its function is to make the impulsion *(javana)* occur. If it is wise attention, the impulsion *(javana)* is for ordinary persons *(puthu·jjana)* and learners *(sekha)* wholesome, and for Arahants only functional *(kiriya)*. When it is unwise attention, the impulsion is always unwholesome, and cannot occur in Arahants.

Question 7.13 Could the Sayadaw please explain the diagram?[453] Is it necessary, in this system of meditation, to practise the more than thirty types of meditation subject *(kammaṭṭhāna)*? What are the benefits in doing so?

Answer 7.13 We are not interested in diagrams. It is based on a diagram drawn by a school teacher, who is very interested in diagrams.

In Pa-Auk we teach many types of samatha meditation to those who want to practise them. If they do not want to practise all of them, but only one, such as *ān·āpāna·sati* (mindfulness-of-breathing), then we teach only that samatha meditation. When they have jhāna, we take them straight to vipassanā, systematically, stage by stage.

[453] This is a diagram that is supposed to describe the practice taught at Pa-Auk.

While practising samatha-vipassanā, there may sometimes be hindrances such as lust *(rāga)*, anger *(dosa)*, and discursive thought *(vitakka)*, which will disturb their concentration and vipassanā meditation. The following meditation subjects are the best weapons to remove those hindrances.

The Buddha gives them in the *'Meghiya'* sutta:[454]

- *Asubhā bhāvetabbā rāgassa pahānāya.*
  You should practise repulsiveness meditation *(asubha·bhāvanā)* **to remove lust** *(rāga)***.**
- *Mettā bhāvetabbā byāpādassa pahānāya.*
  You should practise loving-kindness meditation *(mettā·bhāvanā)* **to remove ill-will** *(byāpāda)***.**
- *Ān·āpāna·sati bhāvetabbā vitakk·upacchedāya.*
  You should practise *ān·āpāna·sati* [mindfulness-of-breathing] **to remove discursive thought** *(vitakka)***.**

Furthermore, a concentrated mind can see ultimate dhammas *(paramattha·dhamma)* as they really are.[455] Of the concentration practices, the eight attainments *(samāpatti)* are very high and powerful; so to those who want to practise the eight attainments thoroughly, we teach kasiṇa meditation too. If you want to understand the diagram thoroughly, you need to practise samatha-vipassanā up to the Path and Fruition Knowledges. Only then will you fully understand the diagram.

Why are we not interested in diagrams? Because it is not enough to show the whole system on one page. We have explained the whole system in more than three thousand six hundred pages in Burmese: one page is not enough.

Question 7.14 Can a hating mind produce many generations of temperature-born octad-kalāpas *(utuja oj·aṭṭhamaka·kalāpa)*, and make the eyes flash?

Answer 7.14 To say 'a consciousness produces light' is only a metaphor, because in fact, apart from the rebirth-linking consciousness *(paṭisandhi·citta)*, all consciousnesses that arise dependent upon the heart base *(hadaya·vatthu)* produce consciousness-born rūpa-kalāpas *(cittaja·kalāpa)*.[456] Among these rūpa-kalāpas there is always colour *(vaṇṇa)*. It is brighter if the consciousness is a samatha-, or vipassanā consciousness. This is discussed in the Pali Texts, Commentaries, and Sub-commentaries. But it does not say

[454] U.IV.1 and A.IX.I.i.3 'The Meghiya Sutta'

[455] These, The Buddha's words, are quoted p.12, and p.23.

[456] For a discussion of consciousness-born materiality, see p.112, and in relation to the light produced by samatha and vipassanā consciousnesses, see also Q&A 4.10, p.156.

that consciousness-born materiality born of a hating mind also produces light.

Question 7.15 Is the seeing mind that sees mentality-materiality itself included in mentality-materiality? Is it included in wisdom?

Answer 7.15 Yes, it is.[457] You can see it at all the stages of vipassanā, especially at the stage of Dissolution Knowledge *(Bhaṅga·Ñāṇa)*. It says in the *Visuddhi·Magga*:[458]

Ñātañca ñāṇañca ubhopi vipassati.

We must practise vipassanā on both the known *(ñāta)* **and the knowledge** *(ñāṇa)*.

'The known' means the five aggregates and their causes, which should be known with vipassanā knowledge. 'The knowledge' means the vipassanā knowledge that knows the impermanent, suffering, and non-self nature of the five aggregates and their causes, which are all formations *(saṅkhāra dhamma)*. Vipassanā knowledge is wisdom, Vipassanā Right View. Usually, Vipassanā Right View arises together with thirty-three or thirty-two mental formations, which gives thirty-four or thirty-three mental formations respectively. They are called 'vipassanā knowledge'. They are mentality dhammas, because they incline towards the object of the impermanent, suffering or non-self nature of formations.

Why do you need to see the vipassanā knowledge itself as impermanence, suffering, and non-self? Because some yogis may ask, or think about whether vipassanā knowledge itself is permanent or impermanent, happiness or suffering, self or non-self. To answer this question, you need to see the vipassanā-process itself as impermanence, suffering, and non-self, especially the thirty-four mental formations in each impulsion moment, headed by that vipassanā knowledge. Furthermore, some yogis may become attached to their vipassanā knowledge. They may become proud, because they can practise vipassanā well and successfully. It is also to remove and prevent these defilements that you need to see the vipassanā knowledge, or vipassanā-process itself as impermanence, suffering, and non-self.[459]

---

[457] For details in this regard, see 'The Seven Ways for Mentality', p.214*ff*, and 'How You Develop the Dissolution Knowledge', p.223*f*.

[458] VsM.xxi.742 *'Bhaṅg·Ānupassanā·Ñāṇa·Kathā'* ('Dissolution-Contemplation Knowledge Discussion') PP.xxi.13

[459] This procedure is explained by The Buddha in S.II.I.iv.4 *'Dutiya·Ñāṇa·Vatthu·Suttaṃ'* ('The Second Knowledge-Subject Sutta'). There, He explains how there is knowledge of each of the factors of dependent origination as operating in accordance with the Dhamma in the present, the past, and the future. And: 'And also that knowledge of the fixity of the Dhamma *(Dhamma·ṭṭhiti·ñāṇaṃ)*, that too is a destructible thing *(khaya·dhammaṃ)*, perishable

(Please see further next page.)

Question 7.16 How to overcome the uninterested and bored mind state that occurs during long periods of meditation, or staying alone in the forest? Is this kind of mind state an unwholesome dhamma?

Answer 7.16 This type of mind state is called indolence *(kosajja)*, and is usually a weak unwholesome dhamma associated with greed or hatred, etc. This type of mind state occurs because of unwise attention. If a person's unwise attention is changed to and replaced with wise attention, then he may succeed in his meditation.

To overcome this mind state you should sometimes recall that our Sakyamuni Bodhisatta's success was due to his perseverance. You should also recall the stories of Arahants who had striven hard and with great difficulty to succeed in their meditation, to eventually attain Arahantship. No one can have great success without striving. It is necessary especially in meditation to persevere. Wise attention too is very important. You should try to pay attention to the nature of impermanence, suffering, and non-self in conditioned things. If you do like this, you may one day succeed.

Question 7.17 Could the Sayadaw please give an example of a wish that is not associated with ignorance *(avijjā)*, craving *(taṇhā)* and clinging *(upādāna)*?

Answer 7.17 If you practise when performing wholesome kammas, and also see the impermanence, suffering, or non-self nature of those wholesome kammas, then ignorance *(avijjā)*, craving *(taṇhā)* and clinging *(upādāna)* do not arise. If you cannot practise vipassanā, then make the following wish: '*Idaṁ me puññaṁ Nibbānassa paccayo hotu*': 'May this merit be a contributing cause for realization of Nibbāna.'

Question 7.18 If the five aggregates are non-self, then who, Sayadaw, is giving a Dhamma talk? In other words, if the five aggregates are non-self, no Sayadaw is giving a Dhamma talk. So is there a relationship between the five aggregates and the self?

Answer 7.18 There are two types of truth: conventional truth *(sammuti·sacca)* and ultimate truth *(paramattha·sacca)*.

You should differentiate clearly between these two types of truth. According to conventional truth there is a Buddha, a Sayadaw, a father, a mother, etc. But according to ultimate truth, there is no Buddha, no Sayadaw, no father, no mother, etc. This you can see if you have strong enough vipassanā knowledge. If you look at The Buddha with vipassanā knowledge, you see ultimate mentality-materiality, which are the five

---

thing *(vaya·dhammaṃ)*, a fading thing *(virāga·dhammaṃ)*, and ceasing thing *(nirodha·dhammaṃ)*.' SA describes this as counter-insight insight *(vipassanā·paṭi·vipassanā)*.

aggregates. They are impermanent, suffering, and non-self. There is no self. In the same way if you look at me, or at a father, or mother etc. with vipassanā knowledge, you see only ultimate mentality-materiality, the five aggregates, which are impermanent, suffering, and non-self. There is no self. In other words, there is no Buddha, Sayadaw, father, mother, etc. The five aggregates and their causes are called formations. So, formations are talking about formations, sometimes about Nibbāna. There is no self at all. So how can we speak of a relationship?

For example, if someone were to ask you, 'Are rabbit horns long or short?' how should you answer? Or if they asked, 'Is the body hair on a tortoise black or white?' how should you answer? If the self does not exist at all, we cannot speak of a relationship between it and the five aggregates. Even The Buddha did not answer this type of question. Why? Suppose you said rabbit horns are long; that would mean you accept that rabbits have horns. And if you said rabbit horns are short; that too would mean you accept that they have horns. Again, if you said a tortoise has black body hair, that would mean you accept that a tortoise has hair. If you said tortoise hair is white, that too would mean you accept it has hair. In the same way, if The Buddha said the five aggregates and the self are related, it would mean he accepted that there is a self. And if he said the five aggregates and the self are not related, it would also mean he accepted that there is a self. That is why The Buddha did not answer this type of question. So we should like to suggest that you try to practise meditation up to the vipassanā level. Only then can you remove this view of self.

Question 7.19 The Buddha taught the 'Snake Mantra' to bhikkhus. Is chanting the 'Snake Mantra' the same as loving-kindness? Is chanting a mantra a Brahmanic tradition brought into Buddhism?

Answer 7.19: What is a mantra? What is the 'Snake Mantra'? We do not know whether mantras have been handed down from Hinduism. But in the Theravāda Texts there is a protective sutta *(paritta·sutta)* called the *'Khandha·Paritta'*.[460] The Buddha taught this protective sutta for bhikkhus to recite every day. There is a disciplinary rule *(Vinaya)* which says that if a forest-dwelling bhikkhu or bhikkhunī fails to recite this pro-

[460] A.IV.II.ii.7 *'Ahi·Rāja·Suttaṁ'* ('The Snake Kings Sutta'), called the *Khandha* (Group) *Paritta* (Protective Chant) because *mettā* is extended to all beings in groups: the four types of snake, beings with no legs (fish, leeches, worms, etc.), with two legs (birds, devas, human beings), with four legs (elephants, dogs, lizards etc.), and with many legs (ants, centipedes, mosquitoes, scorpions, spiders etc.).

tective sutta at least once a day, he or she will have committed an offence.

Once, in The Buddha's time, a bhikkhu was dwelling in the forest when a venomous snake bit him. He died. Because of this, The Buddha taught the '*Khandha·Paritta*'. The purpose of this protective sutta is similar to loving-kindness meditation. In that sutta there are different ways of extending loving-kindness to different types of snake or dragon. There is also an assertion of truth concerning the Triple Gem, and the qualities of The Buddha and Arahants. We shall recite this protective sutta tonight. It is very powerful. You may call it the 'Snake Mantra'. The name is not important. You can call it whatever you like. Some bhikkhus in Myanmar use this protective sutta for those who have been bitten by a venomous snake. It is effective. When they chant this protective sutta many times, and when the victims drink the protective water, the venom slowly decreases in them. Usually they recover. But the effect is not the same in every case. The Buddha taught this protective sutta to prevent bhikkhus from being bitten by venomous snakes. If a bhikkhu recites this protective sutta with respect, and extends loving-kindness to all beings, including snakes, he will meet with no danger. Usually, if he also observes the monastic code, no harm will come to him.

THE BUDDHA'S WISHES FOR HIS DISCIPLES AND HIS TEACHINGS
(Talk given on Vesākha Day)

THE BUDDHA RELINQUISHES THE WILL TO LIVE

The Buddha spent His last rains *(vassa)* in the village of Veḷuva. At that time there arose in Him a severe affliction. On the full-moon day of Asāḷha, a sharp and deadly back pain came upon Him, because of previous kamma.

In one of his past lives, the Bodhisatta, who was to become Sakyamuni Buddha, was a wrestler. Once he threw down an opponent and broke the opponent's back. When mature, that unwholesome kamma *(akusala·kamma)* produced its result, which was ten months before Sakyamuni Buddha's Parinibbāna. The effect of that kamma was so powerful that it would last until death. Such an affliction is called 'feeling ending at death' *(maraṇ·antika·vedāna)*. It ceases only when death occurs.[461]

The Buddha prevented that affliction from arising through entering an Arahant Fruition and making a determination *(adhiṭṭhāna)*. First The Buddha entered the Arahant-Fruition Attainment *(Arahatta·Phala·Samāpatti)* based on the Seven Ways for Materiality *(rūpa·sattaka·vipassanā)* and Seven Ways for Mentality *(a·rūpa·sattaka·vipassanā)*.[462] After those vipassanā practices and just before entering the Arahant Fruition-Attainment, The Buddha determined:

From today until the day of my Parinibbāna, may this affliction not occur.

And then He entered the Arahant Fruition-Attainment. Arahant Fruition-Attainment means that the Arahant Fruition-Consciousness, with Nibbāna as object, occurs continuously for a long time. Because the vipassanā practices were strong and powerful, the Arahant Fruition-Attainment too was strong and powerful. Because of the effort of the vipassanā and the effort of the Fruition-Attainment the affliction did not occur in the ten months that were left until the day of The Buddha's Parinibbāna. But He had to enter that Fruition-Attainment every day until then.[463/A]

---

[461] DA.II.3 (164) *'Mahā·Parinibbāna·Suttaṁ'* ('The Great Parinibbāna Sutta')

[462] For the Seven Ways for Materiality/Mentality, see p.213*ff.*

[463] For details with regard to these The Buddha's practices and attainments, see subsequent endnote A, p.253.

After the vassa, The Buddha wandered from place to place, and eventually reached Vesālī. Three months before Vesākha full-moon day, on the full-moon day of February, at the Cāpāla Cetiya, The Buddha decided to relinquish the will to live *(āyu·saṅkhāra ossajjana)*. What does that mean? On that day He decided:[464]

Temāsamattameva pana samāpattiṁ samāpajjitvā tato paraṁ na samāpajjissāmīti cittaṁ uppādesi.

From today until the full-moon day of Vesākha I shall practise this Fruition Attainment. Then I shall no longer practise it.

THE BUDDHA DECLARES HIS WISHES

So on that day, in front of the assembled Bhikkhu Saṅgha, in the assembly hall of the Mahāvana monastery, The Buddha announced that He had relinquished the will to live. He said to the Bhikkhu Saṅgha:[465]

Tasmātiha bhikkhave ye te mayā dhammā abhiññā desitā, te vo sādhukaṁ uggahetva āsevitabbā bhāvetabbā bahulīkātabbā.

Bhikkhus, you, to whom I have made known the Truths about which I have direct knowledge, having thoroughly learnt them, should cultivate them, develop them, and frequently practise them.

The Buddha taught only the Dhamma about which He had direct experience. Here The Buddha declared His wishes for His teachings, and instructed the Saṅgha as follows:

1) They should learn His Teachings (Dhamma) thoroughly by heart, but learning by heart alone is not enough. This was The Buddha's first wish.
2) He instructed them to cultivate His Teachings (Dhamma). In Pali it is called *āsevitabbā*, and means that we must try to know this Dhamma in practice again and again. It is translated as cultivation. This was The Buddha's second wish.
3) Finally, He instructed them to develop *(bhāvetabbā)* the Truths. When we cultivate, growth and progress are necessary.

   What does that mean? When we practise the Dhamma, only wholesome dhammas *(kusala·dhamma)* must occur in our mental processes. That is, wholesome morality dhammas *(sīla·kusala·dhamma)*, wholesome concentration dhammas *(samādhi·kusala·dhamma)* and wholesome wisdom dhammas *(paññā·kusala·dhamma)*. These wholesome

---

[464] DA.II.3 (169) *'Mahā·Parinibbāna·Suttaṁ'* ('The Great Parinibbāna Sutta')

[465] D.ibid.184

dhammas must occur without a break until Arahantship. If a disciple *(sāvaka)* of The Buddha attains Arahantship, his practice *(bhāvanā)* is over. So a disciple of The Buddha must practise The Buddha's Teachings until he attains that goal: the cultivation must be developed until Arahantship. To reach Arahantship, we must practise again and again. For that reason The Buddha gave the instruction of *bahulīkātabbā*, which means we must practise frequently. This was The Buddha's third wish.

These wishes occured in The Buddha's mental processes. Why?[466]

Yathayidaṁ brahmacariyaṁ addhaniyaṁ assa ciraṭṭhitikaṁ.

So that the pure Teaching may be established and last long.

That is, to maintain the pure Teaching so that it can last for a long time.

OUR DUTY AS BUDDHISTS

It is very important that every Buddhist maintains the pure Teaching, so that it is not lost. We must try. What should we try to do? We repeat:

1) We should try to learn The Buddha's Teachings (Dhamma) thoroughly by heart.
2) We should try to practise The Buddha's Teachings so as to know them through personal experience.
3) We should try to practise The Buddha's Teachings until Arahantship.

These are the duties of all Buddhists. If one is a Buddhist one must follow these three instructions. If one does not follow them then one is a Buddhist in name only: not a real Buddhist. If one follows these three instructions thoroughly, then one is a real Buddhist. So you can today determine:

1) We will try to learn The Buddha's Teachings thoroughly by heart.
2) We will try to practise The Buddha's Teachings so as to know them through personal experience.
3) We will try to practise The Buddha's Teachings until Arahantship.

HOW WE MAY BENEFIT THE WORLD

If we do that, it can be said that we breathe according to The Buddha's wishes. Why should we do so?[467]

[466] D.ibid.

Tadassa bahujanahitāya bahujanasukhāya lokānukampāya atthāya hitāya sukhāya devamanussānaṁ.

For the welfare and happiness of the many, out of compassion for the world, for the welfare and happiness of devas and human beings.

If we practise according to The Buddha's wishes, we will be able to give the Dhamma to future generations as an inheritance.

We will be able to teach devas and human beings the following:

1) To try to learn The Buddha's Teachings thoroughly by heart.
2) To practise The Buddha's Teachings, so as to know them through personal experience.
3) To practise The Buddha's Teachings until Arahantship.

By doing that, those devas and human beings will receive benefits and happiness in this world, up to the attainment of Nibbāna. But if we do not learn the Teachings by heart, and do not practise those teachings, how can we teach devas and human beings to learn the Teachings of The Buddha, and teach them how to practise those Teachings, since we have no knowledge of them? So, if we have strong enough faith *(saddhā)* in the Teachings of The Buddha, we Buddhists should try to learn those Teachings by heart, cultivate them in practice, and develop them until Arahantship.

HOW WE MAY SHOW OUR FAITH

Do you have strong enough faith in the teachings of The Buddha?

It is said in the *'Ghaṭīkāra'* sutta commentary:[468]

Pasanno ca pasannākāraṁ kātuṁ sakkhissati.

True devotees of the Triple Gem can show their devotion through practice.

If a man or woman cannot show devotion, we cannot say that he or she is a real devotee. If you have true faith in The Buddha's Teachings, you should learn those teachings thoroughly, practise them, and not stop before attaining Arahantship. These are important words of The Buddha before He passed away. If we have faith in The Buddha we should obey those words. If we have faith in our parents we should obey their instructions. In the same way we should obey our Father's words; our Father is The Buddha.

---

[467] D.ibid.

[468] MA.II.iv.1 *'Ghaṭīkāra·Suttaṁ'* ('The Ghaṭīkāra Sutta')

WHAT WE MUST LEARN AND PRACTISE

So, what are those Teachings? They are:[469]

- The Four Foundations of Mindfulness *(Cattāro Sati·Paṭṭhānā)*
- The Four Right Efforts *(Cattāro Samma·Ppadhānā)*
- The Four Bases of Success *(Cattāro Iddhi·Pādā)*
- The Five Controlling Faculties *(Pañc·Indriyāni)*
- The Five Powers *(Pañca Balāni)*
- The Seven Enlightenment-Factors *(Satta Bojjhaṅgā)*
- The Noble Eightfold Path *(Ariyo Atthaṅgiko Maggo)*

There are altogether Thirty-Seven Requisites of Enlightenment *(bodhi·pakkhiya·dhamma)*. Let us discuss them briefly. In the Pali Canon, The Buddha taught the Thirty-Seven Requisites of Enlightenment in different ways, according to the inclination of his listeners. The teachings in the Pali Canon can be reduced to just the Thirty-Seven Requisites of Enlightenment. If they are condensed, there is only theNoble Eightfold Path. If it is condensed, there are only the three trainings: morality, concentration, and wisdom.

THE BASIS FOR PRACTICE

We must first learn the training of morality to practise. If we do not know the training of morality, we cannot purify our conduct. Then we must learn samatha meditation to control and concentrate our mind. If we do not know about samatha meditation, how can we cultivate concentration? If we do not practise concentration, how can we control our mind? Then we must learn how to cultivate wisdom. If we do not know the training of wisdom, how can we cultivate wisdom?

So, to purify our conduct, to control our mind, and to develop our wisdom, we must first learn the Dhamma by heart. Secondly, we must cultivate and develop it up to Arahantship.

Therefore, in the *'Mahā·Parinibbāna'* sutta, The Buddha urged His disciples many times:[470]

Iti sīlaṁ, iti samādhi, iti paññā.
Sīlaparibhāvito samādhi mahapphalo hoti mahānisaṁso;
samādhiparibhāvitā paññā mahapphalā hoti mahānisaṁsā.
Paññāparibhāvitaṁ cittaṁ sammadeva āsavehi vimuccati,

---

[469] D.ii.3 (184) *'Mahā·Parinibbāna·Suttaṁ'* ('The Great Parinibbāna Sutta')

[470] D.ibid. e.g. §186

seyyathidaṁ kāmāsavā bhavāsavā diṭṭhāsavā avijjāsavā.

Such is morality *(sīla)*; **such is concentration** *(samādhi)*; **such is wisdom** *(paññā)*. **Great is the result, great is the gain of concentration** *(samādhi)* **when it is fully developed based on morality** *(sīla)*; **great is the result, great is the gain of wisdom** *(paññā)* **when it is fully developed based on concentration** *(samādhi)*.

The mind that is fully developed in wisdom *(paññā)* **is utterly free from the taints of lust** *(kām·āsavā)*, **the taints of existence** *(bhav·āsavā)*, **the taints of wrong views** *(diṭṭh-·āsavā)*, **the taints of ignorance** *(avijj·āsavā)*.

We all have a mind. If, based on morality, we can control our mind, then the power of that concentrated mind is wonderful. That mind can penetrate into ultimate materiality. Materiality arises as rūpa-kalāpas. They are smaller than atoms. Our body is made of those rūpa-kalāpas. The concentrated mind can analyse those rūpa-kalāpas. The concentrated mind can also penetrate into the ultimate reality of mentality. The concentrated mind can penetrate into their causes. The concentrated mind can penetrate into the nature of arising and perishing of mentality, materiality, and their causes. This vipassanā knowledge is called wisdom. This wisdom progresses because of concentration based on morality. The concentrated mind and wisdom are will-power. This will-power can lead to the attainment of Nibbāna, the destruction of all attachment, all defilements and all suffering.

Everybody has a mind. When the mind is fully developed through concentration, the vipassanā knowledge, the wisdom, can free one from the taints of lust and the round of rebirths completely. But that concentration must be based on morality. For laypeople, the five precepts are necessary. They are:

1) To abstain from killing any beings
2) To abstain from stealing
3) To abstain from sexual misconduct
4) To abstain from telling lies
5) To abstain from taking beer&wine liquor[471]

These five precepts are necessary for all lay-Buddhists. If one breaks any of these five precepts, one is automatically not a real lay-Buddhist

[471] beer&wine liquor *(surā·meraya·majja)*: according to The Buddha's analysis in Vin.Pāc.V.vi.2 *'Surā·Pāna·Sikkhā·Padaṁ'* ('Malt-Drink Training-Precept'), and according to the commentary, as well as DṬ.iii.8 *'Siṅgālaka·Suttaṁ'* ('The Siṅgālaka Sutta'), and VbhA.xiv.703 (DD.xiv.1905) *'Sikkhā·Pada·Vibhaṅga'* ('Training Precept Analysis'), *surā* is malt liquor such as beer and ale, *meraya* is vinous liquor such as wine, both fermented and distillable (into whisky, brandy, etc.). *Majja* is a generic term for liquor, spirituous, intoxicating drink.

(upāsaka/upāsikā). One's refuge in the Triple Gem has been made invalid. Buddhists must also abstain from wrong livelihood. They must not use possessions acquired by killing, by theft, by sexual misconduct, by lies, by slander, by harsh speech, or by frivolous speech. They must not engage in the five types of wrong trade: trading in weapons, in humans, in animals for slaughter, in liquor and other intoxicants, or in poisons.

So morality is very important for all Buddhists, not only to attain Nibbāna, but also to reach a happy state after death. If one's conduct is not purified, it is not easy to reach a happy state after death, because at the time of death, those misdeeds usually stick to one's mind, appear in one's mind. By taking one of those misdeeds as the object of the mind, usually one goes to one of the four woeful realms after death. Morality is also important to find happiness and peace in the present life. Without purification of conduct, one cannot find happiness or peace. Someone with a bad character is naturally surrounded by enemies. One who has many enemies cannnot find any happiness.

SAMATHA AND VIPASSANĀ MEDITATION

Then The Buddha taught the following:[472]

Yo ca vassasataṁ jīve, dussīlo asamāhito;
Ekāhaṁ jīvitaṁ seyyo, sīlavantassa jhāyino.

Though one should live a hundred years without morality and without concentration, one's life is not worthy of praise; it is better to live a single day with the practice of morality and concentration.

Why? Because the mind that is fully developed through concentration can produce great wisdom, which can see Nibbāna, the end of the round of rebirths, and can destroy all defilements and suffering.

So we must practise samatha and vipassanā meditation based on morality. In order to practise samatha and vipassanā meditation, we must practise the Four Foundations of Mindfulness *(Cattāro Sati·Paṭṭhānā)*:

1) Body-contemplation mindfulness *(kāy·ānupassanā satipaṭṭhāna)*
2) Feeling-contemplation mindfulness *(vedan·ānupassanā satipaṭṭhāna)*
3) Consciousness-contemplation mindfulness *(citt·ānupassanā satipaṭṭhāna)*
4) Dhammas-contemplation mindfulness *(dhamm·ānupassanā satipaṭṭhāna)*

What is 'the body' *(kāya)*? There are two types of body in vipassanā: the materiality-body *(rūpa-kāya)* and the mentality-body *(nāma·kāya)*. The materiality-body is a group of twenty-eight types of materiality. The mentality-

[472] DhP.viii.10 *'Sahassa·Vagga'* ('Thousands Chapter')

body is a group of consciousnesses and their associated mental factors. In other words, the two bodies are the five aggregates *(khandha)*: materiality, feeling, perception, formations, and consciousness. But samatha meditation objects such as the breath, the thirty-two parts of the body as foulness *(asubha)*, and the four elements are also called body *(kāya)*. Why? They are also compactness of materiality. For example, breath is a group of rūpa-kalāpas born of consciousness. If we analyse those rūpa-kalāpas, we see that there are nine types of materiality in each one: earth-, water-, fire-, and wind element, colour, odour, flavour, nutritive essence, and sound. The skeleton too is compactness of rūpa-kalāpas. If the skeleton is alive, there are a total of five types of rūpa-kalāpa. If we analyse those rūpa-kalāpas, we see that there are forty-four types of materiality.[473]

Thus, under body-contemplation *(kāy·ānupassanā)*, The Buddha taught two types of meditation: samatha and vipassanā. Under body-contemplation, He included *ān·āpāna·sati* (mindfulness-of-breathing), and the thirty-two parts of the body etc. So, if you are practising *ān·āpāna·sati*, you are practising body-contemplation. Those samatha practices go under body-contemplation. After you have succeeded in samatha practice, you change to vipassanā meditation: discerning and analysing materiality and mentality. When you practise materiality meditation *(rūpa·kammaṭṭhāna)*, you discern the twenty-eight types of materiality: that is also practising body-contemplation. When you practise mentality meditation *(nāma·kammaṭṭhāna)*, you discern feelings: that is feelings-contemplation *(vedan·ānupassanā)*; you discern consciousness: that is consciousness-contemplation *(citt·ānupassanā)*; you discern contact: that is dhammas-contemplation *(dhamm·ānupassanā)*. But discerning only feelings, consciousnesses, and contact, is not enough to attain the vipassanā knowledges. So we must discern the remaining associated mental factors. After having discerned mentality and materiality, we must discern their causes in the past, present, and future. This is the Cause-Apprehending Knowledge *(Paccaya-Pariggaha·Ñāṇa)*. After the Cause-Apprehending Knowledge, when you will have reached vipassanā, you can emphasize either materiality, feelings, consciousnesses or contact. 'Emphasize' does not mean you should discern one state only. You can emphasize materiality, but you must not omit mentality. That is, you must discern feeling, consciousness, and dhammas too.[474]

---

[473] For details, see 'How You Analyse the Rūpa-Kalāpas', p.124, and table '2c: The Basic Types of Materiality of the Body', p.139.

[474] There are four foundations of mindfulness: 1) body, 2) feeling, 3) consciousness, 4) dhammas. Dhammas are the remaining constituents of the mentality body *(nāma·kāya)*. The Buddha explains dhammas also as the five aggregates, twelve bases, five hindrances, seven

(Please see further next page.)

You may emphasize feelings instead. But feelings alone are not enough. You must also discern their associated mental formations, their sense bases, and their objects. The five sense bases and their objects are materiality. It is the same for the consciousnesses and dhammas.[475]

So here, vipassanā is contemplating the impermanent, suffering, and non-self nature of mentality-materiality and their causes. Those dhammas perish as soon as they arise, so they are impermanent. They are oppressed by constant arising and perishing, so they are suffering. In those dhammas there is no soul, nothing is stable, permanent and immortal, so they are non-self. Discernment of the impermanent, suffering, and non-self nature of mentality-materiality, and their causes and effects, is called vipassanā meditation. When you practise samatha and vipassanā meditation, we can say you are practising the Four Foundations of Mindfulness.

When you practise the Four Foundations of Mindfulness you must arouse enough of the Four Right Efforts *(Cattāro Samma·Ppadhāna)*. They are:

1) The effort to prevent unwholesome states from arising.
2) The effort to eradicate unwholesome states that have arisen.
3) The effort to produce wholesome states that have not yet arisen (concentration wholesome-dhammas, vipassanā wholesome-dhammas, Path wholesome-dhammas, etc.).
4) The effort to develop those wholesome states up to Arahantship.

How should you practise? You should practise according to the Four Foundations of Mindfulness. When practising you must arouse enough of the four types of effort just mentioned: 'Even if my flesh and blood were to dry up, leaving bones and sinews only, I will not give up my meditation.'

When you practise you should have the Four Bases of Success *(Cattāro Iddhi·Pādā)*:

1) Desire *(chanda)*: we must have strong and powerful desire to reach Nibbāna.

---

enlightenment factors, and Four Noble Truths. It is in fact not possible to separate these many aspects of the Dhamma, because each one includes all the others. For, example, to fully understand the Four Noble Truths is to fully understand the Noble Eightfold Path. To fully understand the Noble Eightfold Path is also to fully understand the seven enlightenment-factors. It is also to fully understand mentality-materiality; and the five aggregates, and the twelve bases etc. Hence, all thirty-seven requisites of enlightenment *(bodhi·pakkhiya·dhamma)* need to be fully understood for enlightenment to take place.

[475] The Most Venerable Pa-Auk Tawya Sayadaw discusses vipassanā by way of discerning only feelings in Q&A 4.6, p.149.

2) Energy *(vīriya)*: we must have strong and powerful energy to reach Nibbāna.
3) Consciousness *(citta)*: we must have strong and powerful consciousness to reach Nibbāna,
4) Investigation *(vimaṁsa)*: we must have strong and powerful vipassanā knowledges to reach Nibbāna.

If we have strong enough desire we will attain our goal. There is nothing we cannot achieve if we have enough desire. If we have strong enough energy we will attain our goal. There is nothing we cannot achieve if we have enough energy. If we have strong enough consciousness we will attain our goal. There is nothing we cannot achieve if we have a strong and powerful mind. If we have strong enough vipassanā knowledge we will attain our goal. There is nothing we cannot achieve if we have enough wisdom.

When we practise the four foundations of mindfulness, we should also have the Five Controlling Faculties[476] *(pañc·indriyāni)*. They are:

1) Faith *(saddhā)*: we must have sufficiently strong faith in The Buddha and His teachings.
2) Effort *(vīriya)*: we must make sufficiently strong effort.
3) Mindfulness *(sati)*: we must have sufficiently strong mindfulness on the meditation object. If it is a samatha object, it must be an object like the *ān·āpāna-nimitta* or kasiṇa-nimitta. If it is a Vipassāna object, it must be mentality, materiality, and their causes.
4) Concentration *(samādhi)*: we must have sufficiently strong concentration on the samatha and vipassanā objects.
5) Wisdom *(paññā)*: we must have sufficient understanding about samatha and vipassanā objects.

These five controlling faculties control the yogi's mind, so it does not go away from the Noble Eightfold Path, which leads to Nibbāna. If you do not have any of these controlling faculties, you cannot reach your goal. You cannot control your mind. These controlling faculties have the power to control your mind, so that it does not go away from your meditation object. This power is also called will-power *(bala)*. From the point-of-view of will-power, the Five Controlling Faculties are called the Five Powers *(pañca balāni)*.

Apart from the Four Foundations of Mindfulness, there are also the Seven Enlightenment-Factors *(Satta·Bojjhaṅgā)*, which are very important. They are:

---

[476] For a discussion of the Five Controlling Faculties, see p.39*ff*.

1) Mindfulness *(sati)*
2) Investigation of Phenomena *(dhamma·vicaya)*: this is vipassanā-knowledge.
3) Effort *(vīriya)*
4) Joy *(pīti)*
5) Tranquillity *(passaddhi)*
6) Concentration *(samādhi)*
7) Equanimity *(upekkhā)*

Finally, there is the Noble Eightfold Path *(Ariyo Aṭṭhaṅgiko Maggo)*:

1) Right View .... *(Sammā·Diṭṭhi)*	5) Right Livelihood .... *(Sammā·Ājīva)*
2) Right Thought ... *(Sammā·Saṅkappa)*	6) Right Effort .... *(Sammā·Vāyāma)*
3) Right Speech .... *(Sammā·Vācā)*	7) Right Mindfulness .... *(Sammā·Sati)*
4) Right Action ..... *(Sammā·Kammanta)*	8) Right Concentration .. *(Sammā·Samādhi)*

It is, in other words, morality *(sīla)*, concentration *(samādhi)*, and wisdom *(paññā)*: the three trainings. We must practise these three trainings systematically.

Altogether, there are Thirty-Seven Requisites of Enlightenment *(bodhi·pakkhiya·dhamma)*. It was The Buddha's wish that His disciples learn these Thirty-Seven Requisites of Enlightenment by heart, and practise them until Arahantship. If we do that, we can give this inheritance to future generations. Doing so, we and future generations will receive benefits and happiness in this world, up to the attainment of Nibbāna.

THE BUDDHA'S EXHORTATIONS TO THE SAṄGHA

The Buddha said further:[477]

Handa dāni, bhikkhave, āmantayāmi vo, vayadhammā saṅkhārā appamādena sampādetha.

Now then, bhikkhus, I exhort you: all formations are perishing things. Strive diligently!

All mentality-materiality and their causes are called formations *(saṅkhāra)*, because they are produced by their respective causes. Formations are always impermanent.

You should not forget about the nature of impermanence. It is because you forget about the nature of impermanence, that you aspire for yourself, for sons, daughters, family, etc. If you knew anything of the nature of impermanence, then throughout your life you would try to escape from it. So you should not forget how The Buddha exhorted us:

---
477 D.ibid.185

Now then, bhikkhus, I exhort you: all formations are perishing things. Strive diligently!

The Buddha then said:

Na ciraṁ Tathāgatassa Parinibbānaṁ bhavissati. Ito tinnaṁ māsānaṁ accayena Tathāgato parinibbāyissati.

The time of the Tathāgata's Parinibbāna is near. Three months from now the Tathāgata will attain Parinibbāna.

That means He would pass away completely. Those words were really sad words to hear. The Buddha said also:

Paripakko vayo mayhaṁ, parittaṁ mama jīvitaṁ.

My years are now full ripe; the life span left is short.

He described His old age to the Venerable Ānanda:[478]

Now I am frail, Ānanda, old, aged, far gone in years. This is my eightieth year, and my life is spent. Even as an old cart, Ānanda, is held together with much difficulty, so the body of the Tathāgata is kept going only with supports.

It is, Ānanda, only when the Tathāgata, disregarding external objects, with the cessation of certain feelings, attains to and abides in the signless concentration of mind,[479] that His body is comfortable.

The Buddha said further:[480]

Pahāya vo gamissāmi, kataṁ me saraṇamattano.

Departing, I leave you, relying on myself alone.

That means He would attain Parinibbāna, and depart from them. He had made His own refuge up to Arahantship.

THE BUDDHA'S ADVICE TO THE BHIKKHUS

That is why The Buddha also said:[481]

Therefore, Ānanda, be islands unto yourselves, refuges unto yourselves, seeking no external refuge; with the Dhamma as your island, the Dhamma as your refuge, seeking no other refuge.

And how, Ānanda, is a bhikkhu an island unto himself, a refuge unto himself, seeking no external refuge, with the Dhamma as his island, the Dhamma as his refuge, seeking no other refuge?

---

[478] D.ibid.165

[479] Arahant Fruition-Attainment with the Signless object of Nibbāna as object. See endnote 1, p.253.

[480] D.ibid.185

[481] D.ibid.165

The Buddha's answer was as follows:[482]

Appamattā satimanto susīlā hotha bhikkhavo. Susamāhitasaṅkappā sacittamanurakkhatha.

Be diligent, then, O bhikkhus, be mindful and of virtue pure. With firm resolve, guard your minds.

Susīlā hotha bhikkhavo means, 'You should try to purify your conduct, bhikkhus. You should try to be bhikkhus who have complete purification of conduct.' This means we must cultivate the training of morality, that is, Right Speech, Right Action and Right Livelihood.

Susamāhita·saṅkappā: *Susamāhita* means we must practise the training of concentration, which is Right Effort, Right Mindfulness and Right Concentration. *Saṅkappā* means the training of wisdom, which is Right Thought and Right View.

Appamattā means to see with vipassanā knowledge the nature of impermanence, suffering, and non-self in formations.

Satimanto means that when we practise the three trainings of virtuous conduct, concentration, and wisdom, we must have enough mindfulness.

So we must be mindful and diligent. Mindful of what? Mindful of the Four Foundations of Mindfulness, of mentality-materiality, or in other words, we must be mindful of formations.

Finally, The Buddha said:

Yo imasmiṁ dhamma-vinaye appamatto vihessati. Pahāya jātisaṁsāraṁ dukkhassantaṁ karissati.

Whoever earnestly pursues the Dhamma and the Discipline shall go beyond the round of births, and make an end of suffering.

So, if we want to reach the end of the round of rebirths, we must follow The Buddha's teachings; that is, the Noble Eightfold Path. Let us strive with effort before death takes place. May all beings be happy.

Endnote

[A] Gotama Buddha had three kinds of Arahant Fruition-Attainment:[A]

1) Post-Path Fruition-Attainment *(Magg·Ānantra·Phala·Samāpatti)*
2) Resorting Fruition-Attainment *(Vaḷañjana·Phala·Samāpatti)*
3) Lifespan-Maintenance Fruition-Attainment[A] *(Āyusaṅkhāra·Phala·Samāpatti)*

1) Post-Path Fruition Attainment: this Arahant Fruition-Attainment comes immediately after the Noble Arahant-Path wholesome-kamma: it has the charac-

[482] D.ibid.185

teristic of immediate fruition, and is referred to as a Momentary Fruition-Attainment *(Khaṇika·Phala·Samāpatti)*. The three fruition consciousness-moments that arise immediately after a Buddha's Noble Arahant Path Consciousness are of this kind.

2) Resorting Fruition Attainment: this is the sustained Arahant Fruition-Attainment that an Arahant may enter at will, is the Fruition-attainment that is the enjoyment of the peaceful bliss of Nibbana, and is also referred to as a Momentary Fruition-Attainment *(Khaṇika·Phala·Samāpatti)*. The Buddha would enter this attainment at all times, even when, during a discourse, the audience applauded by saying *'Sādhu, Sādhu'*.

3) Lifespan-Maintenance Fruition Attainment: this Arahant Fruition-Attainment always follows vipassanā with the Seven Ways for Materiality and Seven Ways for Mentality:[A] they were practised by the Bodhisatta on the threshold of Enlightenment under the Mahābodhi Tree, and daily by The Buddha from the day his back pain arose at Veḷuva village until His Parinibbāna. About to complete the vipassanā, and enter this Arahant Fruition-Attainment, The Buddha would emerge, resolve, 'From today until Mahāparinibbāna day, may this affliction not occur', and then resume the vipassanā to afterwards enter the Arahant Fruition-Attainment.

The difference between the Momentary Fruition-Attainments and the Lifespan Maintenance Fruition-Attainment is the preceding vipassanā. The momentary Arahant-Fruition Attainment that is just the enjoyment of the peaceful bliss of Nibbāna is preceded by an ordinary mode of entering into vipassanā, whereas the Lifespan Maintenance Arahant-Fruition Attainment is preceded by a higher mode of vipassanā that requires greater effort, namely, the Seven Ways for Materiality *(rūpa·sattaka)* and the Seven Ways for Mentality *(a·rūpa·sattaka)*. The difference in effect is that the Momentary Arahant-Fruition attainment suppresses an ailment for only as long as the attainment lasts: like a stone that falls into water clears the water for only as long as the impact of the stone lasts, after which the water-weeds return again. But the Lifespan Maintenance Arahant-Fruition Attainment can suppress an affliction for a determined period (here ten months): as if a strong man were to descend into a lake and clear away the water-weeds, which would not return for a considerable time.

THE MOST SUPERIOR KIND OF OFFERING
(Rejoicement Talk to Donors, Organizers and Helpers)[483]

INTRODUCTION

There are two kinds of offering:

1) The offering with full fruition
2) The offering with no fruition

Which kind of offering do you prefer? Please answer our question.

Let us look at The Buddha's wishes for His disciples *(sāvaka)*, regarding offering in this dispensation. Your preference and The Buddha's preference may be the same or different. To find out The Buddha's preference, let us look at the *'Dakkhiṇā·Vibhaṅga'* sutta.[484]

Once The Buddha was living in the Sakyan country, at Kapilavatthu in Nigrodha's Park. Then Mahāpajāpatigotamī went to The Buddha with a new pair of cloths, which she had had made by skilled weavers. After paying homage to The Buddha, she sat down to one side and said to The Buddha: 'Bhante, this new pair of cloths has been spun by me, and woven by me, specially for The Buddha. Bhante, let The Buddha out of compassion accept it from me.' The Buddha then said:

Give it to the Saṅgha, Gotamī. When you give it to the Saṅgha, the offering will be made both to Me and to the Saṅgha.

She asked The Buddha in the same way three times, and The Buddha answered in the same way three times. Then Venerable Ānanda said to The Buddha: 'Bhante, please accept the new pair of robes from Mahāpajāpatigotamī. Mahāpajāpatigotamī has been very helpful to The Buddha. Although she was Your mother's sister, she was Your nurse, Your foster mother, and the one who gave You milk. She suckled The Buddha when The Buddha's own mother died.

'The Buddha has been very helpful towards Mahāpajāpatigotamī. It is owing to The Buddha that Mahāpajāpatigotamī has gone for refuge to The Buddha, the Dhamma, and the Saṅgha. It is owing to The Buddha that Mahāpajāpatigotamī abstains from killing living beings, from taking what is not given, from misconduct in sensual pleasures, from false

---

483 A talk given after an offering, such as is the case here, is in Pali called an *anumodana* talk: *modana* means rejoicing, and *anu* means repeatedly. An *anumodana* talk is thus a rejoicement-talk (inspirational talk) meant to elevate the minds of the givers, thereby increasing the good kamma and merit of their action, and imprinting it on the mind.

484 M.III.iv.12 'The Offerings-Analysis Sutta'

speech, and from beer&wine liquor, which are the basis of negligence. It is owing to The Buddha that Mahāpajāpatigotamī possesses perfect confidence in The Buddha, the Dhamma and the Saṅgha, and that she possesses the virtue loved by Noble Ones *(Ariya)*. It is owing to The Buddha that Mahāpajāpatigotamī is free from doubt about the Noble Truth of Suffering *(Dukkha·Sacca)*, about the Noble Truth of the Origin of Suffering *(Samudaya·Sacca)*, about the Noble Truth of the Cessation of Suffering *(Nirodha·Sacca)*, and about the Noble Truth of the Way Leading to the Cessation of Suffering *(Magga·Sacca)*. So The Buddha too has been very helpful towards Mahāpajāpatigotamī.'

THE DISCIPLE'S DEBTS TO HIS TEACHER

Then The Buddha replied as follows:

That is so, Ānanda, that is so.

- **When a disciple, owing to a teacher, has gone for refuge to The Buddha, the Dhamma and the Saṅgha, I say that it is not easy for that disciple to repay the teacher by paying homage to him, rising up for him, according him reverential salutation and polite services, and by providing the four requisites.**
- **When a disciple, owing to the teacher, has come to abstain from killing living beings, from taking what is not given, from misconduct in sensual pleasures, from false speech, and from beer&wine liquor, which are the basis of negligence, I say that it is not easy for that disciple to repay the teacher by paying homage to him, rising up for him, according him reverential salutation and polite services, and by providing the four requisites.**
- **When a disciple, owing to the teacher, has come to possess perfect confidence in The Buddha, the Dhamma and the Saṅgha, and to possess the virtue loved by Noble Ones** *(Ariya)*, **I say that it is not easy for that disciple to repay the teacher by paying homage to him, rising up for him, according him reverential salutation and polite services, and by providing the four requisites.**
- **When a disciple, owing to the teacher, has become free from doubt about the Noble Truth of Suffering** *(Dukkha·Sacca)*, **about the Noble Truth of the Origin of Suffering** *(Samudaya·Sacca)*, **about the Noble Truth of the Cessation of Suffering** *(Nirodha·Sacca)*, **and about the Noble Truth of the Way Leading to the Cessation of Suffering** *(Magga·Sacca)*, **I say that it is not easy for that disciple to repay the teacher by paying homage to him, rising up for him, according him reverential salutation and polite services, and by providing the four requisites.**

Here, let us discuss what The Buddha means. If a disciple knows the Four Noble Truths through the guidance of a teacher, his vipassanā knowledge of the Four Noble Truths is more beneficial than his acts of respect, and providing of the four requisites to the teacher. If he knows the Four Noble Truths through Stream-Entry Path Knowledge *(Sot·Āpatti-*

·Magga·Ñāṇa), and Stream-Entry Fruition Knowledge *(Sot·Āpatti·Phala·Ñāṇa)*, then that vipassanā knowledge will help him escape from the four woeful realms *(apāya)*. This result is wonderful. Those who neglect to perform wholesome deeds, usually wander the four woeful realms. The four woeful realms are like their home: *(Pamattassa ca nāma cattāro apāyā sakagehasadisā)*.[485] They only sometimes visit good realms. So it is a great opportunity to be able to escape from the four woeful realms. It cannot be compared to the disciple's acts of respect, and providing of four requisites to the teacher.

Again, if a disciple knows the Four Noble Truths through Once-Return Path Knowledge *(Sakad·Āgāmi·Magga·Ñāṇa)* and Once-Return Fruition Knowledge *(Sakad·Āgāmi·Phala·Ñāṇa)*, he will come back to this human world once only. But if he knows the Four Noble Truths through Non-Return Path Knowledge *(An·Āgāmi·Magga·Ñāṇa)*, and Non-Return Fruition Knowledge *(An·Āgāmi·Phala·Ñāṇa)*, his vipassanā knowledge will help him escape from the eleven sensual realms. He will definitely be reborn in a brahma realm. He will never return to this sensual realm. Brahma happiness is far superior to sensual pleasure. In the brahma realm there is no man, no woman, no son, no daughter, no family. There is no fighting and quarrelling. It is not necessary to take any food. Their lifespan is very long. There is no one who can spoil their happiness. They are free from all dangers. But they are subject to decay; subject to death; subject to rebirth again, if they do not attain Arahantship.

Again, if a disciple knows the Four Noble Truths through the Arahant Path *(Arahatta·Magga)* and Arahant Fruition *(Arahatta·Phala)*, his vipassanā knowledge will lead to his escape from the round of rebirths. After his Parinibbāna he will definitely attain Nibbāna, and he will have no more suffering at all, no more rebirth, decay, disease, death, etc. So these benefits are more valuable than the disciple's acts of respect, and providing the four requisites to the teacher. Even if a disciple offers a pile of requisites as high as Mount Meru, that offering is not enough to repay his debt, because the escape from the round of rebirths, or the escape from rebirth, decay, disease, and death is more valuable.

What are the Four Noble Truths that the disciple has understood?

1) The Noble Truth of Suffering *(Dukkha·Sacca)*: this is the five aggregates If a disciple knows the Noble truth of Suffering, dependent upon a teacher, this vipassanā knowledge is more valuable than acts of respect, and providing the four requisites to the teacher.

---

485 DhPA.I.i.1 *'Cakkhupala·Tthera·Vatthu'* ('The Elder Cakkhupala Case')

2) The Noble Truth of the Origin of Suffering *(Samudaya·Sacca)*: this is dependent origination. If a disciple knows dependent origination dependent upon a teacher, this vipassanā knowledge is also more valuable than acts of respect, and providing the four requisites to the teacher.
3) The Noble Truth of the Cessation of Suffering *(Nirodha·Sacca)*: this is Nibbāna. If a disciple knows Nibbāna dependent upon a teacher, this vipassanā knowledge is also more valuable than acts of respect, and providing the four requisites to the teacher.
4) The Noble Truth of the Way Leading to the Cessation of Suffering *(Magga·Sacca)*: this is the Noble Eightfold Path. In other words, this is vipassanā knowledge *(vipassanā·ñāṇa)* and Path Knowledge *(Magga·Ñāṇa)*.

If a disciple possesses vipassanā knowledge and Path Knowledge dependent upon a teacher, these vipassanā knowledges are more valuable than acts of respect, and providing the four requisites to the teacher, because these vipassanā knowledges lead to one's escape from the round of rebirths, whereas acts of respect, and providing the four requisites, cannot be a direct cause for escape from the round of rebirths. Offering the four requisites can, however, be an indirect contributing cause for one who is practising samatha-vipassanā to attain Nibbāna.

OPPORTUNITIES NOT TO BE MISSED

Here again we should like to explain further. The five aggregates are the first Noble Truth, the Noble Truth of Suffering. In the five aggregates is included the materiality aggregate *(rūpa·kkhandha)*. Materiality *(rūpa)* arises as different types of rūpa-kalāpa (small particle). When one analyses the different types, one sees that there are in all twenty-eight types of materiality. Please consider this problem. Outside a Buddha's dispensation, there is no teacher who can teach about these types of materiality, and how to classify them. Only a Buddha and his disciples can discern these types of materiality, and teach how to classify them. Again, in the five aggregates are included also the four mentality aggregates *(nāma·kkhandha)*. Apart from the rebirth-linking consciousness, bhavaṅga-, and decease consciousness, these mental formations arise according to mental processes. The Buddha taught exactly how many associated mental factors *(cetasika)* are associated with one consciousness *(citta)* in a consciousness moment *(citta·kkhaṇa)*, and he taught how to discern and classify them. There is no teacher outside a Buddha's dispensation who can show and teach these mental formations clearly, because there is no other teacher who fully understands. But if a disciple of this Sakyamuni Buddha practises hard and systematically, according to the instructions of The Buddha, he can discern these mental formations clearly. This is a unique opportunity for Buddhists. You should not miss this opportunity.

Again, dependent origination is the second Noble Truth, the Noble Truth of the Origin of Suffering. The Buddha also taught his disciples how to discern dependent origination. When a disciple of The Buddha discerns dependent origination according to the instructions of The Buddha, he fully understands the relationship between cause and effect. He can gain the vipassanā knowledge which knows that the past cause produces the present effect, and that the present cause produces the future effect. He knows that within the three periods, past, present and future, there is no creator to create an effect, and that there is nothing which occurs without a cause. This knowledge can also be gained in only a Buddha's dispensation. You should not miss this opportunity either.

Again, when a disciple discerns dependent origination, he sees past lives and future lives. If you discern many past lives, you gain the vipassanā knowledge of knowing which type of unwholesome kamma produces rebirth in the woeful realms, and which type of wholesome kamma produces rebirth in good realms. Knowledge of the thirty-one realms, and the Law of Kamma, can be found in the teachings of only a Buddha. Outside a Buddha's dispensation, there is no one who can come to know the thirty-one realms, and the Law of Kamma, that produces rebirth in each realm. You should not miss this opportunity either.

Again, if a disciple discerns cause and effect in future lives, he also sees the cessation of mentality-materiality. He knows fully when his mentality-materiality will cease. This is the third Noble Truth, the Noble Truth of the Cessation of Suffering. This knowledge can be gained in only a Buddha's dispensation. You should not miss this opportunity either.

Again, The Buddha also taught the way, the fourth Noble Truth, that is samatha-vipassanā, to reach the state of cessation. Samatha-vipassāna means the Noble Eightfold Path. The Mentality-Materiality Definition Knowledge and the Cause-Apprehending Knowledge are Right View *(Sammā·Diṭṭhi)*. The Knowledge of the Cessation of Mentality-Materiality is also Right View. The Knowledge of the Noble Eightfold Path is also Right View. Application of the mind to the Four Noble Truths is Right Thought *(Sammā·Saṅkappa)*. Right View and Right Thought are vipassanā. To practise vipassanā we must have samatha concentration, which is Right Effort *(Sammā·Vāyāma)*, Right Mindfulness *(Sammā·Sati)*, and Right Concentration *(Sammā·Samādhi)*. When we cultivate samatha-vipassanā, we should undertake morality purification, that is Right Speech *(Sammā·Vācā)*, Right Action *(Sammā·Kammanta)*, and Right Livelihood *(Sammā·Ājīva)*. To cultivate samatha-vipassanā based on morality *(sīla)* is to cultivate the Noble Eightfold Path. This Noble Eightfold Path can be found in only a Buddha's dispensation. You should not miss this opportunity either. Why? Vipassanā knowledge of the Four Noble Truths leads to a disciple's escape from the round of rebirths.

THE FOURTEEN KINDS OF PERSONAL OFFERING

As mentioned, this escape can be assisted by the disciple's acts of offering. In the *'Dakkhiṇā·Vibhaṅga'* sutta, mentioned in the beginning of this talk, The Buddha explains the fourteen kinds of personal offering *(pāṭipuggalika·dakkhiṇa)*:

Ānanda, there are fourteen kinds of personal offering:

[1] **One makes an offering to a Buddha: this is the first kind of personal offering.**

[2] **One makes an offering to a Paccekabuddha: this is the second kind of personal offering.**

[3] **One makes an offering to an Arahant, a disciple of The Buddha: this is the third kind of personal offering.**

[4] **One makes an offering to one who has entered upon the way to realization of the Arahant Fruition: this is the fourth kind of personal offering.**

[5] **One makes an offering to a Non-Returner** *(An·āgāmi)***: this is the fifth kind of personal offering.**

[6] **One makes an offering to one who has entered upon the way to realization of the Non-Return Fruition: this is the sixth kind of personal offering.**

[7] **One makes an offering to a Once-Returner** *(Sakad·āgāmi)***: this is the seventh kind of personal offering.**

[8] **One makes an offering to one who has entered upon the way to realization of the Once-Return Fruition: this is the eighth kind of personal offering.**

[9] **One makes an offering to a Stream-Enterer** *(Sot·Āpanna)***: this is the ninth kind of personal offering.**

[10] **One makes an offering to one who has entered upon the way to realization of the Stream-Entry Fruition: this is the tenth kind of personal offering.**

[11] **One makes an offering to one outside the dispensation who is free from lust for sensual pleasures due to attainment of jhāna: this is the eleventh kind of personal offering.**

[12] **One makes an offering to a virtuous ordinary person** *(puthu·jjana)***: this is the twelfth kind of personal offering.**

[13] **One makes an offering to an immoral ordinary person: this is the thirteenth kind of personal offering.**

[14] **One makes an offering to an animal: this is the fourteenth kind of personal offering.**

The Buddha then explained the benefits of these fourteen kinds of offering:

- **By making an offering to an animal, with a pure mind, the offering may be expected to repay a hundredfold.**

That means it can produce its result in a hundred lives. Here 'pure mind' means without expecting anything in return, such as help from the receiver. One makes the offering only to accumulate wholesome kamma, with strong enough faith in the Law of Kamma. Suppose someone feeds a dog with the thought: 'This is my dog'. Such a thought is not a pure mind state. But if someone gives food to the birds, such as pigeons, then the offering is pure, because he does not expect anything from the birds. This applies also to the instances mentioned later. For example, if a person offers requisites to a bhikkhu, with the thought that it will bring about success in his business it is not offering with a pure mind. This kind of offering does not produce superior benefits.

The Buddha explained further:

- **By making an offering with a pure mind to an immoral ordinary person, the offering may be expected to repay a thousandfold.**
- **By making an offering to a virtuous ordinary person, the offering may be expected to repay a hundred-thousandfold.**
- **By making an offering to one outside the dispensation who is free from lust for sensual pleasures, due to attainment of jhāna, the offering may be expected to repay a hundred-thousand times a hundred-thousandfold.**
- **By making an offering to one who has entered upon the way to realization of the Stream-Entry Fruition, the offering may be expected to repay incalculably, immeasurably.**
- **What then should be said about making an offering to a Stream-Enterer; or to one who has entered upon the way to realization of the Once-Return Fruition, or to a Once-Returner; or to one who has entered upon the way to realization of the Non-Return Fruition, or to a Non-Returner; or to one who has entered upon the way to realization of the Arahant Fruition or to an Arahant; or to a Paccekabuddha, or to a Buddha, a Fully Enlightened One?**

Here, an offering means one offers food enough for one meal only. If a giver offers many times, such as, over many days or many months, there are no words to describe the benefits of those offerings. These are the different kinds of personal offering *(pāṭipuggalika dakkhiṇa)*.

THE SEVEN KINDS OF OFFERING TO THE SAṄGHA

The Buddha then explained to the Venerable Ānanda:

There are, Ānanda, seven kinds of offerings made to the Saṅgha *(Saṅghika·Dāna)*.

[1] **One makes an offering to a Saṅgha of both bhikkhus and bhikkhunis headed by The Buddha: this is the first kind of offering made to the Saṅgha.**

[2] **One makes an offering to a Saṅgha of both bhikkhus and bhikkhunis after The Buddha has attained Parinibnibbāna: this is the second kind of offering made to the Saṅgha.**

[3] **One makes an offering to a Saṅgha of bhikkhus; this is the third kind of offering made to the Saṅgha.**

[4] **One makes an offering to a Saṅgha of bhikkhunis: this is the fourth kind of offering made to the Saṅgha.**

[5] **One makes an offering, saying: 'Appoint so many bhikkhus and bhikkhunis to me from the Saṅgha': this is the fifth kind of offering made to the Saṅgha.**

[6] **One makes an offering, saying: 'Appoint so many bhikkhus to me from the Saṅgha': this is the sixth kind of offering made to the Saṅgha.**

[7] **One makes an offering, saying: 'Appoint so many bhikkhunis to me from the Saṅgha': this is the seventh kind of offering made to the Saṅgha.**

These are the seven kinds of offering to the Saṅgha. The Buddha then compared personal offerings to offerings to the Saṅgha:

In future times, Ānanda, there will be members of the clan who are 'yellow-necks', immoral, of evil character. People will make offerings to those immoral persons on behalf of the Saṅgha. Even then, I say, an offering made to the Saṅgha is incalculable, immeasurable. And I say that in no way does an offering to a person individually, ever have greater fruit than an offering made to the Saṅgha.

This means that offerings made to the Saṅgha *(saṅghika·dāna)* are more beneficial than personal offerings *(pāṭipuggalika·dakkhiṇa)*. If Mahāpajāpatigotamī offered the robes to the Saṅgha headed by The Buddha it would be far more beneficial. The result would be incalculable and immeasurable. So The Buddha urged her to offer them to the Saṅgha too.

The Buddha also explained the four kinds of purification of offering:

THE FOUR KINDS OF PURIFICATION OF OFFERING

There are four kinds of purification of offering. What are the four? They are:

[1] **There is the offering that is purified by the giver, but not the receiver.**

[2] **There is the offering that is purified by the receiver, but not the giver.**

[3] **There is the offering that is purified by neither the giver nor the receiver.**

[4] **There is the offering that is purified by both the giver and the receiver.**

[1] **What is the offering that is purified by the giver, but not the receiver? Here the giver is virtuous, of good character, and the receiver is immoral, of evil character. Thus, the offering is purified by the giver, but not the receiver.**

[2] **What is the offering that is purified by the receiver, but not the giver? Here the giver is immoral, of evil character, and the receiver is virtuous, of good character. Thus, the offering is purified by the receiver, but not the giver.**

[3] **What is the offering that is purified by neither the giver nor the receiver? Here the giver is immoral, of evil character, and the receiver too is immoral, of evil character.Thus, the offering is purified by neither the giver nor the receiver.**

[4] **What is the offering that is purified by both the giver and the receiver? Here the giver is virtuous, of good character, and the receiver too is virtuous, of good character. Thus, the offering is purified by both the giver and the receiver.**

These are the four kinds of purification of offering.

The Buddha explained further:

When a virtuous person to an immoral person gives, with clear and taintless mind[486] a gift that has been righteously obtained, placing faith in that the fruit of kamma is great, the giver's virtue purifies the offering.

To get superior benefits, the giver should fulfil the four conditions. Because then, although the receiver is an immoral person, the offering is purified by the giver.

The commentary mentions the case of Vessantara.[487] Our Bodhisatta in a past life as Vessantara, offered his son and daughter (the future Rāhula and Uppalavaṇṇā) to Jūjaka Brāhmaṇa, who was immoral, of evil character. That offering was the final one for Vessantara's generosity *pāramī* to be fulfilled. After fulfilling this last pāramī, he was ready to attain enlightenment: He had only to wait for the time to mature. Because of this generosity pāramī, and other previous *pāramī*, he was now certain to attain Omniscient Knowledge *(Sabbaññuta·Ñāṇa)*. So we can say that the offering was a support for his attaining enlightenment. It was purified by Vessantara. At that time Vessantara was virtuous, of good character. His offering had been rightly obtained. His mind was clear and taintless, because he had only one desire: to attain enlightenment. He had strong enough faith in the Law of Kamma and its results. So the offering was purified by the giver.

An offering is purified by the receiver, when an immoral person, whose mind is unclear, full of attachment, hatred, etc., who has no faith in the Law of Kamma, makes an unrighteously obtained offering to a virtuous person. The commentary mentions the case of a fisherman. A fisherman living near the mouth of the Kalyāṇī River in Sri Lanka, had three times offered almsfood to a Mahāthera who was an Arahant. At the time near death, the fisherman remembered his offerings to that Mahāthera. Good signs of a deva realm appeared in his mind, so before he died he said to

[486] With no expectations, attachment, anger, etc.

[487] MA.III.iv.12 *'Dakkhiṇā·Vibhaṅga·Suttaṁ'* ('The Offerings Analysis Sutta')

his relatives, 'That Mahāthera saved me.' After death he went to a deva realm. In this case the fisherman was immoral and of bad character, but the receiver was virtuous. So the offering was purified by the receiver.

An offering is purified by neither the giver nor the receiver, when an immoral person, whose mind is unclear, full of attachment, hatred, etc., who has no faith in the Law of Kamma, makes an unrighteously obtained offering to an immoral person. The commentary mentions the case of a hunter. When he died, he went to the *peta* realm. Then his wife offered almsfood on his behalf, to a bhikkhu who was immoral, of bad character; so the *peta* could not call out, 'It is good *(sādhu)*'. Why? The giver too was immoral, and not virtuous, because she had, as the wife of a hunter, accompanied him when he killed animals. Also, her offering had been unrighteously obtained, as it was acquired through killing animals. Her mind was unclear because had it been clear and understanding, she would not have accompanied her husband. She did not have enough faith in the Law of Kamma and its results, because had she had enough faith in the Law of Kamma, she would never have killed beings. Since the receiver too was immoral, of bad character, the offering could be purified by neither giver nor receiver. She offered almsfood in the same way three times, and no good result occured; so the *peta* shouted, 'An immoral person has three times stolen my wealth.' Then she offered almsfood to a virtuous bhikkhu, who then purified the offering. At that time the *peta* could call out 'It is good' *(Sādhu!)*, and escape from the *peta* realm.

(Here we should like to say to the audience; if you want good results from offering you should fulfil the following four conditions:

1) You must be virtuous,
2) Your offering must have been righteously obtained,
3) Your mind must be clear and taintless,
4) You must have strong enough faith in the Law of Kamma and its results.

Furthermore, if you are the receiver, and your loving-kindness and compassion for the giver is strong enough, you should also be virtuous. If your virtue is accompanied by jhāna and vipassanā knowledge, it is much better. Why? This kind of offering can produce better results for the giver.)

Now, please note the next kind of offering, the fourth kind of purification of an offering: an offering that is purified by both the giver and the receiver.

In that case, the giver has fulfilled the four conditions:

1) The giver is virtuous,

2) The giver's offering has been righteously obtained,
3) The giver's mind is clear and taintless,
4) The giver has strong enough faith in the Law of Kamma and its results,

and the receiver too is virtuous.

As for this kind of offering, The Buddha said:

Ānanda, I say, this kind of offering will come to full fruition.

This offering can produce incalculable, immeasurable results. If the receiver's virtue is accompanied by jhāna, vipassanā knowledge, or Path and Fruition Knowledges, then the virtue of the offering is superior.

THE SIX QUALITIES OF AN IMMEASURABLE OFFERING

Here let us look at another sutta: the *'Chaḷaṅgadāna'* sutta in the *Aṅguttara·Nikāya*, *'Chakka·Nipāta'*.[488] Once The Buddha was living near Sāvatthi, at Jetavana in Anāthapiṇḍika's Park. Then Nanda's mother, a lay disciple of The Buddha, who lived in Velukandaka, offered almsfood. Her offering was endowed with six qualities, and the receiver was the Bhikkhu Saṅgha, headed by the Venerable Sāriputta and the Venerable Mahāmoggallāna. The Buddha saw the offering with his divine eye, and addressed the monks thus:

Bhikkhus, the lay disciple of Velukandaka has prepared an offering endowed with six qualities to the Saṅgha, [which is] **headed by Sāriputta and Mahāmoggallāna.**
How, bhikkhus, is an offering endowed with six qualities?
Bhikkhus, the giver should be endowed with three qualities, and the receiver also should be endowed with three qualities.

What are the giver's three qualities? Bhikkhus,
[1] **Before giving the giver is glad at heart,**
[2] **While giving the giver's heart is satisfied,**
[3] **After giving the giver is joyful.**
These are the three qualities of the giver.

What are the three qualities of the receiver? Bhikkhus,
[1] **The receiver is either free from attachment, or is trying to destroy attachment,**
[2] **The receiver is either free from anger, or is trying to destroy anger,**
[3] **The receiver is either free from delusion, or is trying to destroy delusion.**
These are the three qualities of the receiver.

Altogether there are six qualities. If the offering is endowed with these six qualities, it produces immeasurable and noble results.

488 A.VI.iv.7 'The Six-Factored Offering Sutta'

The Buddha explained further:

Bhikkhus, it is not easy to grasp the measure of merit of such an offering by saying: 'This much is the yield in merit, the yield in goodliness, accumulated for wholesome kamma hereafter, ripening to happiness, leading to heaven, leading to happiness, longed for and loved.' Verily the great mass of merit, wholesome kamma, is just reckoned unreckonable, immeasurable.

Bhikkhus, just as it is not easy to grasp the measure of water in the great ocean, and to say: 'There are so many pailfuls, so many hundreds of pailfuls, so many thousands of pailfuls, so many hundreds of thousands of pailfuls'; for that great mass of water is reckoned unreckonable, immeasurable; even so bhikkhus, it is not easy to grasp the measure of merit in an offering endowed with the six qualities. Verily the great mass of merit is reckoned unreckonable, immeasurable.

Why? The giver was endowed with the four qualities mentioned in the *'Dakkhiṇā·Vibhaṅga'* sutta:

1) She was virtuous,
2) Her offering had been righteously obtained,
3) Her mind was clear and taintless,
4) She had strong enough faith in the Law of Kamma and its results.

The giver's three qualities, mentioned in the *'Chaḷ·Aṅga·Dāna'* sutta, were also fulfilled:

1) Before giving she was glad at heart,
2) While giving her heart was satisfied,
3) After giving she was joyful.

It is very important that these conditions are present in a giver, whether male or female. If he or she expects incalculable and immeasurable good results, he or she should try to fulfil them. But according to the *'Dakkhiṇā·Vibhaṅga'* sutta, the receiver too must be virtuous. According to the *'Chaḷ·Aṅga·Dāna'* sutta, it should be a bhikkhu or bhikkhunī who either has practised samatha-vipassanā meditation up to Arahantship, or who is cultivating samatha-vipassanā meditation to destroy greed *(lobha)*, anger *(dosa)*, and delusion *(moha)*.

OFFERINGS AT RETREAT

There are now, in Yi-Tung Temple, many bhikkhus and bhikkhunīs who are practising samatha and vipassanā meditation to destroy attachment, anger, and delusion totally. They are also virtuous. So we may say:

- Now there are worthy receivers here.
- The givers too may be virtuous.
- Their minds may be clear and taintless.

- What they have offered has been righteously obtained.
- They may have strong enough faith in the Triple Gem, and the Law of Kamma and its results.
- They were glad before giving.
- And were satisfied while giving.
- They were joyful after giving.

So we can say that the offerings made in these two months have been in accordance with The Buddha's wishes. They are noble offerings.

THE GIVER'S WISHES

If the givers expect good results in the future, certainly this wholesome kamma will fulfil their expectation. Why? The Buddha said in the *'Dān-·Ūpapatti'* sutta:[489]

Ijjhati bhikkhave sīlavato cetopaṇidhi visuddhattā.

Bhikkhus, a virtuous person's wish will certainly be fulfilled by purification of conduct.

So, a virtuous person's wholesome kamma can make his wish come true:

- If he wants to become a Fully Enlightened Buddha, he can become a Fully Enlightened Buddha.
- If he wants to become a Paccekabuddha he can become a Pacceka-buddha.
- If he wants to become a Chief Disciple *(Agga·Sāvaka)*, he can become a Chief Disciple.
- If he wants to become a Great Disciple *(Mahā·Sāvaka)*, he can become a Great Disciple.
- If he wants to become an Ordinary Disciple *(Pakati·Sāvaka)*, he can become an Ordinary Disciple.

But this is only when his *pāramī* have matured. Wishing alone is not enough to attain one of those types of enlightenment *(bodhi)*. Again:

- If he wants human happiness after death, he can get human happiness in the human realm.
- If he wants to go to the deva realm, he can go to the deva realm.
- If he wants to go to the brahma realm after death, this wholesome kamma can be a support for him to go to the brahma realm.

489 A.VIII.I.iv.5 'The Offering-Rebirth Sutta'

How? If his offering fulfils the previously mentioned conditions, it means that before, while and after offering, his mind is full of joy, is clear, taintless and happy, and takes the offerings and receivers as object: the receiver becomes his mind's object for the loving-kindness meditation. His loving-kindness for the receiver is strong. If he at that time practises loving-kindness meditation *(mettā·bhāvanā)*, his loving-kindness jhāna will take him to the brahma realm after death. In this way his offering is a support for him to go to the brahma realm. So, if the giver wants to go to the brahma realm after death, he should practise loving-kindness meditation up to jhāna. If he has practised loving-kindness jhāna, and offers almsfood, his wholesome kamma will be a superior and very powerful support for him to go to the brahma realm. So, if you want good results in the future, you should also practise loving-kindness meditation up to jhāna. Among the three kinds of happiness; human happiness, deva happiness, and brahma happiness, brahma happiness is the highest. There is no mundane happiness higher than brahma happiness. It is the most superior happiness in the thirty-one realms.

THE MOST SUPERIOR WORLDLY OFFERINGS OF ALL

That was the first kind of offering mentioned in the beginning of this talk, namely, the offering with full fruition. Do you prefer this kind of offering? If you do, then please listen to the following stanza from the *'Dakkhiṇā·Vibhaṅga'* sutta:

Yo vītarāgo vītarāgesu dadāti dānaṁ
Dhammena laddhaṁ supasannacitto
Abhisaddahaṁ kammaphalaṁ uḷhāraṁ
Taṁ ve dānaṁ āmisadānānamagganti.

Bhikkhus, I say that when an Arahant, with clear and taintless mind, placing faith in that the fruit of kamma is great, offers to an Arahant what is righteously obtained, then that offering indeed is the most superior of all worldly offerings.

In this case, the four qualities present in the giver are:

1) The giver is an Arahant,
2) The giver's offering has been righteously obtained,
3) The giver's mind is clear and taintless,
4) The giver has strong enough faith in the Law of Kamma and its results.

But a fifth quality is necessary, namely:

5) The receiver too must be an Arahant.

The Buddha taught that this kind of offering, one Arahant giving to another Arahant, is the most superior kind of worldly offering. He praised this kind of offering as the most superior. Why? This offering has no result. Why? The giver has destroyed delusion and all attachment to life. Ignorance *(avijjā)* and craving *(taṇhā)* are the main causes for kamma, that is volitional-formations *(saṅkhāra)*. In this case, volitional-formations means good actions like making an offering to the receiver. But this kamma does not produce any result, because there are no supporting causes: there is no ignorance *(avijjā)*, and no craving *(taṇhā)*. If the root of a tree is totally destroyed, the tree cannot produce any fruit. In the same way, an Arahant's offering cannot produce any result, because he has totally destroyed those roots; ignorance and craving. He has no expectation of a future life. In the *'Ratana'* sutta, The Buddha taught the following stanza:[490]

Khīnaṁ purāṇaṁ nava natthi sambhavaṁ
Virattacittā'yatike bhavasmiṁ
Te khīṇabījā avirūḷhichandā
Nibbanti dhīrā yathāyaṁ padīpo
Idampi sanghe ratanaṁ paṇītaṁ
Etena saccena suvatthi hotu.

Arahants have exhausted all old wholesome and unwholesome kamma.
New wholesome and unwholesome kamma do not occur in them.
They have exhausted the seeds of rebirth.[491] **They have no expectation of a future life.**
All their mentality-materiality will cease like an oil lamp, when the oil and wick are exhausted.
By this truth may all beings be happy and free from all dangers.

This is an assertion of truth. By the assertion of this truth all the people in Vesālī became free from dangers.[492]

An Arahant's offering is the most superior because it has no result in the future. If there is no future life, there will be no rebirth, decay, disease and death. This is the most superior. This is the second kind of offering mentioned at the beginning of this Dhamma talk: an offering with no fruition, no result.

But in the case of the first kind of offering mentioned, the offering with result, such as happiness in the human realm, happiness in the deva realm, or happiness in the brahma realm, there is still suffering. The very least is that the giver is still subject to rebirth, subject to disease, subject

---

490 SuN.ii.1 'The Jewel Sutta'

491 The seeds of rebirth: ignorance, craving, and potency of kamma.

492 Vesālī was a city visited by drought, famine, evil yakkhas (lower devas), and epidemic diseases. The people of Vesālī asked The Buddha to help them, and He taught them the *'Ratana'* sutta.

to decay, and subject to death. If the giver is still attached to sensual objects, animate and inanimate, then when those objects are destroyed or have died, he will experience sorrow, lamentation, physical suffering, mental suffering, and despair.

Please consider this question: Can we say that an offering is superior when it produces rebirth, decay, disease, death, sorrow, lamentation, physical suffering, mental suffering, and despair? Please consider also this question: Can we say that an offering is superior when it produces no result: no rebirth, no decay, no disease, no death, no sorrow, no lamentation, no physical suffering, no mental suffering, and no despair? This is why The Buddha praised the second kind of offering as the most superior. Now you may understand the meaning of this Dhamma talk. At the beginning of this Dhamma talk were mentioned the two kinds of offering:

1) The offering with full fruition,
2) The offering with no fruition.

Which kind of offering do you prefer? Now you know the answer.

HOW YOU MAKE A MOST SUPERIOR OFFERING

But if the giver is not an Arahant, how can he then make the second kind of offering? In the *'Chaḷ·Aṅga·Dāna'* sutta mentioned before, The Buddha taught that there are two ways he can do this: when the receiver either is free from attachment, anger, and delusion, or is trying to destroy attachment, anger, and delusion. You can say that the offering is also most superior, if the giver too is trying to destroy attachment, anger, and delusion; if he at the time of offering practises vipassanā:[493]

- If he discerns his own mentality-materiality, and discerns their impermanent *(anicca)*, suffering *(dukkha)*, and non-self *(an·atta)* nature;
- If he discerns the impermanent, suffering, and non-self nature of external mentality-materiality, especially the receiver's mentality-materiality;
- If he discerns the impermanent, suffering, and non-self nature of the ultimate materiality of the offerings.
- If he discerns the impermanent, suffering, and non-self nature of wholesome mentality dhammas, which arise in him while offering.

When he looks at the four elements in the offerings, he sees the rūpa-kalāpas easily. When he analyses the rūpa-kalāpas, he discerns the eight

[493] *Paṭṭhāna (Conditional Relations)* (fifth book of the *Abhidhamma*) *'Kusala·Ttika'* ('Wholesome Triads' §423)

types of materiality: earth-, water-, fire-, and wind element, colour, odour, flavour and nutritive essence. The rūpa-kalāpas are generations of temperature-born materiality *(utuja·rūpa)*, produced by the fire element in each rūpa-kalāpa.[494] Then he discerns their impermanent, suffering, and non-self nature. If the giver is able to do this type of vipassanā, his attachment, anger and delusion are suppressed at the time of offering, and also, his offering will usually produce no result. That way, we can say that also this kind of offering is most superior.

The giver can do this type of vipassanā before, after or while offering. But his vipassanā must be strong and powerful. He must have practised up to the stage of at least Dissolution Knowledge *(Bhaṅga·Ñāṇa)*. Only then can he practise this type of vipassanā. We should not miss this opportunity either. This opportunity exists only in a Buddha's dispensation. But you may ask, how can we make this kind of offering if we have no vipassanā knowledge? We should like to suggest that you then make your offering with the thought: 'May this offering be a contributory cause to attaining Nibbāna.' This is because The Buddha many times taught to make offerings with the wish for Nibbāna.

We should like to conclude our Dhamma talk by repeating the stanza from the *'Ratana'* sutta:

Khīnaṁ purāṇaṁ nava natthi sambhavaṁ
Virattacittā'yatike bhavasmiṁ
Te khīṇabījā avirūḷhichandā
Nibbanti dhīrā yathāyaṁ padīpo
Idampi sanghe ratanaṁ paṇītaṁ
Etena saccena suvatthi hotu.

Arahants have exhausted all old wholesome and unwholesome kamma.

New wholesome and unwholesome kamma do not occur in them.

They have exhausted the seeds of rebirth.[495] They have no expectation of a future life.

All their mentality-materiality will cease like an oil lamp, when the oil and wick are exhausted.

By this truth may all beings be happy and free from all dangers.

May all beings be well and happy.

---

[494] For details regarding the regeneration of temperature-born materiality, see p.113.

[495] The seeds of rebirth: ignorance, craving, and potency of kamma. See the three rounds of dependent origination, p.184.

THE FORTY MEDITATION SUBJECTS

The forty meditation subjects taught by The Buddha,[496] for the development of samatha meditation, with some sutta references.[497]

Kasiṇa	+	Foulness	+	Recollection	+	Divine Abiding	+	Immaterial	+	Perception	+	Defining	=	Total
10	+	10	+	10	+	4	+	4	+	1	+	1	=	40

Ten Kasiṇas

D.ii.2 *'Mahā·Nidāna·Suttaṁ'* ('The Great Causation-Sutta')
M.II.iii.7 *'Mahā·Sakuludāyi·Suttaṁ'* ('The Great Sakuludāyi Sutta')

Ten Foulnesses

D.ii.9 *'Mahā Sati·Paṭṭhāna·Suttaṁ'* ('The Great Mindfulness-Foundation Sutta')
M.III.ii.9 *'Kāya·Gatā·Sati·Suttaṁ'* ('The Body-Related Mindfulness Sutta')

Ten Recollections:

Buddha, Dhamma, Saṁgha

D.ii.3 *'Mahā·Parinibbāna·Suttaṁ'* ('The Great-Parinibbāna Sutta')
S.I.XI.i.3 *'Dhajagga Suttaṁ'* ('The Standard Sutta')

Virtue

D.ii.3 *'Mahā·Parinibbāna·Suttaṁ'* ('The Great-Parinibbāna Sutta')
A.III.II.ii.10 *'Uposatha·Suttaṁ'* ('The Uposatha Sutta')

Generosity

A.VI.i.10 *'Mahānāma·Suttaṁ'* ('The Mahānāma Sutta')

Devas

A.III.II.ii.10 *'Uposatha·Suttaṁ'* ('The Uposatha Sutta')
A.VI.i.10 *'Mahānāma·Suttaṁ'* ('The Mahānāma Sutta')

Death

A.VI.ii.9 *'Paṭhama-'* & *'Dutiya·Maraṇa·Ssati·Suttaṁ'*
('First-' & 'Second Death-Recollection Sutta')

Body-Related Mindfulness[498]

D.ii.9 *'Mahā Sati·Paṭṭhāna·Suttaṁ'* ('The Great Mindfulness-Foundation Sutta')
M.III.ii.9 *'Kāya·Gatā·Sati·Suttaṁ'* ('The Body-Related Mindfulness Sutta')

---

[496] VsM.iii.47 *'Kamma·Ṭṭhāna·Ggahaṇa·Niddeso'* ('Exposition of the Meditation-Subject Obtainment') PP.iii.104-105

[497] The sutta references given are only examples: there are more suttas that mention these meditation subjects.

[498] In the *Visuddhi·Magga*'s listing, body-related mindfulness refers specifically to meditation on the thirty-two parts of the body. The term body-related mindfulness, however, is used by the Buddha in many ways. Thus, in M.III.ii.9 *'Kāya·Gatā·Sati·Suttaṁ'* ('The Body-Related Mindfulness Sutta'), for example, The Buddha explains it as the exact same fourteen body-contemplations (incl. meditation on the thirty-two parts of the body) that He explains in D.ii.9 *'Mahā·Sati·Paṭṭhāna·Suttaṁ'* ('The Great Mindfulness-Foundation Sutta'), as well as the four material jhānas: at each explanation He says: 'That too is how a bhikkhu develops body-related mindfulness.'

Mindfulness-of-Breathing

D.ii.9 *'Mahā Sati·Paṭṭhāna·Suttaṁ'* ('The Great Mindfulness-Foundation Sutta')
M.III.ii.9 *'Kāya·Gatā·Sati·Suttaṁ'* ('The Body-Related Mindfulness Sutta')

Peace[499]

M.II.ii.4 *'Mahā·Mālukyāputta·Suttaṁ'* ('The Great Mālukyāputta Sutta')
A.X.I.i.6 *'Samādhi·Suttaṁ'* ('The Concentration Sutta')

Four Divine Abidings

Loving-kindness

M.I.iii.1 *'Kakac·Ūpama·Suttaṁ'* ('The Saw-Simile Sutta')
A.IV.II.ii.7 *'Ahi·Rāja·Suttaṁ'* ('The Snake-King Sutta')

Loving-kindness, Compassion, Sympathetic Joy, Equanimity

D.i.13 *'Te·Vijja·Suttaṁ'* ('The Three-Sciences Sutta')
M.II.iv.3 *'Maghadeva·Suttaṁ'* ('The Maghadeva Sutta')
A.III.II.ii.5 *'Kesamutti·Suttaṁ'* ('The Kesamutti Sutta')[500]

Four Immaterials

The Boundless-Space Base, The Boundless-Consciousness Base, the Nothingness Base, the Neither Perception nor Non-Perception Base

D.ii.2 *'Mahā·Nidāna·Suttaṁ'* ('The Great Causation-Sutta')
M.I.iii.6 *'Ariya·Pariyesanā·Suttaṁ'* ('The Noble-Search Sutta')[501]
M.III.i.6 *'Āneñjasappāya·Suttaṁ'* ('The Imperturbable-Wards Sutta')
A.IX.I.iv.5 *'Jhāna·Suttaṁ'* ('The Jhāna Sutta')

One Perception

Nutriment

S.V.II.viii.3 *'Āhāre·Paṭikūla·Suttaṁ'* ('The Nutriment-Repulsiveness Sutta')
A.X.II.i.6 *'Paṭhama·Saññā·Suttaṁ'* ('The First Perception Sutta')
A.X.II.i.7 *'Dutiya·Saññā·Suttaṁ'* ('The Second Perception Sutta')

One Defining

Four Elements

D.ii.9 *'Mahā Sati·Paṭṭhāna·Suttaṁ'* ('The Great Mindfulness-Foundation Sutta')
M.III.ii.9 *'Kāya·Gatā·Sati·Suttaṁ'* ('The Body-Related Mindfulness Sutta')

---

499 This is recollecting the qualities of Nibbāna.

500 Also known as 'The Kālāma Sutta'.

501 Also called *'Pāsa·Rāsi·Suttaṁ'* ('The Mass of Snares Sutta').

Editorial Notes

FOURTH REVISED EDITION

For the fourth revised edition, four things need to be mentioned:

1) In the preceding editions' explanation of the five-door process, it said the **'knowing'** of an object taken by a five-door process 'takes place at the fifth subsequent mental processes', which was not only ungrammatical, but also disagreed with the subsequent explanation of visual-cognition. Thus, it should say that the knowing of a five-door object 'takes place at the **fourth** and subsequent mental processes.' See p.168.
2) The **table** describing **the attainment of jhāna** described only attainment of fine-material jhāna: it now includes also attainment of immaterial jhāna: see p.44.
3) The Most Venerable Sayadaw has reported that 'many foreigners' have 'criticized' him because his editor refers to him as **the Most Venerable Sayadaw**. The Sayadaw has thus been questioned: 'Are you the most venerable person in the whole world?' Such a reading of 'Most Venerable', however, has no basis in Standard English.[502] Since such an expression of reverence and respect for the most venerable author of *Knowing and Seeing* is fully in line with the Teachings of The

---

[502] MOST: *Penguin Hutchinson Reference Library*, Helicon Publishing and Penguin Books Ltd, 1996 *(Longman's Dictionary of the English Language)*: '*adv* 2 very <*shall ~ certainly come*> <*her argument was ~ persuasive*> NOTE 1 As an intensifier meaning "very", *most* is generally used only with adjectives and adverbs conveying a judgment of feeling or opinion <*a most handsome gift*><*he argued most persuasively*>'. *Merriam-Webster's Collegiate Dictionary*, 10 Ed., Merriam-Webster, Incorporated, 2001: 'adv. … 2 to a very great degree <was ~ persuasive>. *The Pocket Oxford Dictionary*, H.W. Fowler: Clarendon Press: 1924: 'adv. To a great or the greatest degree or extent or amount (esp. with adjj. & advv. To emphasize or, with *the*, to form superlative…).' *Penguin Hutchinson Reference Library*, Helicon Publishing and Penguin Books Ltd, 1996 *(Usage and Abusage* Eric Partridge*)*: 'MOST AND VERY *Most* can properly (though rather formally) mean "very", as well as meaning "more than all the others".' *Fowler's Modern English Usage* Revised Third Edition by R.W. Burchfield, Oxford University Press, Oxford, 2004: '*Most* governing an adj. frequently has an intensive rather than a superlative function.' Thus the term is used in, for example, *On the Path to Freedom* (Buddhist Wisdom Centre, Selangor, Malaysia) p.441: 'The Most Venerable *Ovadacariya Sayadaw Bhaddanta Panditabhivamsa* [sic]' ; and on p.442: 'The Most Venerable Aggamahapandita Mahasi Sayadaw'; and on the cover of their *The Great Chronicle of Buddhas*: 'The Most Venerable Mingun Sayadaw Bhaddanta Vicitta Sārābhiva sa.' In the same way, 'Most Reverend' is used in the Christian church to refer respectfully to and address an archbishop or cardinal.

Buddha, many have approved of it as only natural, only proper, and even wonderful. For that reason, and in order to avoid causing offence to those many readers, this most venerable term of reference has been left untouched.[503]

4) From a retreat in the USA came a most valuable contribution from successful yogis. They pointed out that '**translucent**' is in fact more accurate than 'transparent', to describe the counterpart sign in, for example, mindfulness of breathing; to describe the 'ice-block' appearance of the body during successful four-elements meditation; and to describe *pasāda·rūpa* (now translated 'translucent materiality').[504] This is confirmed by the *Visuddhi Magga*'s comparing the counterpart sign to a mirror, to mother of pearl, and to the full moon, and its comparing transparent materiality to a pellucid mirror: they are all translucent things rather than transparent ones.[505]

REVISED EDITION (2ND/3RD EDITION)

The first edition of *Knowing and Seeing*, a collection of talks given in Taiwan by the Most Venerable Pa-Auk Tawya Sayadaw[506] was, in spite

---

503 Throughout His Teachings, The Buddha advises one to abandon one's pride and pay due respect to those deserving it. For example, in M.III.iv.5 *'Cūḷa·Kamma·Vibhaṅga·Suttaṁ'* ('The Small Kamma-Analysis Sutta'), He says: 'But here, student, a woman or man is not stubborn, not proud. To one who should be paid obeisance to, she or he pays obeisance; for one for whom one should stand up, she or he stands up; to one to whom one should give a seat, she or he gives a seat; for one for whom one should make way, she or he makes way; one to be honoured, she or he honours, one to be respected, she or he respects, one to be revered, she or he reveres, one to be paid homage to, she or he pays homage to. Because of accomplishing and undertaking such actions, she or he at the breakup of the body, after death, in a good destination, a heavenly world is reborn. But if she or he, at the breakup of the body, after death, in a good destination, a heavenly world is not reborn, if she or he as a human being returns, then wherever she or he is reborn, she or he is high-born.' Stubbornness and pride being unwholesome, the one who does not do these wholesome things gets the opposite results.

504 TRANSLUCENT (translucency/translucence): PHR 'permitting the passage of light: e.g. A clear, transparent <*glass and other ~ materials*> B transmitting and diffusing light so that objects beyond cannot be seen clearly <*a ~ window of frosted glass* > <*~ porcelain*> [L *translucent-*, *translucens*, prp of *translucre* to shine through, fr *trans-* + *luc re* to shine à]'
TRANSPARENT: PHR 'having the property of transmitting light without appreciable scattering, so that bodies lying beyond are entirely visible [ME, fr ML *transparent-*, *transparens*, prp of *transpar re* to show through, fr L *trans-* + *par re* to show oneself - more at APPEAR]'

505 VsM.iv.57 *'Bhāvanā·Vidhānaṁ'* ('Meditation Directions') PP.iv.31 & VsM.xiv.447 *'Rūpa·Kkhandha·Kathā'* ('Discussion of the Materiality Aggregate') PP.xiv.73

506 As there are several 'Pa-Auk' monasteries, the Most Venerable Pa-Auk Tawya Sayadaw

(Please see further next page.)

of the best intentions, published with regrettably very many flaws and errors. They were almost only of language, which could not unfortunately but have an adverse effect on the contents. An attempt has been made, with this revised edition, not only to put things right, but to give the entire text an overhaul, so as to make it less inaccessible to newcomers.

Endeavours have thus been made to streamline the language (one thing referred to by only one term: as far as possible), and on the one hand to remove unnecessary repetitions,[507] and other excess text (incl. the many hyphens); on the other hand to add information where deemed necessary (charts, footnotes, source references, a detailed table of contents, and an index of the questions from meditators);[508] and in some cases even to re-arrange the text. Furthermore, the Most Venerable Pa-Auk Tawya Sayadaw added an introduction to the entire course of meditation, with continual reference to pertinent Pali Texts.[509]

The Most Venerable Pa-Auk Tawya Sayadaw has also made adjustments in terminology, for example, 'mental process' for *citta·vīthi* (instead of 'thought-process'), and 'consciousness' as a countable noun (one consciousness, two consciousness*es*) has been adopted. Capitalization of 'the Buddha' to '*T*he Buddha' has been adopted as an orthographical sign of respect, since the Asian appellations (which can be translated as *Lord* or *His Majesty King* etc. Buddha) are in standard English too restricted in meaning. A Burmese element of proper usage has also been added, namely, the Most Venerable Pa-Auk Tawya Sayadaw's reference to himself in the first person plural instead of the first person singular (*we* and *our* instead of *I* and *mine)*: in Burmese, it is considered immodest to refer to oneself in the first person singular.[510]

For this edition too the Most Venerable Pa-Auk Tawya Sayadaw was consulted, and again he read through the material, adding comments, further explanations, making corrections etc.

---

has asked that *Tawya* (Forest) be included in his name, to specify which one he belongs to.

[507] From an English point-of-view, Burmese (and Pali) are pleonastic languages.

[508] This includes an introduction to Talk 4 'How You Discern Materiality'.

[509] Written by a 'ghost-writer' under the Most Venerable Pa-Auk Tawya Sayadaw's close guidance and supervision.

[510] Modesty by way of the first person plural may be found in also the Commentaries to the Pali Texts. Furthermore, as one of the Most Venerable Pa-Auk Tawya Sayadaw's disciples has pointed out, since the Sayadaw's teaching is nothing other than what is stated in the Pali Texts, his voice is in fact not his own: it is the voice of the tradition handed down through generations of bhikkhus, harking back to the bhikkhus who received instruction from The Buddha Himself.

Given some of the responses to the first editions of this book, and to the Most Venerable Pa-Auk Tawya Sayadaw's teachings as a whole, the following four points need perhaps be made.

1) Although the Pa-Auk system may be used as a convenient term to refer to the teachings of the Most Venerable Pa-Auk Tawya Sayadaw, there is no such thing. The Most Venerable Pa-Auk Tawya Sayadaw's system of instruction is by no means 'his'. It is borne out by, drawn directly and unadulterated from, and in strict accordance with, the authoritative texts of the Theravāda tradition:[511] the ancient Theravāda Canon, Commentaries and Sub-Commentaries: most notably the ancient commentary and meditation manual, the *Visuddhi·Magga*.[512]
2) Yogis who have taken the Most Venerable Pa-Auk Tawya Sayadaw or one of his authorized teachers as teacher have and do fully or partly put into practice the system of instruction that is presented here. The Pali Texts (Vinaya, Suttas and Abhidhamma) are, says the Most Venerable Pa-Auk Sayadaw, aimed entirely at practice. As advised by The Buddha, learning *(pariyatti)* goes hand-in-hand with practice *(paṭipatti)*, practical experience of that knowledge, which leads eventually to realization *(paṭivedha)* of it.
3) The main talks are not descriptive so much as prescriptive. Nevertheless, the book is not to be regarded as a manual but as an overview.
4) Yogis who take the Most Venerable Pa-Auk Tawya Sayadaw or one of his authorized teachers as their teacher should know that there are no hard and fast rules about how he guides the individual yogi: in each case the yogi's preferences, strengths and weaknesses etc. are taken into account. The individual yogi's practice may therefore, in sequence and detail, very well differ from what is presented here.

Once again, the editors beg forgiveness from their readers and from their teacher, the Most Venerable Pa-Auk Tawya Sayadaw, for whatever scratches that still remain after this final polish.

May absolutely all parties involved in the production of this material, from its very inception, reap much merit from their labours. May all the

---

[511] Attention to this was drawn already in the first edition by quoting the Most Venerable Buddhaghosa's and the Most Venerable Pa-Auk Tawya Sayadaw's own words on the matter (now given on the left inside cover). See also the source references inserted throughout the talks.

[512] see footnote 71, p.20.

merit of that work; the merit of reading these talks by future readers; the merit of the meditation assisted and perhaps engendered by these talks; and the merit of the attainments, mundane and supramundane, attained thereby all go towards keeping the Most Venerable Pa-Auk Tawya Sayadaw healthy and happy for long to come.

FIRST EDITION

The talks in this book were given by the Venerable Pa-Auk Tawya Sayadaw of Pa-Auk Forest Monastery, Pa-Auk, Mawlamyine, Myanmar, while he conducted a two-month meditation retreat at Yi-Tung Temple, Sing Choo City, Taiwan. In the course of those two months, apart from giving daily meditation instructions to individual yogis, the Sayadaw read seven main talks, which had been prepared at Pa-Auk prior to the retreat. Those talks were interspersed with seven Question&Answer talks; the questions having been given beforehand by the yogis at the retreat, and the answers then having been likewise prepared beforehand by the Sayadaw. The Sayadaw read a further two talks. One was read to the general public on the occasion of Vesākha day (the anniversary of the Buddha's birth, enlightenment and final perishing). The other was read at the end of the retreat, and was the traditional talk on offerings, for the chief donor, the abbess of Yi-Tung Temple, other donors, and the organizers and helpers at the retreat. All sixteen talks had been prepared in English, and then read in English by the Sayadaw. For the benefit of the audience, who were all Chinese, the talks were also translated beforehand into Chinese, and the Chinese read concurrently with the Sayadaw's reading.

The talks are concerned mainly with the Sayadaw's principal approach to vipassanā meditation: to practise tranquillity meditation first, after which to use it as a vehicle for vipassanā meditation. The Sayadaw teaches also pure-vipassanā meditation, which is why he provides an exposition of the orthodox instructions for both methods.

The talks, as they appear here, are not word-perfect versions of the talks as they were given in Taiwan. This is because the Sayadaw decided that the material should be edited prior to publication. To that end, the Sayadaw requested that the language and contents be changed in any way deemed necessary, and himself added further details etc. The Sayadaw was very frequently consulted during the entire editing process, and his approval secured for changes other than those of only form.

The editing has been mostly of form and not content. Efforts have been made to retain the Sayadaw's particular way of speaking English, when he discusses with and instructs yogis. Since the Sayadaw was addressing

Taiwanese and Malaysian-Chinese Mahāyāna Buddhists, there are considerably fewer of his usual copious references from the Theravāda texts and commentaries. It should here be mentioned that, when the Sayadaw translates a Pali quotation, he usually follows the Burmese custom of including a gloss from the commentaries.

Most of the Pali terms used by the Sayadaw have been translated. The Pali has initially been retained in brackets, after which it has usually been omitted: for example, initially, 'impermanence (*anicca*)', subsequently, 'impermanence'. Conversely, some terms, awkward in English, have been left untranslated, such as: kasiṇa (totality? device?), deva (god? deity?), Brahmā (supreme being in a very high realm of existence?). Appendix 1 is a glossary, which defines rather than translates those terms.

The editorial priorities have been to maintain the required degree of accuracy, and to try to make the talks readable to newcomer, yogi, and scholar alike. Complete uniformity in editing has, for those reasons, been somewhat compromised. In the genesis of this book, diverse helping hands have been involved in the translating, composing, and editing. For any errors or faults in the material, the helping hands alone are responsible.

Editors
Pa-Auk Forest Monastery

Bibliographical Abbreviations etc.
(Used in Source References)

A.	*Aṅguttara·Nikāya (Numerical Collection)*
AA.	*Aṅguttara·Nikāya-Aṭṭhakathā* [513] *(— Commentary)*
AbS.	*Abhidhammattha·Saṅgaho (Abhidhamma Compendium)*
Ap.	*Apadāna·Pāḷi (Narrative Text)*
CMA.	*A Comprehensive Manual of Abhidhamma* [514]
D.	*Dīgha·Nikāya (Long Collection)*
DA.	*Dīgha·Nikāya-Aṭṭhakathā (— Commentary)*
DD.	*The Dispeller of Delusion* [515]
DhP.	*Dhamma·Pada (Dhamma Word)*
DhPA.	*Dhamma·Pada-Aṭṭhakathā (— Commentary)*
DhS.	*Dhamma·Saṅgaṇī (Dhamma Compendium)*
DhsA.	*Dhamma·Saṅgaṇī-Aṭṭhakathā (— Commentary)*
DṬ.	*Dīgha·Nikāya-Ṭīkā (Long Collection Sub-commentary)*
E.	*The Expositor* [516]
M.	*Majjhima·Nikāya (Middle Collection)*
MA.	*Majjhima·Nikāya-Aṭṭhakathā (— Commentary)*
MṬ.	*Majjhima·Nikāya-Ṭīkā (— Sub-commentary)*
PP.	*Path of Purification* [517]
PsM.	*Paṭisambhidā·Magga (Discrimination Path)*
S.	*Saṁyutta·Nikāya (Connected Collection)*
SA.	*Saṁyutta·Nikāya-Aṭṭhakathā (— Commentary)*
SuN.	*Sutta·Nipāta (Sutta Book)*
TG.	*Thera·Gāthā·Pāḷi (Elder's·Verses·Text)*
U.	*Udāna (Inspiration)*
Vbh.	*Vibhaṅga (Analysis)*
VbhA.	*Vibhaṅga-Aṭṭhakathā (— Commentary)*

---

[513] The Pali titles for the commentaries are: AA = *Manoratha·Pūraṇi*; DA = *Su·Maṅgala-·Vilāsinī*; DhsA = *Aṭṭha·Sālinī*; MA = *Papañca·Sūdanī*; SA = *Sārattha·Ppakāsinī*; VbhA = *Sa·Mmoha·Vinodanī*

[514] CMA: English translation of *Abhidhammattha·Saṅgaha* edited and with notes by Bhikkhu Bodhi, Buddhist Publication Society, Kandy, Sri Lanka.

[515] DD: English translation of *Vibhaṅga-Aṭṭhakathā* by Bhikkhu Ñāṇamoli, Pali Text Society, Oxford, England.

[516] Exp: English translation of *Dhamma·Saṅgaṇī·Aṭṭhakathā* by Professor Pe Maung Tin M.A., Pali Text Society, London, England.

[517] PP: English translation of *Visuddhi·Magga* by Bhikkhu Ñāṇamoli, Buddhist Publication Society, Kandy, Sri Lanka.

VbhṬ. *Vibhaṅga·Ṭīkā*[518] *(— Sub-commentary)*
Vin.Pāc. *Vinaya Pācittiya·Pāḷi (—: Expiable Text)*
VsM. *Visuddhi·Magga (Purification Path: Commentary)*[519]
VsMṬ. *Visuddhi·Magga-Mahā·Ṭīkā (— Great Sub-commentary)*

SOURCE REFERENCES

The source references are according to the standard divisions in the Pali:

Collection • Book • Section • Chapter • Sutta.

For example:[520]

M.I.ii.2
M = *Majjhima·Nikāya (Middle-Length Suttas)*
I = Book 1 *'Mūla·Paṇṇāsa·Pāḷi'* ('Root Fifty Texts')
i = Chapter 1 *'Mūla·Pariyāya·Vagga'* ('Root Series Chapter')
2 = Sutta 2 *'Sabb·Āsava·Suttaṁ'* ('The All-Taints Sutta')
S.III.I.i.5
S = *Saṁyutta·Nikāya (Connected Suttas)*
III = Book 3 *'Khandha·Vagga'* ('Aggregates Book')
I = Section 1 *'Khandha·Saṁyutta'* ('Aggregates Section')
i = Chapter 1 *'Nakulapitu·Vagga'* ('Nakulapita Chapter')
5 = Sutta 5 *'Samādhi·Suttaṁ'* ('The Concentration Sutta')

VsM.viii B223/PP.viii.90
VsM = *Visuddhi·Magga (Purification Path)*
viii = Chapter 8 *'Ān·Āpāna·Sati·Kathā'*('Mindfulness-of-Breathing Discussion')
223 = § 223
PP = *Path of Purification* (by Ven. Ñānamoli)
viii = Chapter 8 'Description of Concentration—Other Recollections as Meditation Subjects
189 = § 189

[518] The Pali titles for the sub-commentaries are: VbhṬ = *Mūla·Ṭīkā*; VsṬ = *Param·Attha Mañjūsā*
[519] VsM: *Visuddhi·Magga (Purification Path)* is a commentary, and there is a sub-commentary (VsMṬ) that explains it further.
[520] Please note also references to *Visuddhi·Magga* and *Path of Purification* (third example).

Glossary of Untranslated Pāḷi

This glossary contains the Pali terms left untranslated in the text. They have been left untranslated because the English translation has, in some way or other, been considered awkward or inadequate, if not misleading. The definitions have been kept as concise as at all possible, and refer to the meaning of the terms as they are used in the text of this book: according to the Theravāda tradition. For more extensive explanations, the reader is referred to the text itself, where most of the terms are, at some time or other, discussed. (An asterisk indicates which of the terms are discussed in the text itself.)

Some of the terms in this glossary do have an adequate translation, but have been retained in the Pali when in compounds, as in for example, '*ān·āpāna* jhāna', rather than 'in&out-breath jhāna', for obvious reasons.

Abhidhamma: third of what are called the Three Baskets *(Tipiṭaka)* of the Pali Texts; practical teachings of The Buddha that deal with only ultimate reality, necessary for vipassanā meditation. (cf. sutta)

ān·āpāna:* in&out-breath; subject for samatha meditation and later vipassanā. (cf. samatha)

Arahant:* woman or man who has eradicated all defilements; at his or her death (*Parinibbāna*) there is no further rebirth. (cf. kamma, Parinibbāna)

Bhante: Venerable Sir.

bhavaṅga:* continuity of identical type of consciousnesses, broken only when a mental process occurs; the object is that of near-death consciousness in past-life. (cf. Abhidhamma)

bhikkhu/bhikkhunī: Buddhist monk/nun; bhikkhu with two hundred and twenty-seven main precepts, and hundreds of lesser precepts to observe; Theravāda bhikkhunī lineage broken.

Bodhisatta:* a person who has vowed to become a Buddha; the ideal in Mahāyāna tradition; she or he is a Bodhisatta for innumerable lives prior to his enlightenment, after which he is a Buddha, until He in that life attains Parinibbāna. (cf. Buddha, Parinibbāna)

brahmā:* inhabitant of one of twenty in thirty-one realms very much higher than human realm; invisible to human eye, visible in light of concentration. (cf. deva, *peta*)

Buddha:* one fully enlightened without a teacher, who has by Himself rediscovered and teaches the Four Noble Truths; being also an Arahant, there is at His death *(Parinibbāna)* no further rebirth. (cf. Arahant, Bodhisatta, Paccekabuddha, Parinibbāna)

deva: inhabitant of realm just above human realm; invisible to human-eye, visible in light of concentration. (cf. brahmā, *peta*)
Dhamma:* (capitalized) the Teachings of The Buddha; the Noble Truth.
dhamma:* (uncapitalized) thing, phenomenon; state; object solely of the mind.
jhāna:* eight increasingly advanced and subtle states of concentration on a specific object, with mind aware and increasingly pure. (cf. samatha)
kalāpa:* small particle, cluster of elements; smallest unit of materiality seen in conventional reality; invisible to physical eye, visible to mind's eye.
kamma:* (Sanskrit: *karma*) action; potency from volition that makes good actions produce good results, and bad actions produce bad results.
kasiṇa:* meditation object that represents a quality in conventional reality, e.g. earth, colour, space and light; used for samatha meditation. (cf. samatha)
Mahāyāna: 'Buddhist tradition' prevalent in China, Taiwan, Korea, Japan, Mongolia, Nepal, and Bhutan, and Tibet. (The majority of the listeners at these talks were Mahāyāna monks and nuns.) (cf. Theravāda)
Mahāthera: bhikkhu of twenty years standing or more. (cf. bhikkhu)
Nibbāna:* (Sanskrit: *Nirvana*) final enlightenment; the cessation element; an ultimate reality; attained after discerning and surpassing the ultimate realities of mentality-materiality; it is seen after the vipassanā knowledges have matured; it is non-self and uniquely permanent and peaceful: not a place.
nimitta:* sign; image upon which yogi concentrates; mind-born, depending on perception and level of concentration. (cf. kasiṇa)

- ***parikamma-nimitta***: preparatory sign in meditation.
- ***uggaha-nimitta***: taken-up sign; image that is exact mental replica of object of meditation.
- ***paṭibhāga-nimitta***: purified and clear version of *uggaha-nimitta*; appears at stable perception and concentration.

Paccekabuddha: a man enlightened without a teacher, who has by Himself discovered the Four Noble Truths, but does not teach. (cf. Buddha)
Pali *(Pāḷi)*: ancient Indian language spoken by The Buddha; alive only as records of the Buddha's Teachings, otherwise dead.
pāramī: (*pāra* = other shore = Nibbāna; *mī* = reach) ten *pāramī* (see Question 4.1, p.141); qualities developed with Nibbāna as aim.
parikamma-nimitta: see **nimitta**
Parinibbāna: death of a Buddha, a Paccekabuddha, and any other Arahant, after which there is no further rebirth, no more materiality, and no more mentality. (cf. Arahant, Nibbāna)

pātibhāga-nimitta: see **nimitta**
peta: inhabitant of realm lower than human realm, but higher than animals; invisible to human eye; visible in light of concentration.
rūpa/arūpa:* materiality/immateriality.
samatha:* serenity; practice of concentrating on a single object to develop higher and higher states of concentration, whereby the mind becomes increasingly serene. (cf. jhāna, vipassanā)
Saṅgha: multitude, assembly; bhikkhus of past, present and future, worldwide, as a group; separate group of bhikkhus, e.g. bhikkhus in one monastery. (cf. bhikkhu)
sīla: for laity the five/eight precepts, for bhikkhus two hundred and twenty-seven main precepts. (cf. bhikkhu)
sutta: single discourse (thread, guideline) in second basket of what is called the Three Baskets (*Tipiṭaka*) of Pali Texts; teachings of The Buddha on a general and conventional level. (cf. Abhidhamma)
Tathāgata: one who has gone thus; epithet used by The Buddha when referring to Himself.
Theravāda: 'Buddhist tradition' prevalent in Sri-Lanka, Thailand, Myanmar (Burma), Laos, Cambodia. (The Most Venerable Pa-Auk Tawya Sayadaw is a Theravāda monk.) (cf. Mahāyāna)
uggaha-nimitta: see **nimitta**
vipassanā: insight, discernment of natural characteristics of materiality and mentality, causes and results, in ultimate reality, and their general characteristics of impermanence, suffering, and non-self. (cf. Abhidhamma, Arahant, Nibbāna)
Visuddhi·Magga *(Purification Path)*: authoritative and extensive instruction manual on meditation, compiled from ancient, orthodox Sinhalese translations of the even earlier Pali Commentaries (predominantly 'The Ancients' *(Porāṇā)*, dating back to the time of The Buddha and the First Council), as well as later Sinhalese Commentaries, and translated back into Pali by Indian scholar monk Venerable Buddhaghosa (approx. 500 A.C.).

Contact Addresses

Myanmar, Union of

Meditation Centres

tel./e-mail

- Pa-Auk Tawya Meditation Centre[521] (95) 57-27-853/-548
  Mawlamyine, Mon State
- International Buddhasāsana Meditation Centre (95) 56-21-927
  (Pa-Auk Tawya Branch)
  Thilawar Road (Near Kyaik-Khauk Pagoda)
  Payargon Village, Than Lyin Township, Yangon

Personal

- Mr & Mrs Yip Seng Foo (95) 50-4011/70-4314
  No.69 (A) University Avenue Street bluestar@mptmail.net.mm
  Bahan Township, Yangon
- Daw Amy (Ms Amy) (95) 1-54-8129/1-55-6355
  66A, Sayarsan Road, attbbpp@myanmar.com.mm
  Bahan Township, Yangon
- U Aung Pyone (Mr Aung Pyone) (95) 1-29-3847
  No. 32, Kwet Thit Street, Yay Kyaw uap@mail4u.com.mm
  7th Quarter, near YMBA
  Pazundaung Township, Yangon

International

(in alphabetical order)

America, United States of

- Mr Robert Cusick (1) 415-847-1302
  P.O. Box 151533-1533 robertcusick@gmail.com
  San Rafael CA 94915 Skype ID: robertcusick
- Mr Roland K. Win (1) 650-994-3750
  15 Palmdale Avenue rolandwin15@gmail.com
  Daly City CA 94015-3708

China, People's Republic of

- Mdm Liang Xinxin
  Att: Ms Ah Min (86) 20-8423-2438
  Guangzhou kaixinhuanzhaonin@126.com

---

[521] Also called Pa-Auk Forest Monastery.

China, Republic of (Taiwan)

- Buddhist Hong Shi College
  No. 121-5 Ta-Tung Village, Guan Yin
  Tao Yuan
- Taiwandipa Theravada Buddhist College (886) 6-230-1406
  No.1 Lane 85 Ming Chuen Street 8 fax: (886) 6-239-1563
  Guei Ren Siang 71148 Taiwan taiwandipa@gmail.com

Malaysia, Federation of

- Nibbinda Forest Monastery
  Mukim 5 Tempat Bukit Balik Pulau, Penang
  Contact: Mdm Lee Hooi Chin
  8N Jalan Tunggal off Jalan Satu + 6012-4811-984
  11400 Air Hitam, Penang hclee7319@yahoo.com

- Tusita Hermitage (a monastery)
- Bodhivana Buddhist Hermitage (a nunnery)
  c/o Kuching Bhagavan Buddhist Society jongjyi@gmail.com
  Contact: Sister Subha
  52 Lot 3700 Dogan Garden, Jalan Dogan
  93250 Kuching, Sarawak

Japan

- Myanmar Theravāda Buddhist Association (81) 90-2220-9886
  Att: Ko Ye Tun, Tokyo

Singapore, Republic of

- Cakkavala Meditation Centre cakkavala_sg@yahoo.com.sg
  Dr Ng Wai Chong (65) 98-48-8384

- Pa-Auk Meditation Centre tel/fax: (65) 66-11-9242
  15 Teo Kim Eng Road, Singapore 416385 paauk.mc.07@yahoo.com

- Visuddha Meditation Centre (65) 90-10-1663
  visuddha77@yahoo.com.sg

Sri Lanka

- Nā-Uyana Āraññā Senāsana (a monastery) (94) 37-567-7328
  Pansiyagama 60554 60-237-9036
  nauyana@gmail.com

- Dhammika Ashrama (a nunnery) (94) 37-567-1258
  Angulgamuwa, Pansiyagama 60554 dhammikashrama@gmail.com

Websites

- **America, United States of** www.paauk.org
- **Malaysia** (Chinese text) www.Dhamma-s.org
- **Singapore, Republic of** (English text) www.paaukforestmonastery.org

Index of Questions from Yogis

(Arranged sequentially according to subject.)

The first number refers to the talk; the second number to the question.
e.g. **1.2** = *Questions-&-Answers* No. 1, Question No.2
2.1 = *Questions-&-Answers* No. 2, Question No.1

MEDITATION (**PRACTICAL**) PAGE

MEDITATION **(DOCTRINAL)**

DOCTRINE **(BODHISATTA PATH ETC.)**

SUNDRY

MAIN INDEX

The main headings are in bold script. For the main discussion of a subject, reference is made only to the first page: the discussion may therefore continue onto the next page or more.

Abbreviations
- tbl = table
- qtn = quotation

A

abnormal person
meditation,&?, 205
absorption*(appanā)*
concentration. (see 'concentration, absorption')
accident
cause of, 198
afflictions
causes, 103
aggregate*(khandha)*. (see also 'consciousness-', 'feeling-', 'formations-', 'materiality-', 'perception aggregate')
arise&perish
  knowing, 216
arising, past/future/present
  seeing, 217
cause/effect, discerning, 183
cessation, 22
clinging-*(upādāna-)*
  five
    definition(qtn), 4
    mentality-materiality =, 5
    suffering =, 73
      quotation, 3, 4
five
  definition, 72, 176
    quotation, 210
  discerning
    w/o dependent origination, 207
  First Noble Truth =, 257
  formations =, 239
  impermanence =, 78, 176
  mentality-materiality =, 177
  personality =, 234
  possessed of, 22
  self,&, 238
  the known =, 237
  two bodies*(kāya)* =, 248
  world =, 3
knowing requires
concentration, 152
known, how, 94
mentality-, 73
mentality-materiality &, 72
past, future, present, discerning, 183
all, the
defin/discuss, 152
ān-āpāna-sati. see 'mindfulness-of-breathing'
anger
heat caused by, 112
overcome, how to, 14
Arahant
description(qtn), 269
Arahantship
Buddha's, 154
delayed, 143
disciples, three types, 154
easy, not, 200
eight attainments, w/o, 148
one dhamma, contemplating, 154
own, seeing
  Arahantship, not, 23, 218
present suffering, still, 22
psychic powers, no, 148
pure-vipassāna,by, 148
rebirth, no new (qtn), 179
skeleton meditation, w/, 158
the end =, 179
time to attain, 177
arise&perish
Knowledge. (see 'Knowledge, Arise&Perish')
arising*(udaya)*
causal
  defin/discuss, 217, 221
Contemplation of*(Anupassi)*
  defin/discuss, 217
momentary
  defin/discuss, 217
perishing*(baya)*,&
  causal
    defin/discuss, 216, 220, 222
  Contemplation of*(Anupassi)*
    defin/discuss, 220
  momentary
    defin/discuss, 216
Ariya Aṭṭhaṅgika Magga. see 'Path,Noble Eightfold'
asceticism
goal of (qtn), 23
attainment*(samāpatti)*. (see also 'jhāna')
eight
  consciousness-purification =, 77
  definition, 69
attention*(manasikāra)*
best, 234
enlightenment factors &, 235
images during meditation, 101
three types, 235
unwise*(ayoniso)*
  boredom, cause of, 238
  defin/discuss, 100, 166
  hindrances, cause of, 100
  unwholesome kamma, 165
wise*(yoniso)*
  daily life, in, 234
  defin/discuss, 100, 166
  removes greed/hatred, 104
  vipassanā best, 104
  wholesome kamma, 165
wise/unwise
  defin/discussion, 165

B

D

G

H

I

J

K

L

M

T

U

V

W

Y

Z

33020229R00183

Made in the USA
Middletown, DE
27 June 2016